D1199870

hotch

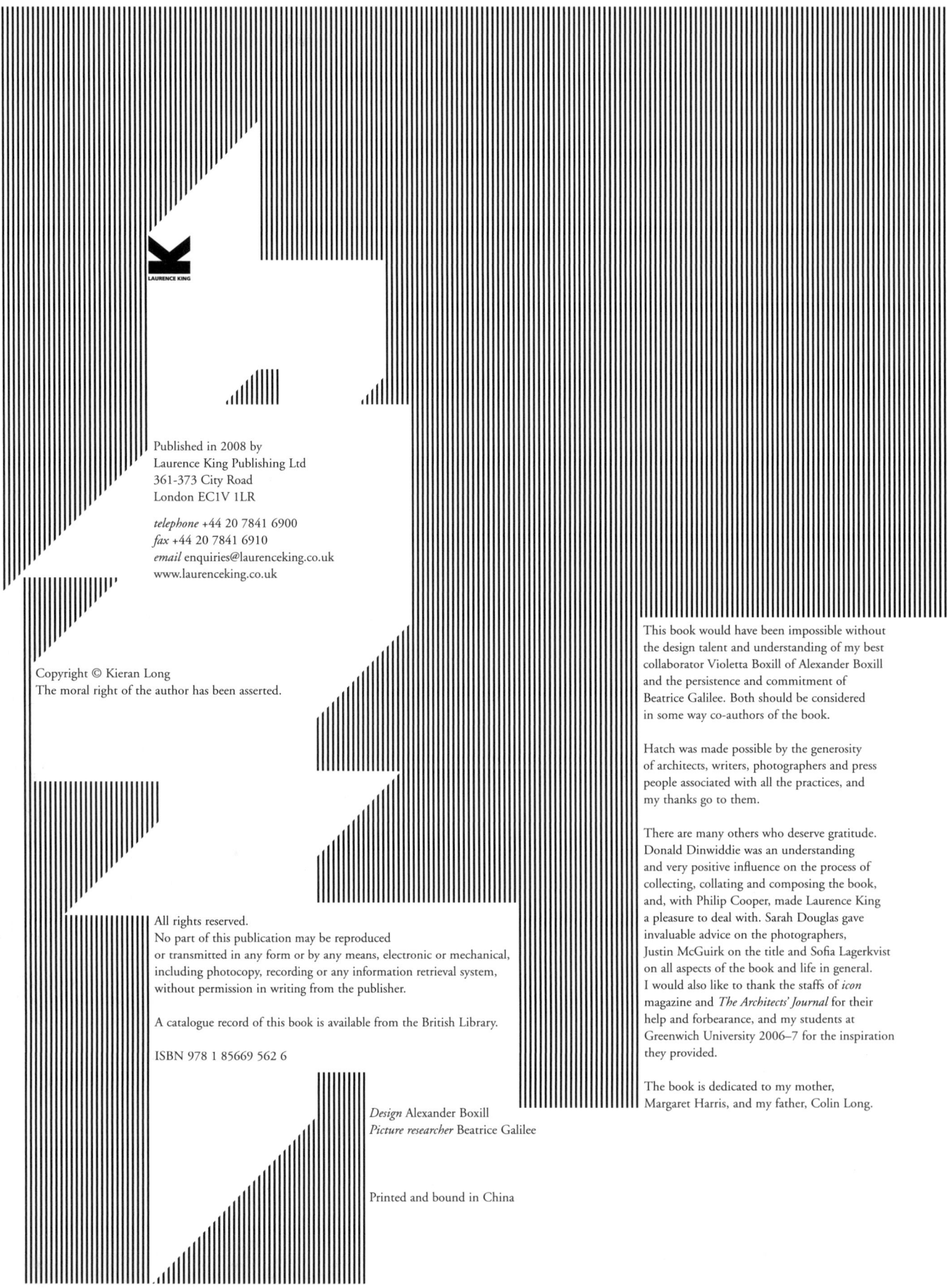

**LAURENCE KING**

Published in 2008 by
Laurence King Publishing Ltd
361-373 City Road
London EC1V 1LR

*telephone* +44 20 7841 6900
*fax* +44 20 7841 6910
*email* enquiries@laurenceking.co.uk
www.laurenceking.co.uk

A catalogue record of this book is available from the British Library.

ISBN 978 1 85669 562 6

*Design* Alexander Boxill
*Picture researcher* Beatrice Galilee

Printed and bound in China

This book would have been impossible without
the design talent and understanding of my best
collaborator Violetta Boxill of Alexander Boxill
and the persistence and commitment of
Beatrice Galilee. Both should be considered
in some way co-authors of the book.

Hatch was made possible by the generosity
of architects, writers, photographers and press
people associated with all the practices, and
my thanks go to them.

There are many others who deserve gratitude.
Donald Dinwiddie was an understanding
and very positive influence on the process of
collecting, collating and composing the book,
and, with Philip Cooper, made Laurence King
a pleasure to deal with. Sarah Douglas gave
invaluable advice on the photographers,
Justin McGuirk on the title and Sofia Lagerkvist
on all aspects of the book and life in general.
I would also like to thank the staffs of *icon*
magazine and *The Architects' Journal* for their
help and forbearance, and my students at
Greenwich University 2006–7 for the inspiration
they provided.

The book is dedicated to my mother,
Margaret Harris, and my father, Colin Long.

# The new architectural generation

## KIERAN LONG

*Hatch* is a portrait, partial and subjective, of the architectural work of a generation that will soon take the lead in the practice and discourse of architecture across the world. The *Hatch* generation is composed of many disciplines, and I have included not just architects, but multi-disciplinary collaboratives, designers, critics (represented by pieces of their own writing) and photographers (represented by curated selections of their photographs) in an attempt to describe a conversation, and a set of incoherent but interlocking professional and cultural networks that contain and enable the leaders in the discipline today. They do not all know each other, but many of them do – or will soon. Who knows? Perhaps this book might also encourage that process.

Implicit in *Hatch* is the impossibility of generalizing. There are practices here diametrically opposed to others within the book, and the book's system of cross-references proposes correspondences and sympathies, but also highlights the different paths taken by those who perhaps started out in similar territory only to diverge later. *Hatch* nevertheless is obviously only a fraction of the whole picture in the sense that there are few practitioners in these pages who are interested in

commercial practice. There are probably more art installations on these pages than there are completed buildings. Also, many of these practices have had an international focus, allowing them to be discovered and written about by journalists and critics like me. The media is an important part of architecture, and you can think of this selection as having been curated magazine-style into a loose-fit coherence.

So what are the criteria for inclusion in *Hatch*? There are no hard and fast rules. Most are under or around 40 years old – young in architectural terms but old enough to have achieved something. All of the practices here have some kind of media profile, whether for a single project or in their own right. In my initial call for entries, quite a few practices recommended colleagues. Many of these were new to me and made it into the book. Omissions, too, no doubt abound, but I have tended towards those striking an identifiably individual tone. I have avoided some practices that are perhaps higher profile, more successful and younger than many included in the book, partly because I wanted this to be a rattlebag, a critical

introduction to contemporary architectural practice.

There was some desire to limit certain geographical areas that have a very well-developed PR industry, but those countries are still disproportionately present. Practices from the US (the overwhelming majority of whose work remains unbuilt), the UK, Germany, Spain and the Netherlands are unsurprisingly well represented. Africa and Southeast Asia less so. But this is part of the story – there is no doubt that a large part of attaining an international reputation in architecture involves engaging with a global press.

The writers, critics and curators are almost all people that I have met and whose work I have read over the years, and most are involved in pretty traditional architectural academia and publishing. When I began the research for this book, I expected to find a new generation of critics emerging through the web. The internet has some extremely successful (in terms of visitor numbers) sites about architecture that do play a role in the discourse. But when I looked hard I found little criticism of the highest order there.

The internet is still dominated by enthusiasts in this discipline, or those writers ploughing a very individual and non-academic furrow. It is difficult to perceive their influences in terms of education, politics or policy. There is only one blogger here – the author of Aggregät 4/5/6 – and he is an academic at an American university. This is not to dismiss the important role that the web has in dissemination, but I think that a new way of talking about architecture has yet to emerge there. Certainly it would be hard to name a site that gets interaction from the leaders in the profession, in contrast to disciplines such as graphic design, where a thriving and serious commentary does exist on the web.

The photographers are a much more whimsical and subjective selection. They are the authors of photographic projects that I enjoy, and are intended to suggest a variety of ways of looking at the built environment. In their work, it is the city that matters, not the authorship of the architect. Most are more likely found on the pages of books or in galleries, and have taken on very few commissioned works of architectural photography. They are all European, too – inevitably only a tiny part of contemporary photographic work on the subject of the city.

The intention of the book is to show the work of each entry in a certain depth. Most of the architects in the book show just one or two projects, the writers just one piece of writing. Some architects have made projects so iconic that it would have been perverse to publish anything but their best-known works. However, most pleasing are those who have completed buildings, but have chosen instead to show a work for a competition, or a prototype that reflects an approach, rather than trying to compete in terms of enclosed square metres with others in the book.

While there is no one emerging paradigm, it is clear that what is developing is a highly competitive situation. Most of the people in the book do not work in national networks, but between groups of practitioners, loosely aligned in terms of disciplinary boundaries but not bounded by national territories.

Having said that it is not possible to generalize, it does seem reasonable to speculate about why that might be. It is, significantly, nothing to do with the geographical spread. Cities with several entries (London, New York, Berlin) are likely to have a diversity of practitioners rather than an identifiable style. Even countries with which you might associate a particular approach show different sides to themselves. Hailing from Spain, a country known for the restrained modernism of Rafael Moneo and the urbanism of Barcelona, is Enric Ruiz-Geli (Cloud 9) and Andrés Jaque, practitioners apparently outside of the strict definition of those traditions. From Scandinavia we see a little blonde timber and glass (Tham and Videgård Hansson), but more that avoids that cliché (N55 and Force4, for example).

The most significant thing that characterizes this book (as it may not have done a decade ago) is the focus of so many practitioners on the possibilities of digital design to generate architecture. That many of these have nothing built to show for a decade or so's work also demonstrates how accepted this kind of design methodology is within architectural education. Without their seats in universities, those who follow what might loosely be described as the 'Emergent' design school might go hungry. They dominate architecture schools from LA to New York, from London to Barcelona. This influence is now in its second generation, with the fathers and grandfathers of the scene (Greg Lynn, Thom Mayne, etc.) already accepted as part of the establishment.

As for these digitally inclined architects (see Emergent, Elena Manferdini, Qua'Virarch, Xefirotarch, Zellner Plus, the late George Yu and others), my instinct is that this generation will enter history as one caught between two worlds: the analogue and the digital. It is a paradox that the architecture schools that are now dominated by the computer (Architectural Association, GSD Harvard, SCI-Arc) are also the schools making the most sophisticated physical models. But these are not models or maquettes in any conventional sense. Rather they are conceived as prototypes, machines that test a mechanical effect,

rather than miniatures that test spatial ideas. The works of most of the current generation exist at their largest in pavilions and gallery installations. You can recognize them by their quasi-organic shapes, faintly sinister plant-like forms and references to biological and mathematical inspirations.

Despite few chances to build, the American establishment has encouraged this kind of architecture by allowing its exponents to become professors at major educational institutions, and rewarding it with commissions such as the MOMA/PS1 Young Architects Programme (whose winners overwhelmingly come from the digital design camp). It illustrates the ongoing remoteness of American architectural practice from education. American praxis (and the foreign architect who studies there) is still mainly in the realms of imaginary projects of high but unproven technological sophistication. That country's lack of interest in architecture at the level of clients means that for young practices, academia is the way forward.

But enough people are now doing it and it has critical mass.

In the hallways of the Architectural Association in my home town of London, adherents to a new computer-generated visual language line up to tell you that it could be built, that these theories are just awaiting advances in manufacturing or an enlightened client. The critics who jet in to ask questions of the students of the Association's Design Research Laboratory are most likely to be from America, rather than mainland Europe. The head of the school is American. The network is organised, too, often entering international architectural competitions en masse (see the Czech National Library or Stockholm City Library competitions, both in early 2007).

Although it hasn't quite happened yet, it is surely just a matter of time before one of these practices wins a competition.

Architecture in the twentieth century saw many extreme proposals emerge from times of economic hardship and lack of opportunity for young architects. But high technology is not the only possible response. Contrast the high sheen, computer-generated world described above with another place where building opportunities are hard to come by. In Berlin, where recession has gripped the construction industry for the best part of a decade, a wholly different character of work has emerged. There,

practices have mixed a close relationship with galleries and art practice, and with a sub-cultural attitude characteristic of the German capital, produced a quite distinct body of work. It consists of strange nightclubs, temporary installations in communist monuments or tower blocks, and warehouses full of motor cars with their radios on. Some of it is meretricious in an arty way, and some of it is a profound meditation on the role of architecture in a city that is shrinking, divided and suffering something of an identity crisis. It is a fascinating and influential scene. There is a band of central Europe fascinated by these strategies, from Germany (Die Baupiloten, Raumtaktik, Raumlabor, etc.) to Austria, and Italy (Stalker). In Scandinavia, too, this tendency is strong (see Fantastic Norway and Testbedstudio). Many of these have an interest in consultation and public interface of some kind, and the approaches are contrasting but have as their goal a politically-motivated and community-driven architecture.

The missing middle is composed of those interested in good background architecture, the simple and existing qualities of cities that we enjoy now and would like to go on enjoying. There is little housing or office design in this book (excepting one-off dwellings). While there are countries with immense strength in laconic city making – Switzerland, Portugal and Spain among them – the younger generation from each of those countries does not reveal

the kind of interest in context and character that distinguished the early work of Herzog & de Meuron, Rafael Moneo or Alvaro Siza. Many younger architects in Spain and Portugal currently seem to be in the middle of a backlash against their masters, and, to be frank, few of them are included in the book.

Perhaps the place with the strongest interest in those issues is London, with practices such as Lynch, DRDH and Dow Jones (who all know each other) forming a convincing generation that is now beginning to win bigger work. However, it can hardly be called dominant. In actual fact, no one thing is or could be dominant here, apart from the egos and reputations of the clutch of architectural superstars who win most of the city's high-profile public commissions.

*Hatch* is intentionally plural in its outlook, but it is not universal. The work shown in these pages is not representative of what is happening in cities, but it is about what is aspirational in emerging architecture. And the seemingly tenuous connections made in the book could turn out to be defining meetings and collaborations in the history of architecture.

# 6A

6A's cultural background is eclectic. Despite a strong tendency towards a sensitive, Cambridge University, modernism, it has been their far less conventional projects that have built the practice's considerable profile in the UK. First came the simple but beautiful interior for fashion label Oki-Ni on Savile Row in London. More recently, their temporary summer installation for the Architecture Foundation's Yard Gallery in Clerkenwell, London, worked as a beautiful calling card, and demonstrated their ability to collaborate across disciplines (in that case with fashion design company Eley Kishimoto).

But it is their victory in the high-profile competition for 35 low-cost housing units in Savigny-le-Temple in the south Parisian suburb of Senart in 2005 that has revealed the social intent behind the practice's work.

Their proposal consists of a perimeter block on a site in a suburban context and bounded on one side by a public park. Access to the apartments is from open decks on the courtyard side of the building. So far, so conventional. But part of 6A's proposal was for the development to integrate a 'Hall'

building, for use by the residents and the wider community. Partner Tom Emerson writes: 'The Hall mediates spatially and socially between inside and out. It is intended for residents' leisure activities that cannot be accommodated within the apartments, such as table tennis, yoga and children's birthday parties, where it would open onto the communal garden. On more ceremonial occasions it can extend onto the public green and may also be used by the broader community.'

Materially, the project is beautiful and slightly whimsical, with pink cement-board cladding ('recalling

the farmsteads of the Low Countries,' says Emerson). Also, the south façade and the communal courtyards have narrow tree trunks (or 'thinnings') for columns, an explicit reference to the forested landscape of Senart. Inside, the apartments are long and relatively narrow, with each room well lit and naturally ventilated. Both living areas and bedrooms have access to south- and west-oriented balconies.

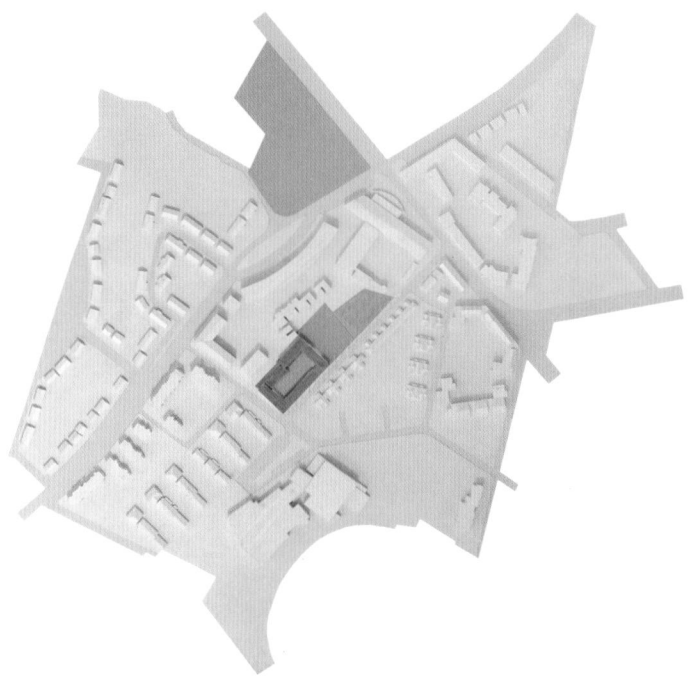

Clockwise from right: Detail of *Hairywood* installation, showing the laser-cut plywood tracery; *Hairywood* made a small elevated room overlooking Old Street in east London; Elevation and site model for low-cost housing in Savigny-le-Temple, France.

| Location | London, UK |
|----------|-----------|
| Nationality | British |

A

Tom Emerson and Stephanie Macdonald founded 6A Architects in London in 2001 after they met while studying at the Royal College of Art in London. Emerson studied at Cambridge University before that (where he still teaches), whereas Macdonald has a diverse CV including a stint in Japan, and collaborations with artists and product designers (she was a welder for designer Tom Dixon). Both partners have lectured and taught widely, and Emerson is a member of the governing council of the Architectural Association. In 2006, 6A won a D&AD Yellow Pencil Award for its temporary installation *Hairywood*. Projects in progress include the South London Gallery and a contemporary art gallery in Spitalfields.

6A has collaborated with German artist and photographer Oliver Godow (pp. 130–133).

Aggregät 4/5/6 is one of a new breed of blogs that has found a platform on the net for cross-disciplinary architectural theory. This post, on the film sets of expressionist architect Hans Poelzig, is typically pithy and insightful. It originally appeared on the site on 29 November, 2006.

Laura Mulvey, in her essay on *Citizen Kane* (Orson Welles, dir., 1941), comments on the 'empty, shell-like constructions' of Charles Foster Kane's neo-Hearstian Xanadu. This is a powerful idea indeed, for the pastiche of gaudy European bric-à-brac depicts an architecture that is literally and figuratively empty. In other words, art director Van Nest Polglase's sets create a true shell of a building, and perhaps nothing more. For the sake of being purely historical, I only suggest that this idea is at once reminiscent of Karl Scheffler's 1919 pronouncement that the interiors of Max Reinhardt's Großes Schauspielhaus, designed by Hans Poelzig, comprised a 'glittering stage set, a complicated, artistic, architectural mask of plasterboard' amounting to an architecture that was merely 'playacting.'[1]

In 1918, the film director Paul Wegener asked Poelzig to design the sets for a third film version of *Der Golem* (*The Golem*).[2] Poelzig readily accepted Wegener's offer – their 'shared interests in the mysterious and fantastic' undoubtedly 'made the collaboration on *The Golem* easy and fruitful.'[3] As for the 1920 film, it was Wegener's third version of the Austrian writer Gustav Meyrink's 1915 novel of the same name. The film has a distinct urban flavour – set in the sixteenth century, it tells the tale of the scrupulous and shrewd Rabbi Löw, the most outspoken of Prague's Jewish community. In response to a premonition that a terrible disaster would befall Prague's Jewish population (shortly afterwards, local secular authorities would issue an edict to expel and relocate the city's Jewish population), Rabbi Löw consults his own circle and they decide to build a Golem, an anthropomorphic clay-hewn monster that will protect the people. However, the monster loses control and begins destroying Prague.

Along with his wife, the sculptor Marlene Moeschke, Poelzig designed a whole city for the production. Entrusted with the design of 'buildings, streets, and interiors which were a formal equivalent of the ideas of mystery and the supernatural which underlie the film,' Poelzig created a three-dimensional space, 'a concept foreign to motion pictures up to that time … which forced the camera eye to view it obliquely.'

The finished sets thus have an angular, exaggerated feel, a true architecture of playacting. The only sense of verisimilitude that Poelzig deploys is not architectural – his sets convey a sense of psychological and spiritual dread. For example, in the

Location       Princeton, USA

Nationality   American

A

Aggregät 4/5/6 is the blog of Enrique Gualberto Ramirez (above), an architectural historian who writes about the built environment, technology and armed conflict. He completed a research project at Yale University on the World War Two-era work of Erich Mendelsohn, Konrad Wachsmann and Antonin Raymond in 2007, and has been published in *RES Magazine* and *Critical Planning*. He has publications forthcoming in *Thresholds* and *Perspecta: The Yale Architecture Journal*. Trained as an attorney and urban planner, Enrique says his site 'has no qualms about the messy connections between spatial practice, cultural criticism, technology studies, art history, architecture and other realms.' Ramirez recently began his studies in the PhD program at Princeton University. The website can be found at www.aggregat 456.blogspot.com

opening moments of the film, a group of Rabbinic elders watch the stars, awaiting the fateful premonition that a terrible event will befall Prague's citizens. On a dark-indigo tint screen, a mysterious constellation of stars hovers above an array of sharp, cragged artichoke-shaped silhouettes. There is no way in which a viewer can get a sense of the size or massing of these crags, but in silhouette they look like a set of broken, upturned teeth (A). Poelzig replicates these angular, pointy motifs in his urban set pieces. In a long shot of a Prague city scene (B), steep, crooked, cracked gables retreat into the distance, creating a successive layering of light and shadow that only serves to frame and surround the masses of city dwellers in the middle. The triangular shapes are twisted and mangled, inadvertently showing the sections of the individual buildings. This layering of light and shadow is more evident in another frame, this one featuring a set of stairs reaching upwards underneath a large, arched bridge (C). A closer inspection reveals a complex interplay of surfaces – whereas in the previous scene the houses reveal a type of plaster and wood-beam construction, here it looks as if the surfaces were hand-cut from stone.

The tall, pointed, twisted city gate also combines the elements of light, shadow and rough surface, creating an undulating structure that spins upwards in an angle, coming together at a point that mimics the very same artichoke silhouettes from the night scene. Poelzig also uses these elements in set pieces that emphasize landscape. In one scene, for example, the Golem follows Rabbi Löw across a serpentine, rocky bridge (D). Far away, beyond the unseen end of the bridge, a city's gnarled and pointed towers and spires rise in the distance. On the side of the bridge, a witness to the curving, malevolent shapes unfurling across the landscape, a stone Madonna holds her own child. The venerated creator and created, mother and child thus gazes on its tragic analogue: a monster following its inattentive creator into an uncertain future. *The Golem* can be interpreted as a tragic tale about the relationship between a creator and the maligned offspring created in its image. And this is not insignificant as different variations of this relationship become more and more evident. For example, there is Paul Wegener himself, who played The Golem in all three films. Here, the creator of the film depicts himself as the errant, uncontrollable creation in the movie. Hans Poelzig's sets for the film are almost an inverse of this relationship. Poelzig's own errant, maligned 'playacting' architectures (such as the 'plaster and wire' Schauspielhaus) find a home within the dark, twisted logic of Wegener's film. They even find an unlikely apotheosis in Van Nest Polglase's sets for Welles' *Citizen Kane*.

1   Karl Scheffer, 'Das Große Schauspielhaus', *Kunst und Künstler* 18 (1920), in Julius Posener, *Hans Poelzig: Reflections on His Life and Work* (Cambridge: MIT Press, 1992): 126.

2   The title of Wegener's 1920 version is *Der Golem, wie er in die Welt kam* (*The Golem: How He Came Into the World*).

3   John R. Clarke, 'Expressionism in Film and Architecture: Hans Poelzig's Sets for Paul Wegener's *The Golem*', *Art Journal* Vol. 34, No. 2 (Winter, 1974–1975): 115.

# Anteeksi

Anteeksi occupies a space in 300sq m (3,230sq ft) of undistinguished office space in Kallio, Helsinki, very near to an Alvar Aalto-designed church in that city of beautiful, tasteful modernism. Inside are racks and shelves full of models and prototypes of every kind, with desks ranged around the edges full of young creative types. When I visited, a dog yapped around my ankles as four members of the collective sat on a sofa and tried to explain the diversity of their work.

It is impossible to describe all the facets of Anteeksi here, but suffice it to say that the members hail from disciplines including fashion, graphics, product design and architecture, and they hold in common a humourous and subversive sensibility. This has produced works, often quite ephemeral, that turn architecture and design into a spectator sport and a social enterprise. Anteeksi means 'excuse me' or 'sorry', a self-effacing name that seems to sum up the group's strange passive-aggressive alternativeness.

As a collective, their most important achievements have been events. Their series of fashion shows, Anteeksi Fäsäri, have become cult happenings in their home city, attracting hundreds of spectators to see an anarchic mix of clothes, installations and performances from members of the collective. The 2006 event took place at an ice rink, and featured a 'Peffletts collection, Chairman and Chairwoman collection, some hockey-helmet-inspired thing' by product designers Company, and a 'city on skates' by architect Tuomas Siitonen of architecture office M41LH2.

Anteeksi also publishes an occasional magazine called *Uutiset*, and organizes a bizarre annual parody of the Milan Furniture Fair on a street corner near their office. This involves a small glass case (the Milaribox on the corner of Sturenkatu and Kirstinkatu) with products inside, accompanied by a party for anyone willing to stand around it for a while. More conventional projects include extensive teaching and a large club interior in Helsinki, completed in 2003.

Clockwise from above: *Portable Home* in open and closed configurations; *Tree Stool*; Exhibition installation showing a variety of Anteeksi products; *Domestic Clothing*; *Lidl by Lidl Chair*; *Dresschair*.

A

| Location | Helsinki, Finland |
| --- | --- |
| Nationality | Finnish |

Anteeksi (Finnish for 'excuse me' or 'sorry') is a collective of 14 people based in Helsinki, Finland, that spans disciplines from fashion to architecture. There are several independent offices within the collective, three of which are principally involved in architecture, but the work of the collective spans activities from events and installations to art projects, furniture and product design and conceptual provocations. Most significant are their regular fashion shows entitled Anteeksi Fäsäri, where they design everything from clothes to installations. Formed in 2002, the space Anteeksi occupies takes 14 people – when one moves on, they invite someone new to occupy the vacant space. Firms currently in the collective include Company, M41LH2, NOW Office, Vire Design, Lacquer and Janne Suhonen.

The only other Finnish practice in this book, Anttinen Oiva Arkkitehdit (AOA; pp. 20–21), is a member of Anteeksi.

# AOA

The commission for the *Lilja Chapel* was won by Anttinen Oiva Arkkitehdit (AOA) partner Vesa Oiva in competition when he was still at university. *Lilja* (which means 'lily') was the result of a competition sponsored by the paper and timber company UPM to create a transportable ecumenical chapel to be built at a housing fair in Oulo, 190km (120 miles) south of the Arctic Circle in Finland. The chapel was intended as a place of repose and silence for visitors.

The result was a very simple, 100sq m (1,080sq ft) building, built entirely from prefabricated timber elements. The plan is a three-pointed star, and each arm of the plan has a triangular cross-section. One arm is slightly larger than the others, and has an intricate fretwork pattern evoking a tree. Vesa Oiva explains: 'There are no recognizable religious symbols in the chapel. I wanted the only symbol to be of the forest, the first sacred space for most Finnish people.'

Inside, the building is sparsely fitted out, with concealed light fittings in the floor, and the most minimal of furniture – there are two simple timber blocks for seating.

This spread:
The demountable
*Lilja Chapel.*

AOA is part of the Anteeksi (pp. 18–19) collective.

| Location | Helsinki, Finland |
| --- | --- |
| Nationality | Finnish |

Anttinen Oiva Arkkitehdit (AOA) was founded in 2006 by Selina Anttinen and Vesa Oiva, and is based in Helsinki. It focuses on a wide variety of tasks from building design to urban planning studies. Its main projects so far are the *Poltinaho* housing area, the *Lilja Chapel*, housing blocks in Hämeenlinna and an ice-swimming centre in Rovaniemi, all in Finland. AOA has won prizes and honourable mentions in several international and domestic competitions. It currently employs five people.

# AOC

AOC (Agents of Change) burst on to the London scene in 2004 when it was shortlisted in the high-profile competition to design a new home for the Architecture Foundation in the city. Although it didn't win that project, its profile has increased by virtue of an approach almost unique in the capital – a genuinely multi-disciplinary office of a distinctly outward-looking character.

One feature of AOC is that not all the partners work there all the time. Daisy Froud is an interpreter and cultural theory graduate, who adds a dimension of engagement and interpretation to the practice's work that is contained within AOC Participation, an in-house unit specializing in consultation and participation. Vincent Lacovera has the distinction of being an urban designer at the London Borough of Croydon, working from within existing bureaucratic strictures as well as proposing from without with AOC.

The attention paid to communication is a great feature of the practice's work, from their cartoonish drawings of the interiors of their projects, to the development of alternative strategies of communication with a broad public. Their *Polyopoly* proposal makes an accessible front end for a new kind of urban development. 'Polyopoly,' they write, 'is a game of urban cultivation. Players invest Time, Skills and Knowledge in Sites, cultivating Assets, Amenities and Landscapes for the generation of individual and collective wealth. It proposes an alternative to the Monopoly mindset.' The practice is set to develop another consultation

Below: Perspective of *Crown Terrace* in Southwark, south London.

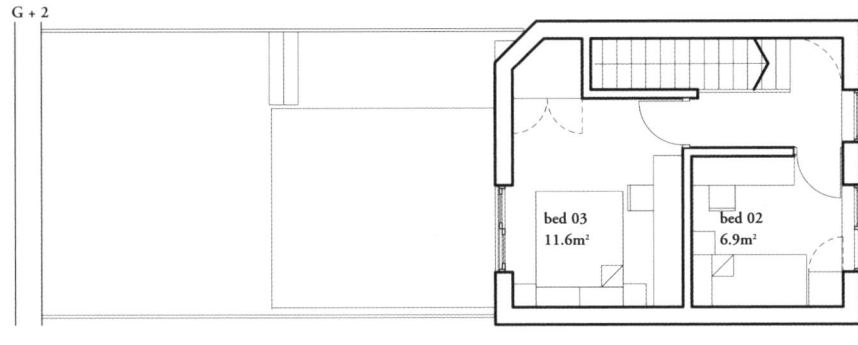

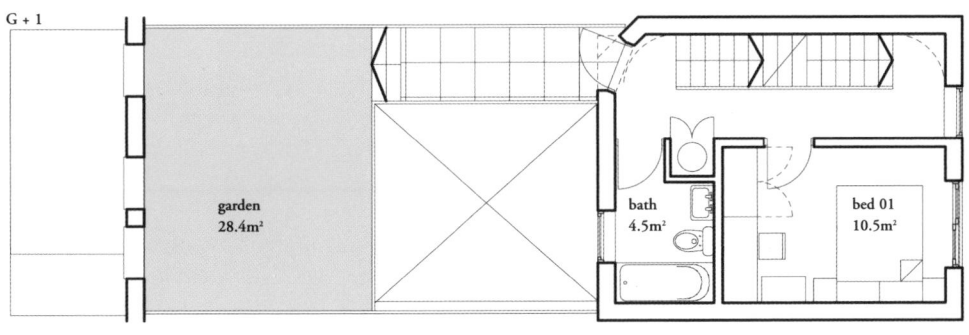

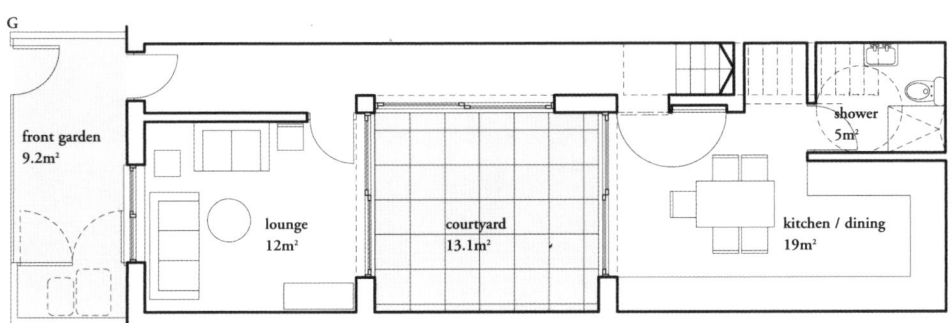

1:100 Plan, Type A 3 bed home

G + 2

bed 03
11.6m²

bed 02
6.9m²

G + 1

garden
28.4m²

bath
4.5m²

bed 01
10.5m²

G

front garden
9.2m²

lounge
12m²

courtyard
13.1m²

kitchen / dining
19m²

shower
5m²

| Location | London, UK |
|---|---|
| Nationality | British |

A

AOC (Agents of Change) was founded as a multi-disciplinary studio in 2004 by Tom Coward, Daisy Froud, Vincent Lacovera and Geoff Shearcroft. The practice came to broader attention when it was shortlisted alongside the likes of Zaha Hadid and Caruso St John for the new headquarters building of the Architecture Foundation in London. That was the four partners' first collaborative venture, but they have since gone on to win other commissions, including several major housing projects. Recent work includes the completion of a nursery at Friars Primary School in Borough, two first-placed housing schemes in south London, and a winning design for 314 homes in south London.

Clockwise from below:
Cutaway perspective of *Crown Terrace*; *Every Home Needs...* drawing; Plans of one of the house types in the terrace.

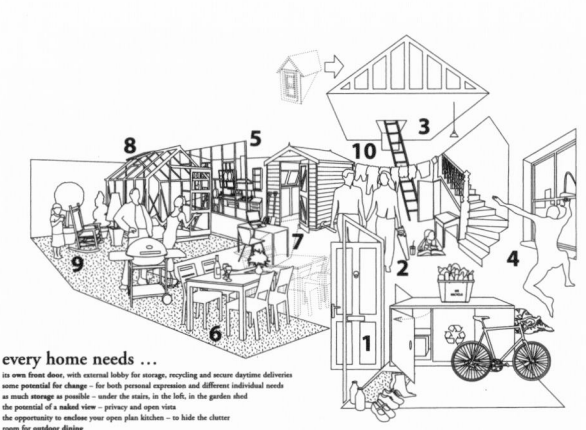

every home needs ...

01_ its own front door, with external lobby for storage, recycling and secure daytime deliveries
02_ some potential for change – for both personal expression and different individual needs
03_ as much storage as possible – under the stairs, in the loft, in the garden shed
04_ the potential of a naked view – privacy and open vista
05_ the opportunity to enclose your open plan kitchen – to hide the clutter
06_ room for outdoor dining
07_ room to do homework
08_ somewhere to grow things
09_ somewhere to sit out and relax in peace
10_ somewhere to air-dry your clothes

Reminiscent of the vacancy built into AOC's *Crown Terrace* project is
Alejandro Aravena's prototype super-low-cost housing in Chile (pp. 26–29).

card game for the Royal Institute of British Architects.

The reference to Monopoly seems very English – board games as generative strategy. AOC's view of their place in architectural history is similarly Anglocentric. They trace a line from an 1850s top-down philanthropic and quasi-scientific drive to house the poor, through Le Corbusier at Pessac, to the nay-saying head of Harvard Design School in the 1930s and 1940s, Joseph Hudnut. To AOC, the spirit of modernism is still valuable and alive as a 'spirit'. But, they wrote in 2006, 'a narrow understanding of use, as merely function – rather than custom and usage – applied in a paternalistic way, led it down the cul-de-sac of what is now understood, and often distrusted, as the Modern style.' AOC's charming (and distinctly postmodern-looking) proposal for a terrace of five houses in Southwark, south London, seeks to incorporate both their instinct to encourage community participation and customization, with an urban façade that can face the city.

This spread: Views of AOC's *Polyopoly* board game, intended as a consultation tool.

A

Currency TKS
*time*
*skills*
*knowledge*

Building Site

Event Card
*global*
*national*
*local*

Amenity

Billboard
*produce*
*make*
*provide*

Landscape

Assets
*produce*
*industry*
*service*

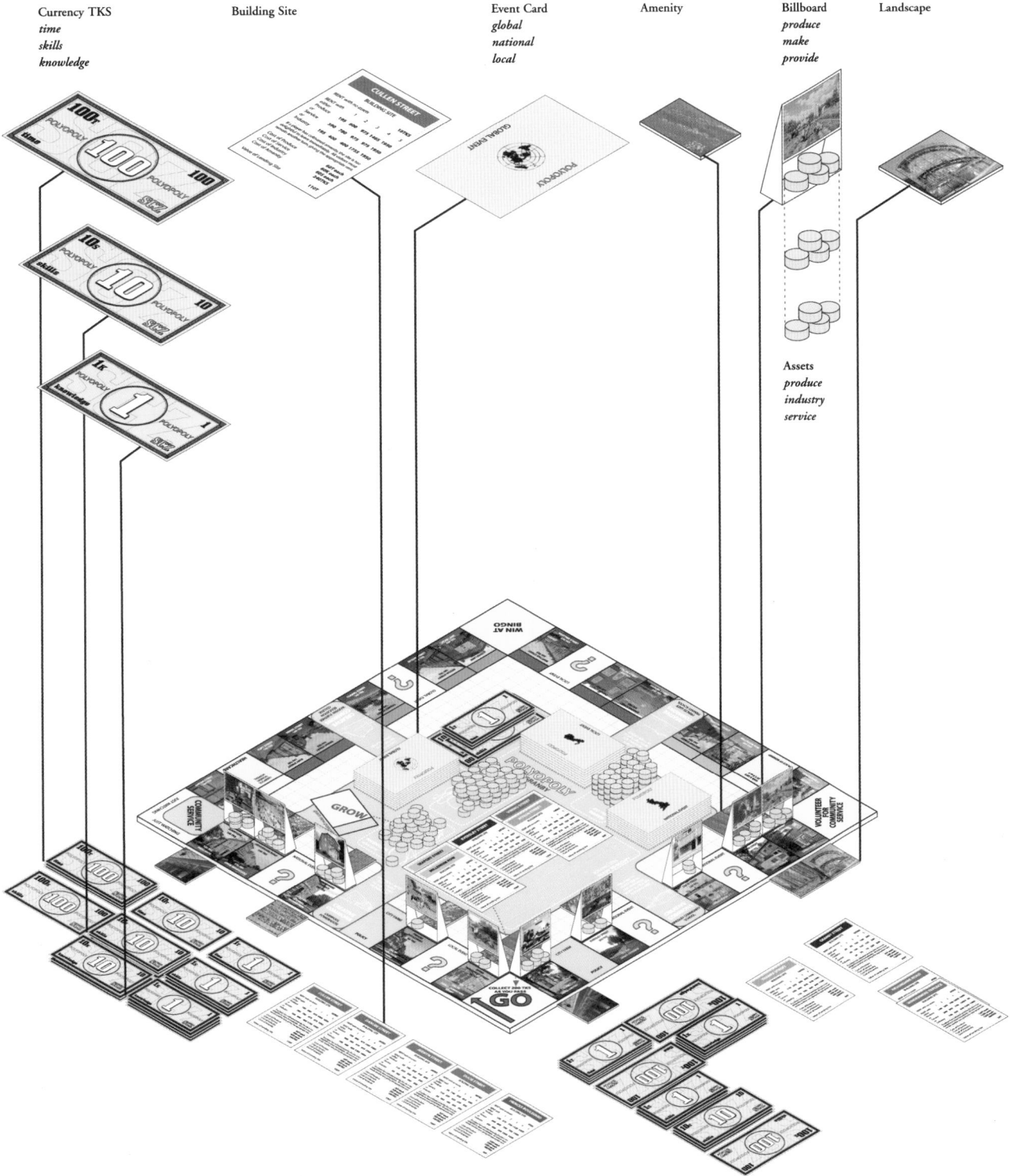

# Alejandro Aravena

It would be easy to categorize Alejandro Aravena's work within a tradition of regionalist modernism – contemporary enough, but essentially generated by the climate and materials of his homeland of Chile and a desire to reach beyond. His high-profile public works are glossy enough to appear in magazines, and hugely distinctive formally. Perhaps the best example is his beautiful *Siamese Towers*, a digital research centre for a university in Santiago, Chile. The tower is a concrete tower with a glass sheath that divides at the top to emphasize its height. This elegance is contrasted with the rough and beautiful base, clad in old railway sleepers.

Aravena's work is now growing beyond that context, with his first building outside Chile – a 27,870sq m (300,000sq ft) student residence at St Edward's University in Austin, Texas in 2008. But the more interesting part of his work lies in driving innovation in social housing in his home country. The Chilean government is investing heavily in plugging the gap in housing for the poorest members of society, but, it was felt, without looking at how some kind of design quality could be achieved for the tiny contract sums available. Aravena was instrumental in setting up Elemental, a research cell based at the Universidad Católica de Chile's

architecture school, and funded with money from the government and from Harvard Design School.

The aspiration was to create housing developments that show how very cheap housing can be created that also allows individual owners to add to it themselves. As Aravena puts it, he was interested in 'looking at the city as a source of equity – with social housing projects, trying to contribute to the country using architecture.' The Elemental project will run a series of competitions to find architects for a number of multi-unit schemes across Chile, but Aravena himself took up the pilot project – a 100-unit development

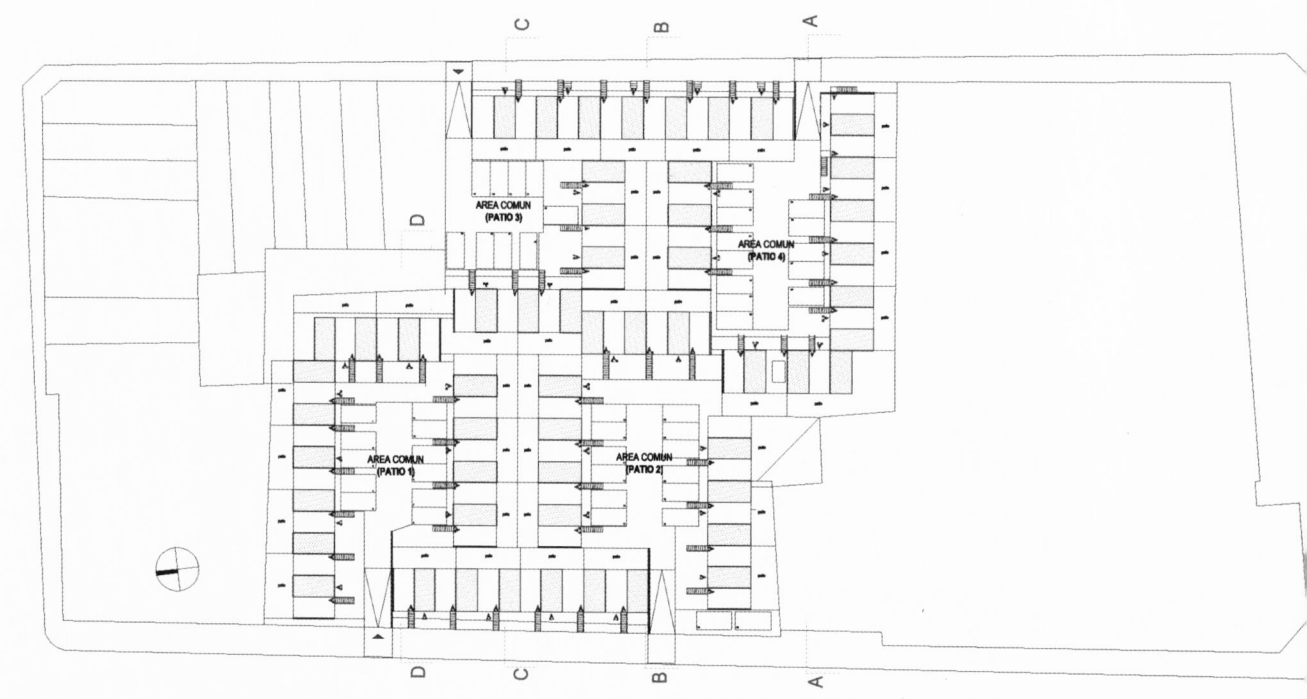

ELEVACION CALLE GALVARINO

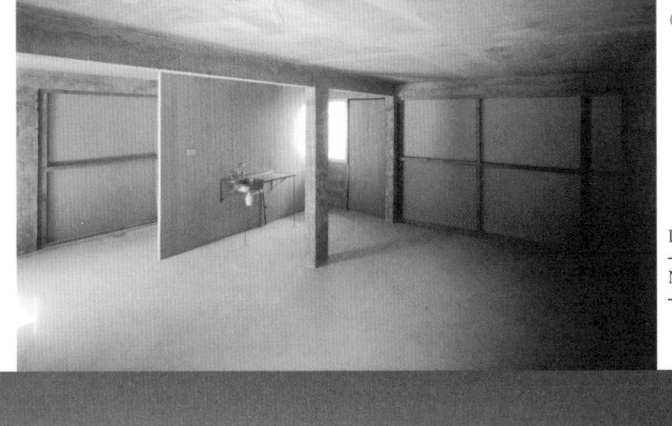

Clockwise from right: Interior of one of the houses at Quinta Monroy; Before and after views, showing the residents' additions to Aravena's initial provision; Layout and elevation of the housing.

| | |
|---|---|
| Location | Santiago, Chile |
| Nationality | Chilean |

Alejandro Aravena was born in 1967, graduated from the Universidad Católica de Chile in 1992, and after a year studying in Venice he set up his own practice in 1994. Since then he has become one of the most decorated and high-profile architects in Chile. His most significant body of work has been a series of buildings at his alma mater at the Universidad Católica de Chile in Santiago, but he is now working on various projects from social housing to a new national concert hall. He has published a number of books, including *Los Hechos de la Arquitectura*, and is professor at the Universidad Católica and a visiting critic at Harvard's Graduate School of Design.

nArchitects (pp. 212–213) and Patterns (pp. 242–243) were also nominated by US magazine *Architectural Record* as Design Vanguard Award winners in 2004. More recent winners include Evan Douglis (pp. 82–83) in 2005.

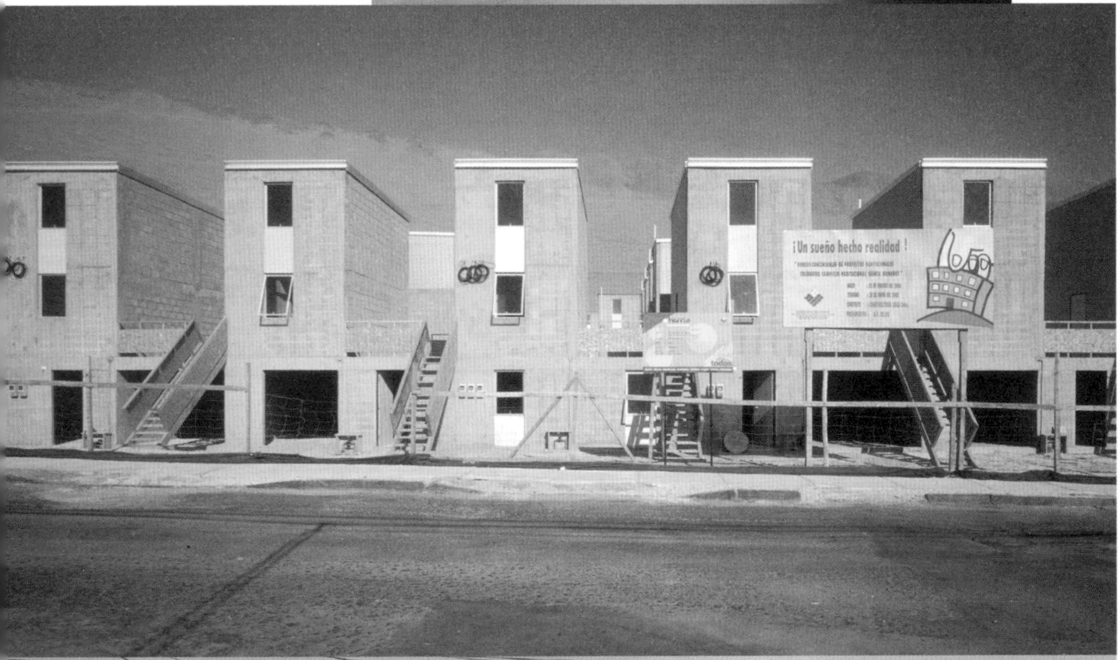

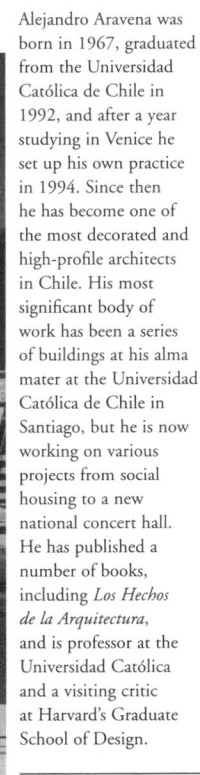

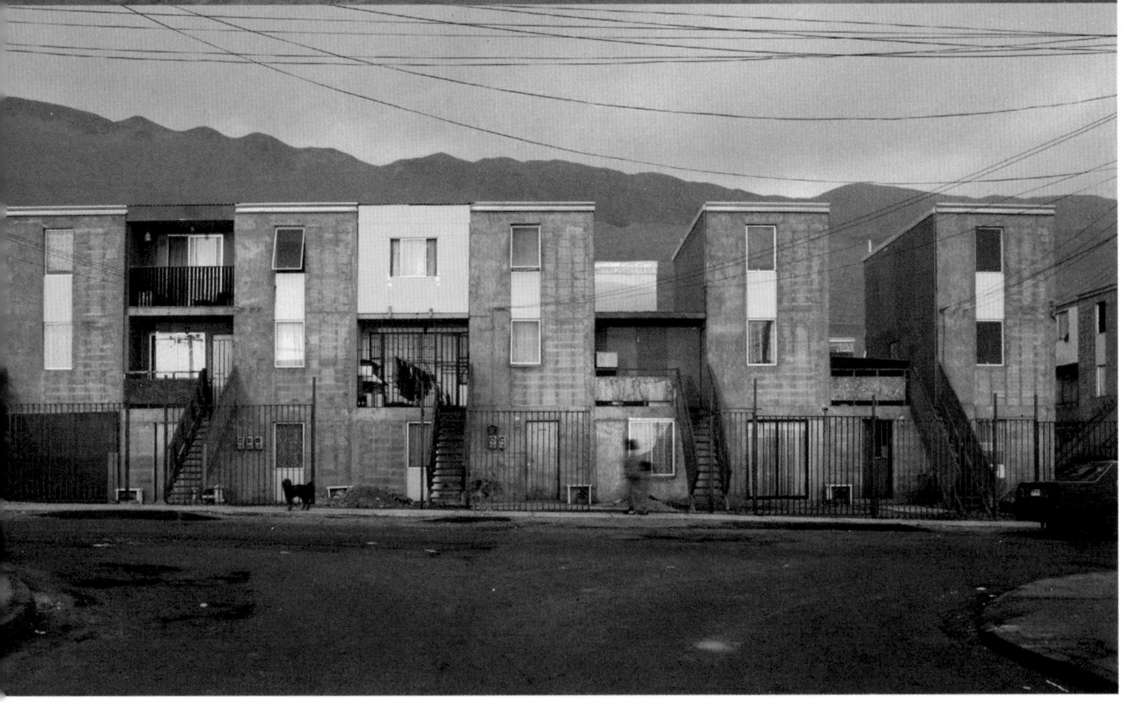

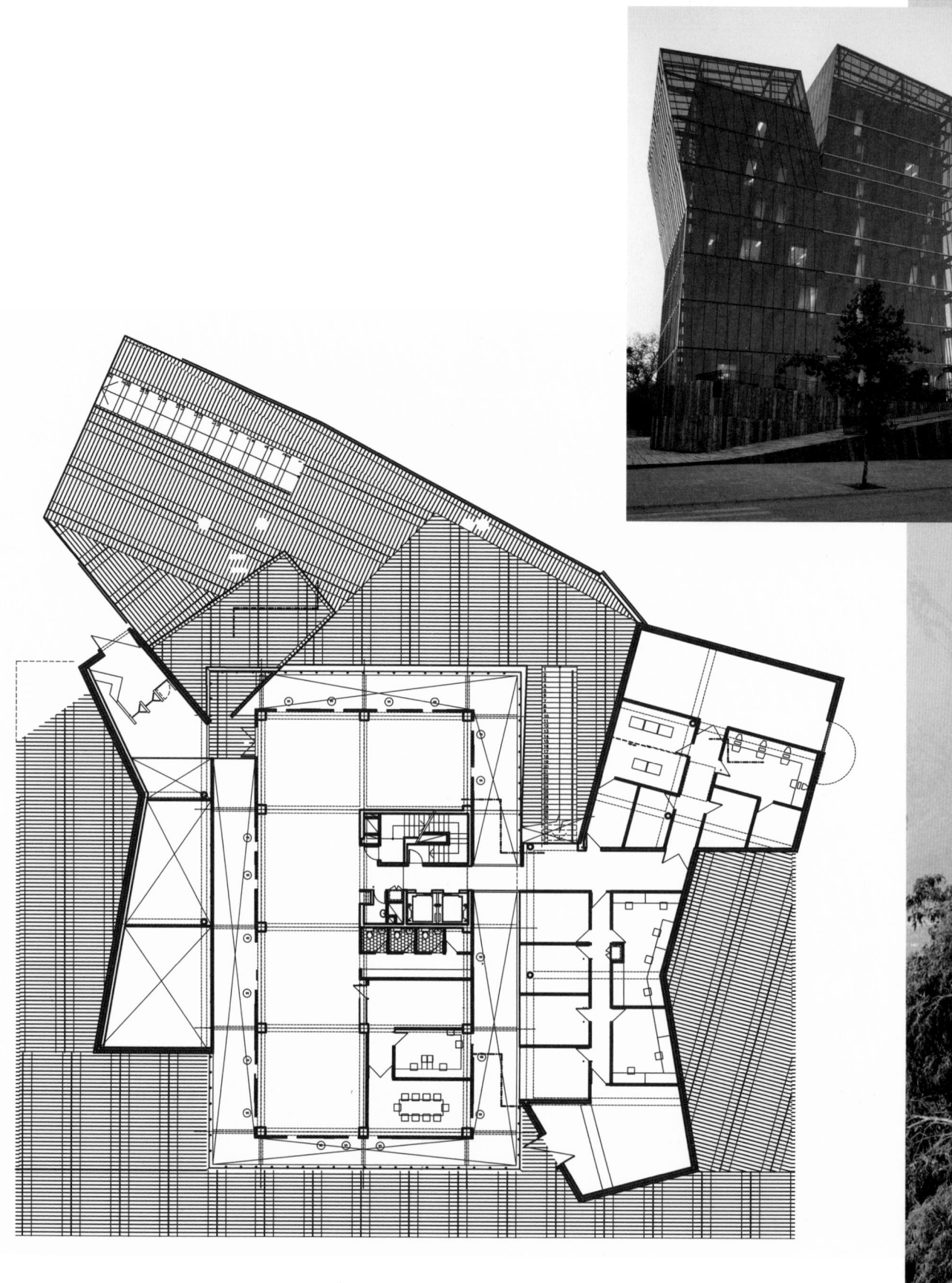

for families living in Quinta Monroy in Iquique in the Chilean desert.

Aravena makes the case for Elemental's importance in the history of architecture by referring to eclectic forebears. He refers to the 'two major moments' in social housing, the first being the *Weissenhofsiedlung* in Stuttgart, masterplanned by Mies van der Rohe, and the *Previ Lima* project in Peru, influenced by Christopher Alexander's *Pattern Language*. While this gives no real clue as to the formal persuasion of the future of Chile's housing, it is clear that Aravena sees it as much more than a local solution to a local problem.

He says of his increasingly public role: 'We are having a lot of influence in policy, housing policy, broader questions that can be answered by architecture.'

This spread: Views of the *Siamese Towers*, a university building in Santiago, Chile, with plan shown bottom left.

A

# Architecture and Hygiene

Quite what Adam Kalkin's work has to do with hygiene is unclear. The founder of Architecture and Hygiene's portfolio consists primarily of large buildings constructed using recycled shipping containers, as well as conceptual works, which have a tangential relationship to any mainstream definition of architectural practice. But it is this kind of obscurantist perversity and desire to exist outside of any orthodoxy that makes Kalkin and his practice such a compelling presence in the global architecture scene.

The majority of Kalkin's built work consists of riffs on the theme of cargo containers. The most extreme of these projects is his own house in Bernardsville, New Jersey. Kalkin bought an 1880s country house and built a brutal industrial shed around it, cutting out the form of a gable on one façade in glazing. This extreme juxtaposition extends to the interior. While the massive volume of the industrial shed is occupied by furniture as a large lounge room, the interior of the original home is given a super-

This spread: Views of Adam Kalkin's home, *Bunny Lane House*, in Bernardsville, New Jersey.

| Location | New York, USA |
| --- | --- |
| Nationality | American |

A

Architecture and Hygiene is the practice of artist and architect Adam Kalkin. Kalkin graduated in philosophy from Vassar College in New York State, before studying at the Architectural Association in London. He won the Young Architect's Award from *Progressive Architecture* magazine in 1991, and has since exhibited his work around the world, including at the Deitch Galleries in New York, Art Basel in Miami and, with Dutch collaborator Aernout Mik, in the Netherlands and Belgium. Kalkin has lectured at the Whitney Museum and MOMA New York, and has completed buildings such as the remarkable *Bunny Lane House* in New Jersey (2005). He has also designed a prototype prefabricated housing range called the *Quik House*.

chintzy makeover. Architect and writer Sam Jacob wrote about this project that 'the original house changes in all kinds of ways. The porch becomes an extension of the lounge. The roof and drainage, which once made the house habitable, become decorative. It explores the Modernist interest in the relationship between the interior and the exterior from an alternative angle.'

Kalkin's abiding interest in containers has led to him seeing the possibility of marketing houses made from containers as a low-cost housing solution for self-builders (the *Quik House* is his own attempt to market 185sq m/2,000sq ft versions of these), and also as disaster-relief housing. Kalkin sees the containers as a narrative device, as well as simple and effective means of enclosure. 'You can look at them both as junk or as something special,' he says. 'To me they are like a treasured antique: they may not be inherently valuable, but the history and the storytelling add value.'

Kalkin's more artistic endeavours are hard to square with the pragmatism of his container architecture. An example is his *Adam Kalkin Day Trader* project, about which he wrote: 'Believing that America is a machine designed for the efficient allocation of capital, and further, that it is its citizens'

obligation to energetically exploit any pricing inconsistencies in its broad and deep capital markets, [I] borrowed $1,000,000 to day trade in the stock market.' Stockbroker Charles Schwab lent him the money, and he made a net profit of £51,458 which funded the manufacture of his *Push Button House* prototype. He also donated $10,000 to a Tasmanian orphanage. Other artistic projects include an edited montage of Jerry Lewis movies, shown at the Shelburne Museum in Vermont in 2006.

Below: *Push Button House*, a container that unfolds into a dwelling. Right: *Adriance House* in Brooklin, Maine.

A

Other architects in this book who have worked with cargo containers include Lot-ek (pp. 176–177)
and Jennifer Siegal (pp. 290–291)

# As-If Architects

As-If's most significant project is its single-storey exhibition building at the Museum of Contemporary Art in Leipzig, Germany. The building, which has an irregular plan composed from a set of polygons and an abstract architectural language, is on a wooded site adjacent to the existing museum.

The project is intentionally very far from the classical contemporary art space, say the architects. 'In opposition to the idea of the classical notion of the "White Cube", which at the same time neutralizes social implications as well as producing an atmosphere of aura, the design enhances a principle of permanent engagement and a dialogue with the institutional parameters and its architectural representation.'

This institutional critique can perhaps be seen as characteristic of much Berlin art practice, which is highly engaged with rethinking the locations of cultural events. The main intervention of As-If in these terms was the use of a series of sliding walls, which open up views across the gallery space, and allow surprising juxtapositions within exhibitions. As well as giving curatorial freedom, the project allows a flexibility of use. There are three entrances to the building; one of them leads to the café and cinema, which can be kept open when the rest of the gallery is closed.

The façade of the building, with its rhythmic mullions, is intended to heighten a sense of perspective in the viewer, and also betrays a certain influence from fellow Berlin practice Barkow Leibinger, for whom two of As-If's partners previously worked.

The Leipzig project questions curatorial conventions in the art world.

Also interesting in this context are Anteeksi (pp. 18–19), Deadline (pp. 76–77), Evan Douglis (pp. 82–83) and ReD Research + Design (pp. 270–271).

| Location | Berlin, Germany |
| Nationality | German |

As-If was founded in 2003 by Paul Grundei, Stephanie Kaindl and Christian Teckert in Berlin. It is an interdisciplinary team working between architecture, urbanism, theory and art. All its members work with As-If and in other configurations, including Teckert's so-called Office for Cognitive Urbanism. As-If's work has been widely published, and exhibited in Germany, Austria, the USA and the UK.

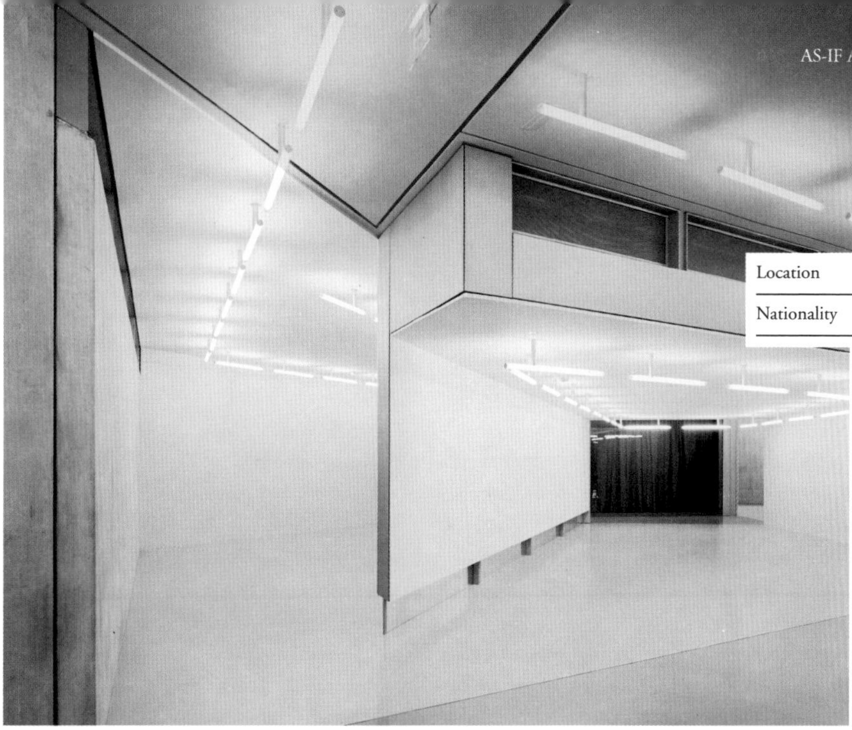

This spread: Views of As-If's project for the Museum of Contemporary Art in Leipzig, Germany.

# AWP

AWP's work has a strong landscape focus, and it is a garden that forms its most poetic built work yet.

The Royal Abbey of Fontevraud was founded in 1101 by Robert d'Arbrissel and was, before the revolution, the richest and most important monastery in France. In the nineteenth and twentieth centuries it was used as a prison, and was later converted into a cultural centre. AWP was commissioned to make a new landscape intervention on the occasion of an exhibition about Eleanor of Aquitaine (wife of Henry II of England, who became a nun at the abbey). Surrounding the abbey, AWP made what it describes as a 'fabric of moving green lines' out of high grasses, which accentuates the existing topography and leads the visitor to vantage points from which to view the abbey itself.

The architects write: 'These lines are drawn over the existing grass, and they are made of sensual textures and different types of greenery (including so-called Pheasant Grass). On the top of the hill, underneath a big tree, there is a place to rest, an observatory to the abbey and the distant landscape. This garden is a contemporary tribute to the intelligence and the vision of Eleanor of Aquitaine.' The project was selected for exhibition at the Barcelona Landscape Biennale in 2006.

AWP's *Troll* project (conceived by group member Matthias Armengaud) has very much more contemporary concerns than a dead queen. The art programme, carried out for the Institut pour la Ville en Mouvement (City on the Move Institute) in Paris, invites a range of different artists in many different European cities to make artworks and research projects about movement at night. A book about the project was published in 2007, recording the various activities of the project.

Below: Views of the *Troll* project, which examines the effect of mobility at night on the city.
Opposite: AWP's project at the Royal Abbey of Fontevraud. The landscape is described as a 'fabric of moving green lines.'

| Location | Paris, France |
|---|---|
| Nationality | French<br>Italian |

AWP was founded in Paris in 2003 by Matthias Armengaud, Sébastien Demont, Arnaud Hirschauer and Aurélien Masurel (who began working together in 1997), philosopher and artist Marc Armengaud, and architect and landscape designer Alessandra Cianchetta. The practice now employs around 20 people from multi-disciplinary backgrounds, making it one of the biggest offices in this book. Projects include the renovation of the Evry sewage treatment plant and a cultural centre in Bois-le-Roi, as well as projects in Italy, Germany, Scandinavia and the UK. In 2005, AWP came second in the high-profile competition for a new building for the Architecture Foundation in London, losing out to Zaha Hadid.

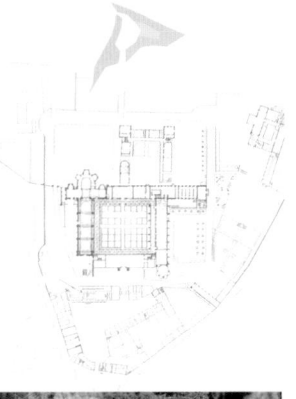

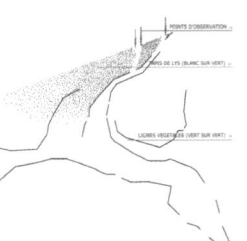

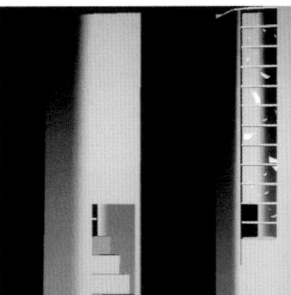

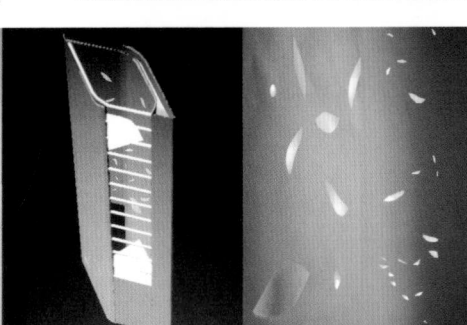

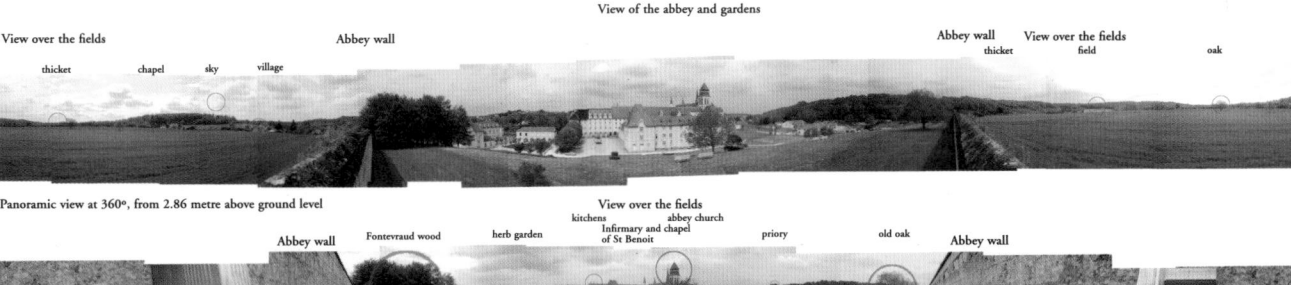

View of the abbey and gardens

View over the fields          Abbey wall                                          Abbey wall  View over the fields

thicket     chapel    sky    village                                                    thicket          field              oak

Panoramic view at 360º, from 2.86 metre above ground level

View over the fields
Abbey wall    Fontevraud wood    herb garden    kitchens    abbey church    priory    old oak    Abbey wall
Infirmary and chapel of St Benoit

Panoramic view at 180º, from 1 metre above ground level

# Ball Nogues

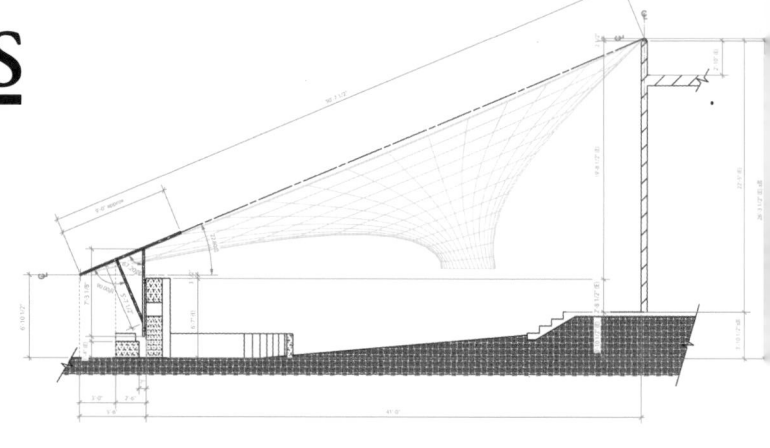

Ball Nogues is a practice with a very coherent portfolio. Each of the practice's remarkable installations exhibits the same fascination with material research and advanced computational processes, allied to a sensuous and organic imagery that adds spectacle and delight.

The practice's most high-profile success so far has been the *Maximilian's Schell* installation, a canopy that shaded the courtyard of the Materials & Applications Gallery in Los Angeles in 2005. The project was named after an actor in the Disney movie *The Black Hole*, who had a maniacal mission to 'harness the power of the vortex'. The form of the canopy is a vortex composed of 504 translucent petals made of reinforced Mylar polyester film.

The architects explain: 'Every petal connected to its neighbours at three points using clear polycarbonate rivets to form the overall shape of a vortex. As though warped by the

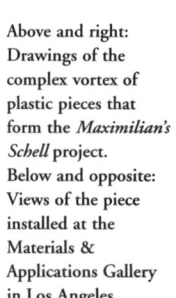
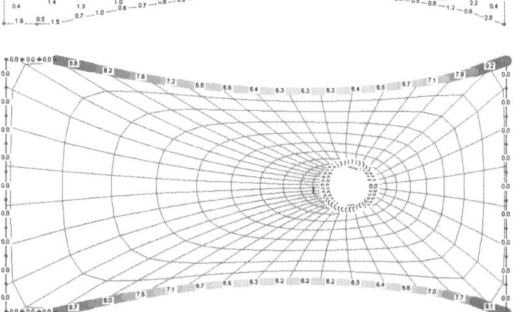

**Above and right:** Drawings of the complex vortex of plastic pieces that form the *Maximilian's Schell* project. **Below and opposite:** Views of the piece installed at the Materials & Applications Gallery in Los Angeles.

| Location | Los Angeles, USA |
| --- | --- |
| Nationality | American Argentinian |

**B**

Benjamin Ball and Gaston Nogues began working together as Ball Nogues in 2005, and have since completed a number of works at the scale of the art gallery or temporary installation. Both partners studied architecture at the Southern California Institute of Architecture (SCI-Arc) in Los Angeles, and both worked for Frank Gehry, before setting up on their own. Ball's previous experience includes designing and building film sets (for films such as *The Matrix*), while Nogues worked for Frank Gehry making mock-ups and prototypes using advanced computerized processes. Ball Nogues has carried out a number of high-profile and widely published installations, including the award-winning *Maximilian's Schell* in 2005. In 2007 they won the annual competition to build a temporary installation at the PS1 Gallery in New York.

gravitational force of a black hole, the petals continually changed scale and proportion.' The entire structure was modelled in a computer and is constantly in tension across its surface, giving the piece a smooth appearance. The amber canopy cast a remarkable series of fractal shadows on the floor when it was installed, and was combined with a sound installation by American composer James Lumb.

The two partners both spent time working for Frank Gehry in Los Angeles, an office renowned for its use of advanced computer technologies to realize its formally hyperactive buildings. Nogues says that while the sensibility of that office was influential, the practice's formal repertoire is influenced by much more than just computer technology: '[At Gehry's office] we built tons of mock-ups to test everything, and that influenced me. But also my childhood. My father used to take me to aircraft factories and I would walk around there completely fascinated by materials, by machinery, by process.'

The practice's projects always seem to be made in a context where they are intended to animate a space temporarily, for parties or exhibitions, and attempt a theatrical effect that goes beyond the technology of the projects' making. Their sinuous series of CNC-cut cardboard forms at the Rice Gallery in Houston, Texas entitled *Rip Curl Canyon* (2006) used advance computation again, but, Ball explains, was inspired by the mythical forms of the American landscape. 'The topography of it, the forms, for me come out of a background of living in Colorado. They just seemed very natural to me,' he says.

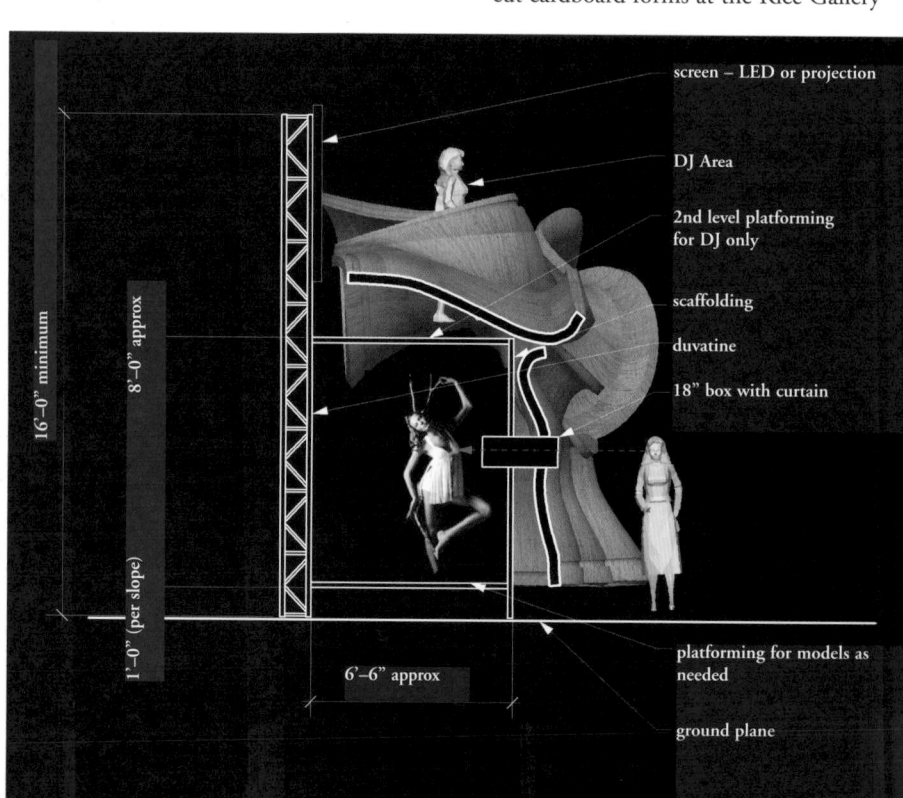

screen – LED or projection

DJ Area

2nd level platforming for DJ only

scaffolding

duvatine

18" box with curtain

16'–0" minimum

8'–0" approx

1'–0" (per slope)

6'–6" approx

platforming for models as needed

ground plane

B

Nogues adds that the tangible reality of mock-ups is vital to the practice's working processes. 'We're interested in being able to pull it off – and to do that you have to know the material you are working with. It's a lot easier to take a 5-axis milling machine and have it mill a form that you want, but we're not interested in that.'

Right and bottom: Views of the *Rip Curl Canyon* installation at the Rice Gallery in Houston in 2006. Opposite bottom: Drawing for design of Gehry Jewelry Launch on closed section of Beverly Hill's Rodeo Drive for Tiffany & Company in 2006.

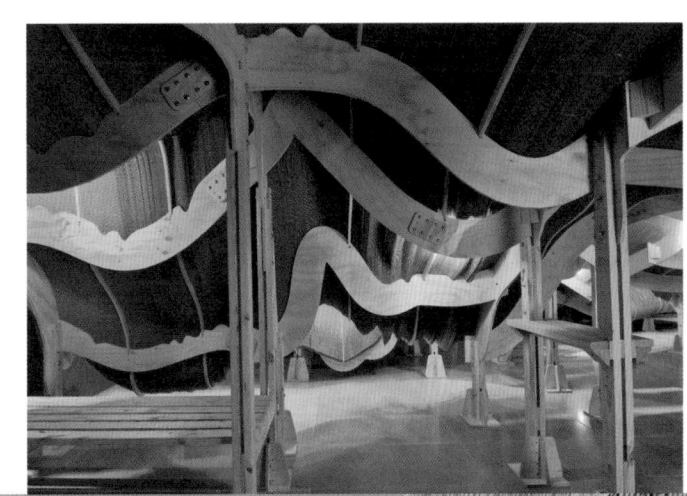

# Baumann Roserens

Baumann Roserens' work can look austere, with their housing projects in particular taking on a geometrical rigour that verges on intimidating, but with the practice's competition-winning project for a tram station on the Limmatplatz in Zurich, the practice made an ovoid roof, punctured by existing trees, that belies their apparent rationalism.

This project replanned the busy intersection of the Limmatplatz with an almost circular floating roof with a gulley down the middle for the trams to pass through. The two independent roof forms give the place a coherent form and identity. Beneath the roof are six cylinders in steel and glass that the roof floats above. Inside these are a kiosk, ticket machines, a toilet and a café bar. Ellipses are also cut out of the roof to accommodate the four huge plane trees that already existed on the site.

Of a quite different nature is the hospital for small animals that Baumann Roserens designed for the University of Zurich. This is characteristically laconic as a building, creating a new space in relation to the existing veterinary hospital complex built in the 1960s. Functionally, the building is straightforward, with a ground floor dedicated to admissions and consultation rooms, and an upper floor with treatment rooms.

Below: Views of the Limmatplatz tram station in Zurich. Opposite, top: Project for a veterinary hospital at the University of Zurich, which will be completed in 2009. Opposite, below: Ski lodge in Stockhütten, Switzerland, completed in 2007.

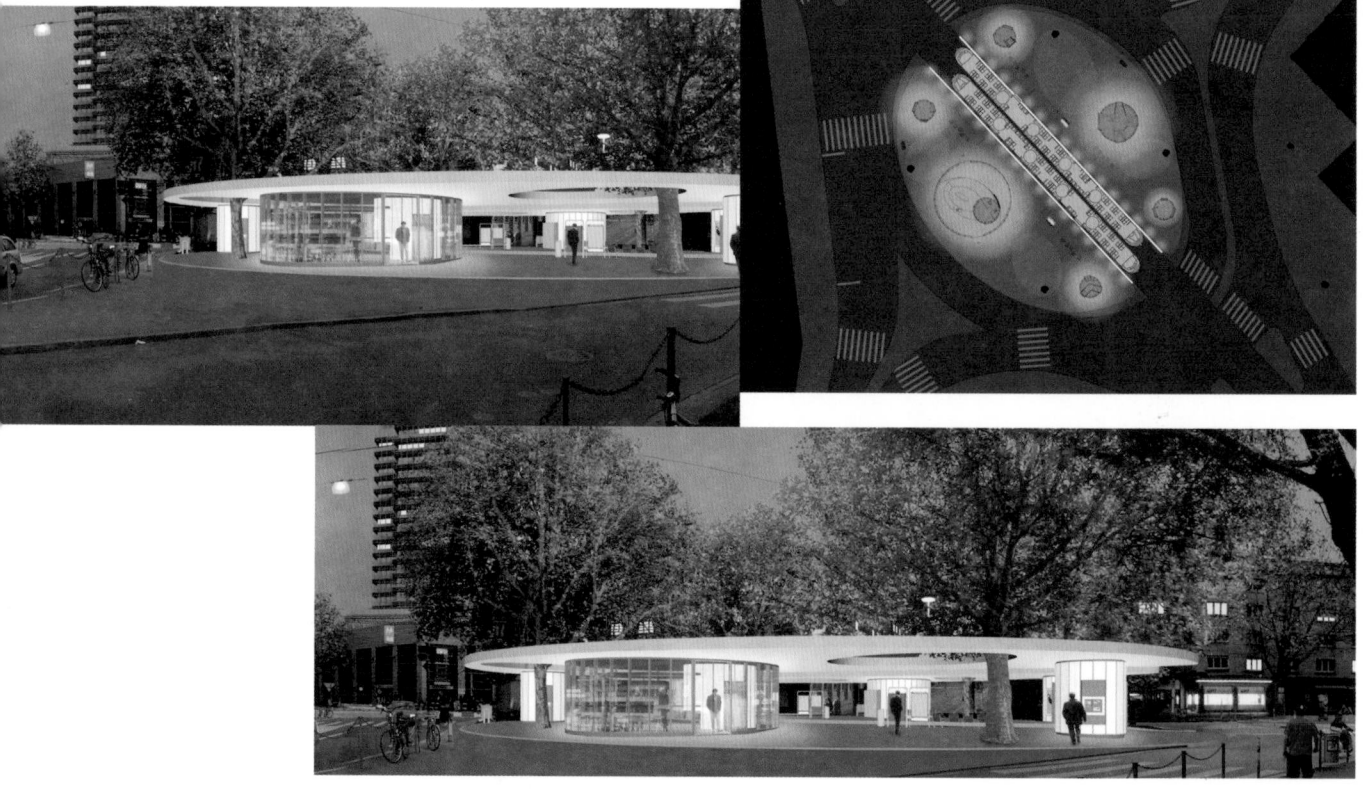

| Location | Zurich, Switzerland |
| --- | --- |
| Nationality | Swiss |

Lorenz Baumann and Alain Roserens began their practice together in 1998 in Zurich. Both partners studied at the ETH in Zurich, and the practice now employs five architects. Alain Roserens is a board member of the Architekturforum in Zurich. The practice has undertaken work at every scale, from urban planning to one-off houses, and much of their success has come in competitions. In 2004 they won the project for a new tram station in Zurich; in 2003 they won first prize in the competition for a residential building in Zurich-Albisrieden.

Baumann Roserens was part of the *Young Swiss Architecture* exhibition at the Swiss Architecture Museum in 2003. Although no other practices from that exhibition are in this book, Santiago Cirugeda (pp. 54-57), Andrés Jaque (pp. 154-157), Modulorbeat (pp. 206-207) and NL Architects (pp. 226-229) have subsequently appeared in SAM exhibitions.

# Die <u>Baupiloten</u>

An oft-cited criticism of architectural education is that it is unable to produce graduates who are prepared for the real world of practice. Die Baupiloten was created as a response to this polemic. Architect Susanne Hofmann began the hybrid studio at the Technical University in Berlin in 2003 to try to prove that education could teach experimental architecture, as well as providing real skills in design, technology and management.

Hofmann is responsible for bringing the projects to the university, and the clients employ her as the legally responsible architect. But the students are also given responsibility for developing and detailing their designs within a given budget, chairing meetings and working as a team. Hofmann writes: 'Through Die Baupiloten I have come to realize that students enjoy the challenge of transforming their design into something tangible. [They] work on such a project with an endurance, intensity and impartiality that can only be admired. In fact, it is the students' lack of experience, reflected in a certain openness and naïveté, continuous questioning and ambition, that very often lends wings to the project.'

The studio's most important project yet is the *Erika Mann Elementary School* in the very poor Berlin suburb of Wedding. In an austere Prussian early twentieth century building, Die Baupiloten wanted to give an identity to the school that the ethnically diverse student body could buy into, as well as to solve problems of storage.

The response was to involve the pupils at the school in workshops where they came up with concepts that went on to define the treatments of the interiors. 'Listening to the pupils describing their imaginary landscape with a very evocative and sensuous vocabulary was inspiring,' says Hofmann. 'They led us through an airy, golden, icy, soft, cushioned, fluffy, feathery, furry, cuddly, tight, bright, dreary, wispy, stretchy, prickly world.' The scheme developed around the story of an imaginary dragon, and the imagery of wings, tails and even dragon's breath generated spaces with sinuous lit roofscapes, a staircase with musical balustrades, and hallways full of nooks for children to play or quietly read in. Many of the furniture pieces were produced to drawings by inmates at a local prison, and mentally and physically handicapped people helped in the sewing of textiles and the production of wardrobes.

| Location | Berlin, Germany |
| --- | --- |
| Nationality | German |

**B**

Die Baupiloten is an experimental design course at the Technical University of Berlin, Germany. Led by architect Susanne Hofmann as tutor, the course aims to give students real experience of designing and building projects, bridging the gap in education between theory and practice. Die Baupiloten has carried out several projects in Berlin, including a lecture hall, the transformation of a school and two kindergartens. Susanne Hofmann studied in Berlin, Hamburg and London, and began Die Baupiloten in 2003. Its work has been published widely. The *Erika Mann Elementary School* received an honourable mention in the AR&D Awards in 2004 and received a Socially Integrative City Award in the same year.

The 2004 AR+D Awards was a good year for architects in this book. Other architects of highly commended projects include: Manuel Clavel Rojo (pp. 58–61), Ofis Arhitekti (pp. 234–235), Atelier Tekuto (pp. 300–303) and Theskyisbeautiful (pp. 316–317).

Opposite: The *Erika Mann Elementary School* in Berlin. Each floor was given a whimsical title according to its atmosphere. This is the third floor, entitled *Flying on the Dragon's Tail.*
Above left: First floor of the school, *A Breath of Gentle Air.*

Above right: Second floor, *The Throne on the Beat of the Wings.*
Left: The *Tree of Dreams Kindergarten*, also in Berlin and completed in 2005. The lighting of the installation changes according to the weather and seasons.

# Biothing

Despite the seductive forms that Alisa Andrasek, founder of Biothing, creates, she is puritanically uninterested in their aesthetic effects. 'I'm not interested in creating a beautiful pattern,' she claims. 'I want to stretch the potential of the fabrication process so it can produce rich, differentiated designs that learn and change over time.'

This makes Andrasek pretty much a fundamentalist, even within the hardline world of contemporary digital design. Her approach brings together advanced mathematics and the potential of new computer software to generate forms, surfaces and shapes that respond to measurable parameters in the environment and learn from that data.

However, Andrasek's work differs from much of the now-common school of 'emergent' design, influenced by the work of writer Steve Johnson. Johnson's most influential book, called *Emergence*, documented the behaviour of 'bottom-up' communities, such as ant colonies, which organize themselves without an overarching, controlling intelligence. While many architects have used emergent design strategies to make new forms (Greg Lynn and Lars Spuybroek, for example), Biothing combines this theoretical viewpoint with computational power to design 'behaviours', as Andrasek calls them, most often regarding particular materials.

Andrasek's gallery installation *Bifid* (2006) used scripts in Maya to generate an intersecting form that required no glue or other framing to hold it together. The computer program instructed a laser-cutting machine to make incisions wherever a junction was required. The fabric created is intricate and is, despite Andrasek's claims, also very beautiful.

Other projects include reactive architectural elements that respond through movement, such as the *Invisibles* installation at the Prague Biennale in 2004, or the *Reticular* screening system that can change its opacity according to how the components are orientated.

Bottom left: Part of the the *Reticular* project for a screening system made of components that rotate and change in opacity.
Below and opposite bottom: Images from the *Bifid* installation, which was installed on the ceiling of the New Museum in New York in 2006.
Opposite top: A sequence of images from the *Invisibles* installation, an interactive sound and art piece carried out in collaboration with artist Mario Rizzi and actress Isabella Rossellini.

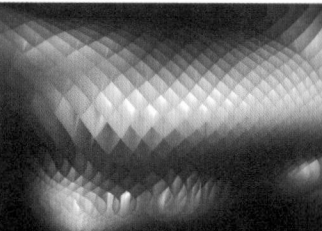

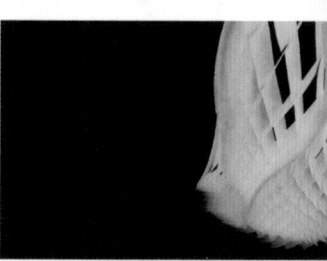

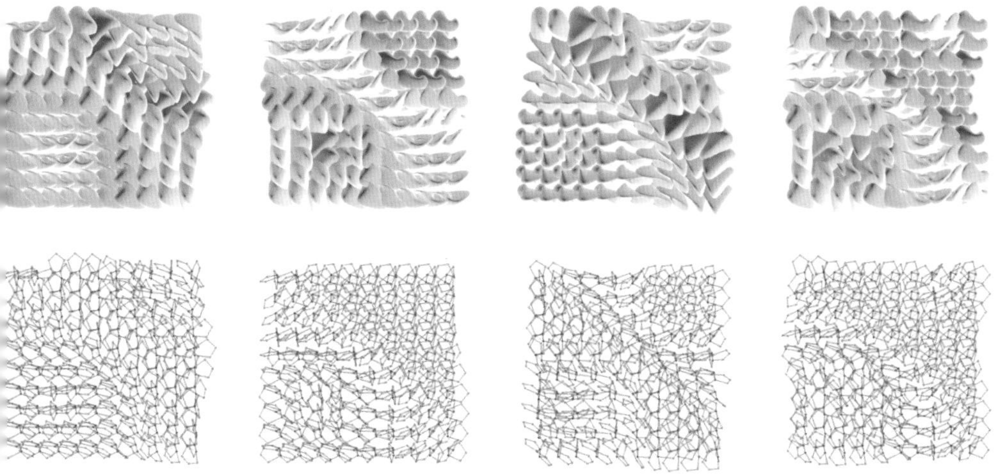

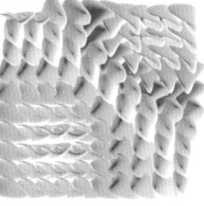

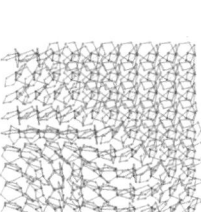
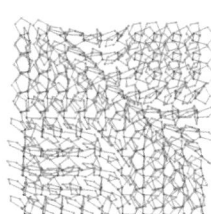
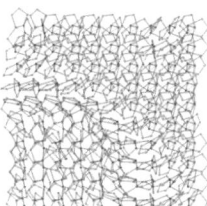

| Location | New York, USA |
|---|---|
| Nationality | Croatian |

Alisa Andrasek studied first in Zagreb in her native Croatia, before going to Columbia University in New York to complete a Masters in advanced architectural design. Since then she has taught at Columbia and other universities and lectured widely. She founded Biothing in 2001, and has worked on projects from clothing to gallery installations, as well as collaborating on large-scale architectural projects, such as the East River masterplan competition with Rem Koolhaas' Office for Metropolitan Architecture (OMA) in 2001.

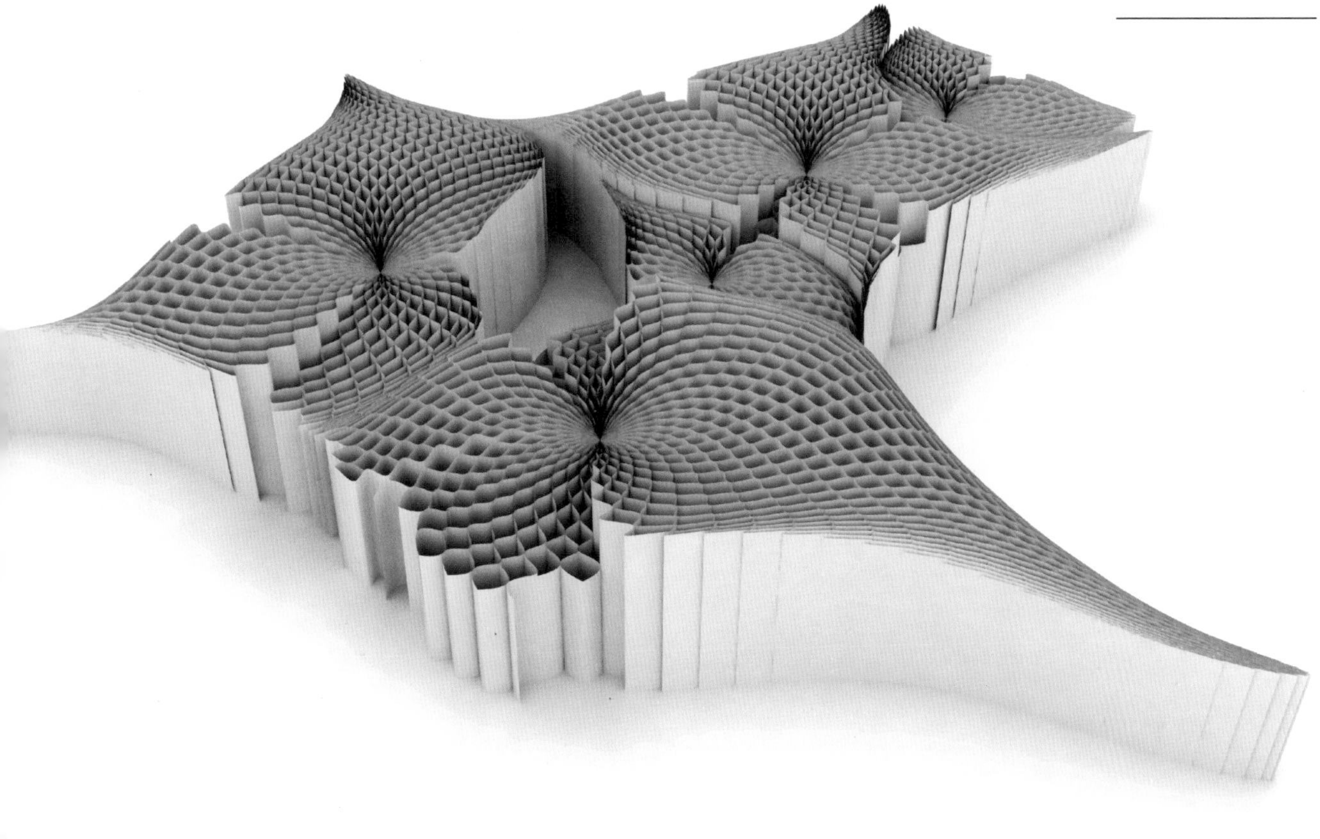

**B**

Other practices in this book in the emergence school (almost all of which come from the US) include Emergent (pp. 94–97), Elena Manferdini (pp. 190–191), Patterns (pp. 242–243), ReD Research + Design (pp. 270–271), Servo (pp. 282–285), UFO (pp. 324–327) and Xefirotarch ( pp. 340–343), among others.

# Bureau des Mésarchitectures

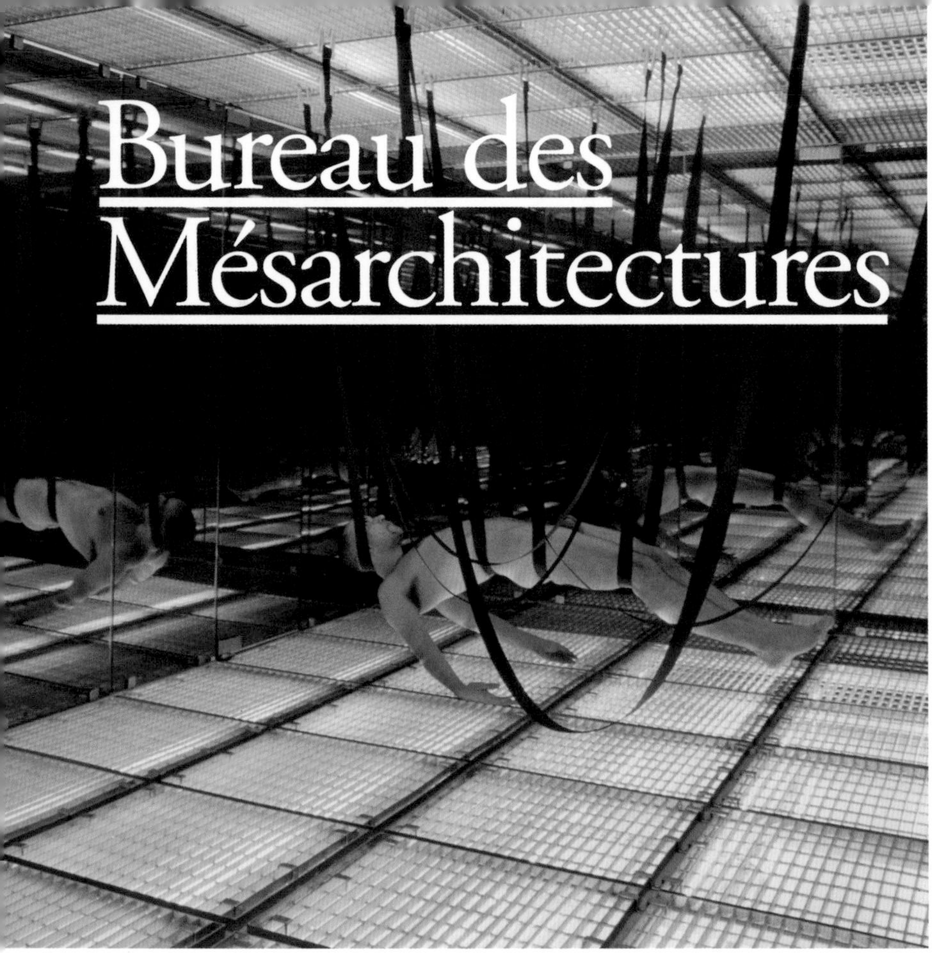

Didier Fiuza Faustino, the leader of Bureau des Mésarchitectures, begins the description of his approach with an attack on mainstream architectural modernism, railing against 'empty interiors that claim to be micro-universes but which are nothing more than an assembly of walls and partitions. Minimalist spaces in want of experience and sensations.' He continues: 'Architecture that remains insensitive to the movements of the mind or body, contenting itself with a glut of details while failing to grasp the richness of daily life. This architecture – who is it trying to fool?'

While Faustino does not (in his writing) name those he blames for such crimes, the work of his practice Bureau des Mésarchitectures is engaged in making spaces and installations that appeal directly to the human body, to our personal sensory and psychological fragility. But the work does not reassure us, instead seeking to remind us of things Faustino considers to have been lost by a 'straitjacketed

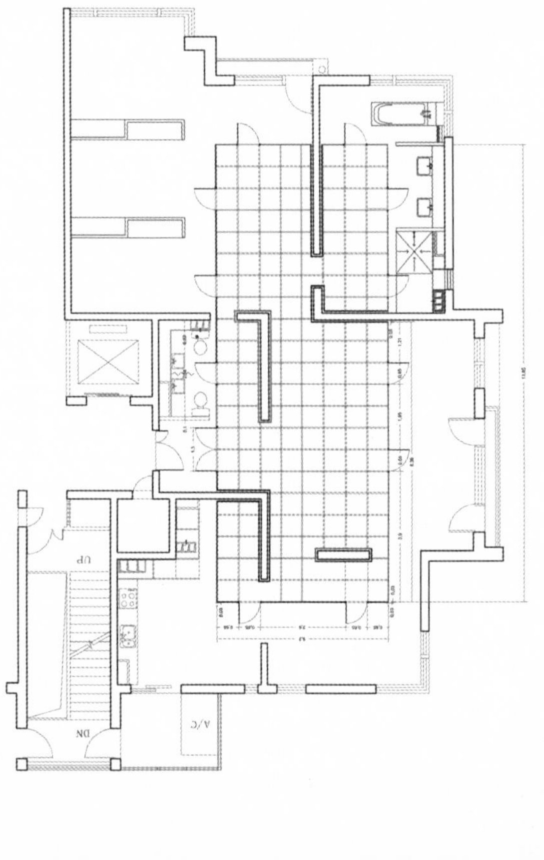

This page: The *Homepalace* project, with unconventional sleeping arrangements shown above.

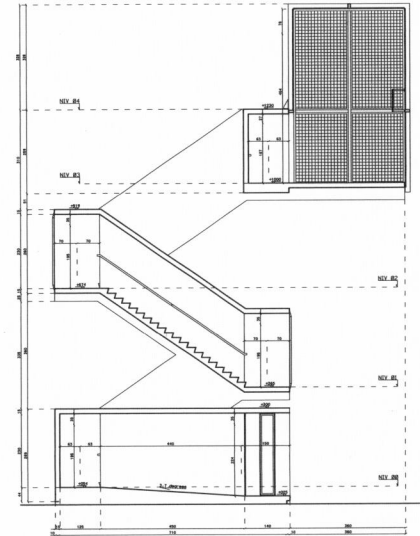

This page: *Stairway to Heaven*, a viewing platform on a Portuguese housing estate, completed in 2001.

| Location | Paris, France |
| --- | --- |
| Nationality | French, Portuguese |

**B**

Bureau des Mésarchitectures was set up in 2002 by Didier Fiuza Faustino and Pascal Mazoyer, who were later joined by Mathieu Herbelin and Cláudia Martinho. All four are qualified architects, but their work exists in the boundaries between public art and architecture – the members have been involved in arts festivals, publications, public art, performance art and architecture. Their work has won prizes from the French and Portuguese culture ministries, and is included in the collections of the Musée National d'Art Moderne in Paris and the FRAC Centre in Orléans, among others. Faustino has taught in architecture schools in France, Portugal, the US and Japan.

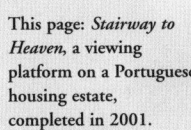

Paris is making a comeback as a place of provocative architectural production. Others in this book from the French capital include:

AWP (pp. 36–37), Périphériques (pp. 244–245), R&Sie (pp. 258–261), Phillippe Rahm (pp. 262–263) and Theskyisbeautiful (pp. 316–317).

and muzzled' hyper-hygienic contemporary culture.

Perhaps the office's most iconic project is *Stairway to Heaven* erected on a housing estate in Castelo Branco, Portugal in 2001. This project is an enclosed concrete stairway that leads to a caged viewing platform of just 4sq m (43sq ft) at first-floor level, described by Faustino as 'a sort of individual basketball court.' Along with the reference to a basketball court, it

contains other resonances of troublesome or loaded spatial typologies, such as the concrete stairwells of modernist housing estates, or indeed the cages of police vans. The project gives the occupier a bird's-eye view, but also puts him or her on uncomfortable display. Faustino explains: 'I always question notions of the individual and the group, what is public and what is private. Even going as far as to invert these relationships so as to restore their true meaning.'

The punning title of the practice's proposal for a médiathèque (a French library with a range of other digital-age services), for an invited competition held in 2003, would by some be considered a title in search of a project. But the *Casa Nostra* proposition is intended to subvert the supposed publicness of médiathèques by creating a series of boxes, connected to a central public space. The golden-coloured boxes, full of books or other cultural products, could be disassembled from the main body of the building and

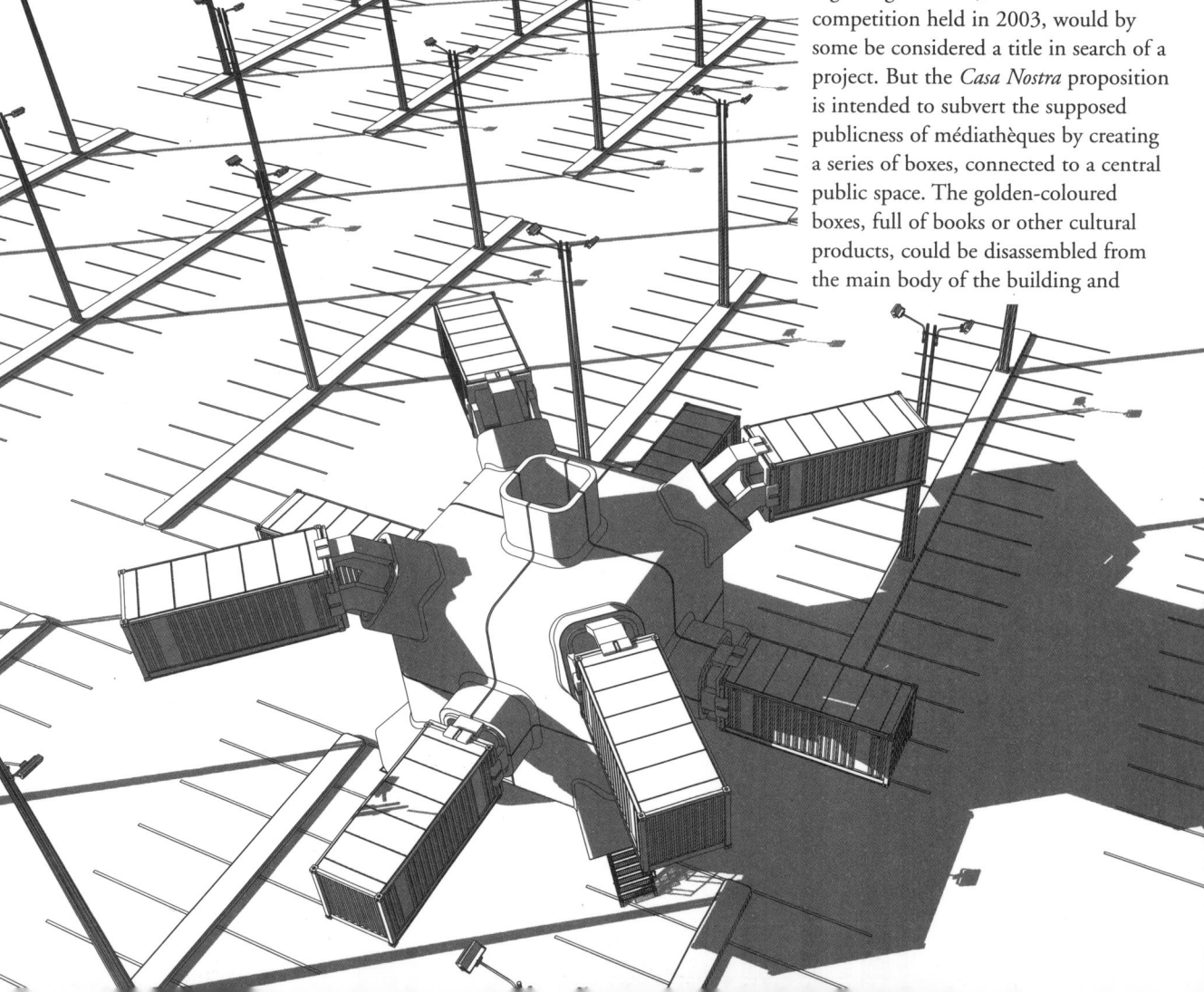

Some other practitioners in this book who are dealing with the maligned medium of public art include: Lead Pencil Studio (pp. 170–173), Modulorbeat (pp. 206–207), nArchitects (pp. 212–213), Pezo von Ellrichshausen (pp. 246–249) and Realities United (pp. 268–269), among others.

B

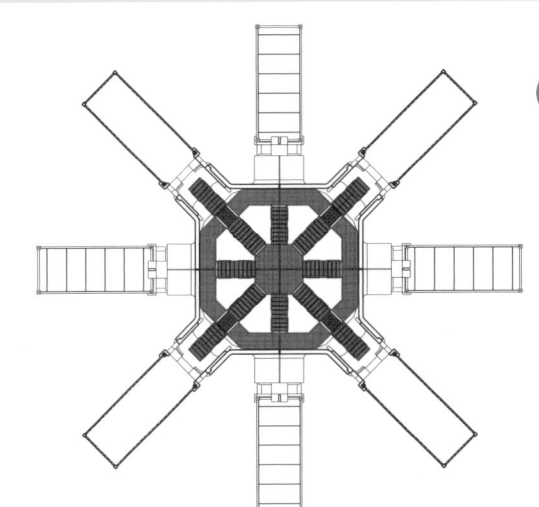

distributed throughout the city. The practice didn't win the competition: 'People didn't like the joke of the title,' Faustino jokes.

Faustino's approach leads to his involvement in some extreme and fraught architectural situations, such as a proposal for a memorial to the dying shipbuilding industry in Cherbourg in northern France. But, he explains, that is the essence of his work. 'That is why my office is called the Bureau des Mésarchitectures,' he says. 'Because we believe there is no bad situation for architecture. It is not about solutions but about finding ways for new possibilities and new arrangements.'

This spread: The *Casa Nostra* proposal for a médiathèque (digital-age library). The project's golden boxes are full of books, and can be detached and dispersed around the city.

# Caramel

Caramel Architekten's work has its share of spectacular modernist one-off houses, but it is an interest in industrial typologies that marks this practice out as one to watch.

The most significant of these projects is the *Central Garage* in Ansfelden, Austria, completed in 2006, which uses a limited palette of industrial materials to striking effect. The complex consists of 1,300sq m (14,000sq ft) of automotive garage, with three large mechanics' pits, vehicle hoists, and various other infrastructure, along with surrounding facilities of other workshops, paint shops, warehouses and a two-storey office building.

Caramel won the project in a limited competition in 2002 with a scheme that ignored the organizers' request that the buildings should be arranged in a linear manner, preferring a courtyard arrangement featuring an interior yard with a transparent covering. This creates an internal street, flooded with light from a transparent ETFE membrane roof, which can be accessed from either end.

The building was constructed in just 18 months, despite a very harsh winter, using an advanced steel-frame construction method. Long spans of 20m (65ft) were achieved with 1.6m-high (5ft) plate girders, and the whole building was made using mass-produced, standard beams and posts. Transparency is a feature of the building, but it is the reflective section of façade that really catches the eye. This may look like steel in the pictures, but it is in fact a synthetic EVA plastic membrane, and the rivets holding it in place make it look like a quilt, almost like a piece of fabric. What the architect describes as an 'industrial vernacular' continues inside the building, apart from the bathrooms which are entirely painted in green.

The practice's work ranges from art projects (their radio-controlled rain cloud was a low-key hit at the Venice Biennale in 2004) and small-scale installations to industrial buildings, but at Ansfelden they have showed themselves to be masters of a glamorous form of modernism.

The Ansfelden *Central Garage* was photographed by prominent architectural photographer Hertha Hurnaus, who has also shot buildings for Purpur (pp. 252–253) and many of the best emerging Austrian architects.

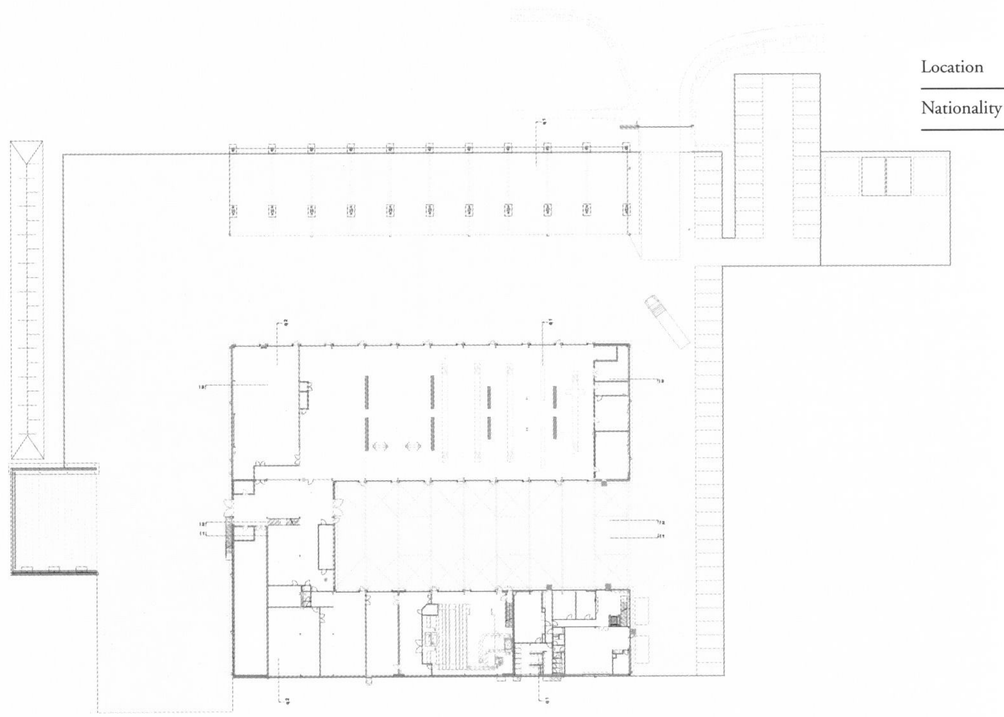

| Location | Vienna and Linz, Austria |
|---|---|
| Nationality | Austrian |

Caramel partners Martin Haller and Günter Katherl have worked together as Haller Katherl since 1997, but they founded Caramel together with Ulrich Aspetsberger two years later in 1999. They have since completed a wide range of projects across Austria, many as the result of winning competitions, particularly for medical and science buildings. Caramel's most significant completions include *Haus Lina* and *Haus H* in the practice's home town of Linz, the *MA48* office building in Vienna, and the *Voest Visitors' Platform*, also in Linz. The partners have lectured widely across the German-speaking world.

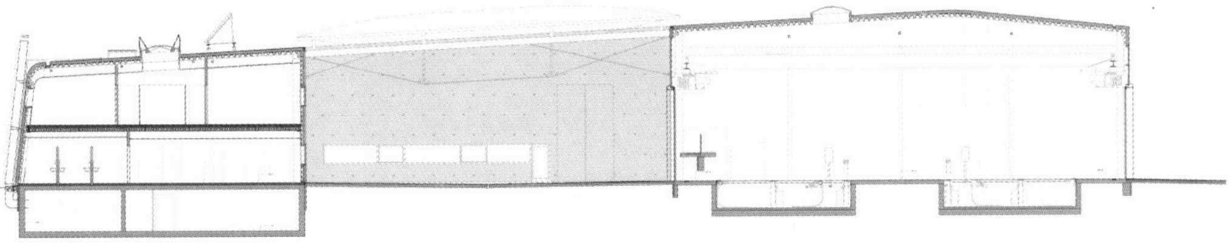

C

All pictures: The Ansfelden *Central Garage*, a bus garage in Austria, arranged around a semi-open maintenance courtyard.

# Santiago <u>Cirugeda</u>

Santiago Cirugeda's work is as near as architecture can come to protest. His small-scale interventions engage critically with planning law, building regulations and the other legislative frameworks of the built environment, pushing the limits of these rules and attempting to create new ways for the individual to affect his or her environment.

   He has said, of his motivations: 'I was arrested when I was very young. I didn't know what to do because I was very young and afraid. It is interesting that when an artist wants to do an exhibit, art installation or anything else, he can get permission to do whatever he wants and to show it in the street. But as a citizen, even if you ask for permission, you don't get it, because you are not an artist. Therefore, I work from a citizen's point of view, because as an architect I can get the permission required for my installation. But really I want to be a citizen.'

Santiago Cirugeda was part of *Projekt Migration*, a lecture series in Cologne in 2002 on migration and architecture, curated by Ilka and Andreas Ruby of Textbild (pp. 312–313).
Others involved included François Roche of R&Sie (pp. 258–261) and Eyal Weizman (pp. 336–337).

| Location | Seville, Spain |
| --- | --- |
| Nationality | Spanish |

Santiago Cirugeda was born in Seville in 1971, and still works there. Since 1994 he has produced architectural projects, written articles and participated in different educational and cultural projects, particularly in the field of semi-legal or guerilla interventions in the city. He is currently working on a cultural and visual arts centre in Seville, and is carrying out research on emergency dwellings. He has been a professor in Bogota's Javeriana School, and his work has been widely published and exhibited, including at the Venice Architecture Biennale and the Transformers Conference in Berlin in 2003.

All pictures: Cirugeda's *Insect House*, a way for protesters to temporarily occupy trees.

This attitude has led to several extraordinary projects, often presented in the form of manuals that his fellow citizens could use to pursue Cirugeda's reasoning. For instance, in the project *Building Yourself an Urban Reserve* Cirugeda gives a step-by-step guide to creating a tiny extension to your property, using rules that are usually intended to allow the painting of façades in historic areas of the city. The result, in an example built by Cirugeda, is a tiny module built at first-floor level on a street corner in Seville, and demonstrates, in his view, 'the incapacity of an institution to set boundaries to the complex human reality.'

Another politicized project, cosmetically a little similar but different in intent, is Cirugeda's *Insect House*, constructed in 2001. The project is a temporary bunker for those involved in political protest, its protective shell suspended 4.5m (15ft) off the ground and cantilevering off a sturdy tree.

Cirugeda's work is now growing in scale and tackling more permanent types of building, but his politics seem unshaken. His cultural centre, entitled *Institutional Prosthesis*, is likely to take a polemic about temporary buildings and urban planning to a more mainstream audience.

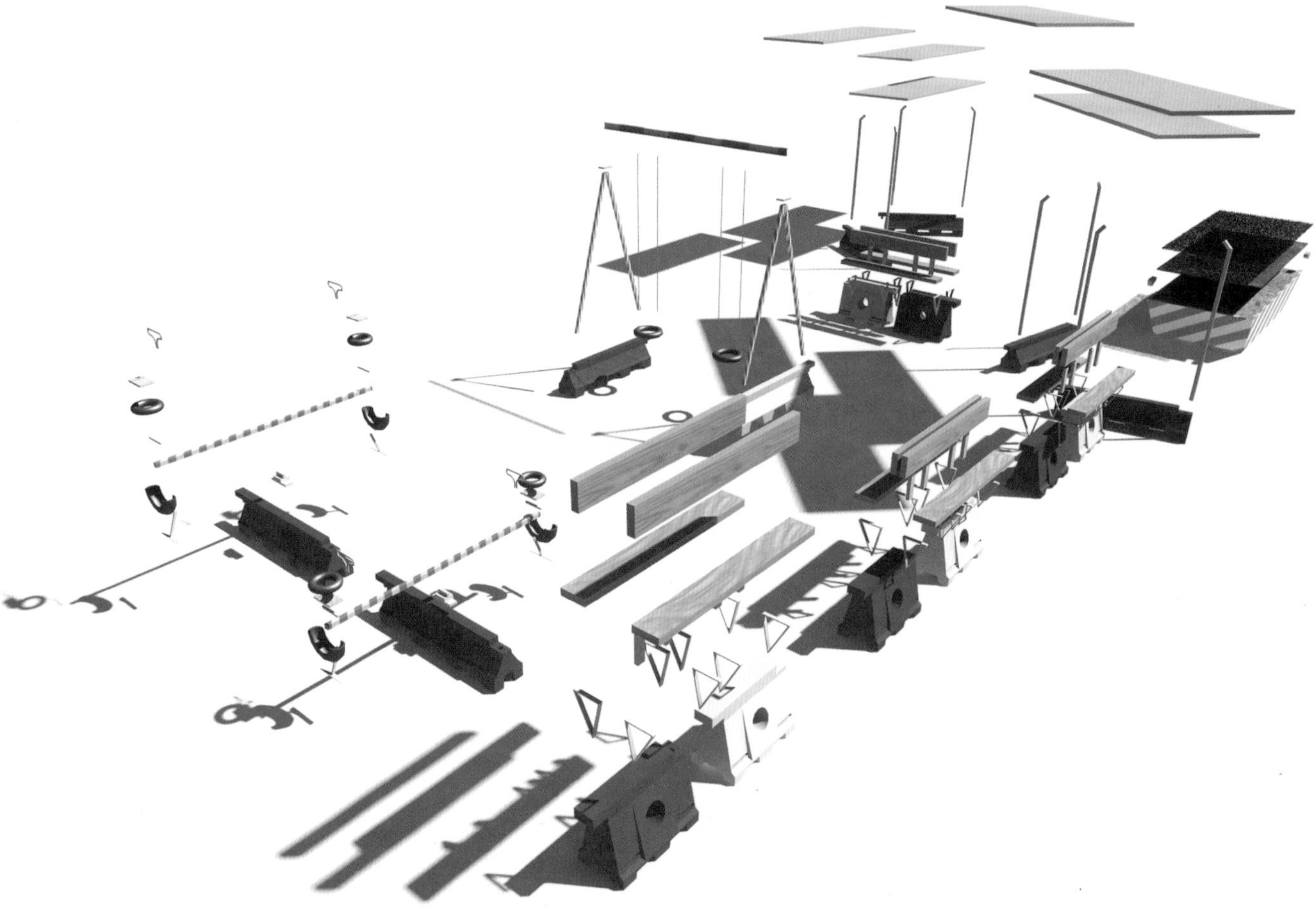

This page: Views of Cirugeda's *Institutional Prosthesis* project. In 1999 he installed this pod in the midst of the Finnish pavilion from the 1992 Seville Expo. Cirugeda invited people to stay in the pavilion during the time of the pod's installation, to question curatorial conventions. He writes: 'No reality, least of all the artistic (architectural), is immutable or static.'

Opposite: The occupation of an empty building lot in Seville with a temporary playground, made from elements of temporary architecture from the public realm.

# Manuel <u>Clavel</u> Rojo

Manuel Clavel Rojo qualifies as a prodigy. For his age (he was born in 1976), he has more built work than most architects, but he has recently made his name with two mausoleum buildings – perhaps the most loaded architectural type of all – that show a virtuoso poetic and tectonic sense rare at any stage of a career.

The first of these was the fêted mausoleum he made at the *Alberca Cemetery* on the edge of Murcia in Spain. This project takes a modernist sensibility towards the manipulation of volumes, and gives it a distinctly

Below: The *Panteon Mausoleum* in Espinardo, Murcia, in its closed state. Opposite: The sheer façade is transformed when opened, as the two rectangular planes disappear and the depth of the building is revealed.

| Location | Madrid, Spain |
| --- | --- |
| Nationality | Spanish |

Manuel Clavel Rojo was born in Murcia, Spain, in 1976, making him one of the youngest architects in this book. He studied in Madrid, and has been collaborating with London-based Foreign Office Architects since 2000. He has a considerable amount of built work for his age, including the *Nautical Club* in Cartagena (1999), a school in Iniesta and the *F+S Mirror House* in Murcia. His most famous project is his *Alberca Mausoleum*, for which he was commended in the 2004 AR&D Awards.

Also commended in the 2004 AR+D Awards was Ofis Arhitekti (pp. 234–235).

symbolic material expression. A travertine plinth houses the below-ground mausoleum, and a slate tower marks the entrance, with a rusting steel cross in front of a stacked glass skylight the only representational element. Most lavishly, an onyx skylight allows light down into the crypt from above.

Clavel followed this with another mausoleum, the *Panteon* in Espinardo, Murcia, which is a house for burial that takes its place in a historic row of such buildings. The building is clad entirely in white render, with two huge black doors ('with scale and shapes beyond human reference,' says Clavel). Inside there is space for 14 bodies and 16 niches for ashes. The crypt is reached by some smooth stone steps, and the upper floor, for the ashes, by a steel staircase. The composition is completed by an inaccessible light well. He says: 'The third space is nothing – it represents an absence of everything. It's as if to say, there is a light beyond but you can't get there as a human.'

This spread:
*Alberca Cemetery* in
Murcia, Spain.
Right: The onyx
skylight allows light
into the room
containing niches
for cremains.

# Cloud 9

Welcome to the world of Enric Ruiz-Geli. 'Let's try to mix,' he proposes on his website, 'Roberto Benigni, Amadeus Mozart, *Rainman*, the man on the moon, *Forrest Gump*, Luke Skywalker, Sergei Eisenstein, Yago Conde, Oscar Wilde, Bob Wilson, Paul Virilio, *Orlando*, Antonin Artaud, El Flautista de Hammelin, Ignasi de Sola Morales, *Shine* … and an eight-year-old kid.'

This eclectic and possibly faux-naif opening belies a technocratic approach to making architecture that Cloud 9 is now developing into some of the most hotly anticipated architectural projects of the early twenty-first century. Ruiz-Geli's background was in stage-set design, but his architectural work has always had a strong data-driven motivation. Critic Kristine Feireiss described Ruiz-Geli's 2001 proposal *Lifescan Plot House* as the 'first plotted house'. His approach to that proposal combined a strict functional analysis of activities within a home and a material responsiveness that allowed the 40m-long (130ft) building to constantly adjust its shape to the inhabitants. Ruiz-Geli described this as an 'interface house', which neatly sums up much of the rest of his work.

Ruiz-Geli's two most recent projects of note have been private houses in Spain: *Villa Bio* and *Villa Nurbs*. *Villa Bio* is a neat, two-storey house with a bifurcating form and

Below: *Morphorest*, Ruiz-Geli's project at the Barcelona Forum in 2004.
Opposite: *Villa Nurbs* in Empuriabrava, Spain, a keenly anticipated project here shown under construction. The elaborate formwork for the concrete undercroft is shown at the bottom of the page.

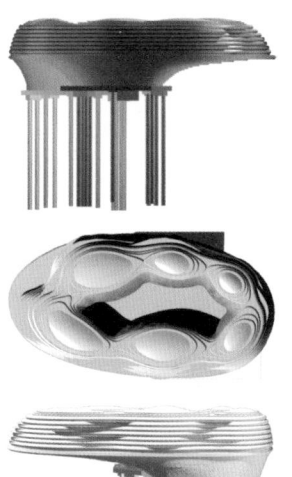

| Location | Barcelona, Spain |
| --- | --- |
| Nationality | Spanish |

Enric Ruiz-Geli studied architecture in Barcelona and Mississippi before moving to Paris to study scenographic design. He founded Cloud 9 in 1995, and began by designing stage sets for artists such as Philip Glass and Yoko Ono. He has directed theatre projects, ephemeral architecture, exhibitions, interventions and events, and more recently has completed two extraordinary private houses. Spanish publisher Actar is to publish a book about one of these – *Villa Nurbs*. As a curator he was commissioner of the Spanish pavilion at the 2003 Architecture Biennale of Sâo Paulo, and co-director of Metapolis, the Barcelona architecture festival. His work has been published and exhibited widely, and the model of *Hotel Habitat* is held in the permanent collection of MOMA New York.

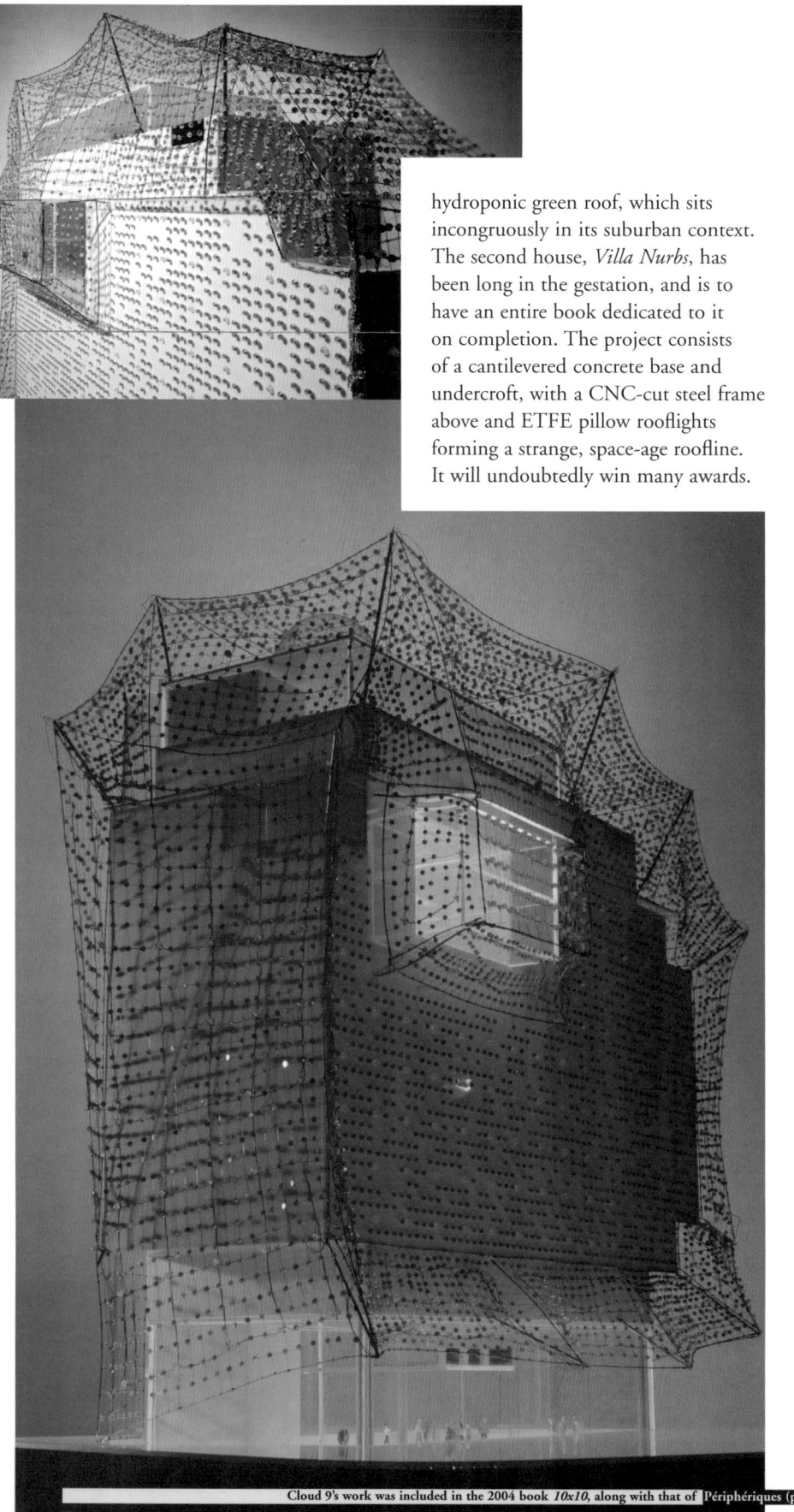

hydroponic green roof, which sits incongruously in its suburban context. The second house, *Villa Nurbs*, has been long in the gestation, and is to have an entire book dedicated to it on completion. The project consists of a cantilevered concrete base and undercroft, with a CNC-cut steel frame above and ETFE pillow rooflights forming a strange, space-age roofline. It will undoubtedly win many awards.

Ruiz-Geli's most important project, the *Hotel Habitat* in Barcelona's L'Hospitalet area, was due to be completed in 2008. The project is defined by its responsive skin. Consisting of a light mesh by interactive lighting designer James Clar, it has 500 computer-controlled lights and embedded photosensors that map the movement and intensity of the sun across the façade during the day. At night, the colour and pattern of the 500 lights will recall this solar movement. Collaborating with Cloud 9 on the project are other high-profile designers such as Vito Acconci and Dutch product designers Droog. The model of the project was acquired by MOMA New York after it appeared in its 2006 exhibition of contemporary Spanish architecture.

Until this project is completed, it will be difficult to know just how big a name Cloud 9 will become. But its mix of sloganeering (a typical quote from Ruiz-Geli: 'We perform architecture like a graffiti artist: full of ideas searching for the right wall-site to place them. We try to move mountains every week. Just do it.'), techno-babble and eccentric form-making seems to guarantee success in today's architectural market.

Enric Ruiz-Geli gave a joint lecture with Jürgen Mayer H (pp. 194–197) in Barcelona in November 2006 on the subject of national and international languages of architecture.

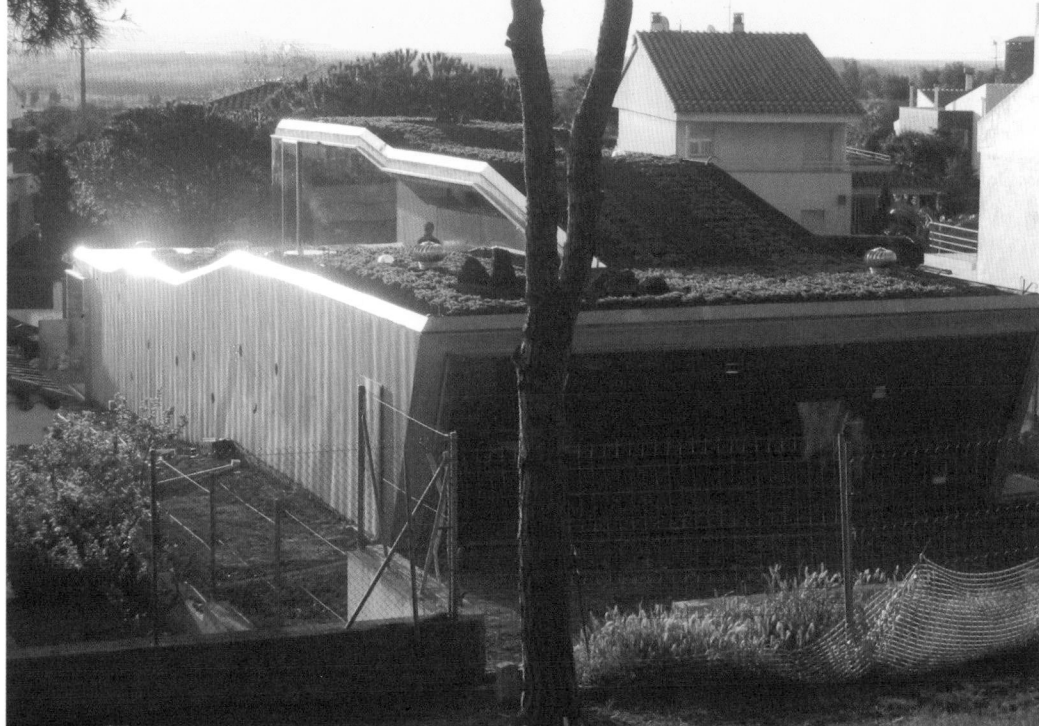

Opposite: The model of *Hotel Habitat* in Barcelona. The whole building is covered in a light-responsive mesh. Luminaires on the mesh will change colour according to how much sun they are exposed to over the course of a day. The model is in MOMA New York's permanent collection. Right and below: The bifurcated *Villa Bio* in Figueras, Spain, completed in 2003.

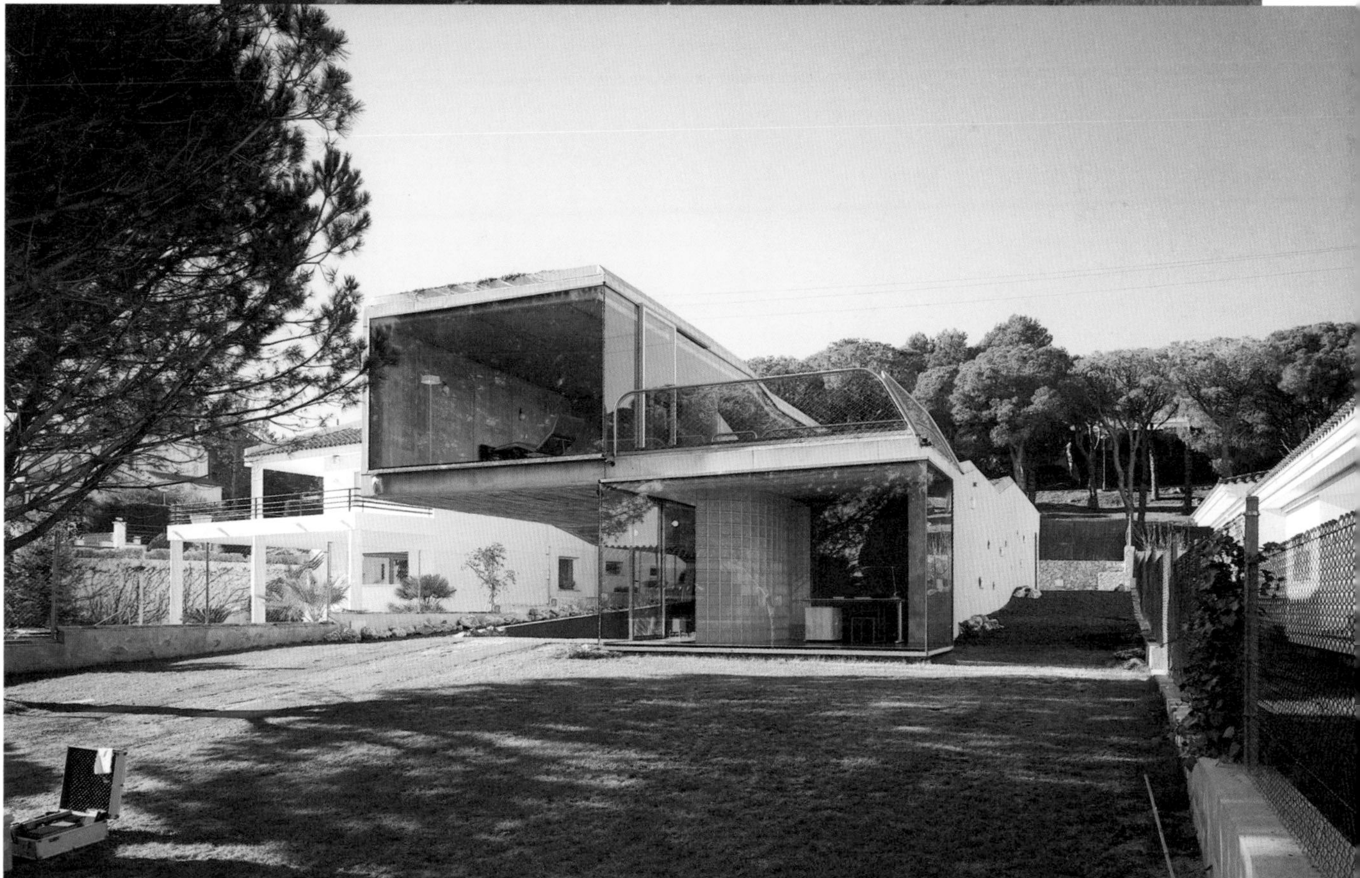

# Michael Collins

These photographs are part of Collins'
series of *Record Pictures*, documenting
seemingly banal urban landscapes that
are undergoing periods of transition.
His work is interested in returning
to the roots of photography's use
as a medium that fixes memories in
images, but it is equally influenced
by seventeenth-century Dutch
topographical painting, which sought
to reveal the impact of industrial
processes on the landscape.

Below: Bourdon Street,
London, 2005.
Opposite top: Battersea
Power Station Turbine
Hall A, London, 2006.
Opposite below:
Battersea Power Station,
London, 2006.

| Location | London, UK |
|---|---|
| Nationality | British |

Michael Collins is an artist and photographer based in London. He was born in Calcutta, India, and studied international relations before turning to photography. His work is strongly influenced by the seminal German photographers Bernd and Hilla Becher, and he has completed several series of what he calls *Record Pictures*, objective studies of sometimes banal urban contexts. Collins has lectured in Europe and America, and has published articles in the UK's *Tate Magazine* and the *Daily Telegraph* newspaper.

Below: Jaguar, Castle
Bromwich, 2006.

C

Below: R.J. Nash,
Birmingham, 2006.

Collins was commissioned in 2007 by art director Sarah Douglas to undertake photoshoots for UK magazine *The Architects' Journal*, as was Oliver Godow (pp. 130–133).

# Concrete

Concrete is one of the most successful young offices in the Netherlands, with a marketing-led approach that seems to owe as much to contemporary advertising agencies as it does to architecture offices.

The practice's career so far has been characterized by ambition. When it won the Mart Stam Incentive Prize for young designers in 2001, the citation read: 'In the first place, it is not necessary; the winner has absolutely no need of encouragement. Production is moving at high speed ....' Its interior design was also characterized well by this citation, which said the practice has a feeling for 'the things people like to do best: eat, drink, socialize, dance, converse, see and be seen', and this has been demonstrated in Concrete's many club interiors, including, most importantly, possibly the coolest restaurant in Europe in the 1990s – *Supperclub Amsterdam*.

For this remarkable space, in an old gym in a backstreet in the Dutch capital, the designers took a double-height space and turned it into a retro-futurist temple of decadence. An upholstered mezzanine accommodated recumbent diners at various levels of intoxication, and the performance dining concept (with dishes such as crucified guinea fowl) and array of entertainment took place in what Concrete founder Rob Wagemans describes as a 'blank canvas where people can do their own thing'. The concept was a huge success, and Concrete's work has since extended to fitting out a boat for Supperclub Cruise, and interiors in Rome and San Francisco.

The Supperclub concept, although not exclusively Concrete's, seems to be characteristic of the office's work. All its projects seem to have a concept that extends beyond just the physical fabric of a building to packaging, furniture and even graphic-design briefing. Its award-winning Lairesse Chemist is a working chemist, but clearly influenced by Damien Hirst's *Pharmacy* installation. Wagemans admits that Hirst is one of his favourite artists, and the translation of this work into a commercial sphere is typical of Concrete's pragmatic and commercial conceptualism.

Most recently, Ben van Berkel of UN Studio has acted as a patron, and brought the practice in to make the interior for the shop and restaurant of the Mercedes-Benz Museum in Stuttgart. It created a series of hanging threads of silver beads, separating spaces in vortices of silver, with sinuous ceiling tracks and curving furniture recalling the helical plan of UN Studio's building.

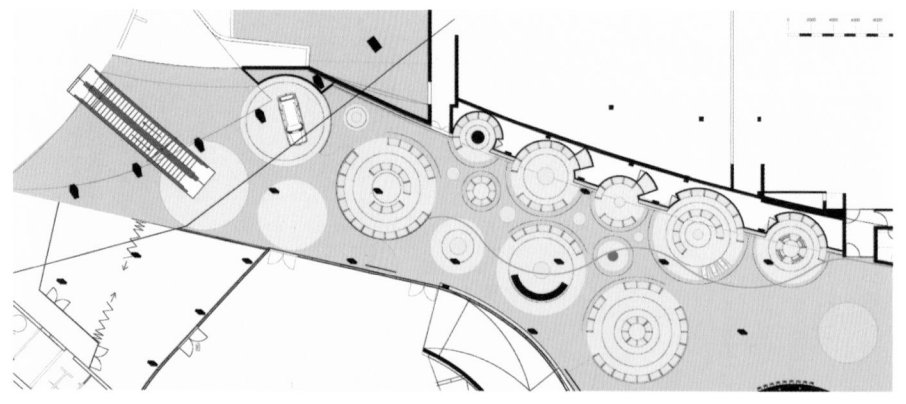

| Location | Amsterdam, The Netherlands |
| --- | --- |
| Nationality | Dutch |

Concrete was formed in 1997 in Amsterdam by architect Rob Wagemans, interior designer Erik van Dillen and designer Gilian Schrofer, who later left the partnership. The practice consists today of three parts: Concrete Architectural Associates, Concrete Reinforced, which works on architecture and urban design at a larger scale, and a model-making studio called Models Monsters. The practice employs around 25 people. Concrete's most high-profile early work was the *Supperclub* restaurant in Amsterdam, a concept restaurant that spawned a thousand imitators. Since then the practice has been prolific in architecture, urban design and interiors. This includes the interior design of the restaurant and shop at UN Studio's Mercedes-Benz Museum in Stuttgart, Germany. In 2001, Concrete won the Mart Stam Incentive Prize, and in 2004 the Lensvelt de Architect Interior Design Prize for a boat for Supperclub Cruise.

All pictures: Views of Concrete's restaurant on the ground floor of UN Studio's Mercedes-Benz Museum in Stuttgart, Germany, which was completed in 2006.

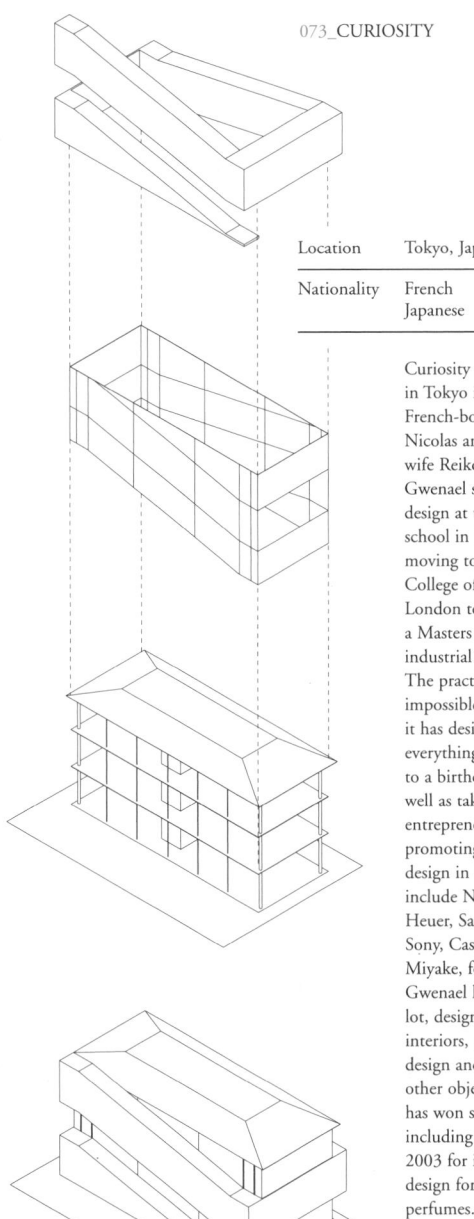

Curiosity must have the most diverse portfolio of any practice in this book. Its work includes perfume bottles, mobile phones, televisions, sofas, boutique interiors and houses. The practice even counts a specially designed birthday cake among its products.

More recently, the completion of two remarkable houses has announced Curiosity as a distinct voice in architectural design, even if the practice's product design background might irritate purists. The first, the *C-1 House* in Tokyo, is an ultraminimalist effort that doesn't really look like a house at all, consisting on the exterior of a band of white render with glass above and below. This scaleless apparition makes sense when it is described by the architect as a work of design rather than architecture. 'It is designed as a product, unique, independent, a seamless space where architecture, interior, furniture and products will become an unique emotional experience,' writes co-founder Gwenael Nicolas. He admits that the project was designed before a site was found, built from the needs of the user rather than responding to context.

| Location | Tokyo, Japan |
| --- | --- |
| Nationality | French Japanese |

Curiosity was founded in Tokyo in 1998 by French-born Gwenael Nicolas and his Japanese wife Reiko Miyamoto. Gwenael studied interior design at the ESAG school in Paris, before moving to the Royal College of Art in London to complete a Masters degree in industrial design. The practice's work is impossible to categorize; it has designed everything from a hotel to a birthday cake, as well as taking an entrepreneurial role in promoting Japanese design in Europe. Clients include Nintendo, Tag Heuer, Sanyo, Nissan, Sony, Cassina and Issey Miyake, for whom Gwenael has worked a lot, designing boutique interiors, packaging design and a host of other objects. Curiosity has won several awards, including an IF Award in 2003 for its packaging design for Issey Miyake perfumes.

This spread: The *C-1 House* in Tokyo, completed in 2005. Right: Diagram showing how the house was conceived, with a simple frame wrapped in glass and then in a staircase, which gives access to all floors. Below right: Gwenael also designed the furniture for the house.

**Gwenael Nicolas is probably better known for his product and furniture design than for architecture.**
**Others keenly interested in designing objects, from door handles to furniture, include 6A (pp.14–15),**
Anteeksi (pp. 18–19), Concrete (pp. 70–71) and NL Architects (pp. 226–229), among others.

The arrangement is relatively simple, consisting of a glass box with a walkway processing around it. The procession of the user is paramount in the project, even extending to the specification of the extremely thin steel floorslabs (6mm [¼in] deep, claims Gwenael) that give a barely perceptible sense of inhabitants appearing and disappearing between floors. Every detail is designed to suppress a sense of scale. Gwenael adds: 'The kitchen's identity, usually revealed by the tap and hood design, disappeared as the tap (just a metal line) and hood (integrated vertically within the wall) were

C

This spread: The *C-2 House*, in its wooded context in Yamanashi, Japan, completed in 2006. Getting to the house involves a long walk through the forest.

developed, so that the kitchen function does not seem to exist.'

The *C-2 House* continues this approach, and is characteristically shorn of all details. However, this house is in the countryside, and responds much more specifically to that location. The angled roof, designed to deal with heavy snow-loading, rises in sympathy with the topography of the site. The interior, though, is designed, says Gwenael, as 'a mini-loft. For a second you forget you are in the middle of a forest.' The entrance is through a covered bridge into an 'almost religious' large and simple space with a 6m (20ft) ceiling.

# Deadline

Perhaps it is the difficult economic climate of contemporary Berlin that encourages the tendency, but Deadline is one of many Berlin practices that has taken to generating its own work rather than waiting for rare commissions in the German capital.

Deadline have made a virtue of this entrepreneurship in their work. They write: 'We see no separation between the end product, and the processes and structures we needed to realize it. To maximize our creative freedom, we first seek to improve our influence on these structures. In many instances this has meant creating extensive supporting structures before embarking on a project. We operate as architects, graphic designers, computer programmers, curators, and developers.'

Such support structures include the gallery they founded in a building in the former East Berlin district of Mitte, and their role as developers of an apartment hotel in which their office also resides. They term their intimate involvement with the technical and financial aspects of a project as a 'prestructural' approach, attempting to free themselves from constraints normally acting on the architect's work.

The partners share an interest in investigating the impact of communications technologies on the built environment. An artistic intervention in Berlin in 1999 was one of the first manifestations of this interest. *Space Race* was a project that would perhaps only be possible in a city like Berlin. Deadline (in collaboration with Büro Genial) orchestrated a host of people to bring their cars to an abandoned railway hall, and parked them in a line on a precarious 400m-long, 5m-wide (1,310 by 16ft) platform. At an appointed time, the cars turned on their lights, warning lights and radios, creating a *son et lumière* show composed entirely of automobiles. Partner Matthew Griffin explains: 'Information technology offers us new ways of relating to space. Resources can now be used flexibly because we can communicate more effectively and manage information more precisely. This enables us to realize large structures by temporarily reorganizing existing material. *Space Race* created a monumental intervention with no physical material by diverting existing traffic flows using communication technology.'

*NR 63*

This spread: Scenes from Deadline's *Space Race* project (1999), where cars were invited to a Berlin warehouse to participate in an automotive performance piece.

Deadline were part of the German pavilion at the Venice Biennale in 2004. The *Deutschlandschaft* exhibit, curated by Francesca Ferguson, also included Heide von Beckerath Alberts (pp. 148–151), Jürgen Mayer H (pp. 194–197), Raumlabor (pp. 264–265) and Regina Schineis (pp. 280–281).

NR 8

BCR 4648    NR 10

**Location**    Berlin, Germany

**Nationality**    New Zealander
                   German

Deadline was founded in 1993 in Berlin by German Britta Jürgens and New Zealander Matthew Griffin. Jürgens was educated in Berlin, and practised in London and Berlin before founding Deadline. Griffin studied at McGill University in Montreal, Canada, and the Architectural Association in London. The practice's work has a strong entrepreneurial streak. Their early installations were carried out in the Urban Issues Gallery that they started in Berlin in 1997. They are themselves the developer of their major built work, the *Slender/Bender* residential and apartment hotel in Mitte, Berlin. They received a Berlin Architecture Prize for the building in 2003.

NR 26

# Disc-O Architecture

Disc-O Architecture's victory in the competition for a memorial to those who died in the 2004 Asian tsunami was certainly a career-defining moment, and looked as if it might also signal a step change in memorial design orthodoxy. The expressive landscaped spires of Disc-O's *Mountains of Remembrance* competition proposal represent a rediscovery of the symbolic order of memorials at the expense of the minimal. However, in 2007, the Thai government suspended work on the project due to what it claimed were escalating costs. Disc-O hit back at this with an international press release, saying that they had never been given a budget for the project. At the time of writing, the project had been put on hold indefinitely.

The proposal is for a cluster of five towers on a headland of the Khao-lak Lamru National Park in Thailand. The forms of the towers, like elongated volcanoes or enlarged stalagmites, are intended to recall various parts of the Thai landscape, from underwater caves to forests and coral reefs. Two public spaces are defined between them, one open and elevated, and the other covered and functioning as the main hall for visitors. The square could accommodate 2,000 people for annual memorial services.

The largest of the towers, 30m (98ft) high, is the memorial tower. It is intended as a place of contemplation, with a single, symbolic mangrove tree in it. The second highest is a museum dedicated to the tsunami, arranged on a spiralling walkway. The other three towers contain an education space, restaurant, shop and an amphitheatre.

The three taller towers have a double structure, one a tubular steel frame, and a secondary structure of cables, making the cones almost tent-like. The cables will have plants growing up them, further associating them with the forested surroundings.

The project is very sincere and serious about referencing the Thai landscape and the vernacular architecture of tropical climes. It is extremely well resolved for a competition entry, and this may have prompted the jury's only reservation – that it is too complex. The citation read: 'The Jury was impressed by the openness, generosity and ecumenical quality of this scheme, which combines references from many different cultures and religions in providing an iconic landmark and place of reflection for the families of victims and survivors of the Tsunami.'

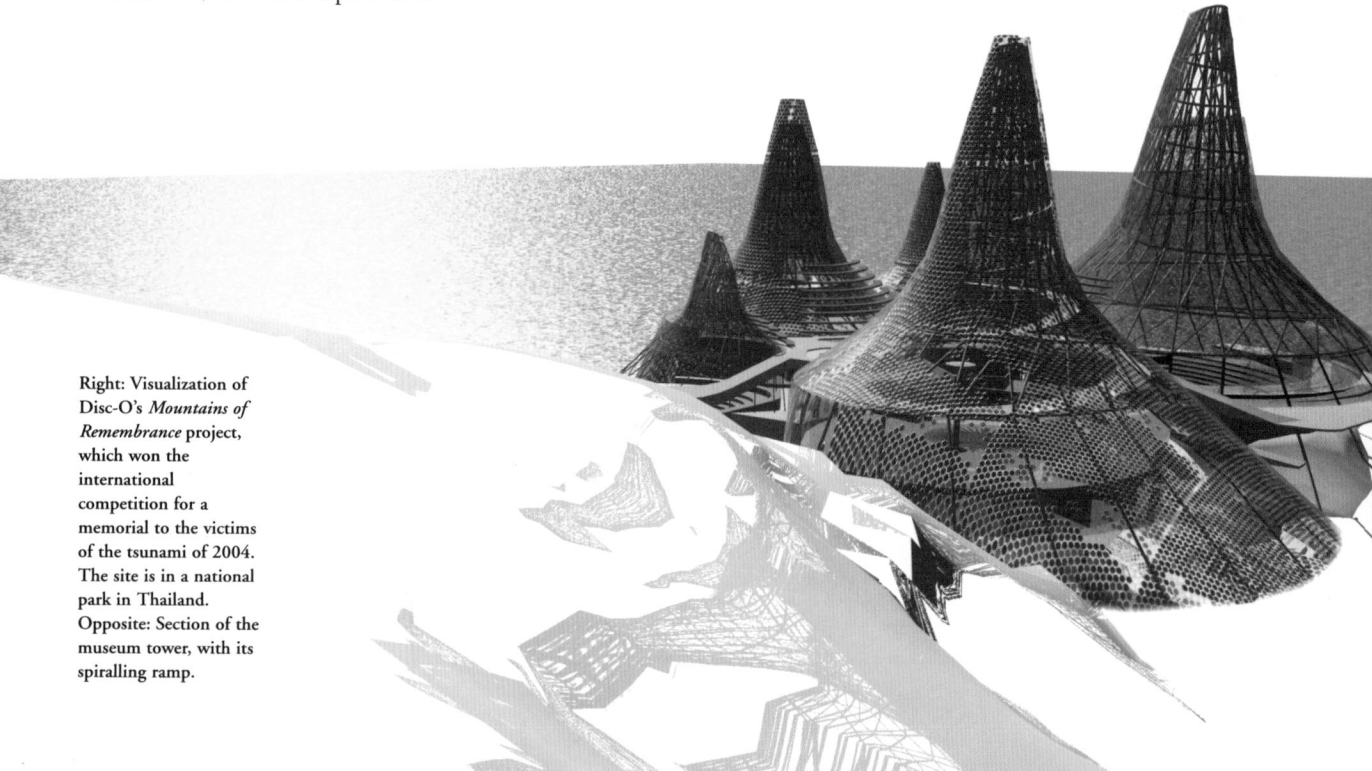

**Right:** Visualization of Disc-O's *Mountains of Remembrance* project, which won the international competition for a memorial to the victims of the tsunami of 2004. The site is in a national park in Thailand. **Opposite:** Section of the museum tower, with its spiralling ramp.

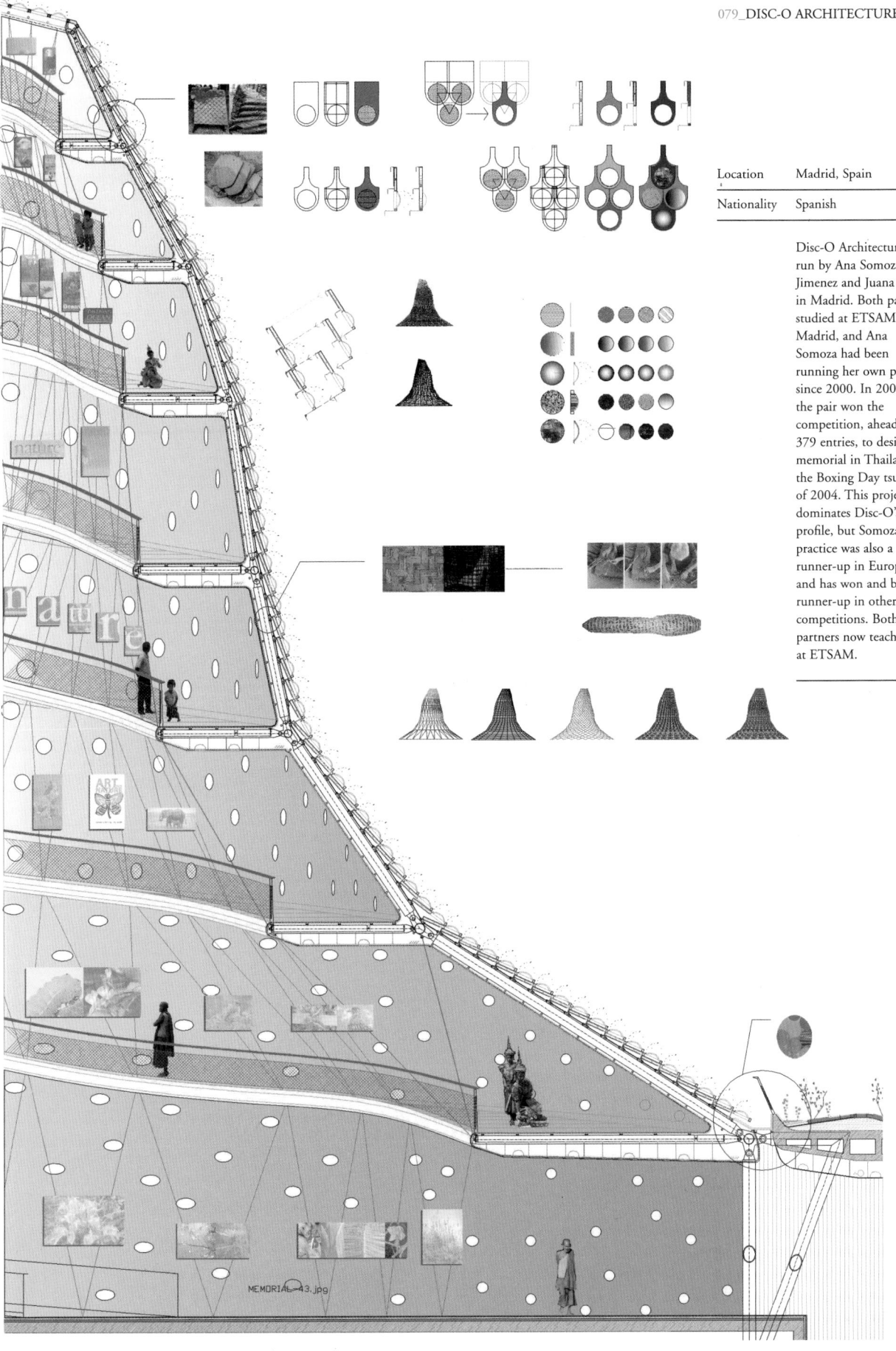

| Location | Madrid, Spain |
| --- | --- |
| Nationality | Spanish |

Disc-O Architecture is run by Ana Somoza Jimenez and Juana Canet in Madrid. Both partners studied at ETSAM in Madrid, and Ana Somoza had been running her own practice since 2000. In 2005 the pair won the competition, ahead of 379 entries, to design a memorial in Thailand to the Boxing Day tsunami of 2004. This project dominates Disc-O's profile, but Somoza's practice was also a runner-up in Europan 7 and has won and been runner-up in other competitions. Both partners now teach at ETSAM.

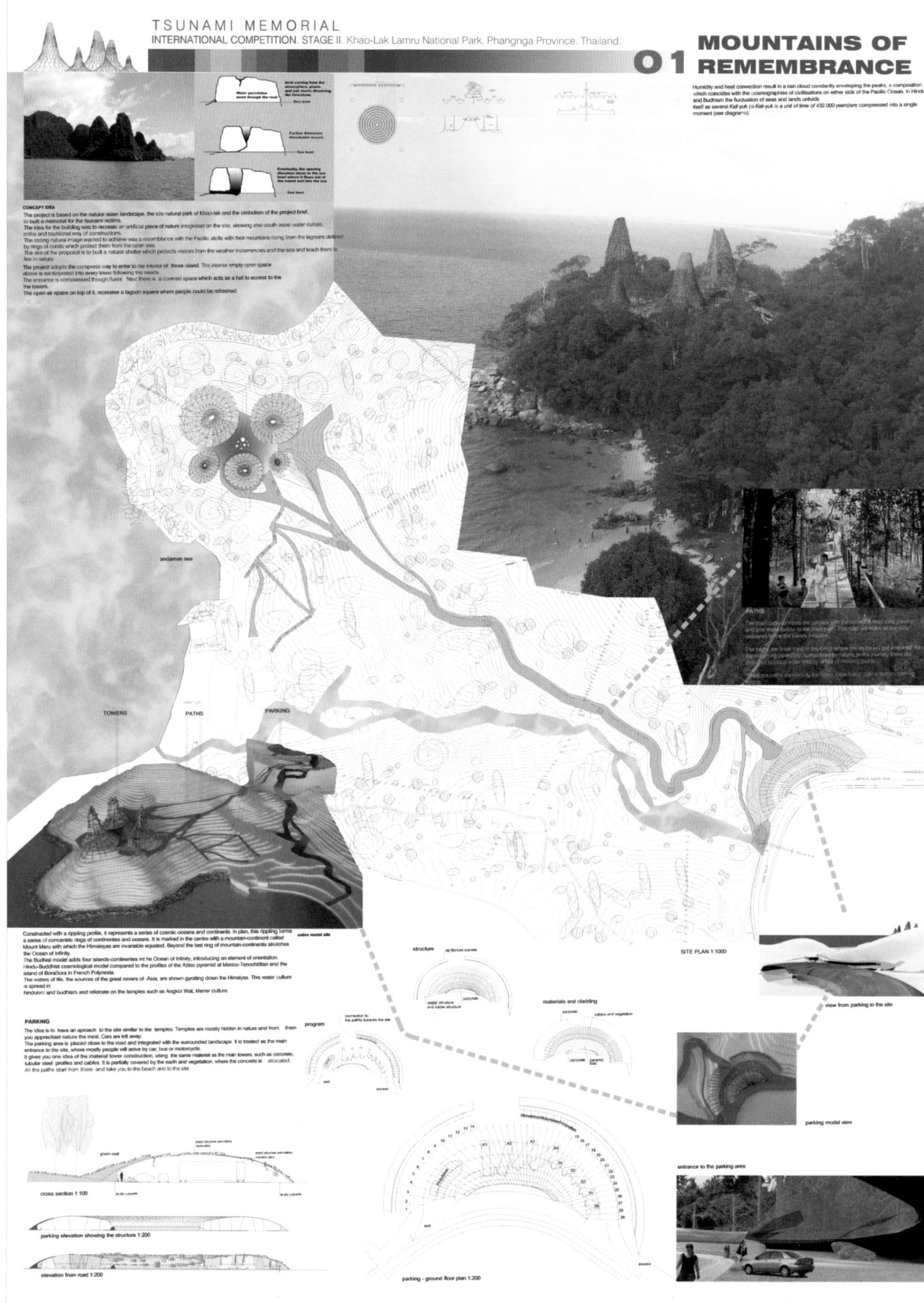

TSUNAMI MEMORIAL
INTERNATIONAL COMPETITION. STAGE II. Khao-Lak Lamru National Park. Phangnga Province. Thailand.

01 MOUNTAINS OF
REMEMBRANCE

Humidity and heat convection result in a rain cloud constantly enveloping the peaks, a composition which coincides with the cosmographies of civilisations on either side of the Pacific Ocean. In Hindu and Budhism the fluctuation of seas and lands unfolds itself as several Kali-yuk (a Kali-yuk is a unit of time of 432,000 years)are compressed into a single moment (see diagrams)

**CONCEPT IDEA**

The project is based on the natural asean landscape, the site natural park of Khao-lak and the simbolism of the project brief, to built a memorial for the tsunami victims.
The idea for the building was to recreate an artificial piece of nature integrated on the site, showing also south asian water culture, miths and traditional way of constructions.
The strong natural image wanted to achieve was a resemblance with the Pacific atolls with their mountains rising from the lagoons defined by rings of corals which protect them from the open sea.
The aim of the proposal is to built a natural shelter which protects visitors from the weather inclemencies and the sea and teach them to live in nature.
The project adopts the compress way to enter to the interior of these island. The interior empty open space above is reinterpreted into every tower following this needs.
The entrance is compressed though fluent. Next there is a covered space which acts as a hall to access to the towers.
The open air space on top of it, recreates a lagoon square where people could be refreshed.

andaman sea

TOWERS          PATHS          PARKING

Constructed with a rippling profile, it represents a series of cosmic oceans and continents. In plan, this rippling forms a series of concentric rings of continentes and oceans. It is marked in the centre with a mountain-continent called Mount Meru with which the Himalayas are invariable equated. Beyond the last ring of mountain-continents stretches the Ocean of Infinity.
The Budhist model adds four islands-continentes int he Ocean of Infinity, introducing an element of orientation.
Hindu-Buddhist cosmological model compared to the profiles of the Aztec pyramid at Mexico-Tenochtitlan and the island of Borallora in French Polynesia.
The waters of life, the sources of the great reivers of -Asia, are shown gyrating down the Himalayas. This water culture is spread in
hinduism and budhism and refelcate on the temples such as Angkor Wat, khemer culture.

native model site

**PARKING**

The idea is to have an approach to the site similar to the temples. Temples are mostly hidden in nature and from them you appreciatet nature the most. Cars are left away.
The parking area is placed close to the road and integrated with the surrounded landscape. It is treated as the main entrance to the site, whoere mostly people will arrive by car, bus or motorcycle.
It gives you one idea of the material tower construction, using the same material as the main towers, such as concrete, tubular steel profiles and cables. It is partially covered by the earth and vegetation, where the concrete is  allocated.
All the paths start from there  and take you to the beach and to the site.

**PATHS**

The main path connects the complex with the seront´s main cars parallel and one ramp below to the main part. The main path will relive at the daily containers to the the towers hospoce.

The beach are lineer cimal in the forest where the visitor will get prepeired  for the welcoming ceremony surounded by nature. In this journey there are ...... important while travelling ritual of morning mortem.

.... are paths connecting the forest, beach and native memorial part.

structure
reinforced concrete
metal structure
and cable structure

materials and cladding
concrete
cables and vegetation

SITE PLAN 1:1000

view from parking to the site

program
connection to
the paths towards the site

parking model view

green roof
metal structure and cables
cross section 1:100

parking elevation showing the structure 1:200

elevation from road 1:200

parking - ground floor plan 1:200

entrance to the parking area

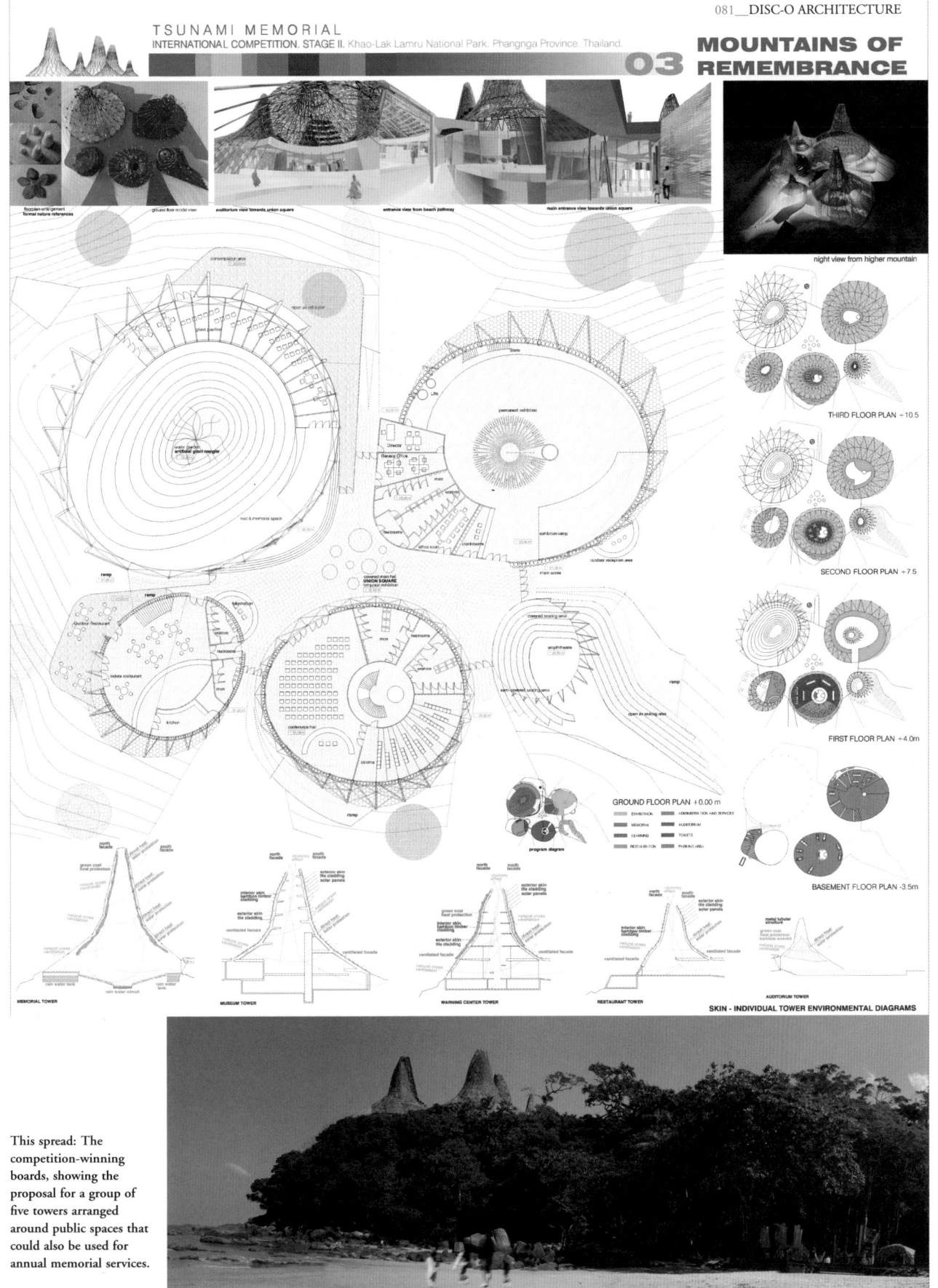

TSUNAMI MEMORIAL
INTERNATIONAL COMPETITION. STAGE II. Khao-Lak Lamru National Park. Phangnga Province. Thailand.

**03 MOUNTAINS OF REMEMBRANCE**

night view from higher mountain

THIRD FLOOR PLAN +10.5

SECOND FLOOR PLAN +7.5

FIRST FLOOR PLAN +4.0m

GROUND FLOOR PLAN +0.00 m

BASEMENT FLOOR PLAN -3.5m

MEMORIAL TOWER

MUSEUM TOWER

WARNING CENTER TOWER

RESTAURANT TOWER

AUDITORIUM TOWER

SKIN - INDIVIDUAL TOWER ENVIRONMENTAL DIAGRAMS

This spread: The competition-winning boards, showing the proposal for a group of five towers arranged around public spaces that could also be used for annual memorial services.

# Evan Douglis

Evan Douglis's work has taken the rapid-prototyped, scripting-generated language of the new digital architecture and applied it in the real world, even if most of those applications so far are at the scale of interior installation or exhibition infrastructure. Douglis's work is compelling for the sheer complexity of the components that he has been able to produce, and these forms have become, in some cases, almost implausible typologies.

Take Douglis's *Helioscope* forms – helical 'tails' that look a little like avant-garde cake decorations. Douglis envisages them as part of a capitalist consumer infrastructure of increasing desire, hanging from the ceiling in 'a hyper-excitable cloud-scape comprised of swirling helical tails magically suspended above a frenzied crowd of thrill-seeking consumers.'

Other more tangible projects include his interior for the Japanese restaurant Haku in New York City. Along one wall is a wallcovering inspired by a reptile's skin. It is a decorative effect that Douglis hopes suggests an architecture in motion, an effect created by using scripting software to make alterations to a basic pyramidal shape. Douglis feels that the project brings together his practice's interest in emergent architectural forms with cultural and mythological themes that are specifically Japanese – in particular in the ambiguous imagery of the reptilian skin.

Douglis's interest in curatorial practice (he is the former director of the architecture gallery of Columbia University) also led him to design the gallery installation for an exhibition of the work of French modernist architect Jean Prouvé. The *Auto Braids/Auto Breeding* piece created a wavy blue surface on which the pieces were placed, as if they were floating in what the architect describes as a 'sea of surface intensities'. The project is a celebration of advanced computer technology and rapid-prototyping techniques.

Below and opposite top: Douglis's interior for the Japanese restaurant Haku in New York. This page bottom: Exhibition installation displaying pieces of furniture by Jean Prouvé. The project was called *Auto Braids/Auto Breeding*.

Opposite bottom: *Helioscope*, what Douglis describes as a 'travelling mediscape'. These CNC-milled fibreglass spirals integrate video displays.

| Location | New York, USA |
|---|---|
| Nationality | American |

Evan Douglis started his independent studio in 1990 in New York, after working for practices such as Tod Williams Billie Tsien and teaching at universities including the Pratt Institute, Columbia and Cooper Union. In 1999, the Architectural League of New York recognized him as an Emerging Voice in architecture, and in 2005 he was chosen in the Design Vanguard Awards by *Architectural Record* magazine. In 2006 he received the Acadia Award for emerging digital practice. Evan Douglis also served as director of Columbia University's architecture gallery, from 1995 to 2003.

**D**

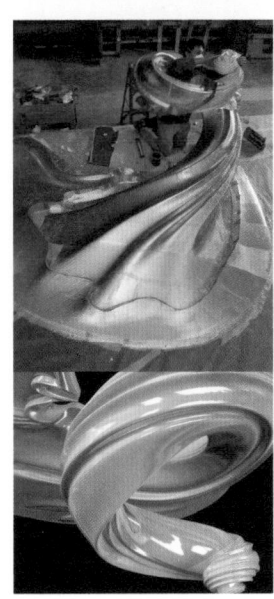

**Douglis teaches at Columbia University in the US, along with Christopher Sharples of SHoP (pp. 286–289).**

# Dow Jones

Dow Jones' architecture is powerfully charged with a phenomenological interest that makes often quite traditional-seeming forms take on a sometimes intimidatingly forceful resonance. This is, in part, explained by both partners' education at Cambridge University in the UK, where a kind of phenomenological modernism has been in vogue for some time. But with projects such as their private houses in Sudbourne and Walberswick in Suffolk, UK, they have taken this referential dimension to an austere extreme.

The house in Sudbourne (2001) was, in many ways, Dow Jones' breakthrough project. A black timber-clad barn with a brick base, the house took its place in the flat landscape in this part of the world as a dark presence. Inside, though, the house was a rich, brick-lined holiday home. Despite its elemental, typological appearance, the siting of the building was carefully tuned. The architects write: 'The house is located on the site to create a threshold between the village, the meadow, and the view to a forest beyond. The house and outbuildings sit at a distance from a hedge in such a way that it creates a room-like space to the front of the house. The house is organized to continue this layering of the spatial experience.'

More recently, Dow Jones have completed their second country house in this part of the UK, this time an extension to an existing cottage in the heart of the village of Walberswick. *Poplar Cottage* (2006) resides between the old and new, retaining three existing façades of a 1920s cottage and creating an entirely new house behind them. Local brick and lime mortar are the principal materials, with the bricks arranged in an English bond. Clay tiles on the floor continue into the garden to form a terrace, and this continuity between inside and outside is a fundamental part of the architectural strategy for the house. Dow Jones partner Alun Jones says: 'The garden is structured as a series of rooms "enfilade", with an existing pathway that runs to the back of the house. The new house is conceived as the culmination of this route.'

The ground floor is arranged around a large brick hearth in the living area that faces the garden. The staircase to the first floor culminates in views to the sea. As Jones says: 'A view to the sea beyond completes your journey; from synthetic nature to nature herself.'

Alun Jones taught at Kingston University in London between 2000 and 2003, with Daniel Rosbottom of DRDH Architects (pp. 86–89) and Patrick Lynch of Lynch Architects (pp. 178–181).

D

| Location | London, UK |
| --- | --- |
| Nationality | British |

Dow Jones was formed in London by husband-and-wife team Alun Jones and Biba Dow. Dow studied architecture at Cambridge University, while Jones took a MPhil in Renaissance humanism there after completing his professional studies in Bath. Jones was the project architect, for Caruso St John, of the Stirling Prize-nominated Walsall Art Gallery before leaving to form Dow Jones in 2000. The practice's work has since been widely published, and was part of the *Encounters* exhibition at the Architecture Foundation in 2001.

This spread: Dow Jones' *Poplar Cottage* in Walberswick, Suffolk, UK, completed in 2006. The project was in fact an extension to an already existing house.

# DRDH Architects

DRDH is at the heart of a group of emerging London practices who have the makings of a new London school. All of them were influenced by the work of architects who, while immensely significant in London architecture, have had limited chances to build in the city. These include Tony Fretton, Florian Beigel and Caruso St John.

But DRDH has always been committed to building, and has spent the best part of a decade undertaking painstaking work in domestic contexts. When it won the competition for a new housing and commercial development within the Hafen City masterplan in Hamburg, Germany, the practice was clearly freed from some of the difficulties of building in the capital, and made a proposal of clarity and maturity.

DRDH's proposal for Baufeld 10 at Hafen City was for 26 apartments, a restaurant and ground-floor commercial spaces on a key gateway site within the new masterplan on the north side of the Elbe River. The site is next door to the Kaispeicher warehouse building, currently being converted by Herzog & de Meuron into the Elb Philharmonie concert hall.

The proposal is greatly influenced by a reading of the city's historic architecture, and uses typical dark and heavy clinker bricks to make a substantial building. The brick is generative for the design. The proportions of the bricks define openings and rhythms on the façade, striving for both economy and harmony, but also the slightly enamelled finish of the high-fired bricks would cause the building to glitter in the sunlight. The kinked façade allows light to hit the building at different times of the day, and the bronzed window frames accentuate this attention to light.

The project shows a rigorous materiality, but also a certain freedom, with the freely modelled roof terrace contrasting with the rational façades and providing a welcome social space for residents.

This spread: Images from DRDH Architects' competition entry for a new university complex in the docks in Hamburg, Germany. The complex is opposite the site of a proposed new aquarium by Rem Koolhaas' OMA.

In 2005, DRDH came second in the Young Architect of the Year Award organized by *Building Design* magazine.
Lynch Architects (pp. 178–181) won the prize.

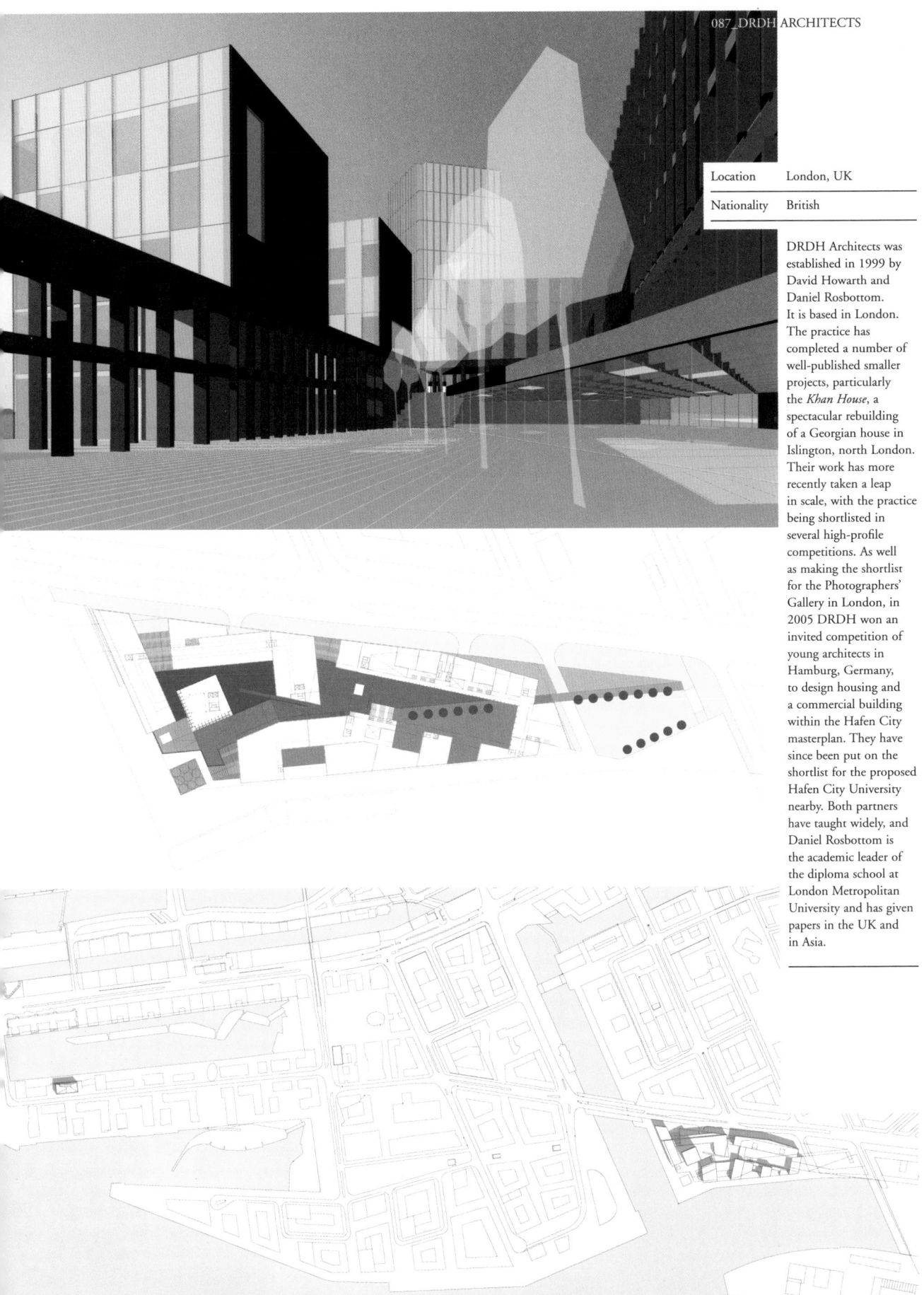

| Location | London, UK |
| --- | --- |
| Nationality | British |

D

DRDH Architects was established in 1999 by David Howarth and Daniel Rosbottom. It is based in London. The practice has completed a number of well-published smaller projects, particularly the *Khan House*, a spectacular rebuilding of a Georgian house in Islington, north London. Their work has more recently taken a leap in scale, with the practice being shortlisted in several high-profile competitions. As well as making the shortlist for the Photographers' Gallery in London, in 2005 DRDH won an invited competition of young architects in Hamburg, Germany, to design housing and a commercial building within the Hafen City masterplan. They have since been put on the shortlist for the proposed Hafen City University nearby. Both partners have taught widely, and Daniel Rosbottom is the academic leader of the diploma school at London Metropolitan University and has given papers in the UK and in Asia.

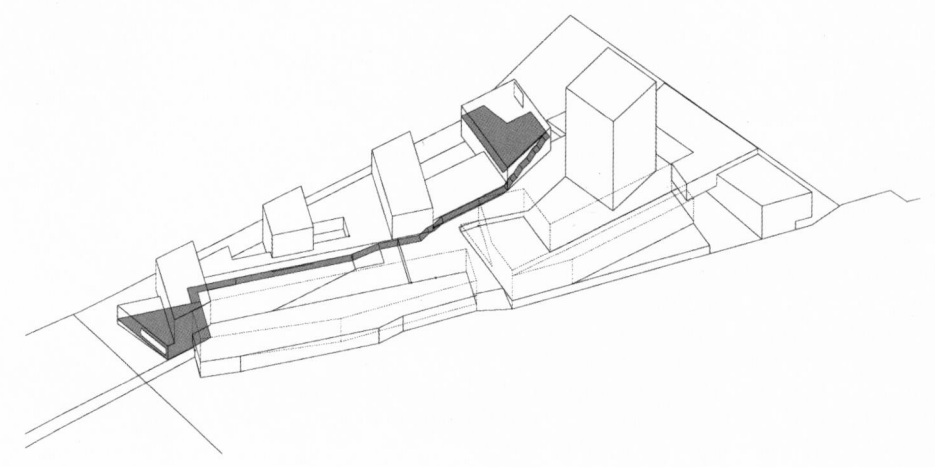

This page: More diagrams of the university proposal in Hamburg, Germany, showing how the project gives routes through the site, rising up on to a plinth. A taller tower unifies the design and is the culmination of the route.

Opposite: DRDH's proposal for the Baufeld 10 residential building, also in Hamburg, near to the site of Herzog & de Meuron's new concert hall. The building was inspired by the historical warehouse architecture of the city, and its inflected façade is made of bricks that reflect the light at different times of the day.

D

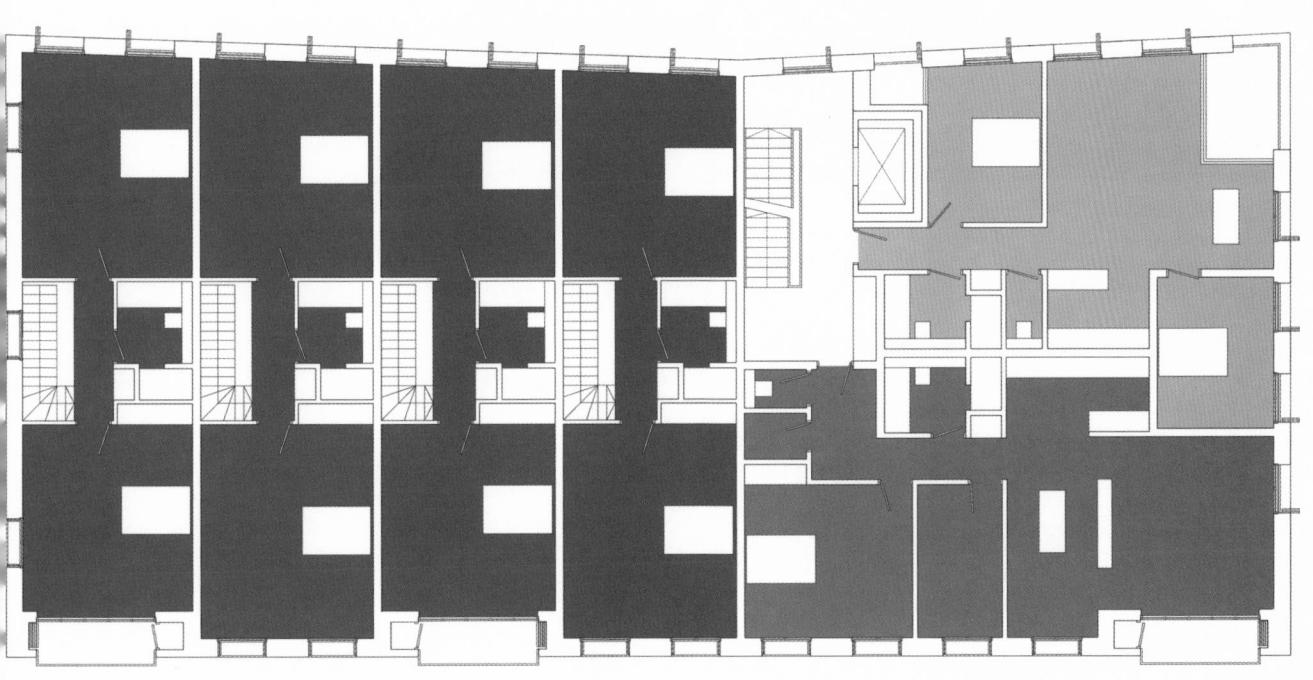

# ecoLogic Studio

Marco Poletto and Claudia Pasquero's studio is almost unique in contemporary London, but could be a herald of things to come. ecoLogic was set up to combine a design sensibility with avant-garde research into how to make buildings more environmentally efficient. The partners themselves see this as an epochal and cultural shift.

They write: 'With the new millennium we are experiencing the definitive passage from the era of "machine" to the so-called era of "ecology". This change in perspective has opened new interpretations of the role of technology, overcoming the modernist enthusiasm for technology and the postmodern refusal of it. Technology in the era of ecology is becoming a tool to evolve new forms of knowledge and architectural practice.'

The partners were trained at the Architectural Association, fully aware of the new 'emergent' design strategies, and look to harness the power of these technologies and practices to solve ecological problems. Their work integrates new prototyping and fabrication technologies into a view of architecture as a system that works from the scale of the component to the city.

The project that demonstrates a pleasingly low-tech approach to emergent design is *STEM*, a screen of algae-filled plastic bottles that ecoLogic showed at the Venice Architecture Biennale in 2006. The bottles are filled with different densities of blanket weed, highly efficient photosynthesizing algae, forming a sunscreen that also produces oxygen. The screen tracks the sunlight – more sun produces a higher density of algae in each bottle, and less produces a clearer bottle, meaning that the screen is aesthetically and functionally responsive as well as ecologically productive. This is what ecoLogic has referred to as an 'eco-machine'.

A more passive example of the practice's work is the light wall they designed for a new-build villa near Turin in Italy. The wall uses the efficient thermal mass of traditional Mediterranean masonry buildings, but reinvented in permeable, sponge-like form. The wall thus acts as a thermally massive wall, but also allows light in and views out. The spiralling cavities in the components were developed using parametric modelling software to retain 70% of the mass of a windowless wall, but with generous openings.

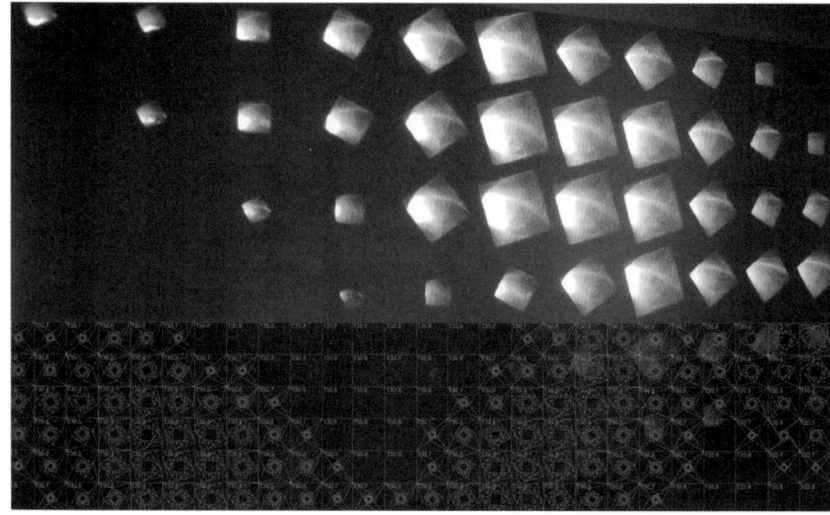

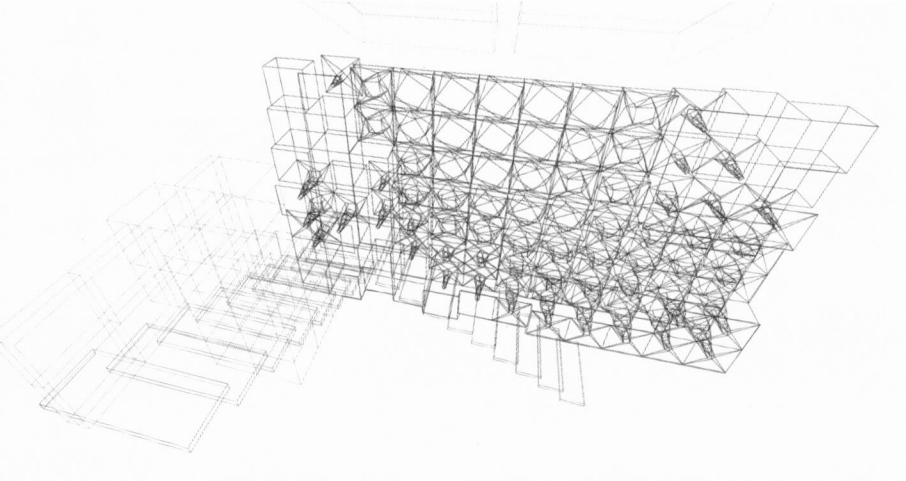

| Location | London, UK |
|---|---|
| Nationality | Italian |

**E**

ecoLogic Studio was founded in London in 2004 by two Italians: Marco Poletto and Claudia Pasquero. Both partners studied in Turin and then at the Architectural Association in London, specializing in environmental design. Their practice is both an architecture office and a research studio, undertaking its own architectural projects (such as the interior of a public library in Cirie, Italy, and a private house in Kent, UK), but more often collaborating with other practices and specializing in the design of energy-efficient systems. Recent collaborations with other architects include the competition for the new Milan Fiera with Foster & Partners and the design of a responsive façade for the *Capital 2 Tower* in Liverpool, UK, by Feilden Clegg Bradley. The partners also teach at the Architectural Association and the University of East London.

**Opposite:** Prototype of the wall of a house ecoLogic is working on in Turin, Italy. The wall has high thermal mass, but also allows light in through the diamond-shaped excavations.

**This page:** *STEM*, on display at the Venice Architecture Biennale in 2006. The bottles are filled with different densities of algae, and form an oxygen-producing shading system.

# Elastik

The Elastik network of architects exists between 13 cities in Europe and China, and describes its architecture in the obfuscating language of so many graduates of the world's computer-driven graduate design schools like Amsterdam's Berlage Institute, the alma mater of Elastik's founders.

They write: 'Elastik's goal is to practise architecture closer to the notion of an industrial product that depends on particular cultural "conditions of existence".' To do this, Elastik claims, architects must compute the best way to combine 'hard' and 'soft' values – 'hard' being material values and 'soft' our psychological and temporal needs. Elastik refers to its projects as 'architectural devices', designed using a method they call 'critical geometry', that can negotiate the competing demands on a building. These demands are 'technological, economical, user's, structural and locational form'.

This method of analysis of the architectural project depends on a large, complex project to be tested in full, and

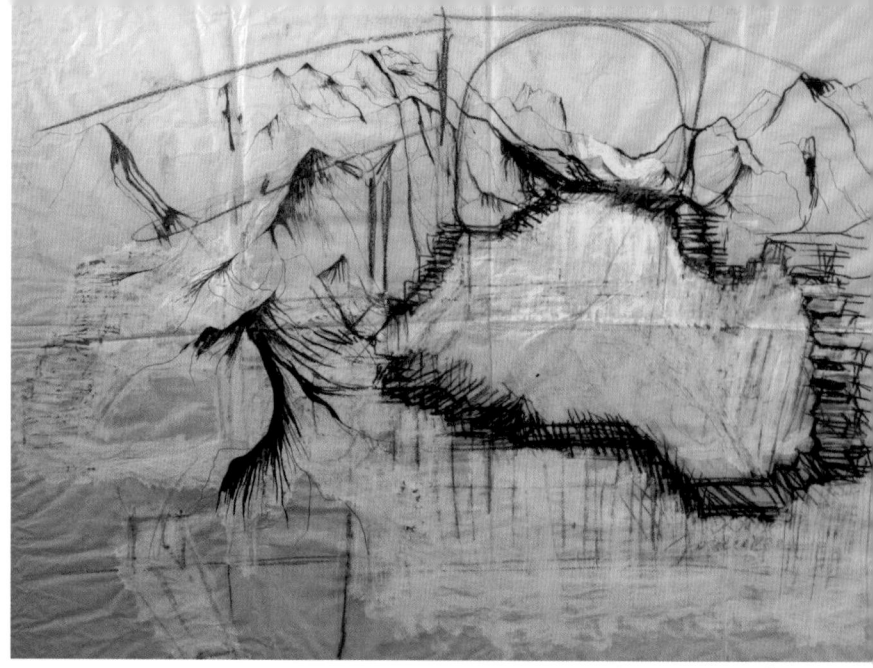

Elastik has come close to winning a commission of this size. They received fourth prize in the competition for a new school of economics in Murska Sobota, Slovenia, with a proposal for a long and sinuous block, with a bulge in the centre of the plan which is a conceptual 'pivot' of the building. This pivot is a public atrium from which can be accessed a series of clusters, defined by the users' activities. The first new-build project that tests their ideas will be a house in Moravske Toplice, Slovenia, the interior of which is an 'endless living room', adjusted using parametric design tools, to the daily routine of the house's inhabitants.

The project you see on these pages, though, is of a very different nature. Created as the background for Italian artist Sissi at the W139 Gallery in Amsterdam in 2003, the project is a white iceberg-like form around the perimeter of the gallery that formed the set for the artist's performance artwork *The Walk*. The beautiful result formed an ethereal backdrop to the white-clad Sissi's long journey. Elastik explains that the installation 'stages Sissi's experience within different dramaturgic environments: from the social gallery space to a transformative corridor, before reaching the intimate, smooth, white, vertically climbing landscape.'

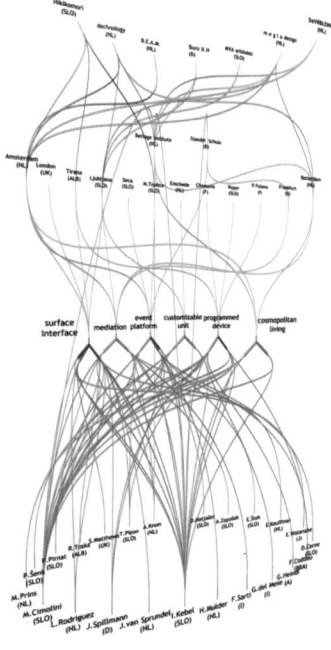

Forming a network of practitioners is an increasingly fashionable approach for practices coming out of the new computer-driven architecture schools like the Berlage (where the two founders of Elastik studied), SCI-Arc or the Architectural Association. See UFO (pp. 324–327).

093_ELASTIK

Mika Cimolini of Elastik is based in Ljubuljana, which may be eastern Europe's most important city for contemporary architecture, following the success of older architects like Sadar & Vuga. See Ofis Arhitekti (pp. 234–235).

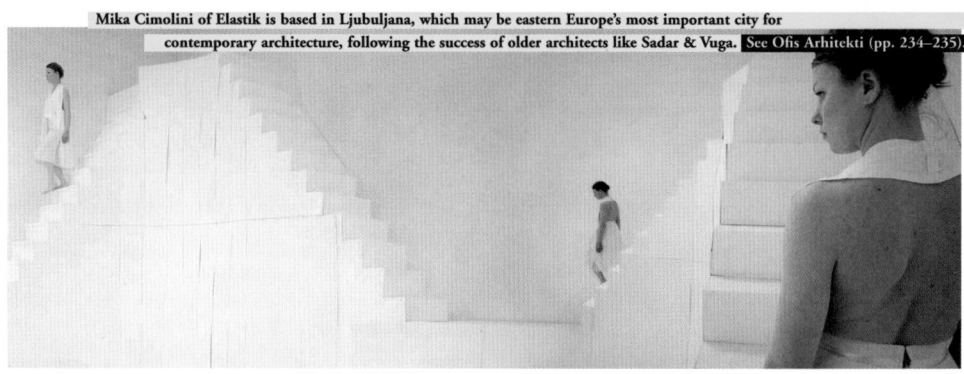

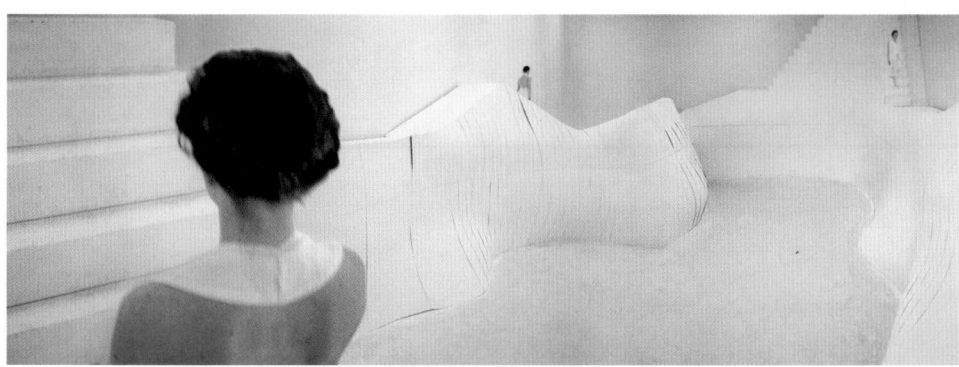

| Location | Ljubuljana, Slovenia Amsterdam, The Netherlands |
| --- | --- |
| Nationality | Slovenian |

Elastik was formed in 2001 by Slovenian architects Igor Kebel and Mika Cimolini as an international network of individuals who come together to form different multi-disciplinary teams according to the requirements of each project. The practice is currently coordinated from Cimolini's office in Ljubuljana and Kebel's in Amsterdam. Nodes in the network now exist across Europe, as well as in China. Both partners studied for their postgraduate degrees at the Berlage Institute in Amsterdam, and both have been back to teach there. Elastik has completed the interior of a hotel in Amsterdam, installations for jewellery designer Lara Bohinc, and recently a private house in Moravske Toplice in Slovenia. In addition, they have carried out two significant research projects, one on the subject of libraries, the other on just-in-time infrastructure.

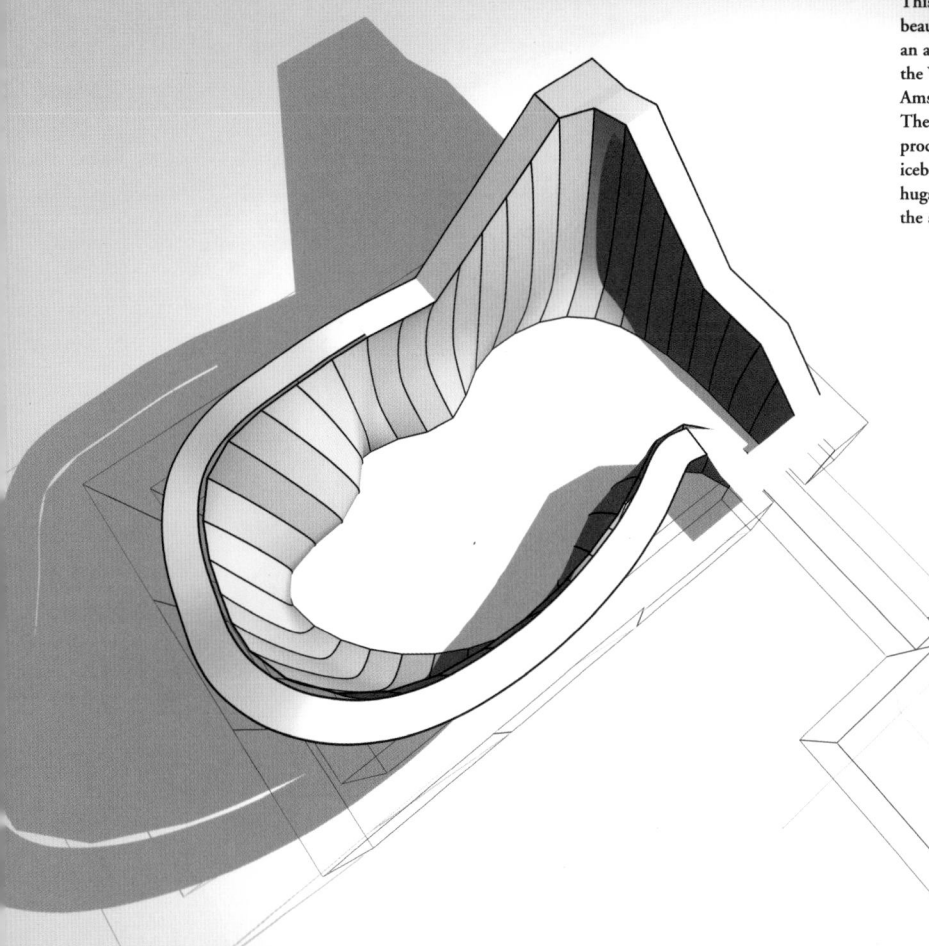

This spread: Elastik's beautiful stage set for an art performance at the W139 Gallery in Amsterdam in 2003. The Italian artist Sissi processed around the iceberg-like route that hugs the perimeter of the space.

# Emergent

It is appropriate that the practice that takes its name from 'emergence', the phenomenon defined by writer/guru Steven Johnson in his 2001 book of the same name, should be perhaps the most eloquent advocate of the advantages of this new design paradigm. Many architecture schools and young practices are now working with so-called emergent design strategies, and Emergent is in the vanguard.

Emergence, as defined by Steven Johnson, is what happens when 'the whole is smarter than the sum of its parts'. The axiomatic example is the ant colony, where, thanks to a multiplicity of quite simple and local rules, relatively dumb components (individual ants) are able to make complex feats of engineering possible without an overarching intelligence directing their actions. Tom Wiscombe, the founder and principal of Emergent, also cites other examples of emergent forms – termite mounds, dragonfly wings, colour-changing octopuses, hyena communities and mould – that inform his work and research.

Many of Wiscombe's projects have a distinctive and robust aesthetic, but he says that his interest is not in designing objects but 'complex adaptive systems' that dovetail building technologies (services, structure, cladding) into mutually supportive or 'optimized' configurations. The same thinking leads to a way of making urban plans in the same way – all the components of a city can be designed to have these relationships.

This spread: Emergent's entry to the competition for a new court house in Paris in 2006. It is part of a larger urban plan for the Rive Gauche. Tom Wiscombe writes: 'The structure is based on dragonfly wings, which are both functional and wildly varied. Dragonfly wings contain two different patterns – one is a ladder-type rectilinear grid, which provides structural stiffness (beam-action), and the other is a multi-directional cellular pattern, which provides flexibility (membrane-action). In the new building, these two systems were deployed.'

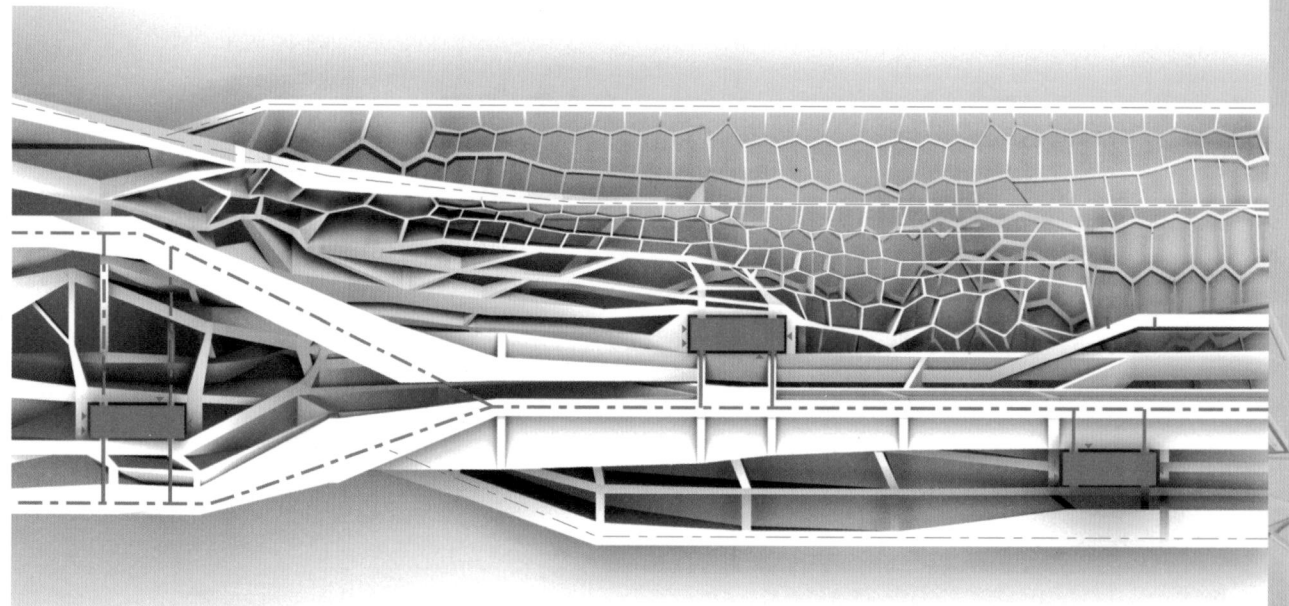

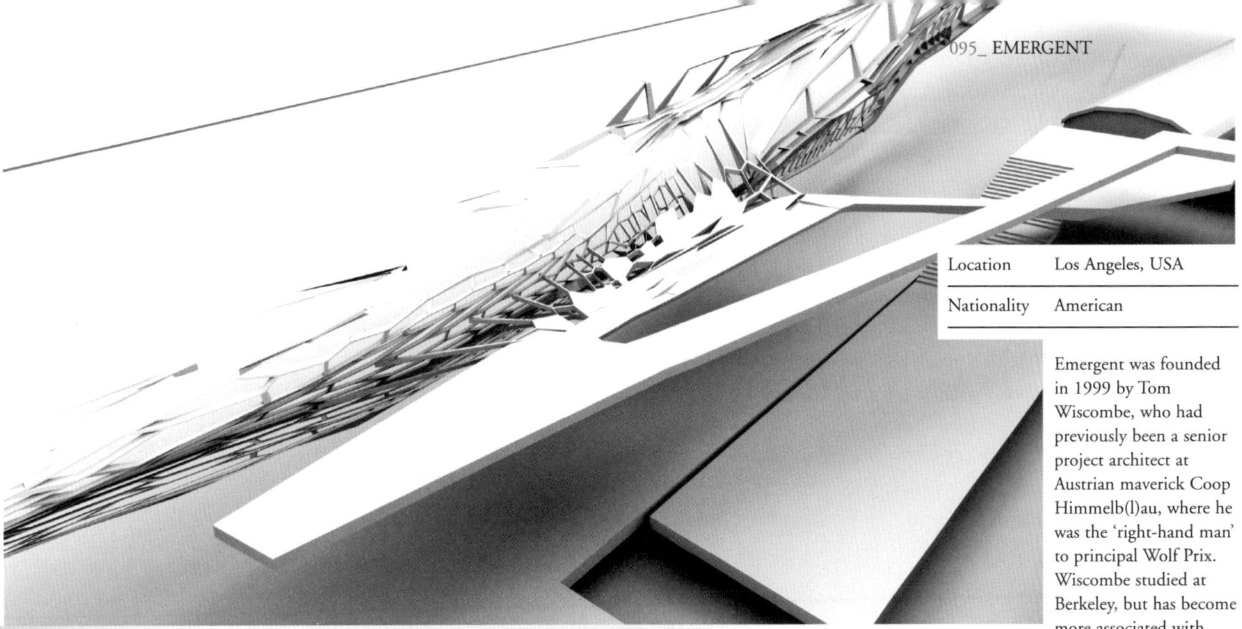

| Location | Los Angeles, USA |
| --- | --- |
| Nationality | American |

Emergent was founded in 1999 by Tom Wiscombe, who had previously been a senior project architect at Austrian maverick Coop Himmelb(l)au, where he was the 'right-hand man' to principal Wolf Prix. Wiscombe studied at Berkeley, but has become more associated with SCI-Arc in Los Angeles, where he now teaches. Emergent's work is part of the permanent collections of the FRAC Centre in Orléans, MOMA San Francisco and MOMA New York, and has been published widely. Emergent also won the PS1/MOMA Young Architects Program competition in 2003.

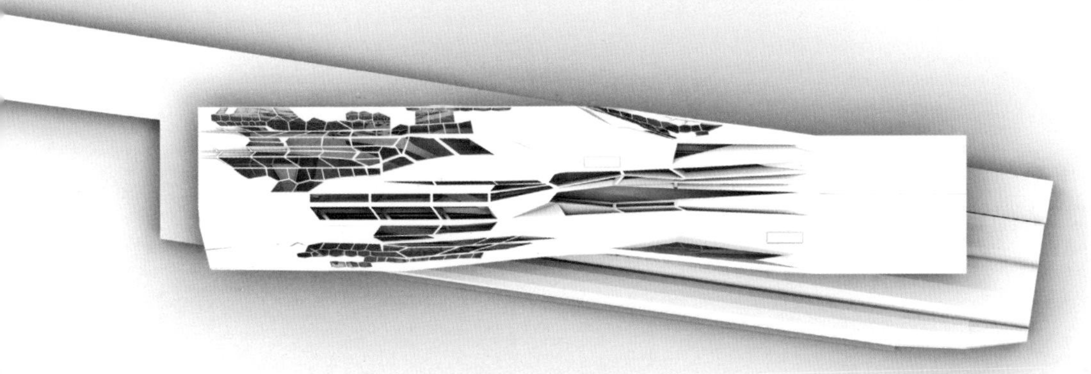

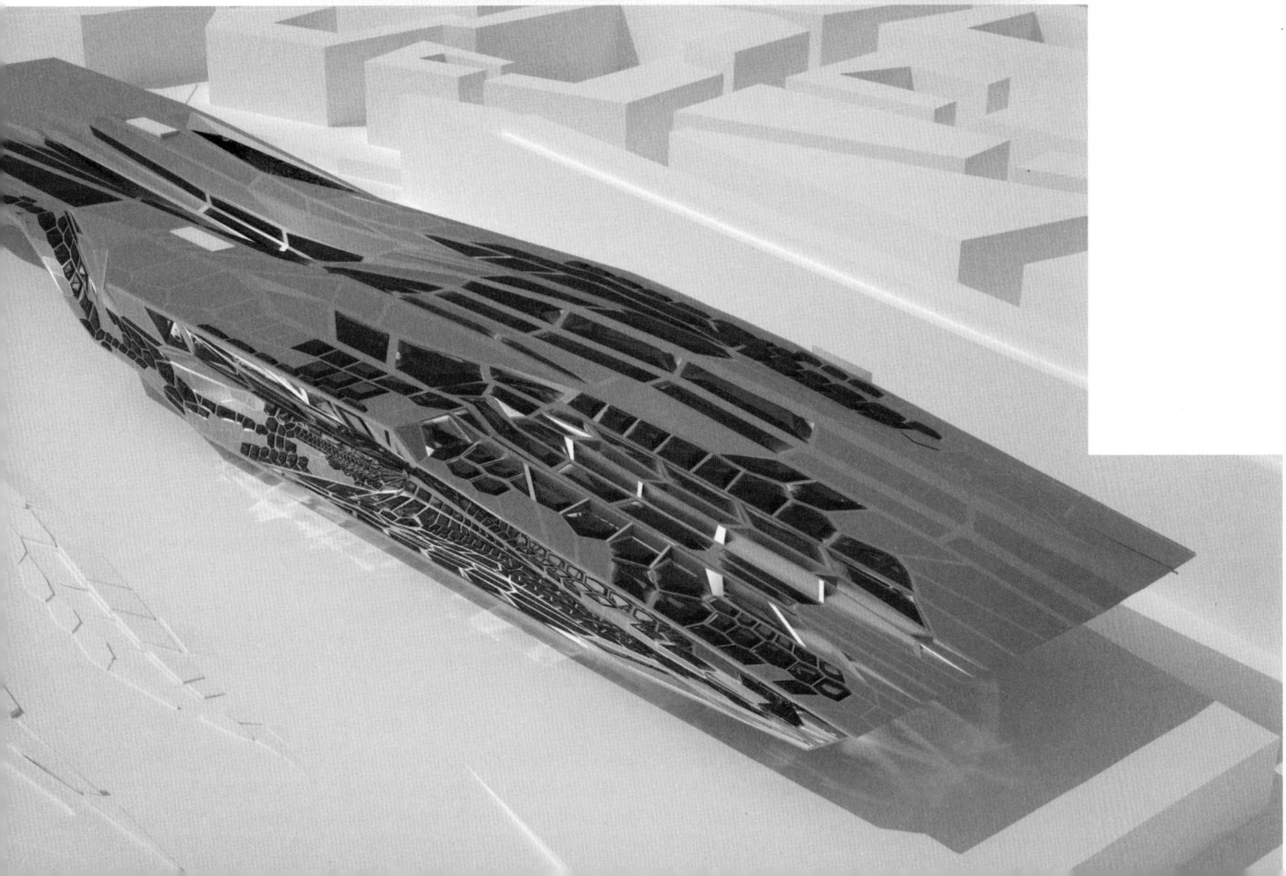

In 2007, Emergent exhibited at the SCI-Arc Gallery with an installation called *Dragonfly*. Other practices in this book that have exhibited there include: Griffin Enright (pp. 136–137), Patterns (pp. 242–243), Marta Malé-Alemany of ReD Research + Design (pp. 270–271), Xefirotarch (pp. 340–343), George Yu (pp. 344–347) and the students of Peter Zellner (pp. 348–349).

Wiscombe writes: 'Emergent's approach is informed by contemporary models of biology and systems theory rather than by the arts. Ecologies and economies are evolutionary, interactive, and resilient – vital qualities that are conspicuously missing from architecture, but necessary for survival in post-industrial culture. [Our] work therefore concentrates on the propagating logic of landscape, infrastructure and network instead of the dead-end logic of ordering, vertical structure and façade composition.'

Examples of Emergent's work include the *Cell House*, designed in 2006 in Los Angeles. Here, the structural frame, floorplates and envelope are understood not as independent components of the house, but as a set of behaviours, between which relationships are optimized for structural efficiency and for formal effect.

It is significant that very little architecture of the emergent school has been built as yet. Wiscombe has come closer than most with his shortlisting for the Prague National Library competition in 2007, but we must wait to see if the built products can match the sophisticated claims made for these neo-modern ideas.

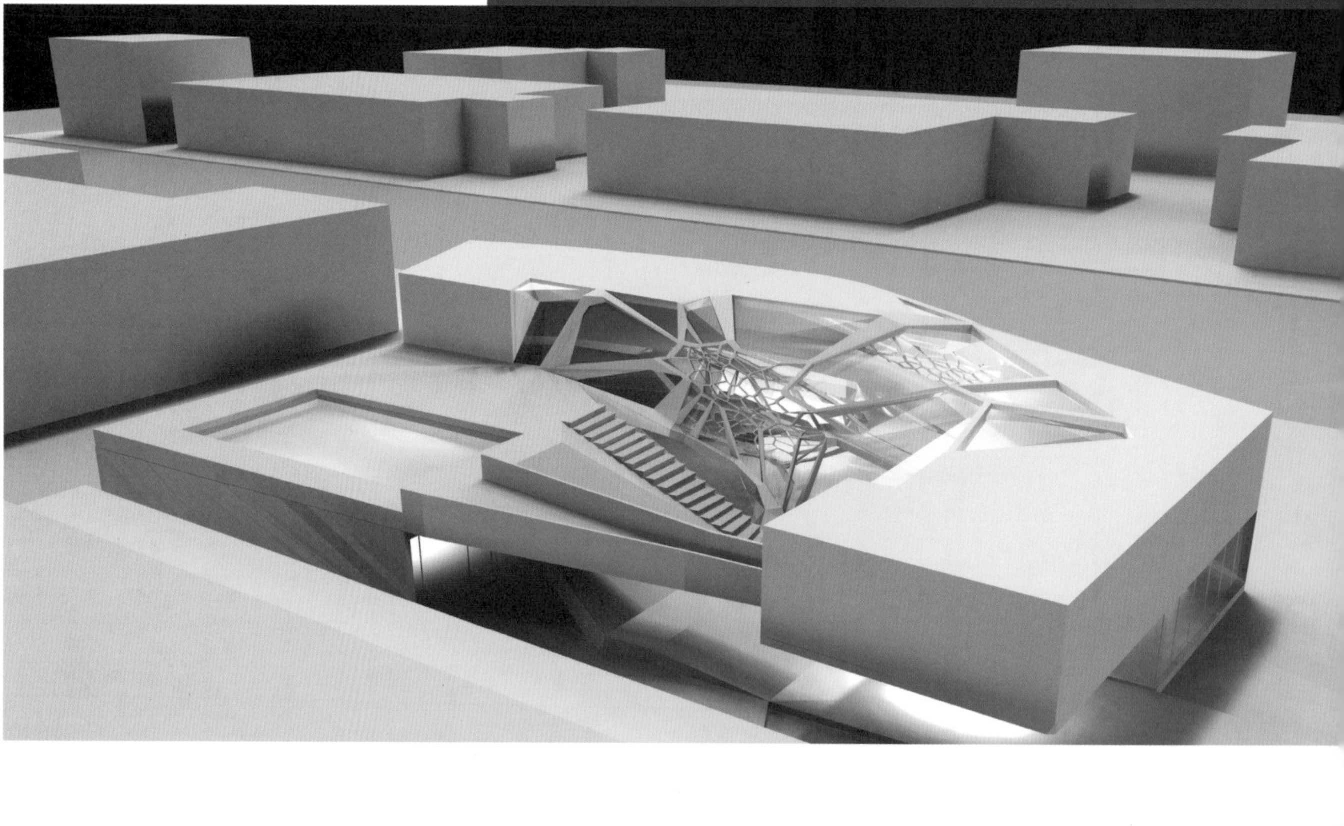

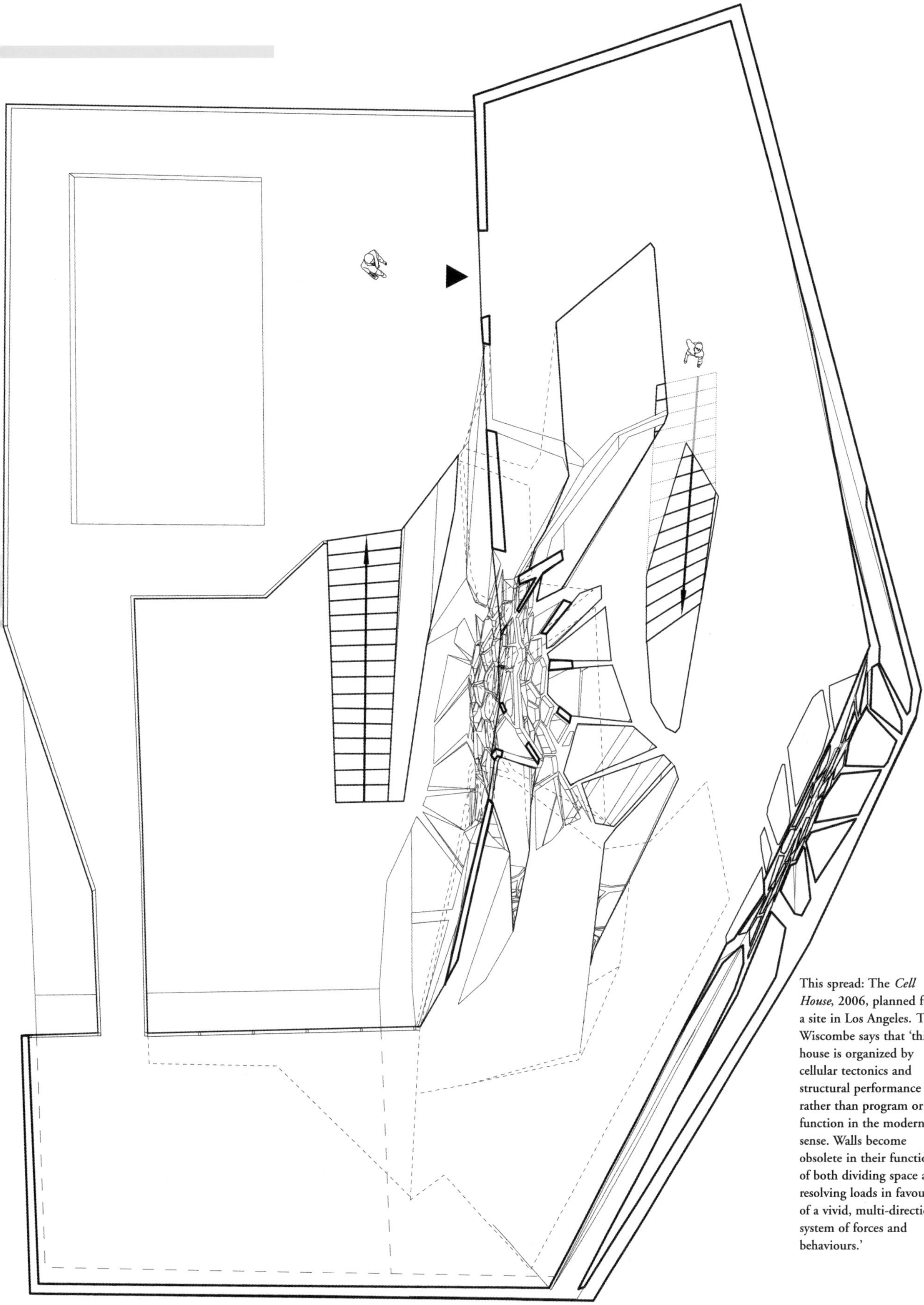

This spread: The *Cell House*, 2006, planned for a site in Los Angeles. Tom Wiscombe says that 'this house is organized by cellular tectonics and structural performance rather than program or function in the modern sense. Walls become obsolete in their function of both dividing space and resolving loads in favour of a vivid, multi-directional system of forces and behaviours.'

# Escher GuneWardena

Escher GuneWardena Architecture's partners are from Switzerland and Sri Lanka, but it is the classic buildings of their immediate surroundings – Los Angeles – that seems to have inspired the best of their work. This is not as surprising as it might seem. While still in his home country of Switzerland, Frank Escher wrote a monograph about the work of California modernist John Lautner (published by Artemis in 1994), and is now on the board of directors of the John Lautner Foundation, lecturing widely on his work. His enthusiasm for the *Case Study Houses* architect's work found its most direct expression in Escher GuneWardena's refurbishment of the historic *Chemosphere* house.

This remarkable flying saucer of a house was perched precariously on a Los Angeles hillside on a fan of concrete supports. But the 1960 Lautner-designed house had been in a sorry state until renowned book publishers Benedikt and Angelika Taschen bought the property and employed the practice to undertake a complete restoration. The project included new furniture and glazing for the house, and also a project for a new guesthouse on the site.

The practice's project most directly influenced by the *Case Study Houses* looks to be the *Jamie Residence*, a 185sq m (2,000sq ft) family house in Pasadena, California. The house sits on a steeply sloping site that creates a long, open-plan building with 180-degree views of the surrounding landscape. The rectangular box of the house sits on two concrete towers. In 2005, artist Olafur Eliasson converted the *Jamie Residence* into a light installation, and it is significant that one of Escher GuneWardena's more modest projects betrays an influence from Eliasson or James Turrell. The interior of the *Electric Sun* tanning salon used indirect ultraviolet light as the only form of decoration in the all-white interior.

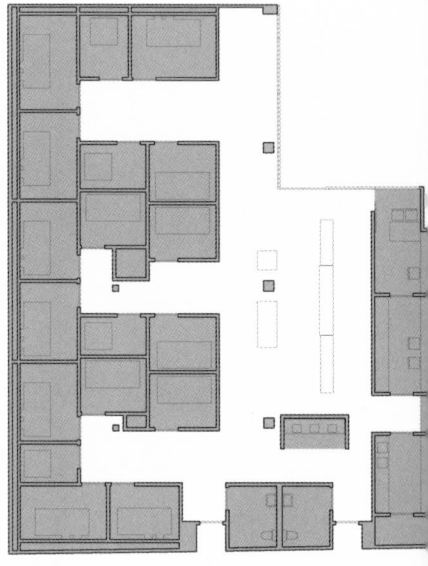

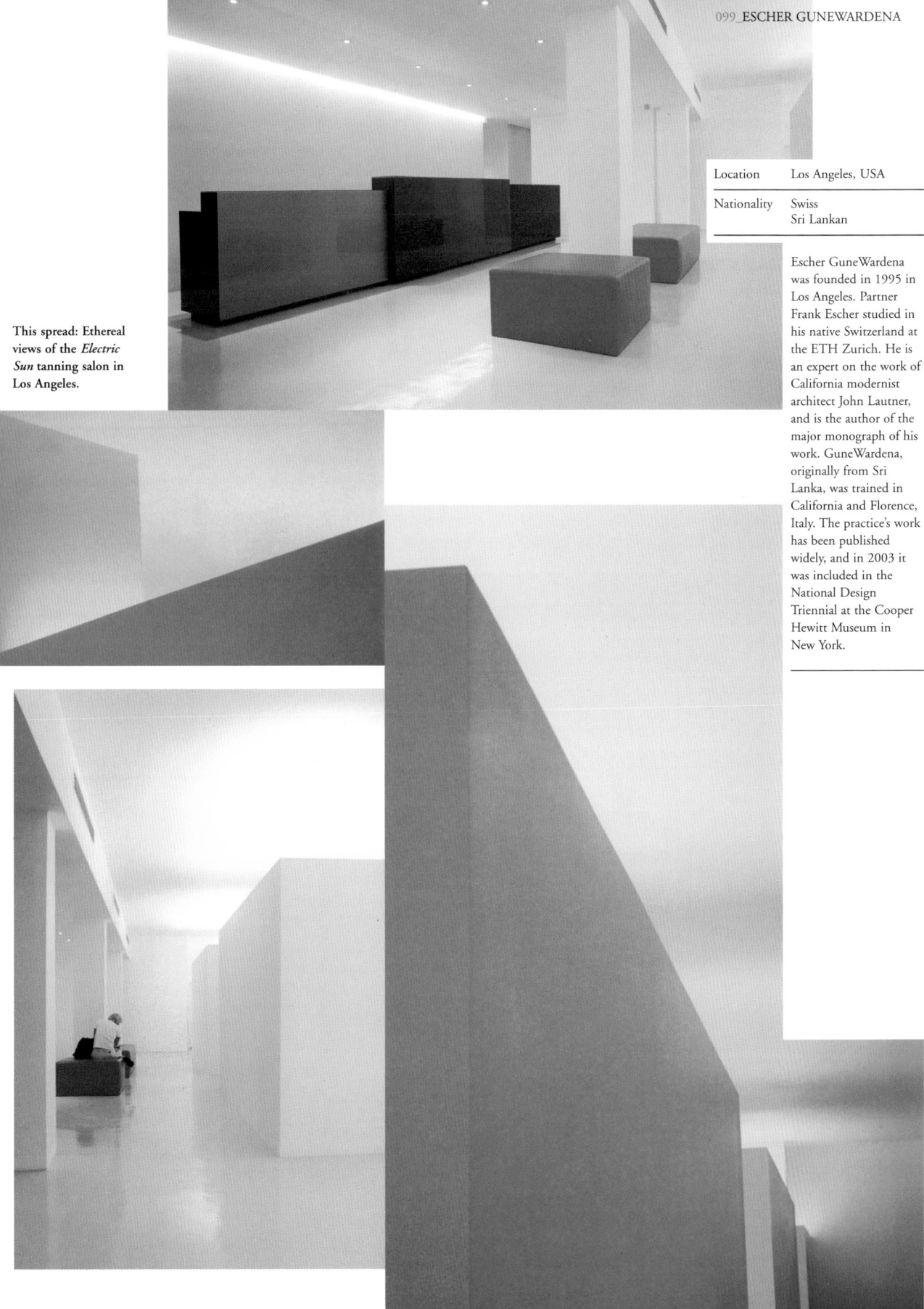

**This spread: Ethereal views of the *Electric Sun* tanning salon in Los Angeles.**

| Location | Los Angeles, USA |
| --- | --- |
| Nationality | Swiss<br>Sri Lankan |

Escher GuneWardena was founded in 1995 in Los Angeles. Partner Frank Escher studied in his native Switzerland at the ETH Zurich. He is an expert on the work of California modernist architect John Lautner, and is the author of the major monograph of his work. GuneWardena, originally from Sri Lanka, was trained in California and Florence, Italy. The practice's work has been published widely, and in 2003 it was included in the National Design Triennial at the Cooper Hewitt Museum in New York.

E

# Fabric

Fabric's work is of the kind that would have been very difficult to understand just a few years ago. Working since 1997, this multi-disciplinary studio undertakes research into the spatial implications of technology, creating new data environments that are designed not just as information-management systems, but as spaces or infrastructures of inhabitation.

To achieve this, encouraging collaboration between computer engineers and architects was key: 'Establishing new collaborations between architects and information scientists was a first step to explore the mutations of "inhabitable" space and contemporary spatialities: digital territories, distributed or media environments, and also non-material, artificial, mobile, displaced or invisible spaces.' Fabric's proposals link the physical world to the worlds existing in networks, proposing that architectural intent can be shown in both.

The *Mix-m* museum project (2005) demonstrates how Fabric's work dovetails these different worlds. Based on the studio's own software (the Java-based rhizoreality.mu framework that attempts to link digital effects to the physical environment), *Mix-m* existed as a physical exhibition at the Centre for Contemporary Art in Geneva, as well as

Clockwise from above: The Centre for Contemporary Art in Geneva, which hosted Fabric's *Mix-m* project in 2005; Images from the virtual part of *Mix-m*. The architects say: '*Mix-m* plays with the nature of its architecture: a mix between a real museum space (1:1 scale), a virtual, "game like", multi-user environment, a digital space based on the dimensions of its host (the Bâtiment d'Art Contemporain), and a model of this "game-like" environment (1:50 scale).' The project was a collaboration between Fabric and the curatorial team Interversion.

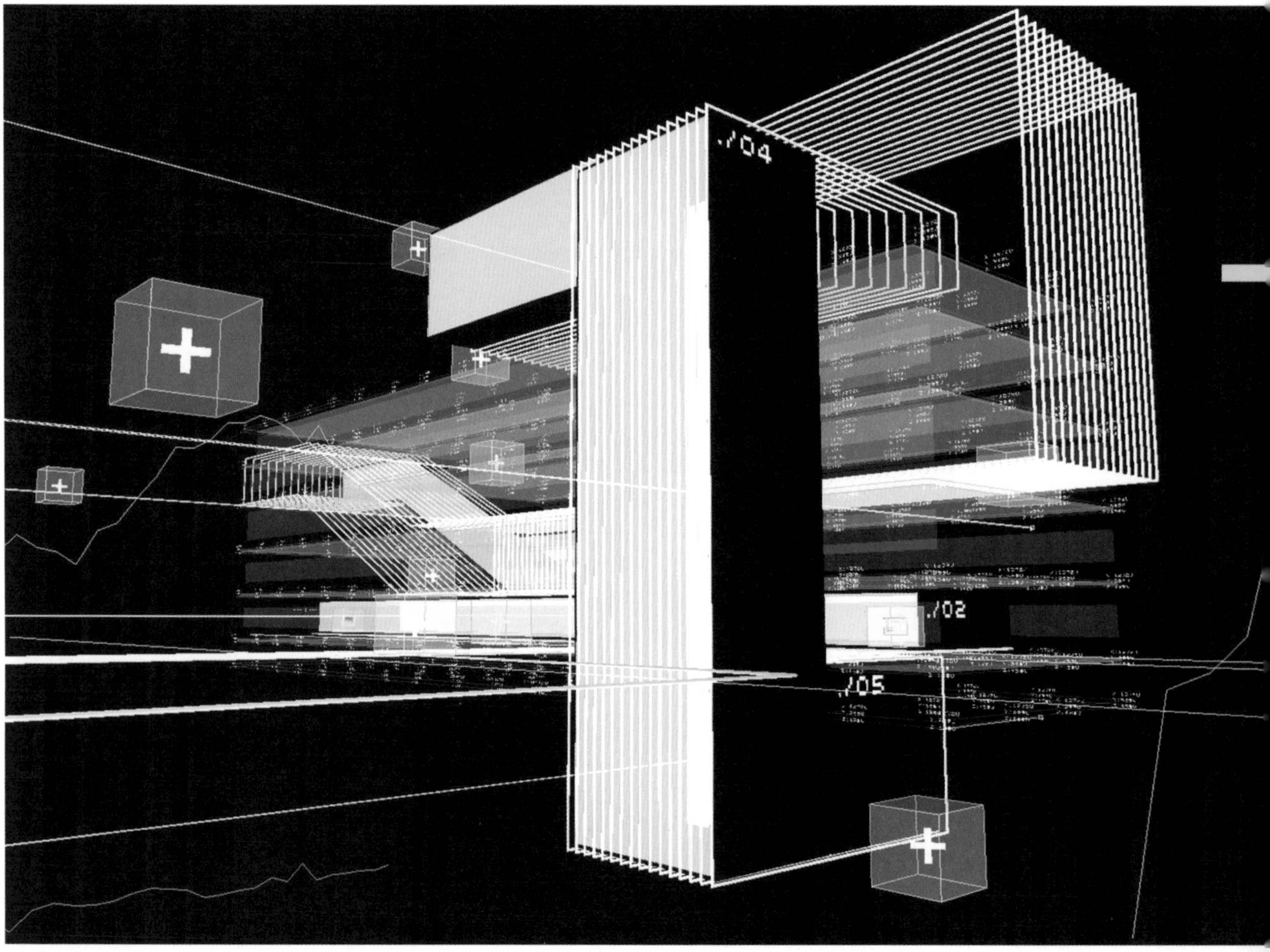

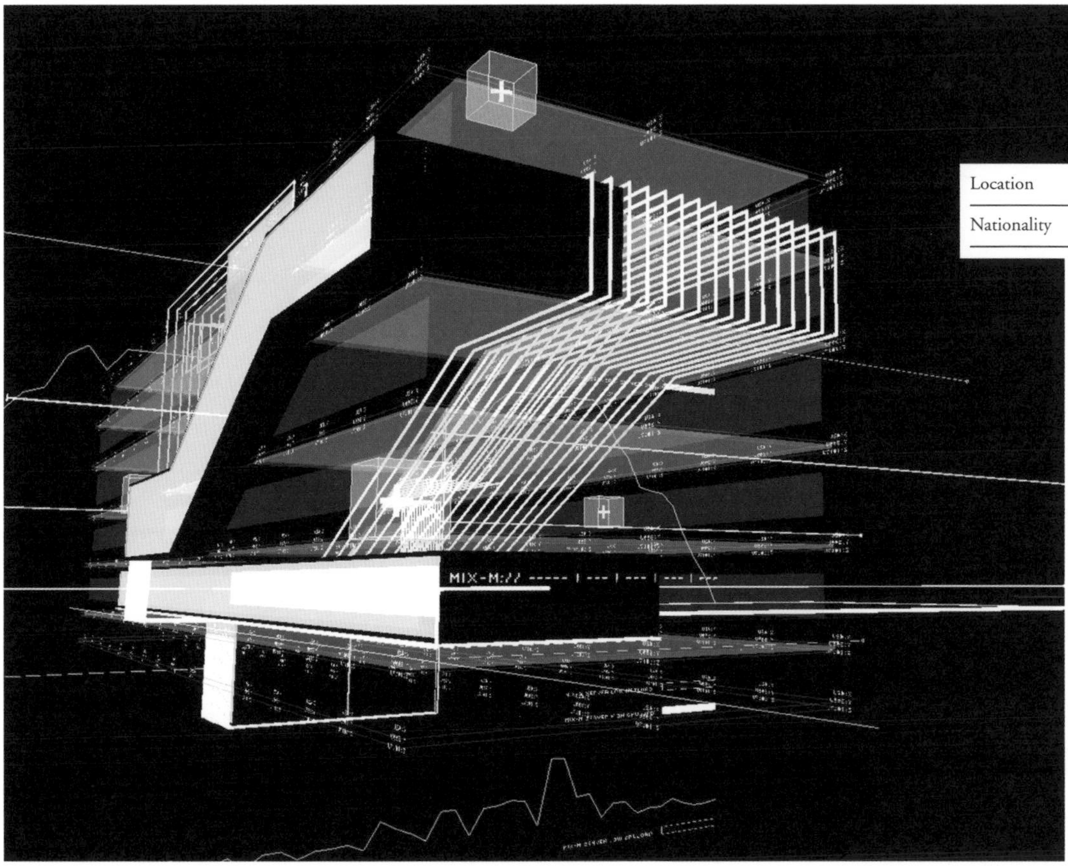

| Location | Lausanne, Switzerland |
|---|---|
| Nationality | Swiss |

Fabric is based in Lausanne, Switzerland. It is a multi-disciplinary practice examining the links between physical and digital spaces. It was founded in 1997 by two architects (Christophe Guignard and Patrick Keller), a telecommunications engineer (Stéphane Carion) and a computer engineer (Christian Babski). The practice's early work was in the creation of new digital networks and data environments (such as the rhizoreality.mu technological framework written in Java). More recently its work has been more physical, such as their experimental project for Nestlé's European headquarters.

In 2005, Fabric collaborated with Philippe Rahm (pp. 262–263) on his exhibition *Architecture Invisible* at the Swiss Cultural Centre in Paris. In the project room at the same time was the work of Joël Tettamanti (pp. 308–311).

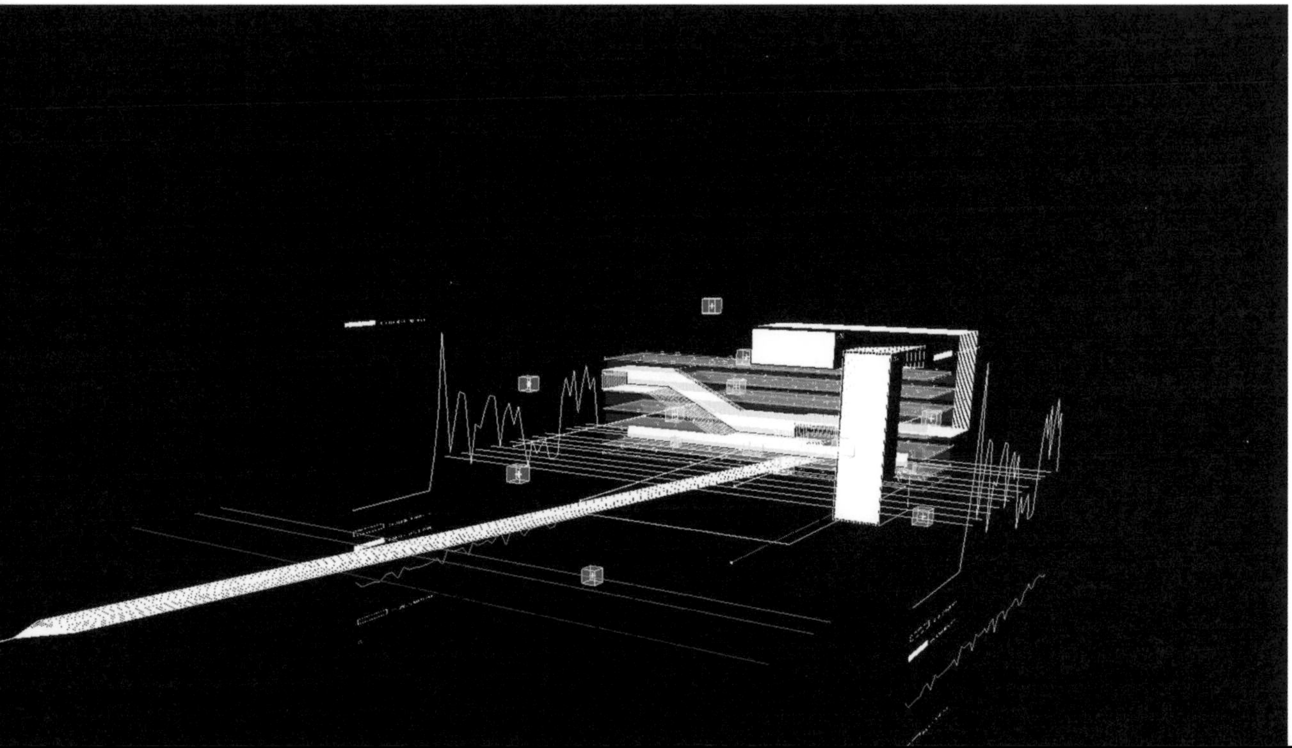

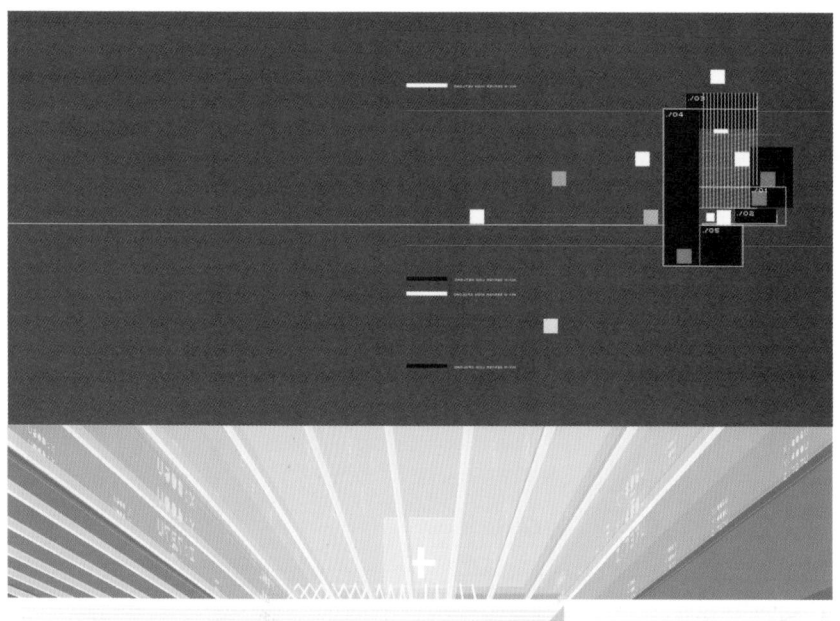

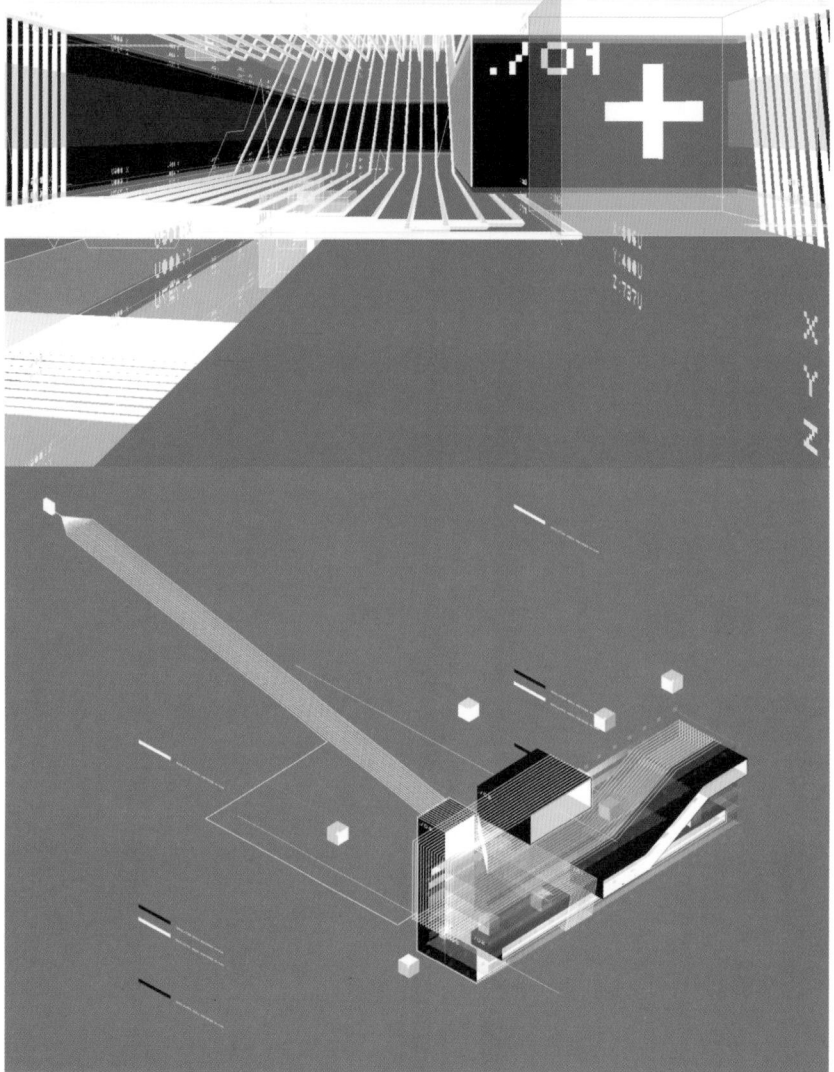

a game-like virtual environment at a variety of scales. Fabric, with the curator Interversion, commissioned works that could exist within both media (such as Joelle Flumet, Yves Mettler and Scanner), with 3-D web-based representations of the artworks allowing an audience well beyond the boundaries of the gallery. Activity in the digital environment was also fed back in to the physical space of the gallery by means of lighting installations that represented the traffic on the website.

Perhaps a more direct example of Fabric's interest in bringing a globalized, networked world into physical form is the *Perpetual (Tropical) Sunshine* installation, created for the Lyon Festival of Light in 2005. Fabric created a virtual representation of the sun, a screen of 300 infrared light bulbs, which 'transposes the state and image of a summer sun on the 23rd South parallel, thanks to live information transmitted by a network of weather stations on the Tropic of Capricorn and all around the globe.' The project was also a comment on the use of infrared heat lamps in public spaces that artificially prolong the summers in Europe, dramatizing it with a 'networked sun' transposed from another part of the globe.

Opposite: More images
from the *Mix-m* project.
This page: The *Perpetual
(Tropical) Sunshine*
installation, which
simulates the sunlight
from all over the globe.
The installation was part
of the Lyon Festival of
Light in 2005.

F

# Leo Fabrizio

This series of pictures is from Fabrizio's book *Bunkers*, which documents modern fortifications in Switzerland. He worked on this series for five years, and it became a meditation on the relationship of built fabric to landscape, and on how military infrastructure resides in traditionally neutral Switzerland.

This spread: Images from Fabrizio's book *Bunkers*. The pictures are Lambda prints on aluminium.

| | |
|---|---|
| Location | Bottens, Switzerland |
| Nationality | Swiss |

Leo Fabrizio was born in 1976 and studied photography at the École Cantonal d'Art de Lausanne. He is a photographer and cameraman based in Bottens in Switzerland whose work has been widely exhibited and published. His photographs are also part of public collections in France and Switzerland, as well as many private collections. In 2005 his work was shown in the *ReGeneration* exhibition at the Musée de l'Elysée in Lausanne, Switzerland. Most recently, he published a book of photographs entitled *Bunkers* with Swiss publisher Infolio. He is represented by the Galerie Kamel Mennour in Paris.

This spread: More of Fabrizio's bunkers. These shelters are disguised in mountains or as false rock formations.

F

# Fantastic Norway

With one of the best names in European architecture, Fantastic Norway makes doing public-spirited architecture sound like a breeze. The architects' approach to a project is to pack up their red caravan (emblazoned with 'Fantastic Norway Architects' across one side), and drive to places they feel are in need of architectural input. This approach is unconventional, but has a streak of northern European pragmatism. 'We wanted to be visible as architects,' says co-founder Erlend Haffner, 'and easy to relate to for the general public.' This seems to be effective, and the strategy of a kind of extreme consultation builds consensus in locations where there often has been none before. 'Once we're there, we find the hidden power structure of the city and then we invade it. We meet powerful locals and explain what we want to do. We write a weekly column in the local paper to get people to the caravan and we publish a project. People come and see us with ideas on how to make it better. Some come to the caravan with dreams, some try to convince us to leave. But from it we build a picture of the place and its secrets.'

The caravan itself is both consultation space and workplace, offering coffee and waffles and conversation to those with ideas about their towns. When Fantastic Norway visited Narvik, in the north of Norway, a group of young people came to the caravan with a suggestion to make a location for a BMX track and sports ground. The architects took the idea and suggested that it be built on a former industrial site where a Lidl supermarket was planned. They got their wish, and the sports arena construction is going ahead.

Other projects also demonstrate that Fantastic Norway is not just about making friends with the locals. The beautiful, sail-like forms of their proposal for the Svartisen tourist centre complements the starkly beautiful landscape of the glacier.

Erlend Blakstad Haffner studied for his Masters degree at London Metropolitan University, where DRDH Architects (pp. 86–89), Lynch Architects (pp. 178–181) and UFO (pp. 324–327) have all taught.

| Location | Norway |
|---|---|
| Nationality | Norwegian |

Fantastic Norway was founded in 2003 by Erlend Blakstad Haffner and Håkon Matre Aasarød. The two partners dropped out of architecture school to take to the road in a red caravan, to carry out a new kind of direct consultation architecture. Their caravan pulls up in a town and carries out a kind of architecture advocacy, asking local people what they want and lobbying politicians and locals to achieve it. Projects include a proposal to build a sports arena in Narvik, northern Norway, a temporary installation, *Daylight Space*, in 2005 in Bodø and a tourist centre in Svartisen.

F

Clockwise from below: Fantastic Norway's caravan. The two partners travel to sometimes remote locations to offer their services as architects; A visualization of the *Black Boxes* proposal for a tourism centre by a glacier in northern Norway. The project will begin construction in 2008; The cartoon-strip story of the *Black Boxes* proposal; Perspectival section of one of the guesthouses.

# FAT

FAT has long been a compelling and awkward presence in the London architecture scene, its members being known as much as artists as architects and punting an extreme postmodern aesthetic that few thought would become mainstream.

And while the world hasn't gone gothic-revival, FAT has found an audience far beyond the art house. Their recent housing project at New

This spread: The Dutch gables of FAT's New Islington social housing project in Manchester, UK. The pattern on the façade is intended as the urban gesture, and behind it the houses are arranged around a protected courtyard space.

| Location | London, UK |
|---|---|
| Nationality | British |

FAT (Fashion Architecture Taste) was founded in London in 1995, and of the current members, Sam Jacob and Sean Griffiths were founders. Charles Holland joined a year later, and the three have been responsible for the best known of FAT's work. Early projects include manifestoes (*Kill the Modernist Within, How to Become a Famous Architect*), art pieces (*New Civic* in 2000, a clock on King's Cross station in London), and interiors (significantly the Kessels Kramer advertising office in Amsterdam, the Netherlands in 1998). New projects include *WIMBY!* (*Welcome Into My Backyard*), a park and community centre in Hoogvliet, the Netherlands. Sean Griffiths teaches at the University of Westminster in London, and the other partners have also taught and lectured widely.

Islington in Manchester, UK, has been published in plenty of magazines, but has also seen the practice win construction industry awards and a second nomination for the Mies van der Rohe Prize. FAT is, in a sense, the kind of architecture office that has kept itself deliberately unfashionable, but critics and clients see much to admire in its work despite that.

The 23-unit housing project in the New Islington masterplan in Manchester is the project that best demonstrates that the practice desires an engagement with the tastes of ordinary people, as opposed to perpetuating the modernist orthodoxies so prevalent in architecture. The houses are a strange

mix of Dutch-gable forms and Pringle-sweater patterning, uniting the terraces behind a brick skin that is deliberately and eclectically characterful. But, as partner Sam Jacob says, their interest is historical, in an authentically postmodern way. 'The traditions we really like are things like the picturesque, the world of follies. We love the sorts of places where people who had a little knowledge made completely the wrong kinds of things out of it. We think that's fantastic.' The project was generated out of a consultation process that observed the kinds of alterations that the tenants had made to their existing homes. The interiors of the new houses are intended to encourage the same self-build interior designs.

Influences are clear – Venturi Scott Brown and others – but FAT's is a more unashamed postmodernism. Sean Griffiths says: 'We are interested in an idea that modernism is actually a historical architectural style and that while High Victorian Gothic is 150 years old, modernism is only 100 years old. It's really asking the question, "Why does everybody do modernist stuff?"'

Perhaps even more extreme is FAT's project for the *Sint Lucas Art Academy* in Boxtel, the Netherlands. FAT's work has always found an audience in the Netherlands (they are currently building a new park and community hall there, too), and this project, with its faux-gothic-ruin façade masking a modernist shed behind, shows the practice's will to use strategies from postmodern culture – quotation, collage and black humour – to impressive effect.

F

This spread: FAT's *Sint Lucas Art Academy* in Boxtel, the Netherlands. The faux-gothic gable is made of precast concrete. Behind the loud façade, FAT carried out a replanning of the entire academy site, including creating a new café at its heart (above). Chandeliers hang in the 1960s building, and more gothic patterns adorn the wall.

It is striking that apart from FAT there is probably not a single architect in this book who would classify themselves as postmodern.

# feld72

feld72 has ambitions at many different scales, evidenced by a long list of urban strategies and art projects on its CV. But it is for its *Wine Centre* in the small south Tyrolean village of Caldaro in Italy that it is best known.

The practice won the project in a limited competition, for a very prominent site on the wine-tourist route through the region. The centre is built very much as a monolith, with a skin of fibre-reinforced concrete in a deep maroon colour with undetailed glass panels that reflect the surrounding landscape. Its form rises around a small courtyard, from a single-storey height to a tower-like landmark on the street that reflects the scale of some of the earlier buildings on the site.

The monolithic exterior contrasts with the sculptural interior.

This spread: feld72's *Wine Centre* in Caldaro, northern Italy. The project rises sinuously to it highest height by the roadside, forming a dramatic landmark for drivers.

feld72 writes: 'Tension arises between perceiving the uniform shell and the single large interior space which it encloses. Here a sculptural landscape unfolds.' Inside, the space of the wine shop is L-shaped in plan. The low section houses the shop, with a counter in the corner for tasting wines. The higher section has a dramatic stepped mezzanine that accommodates an area for more exclusive wines, and at high level what the architects call 'the village pub'. Beautifully made acacia furniture has a certain sophisticated rusticity, and the contrast between the white-rendered perimeter walls and the acacia and concrete mezzanine is cool and pleasing.

This is a fine example of a kind of architecture that could be called typical of recent Austrian architecture, but its more complex geometry and ingenious siting sets it apart from the crowd. feld72 might pride itself on its interdisciplinarity, but this building shows the practice can make something of finely wrought detail and convincing formal gesture.

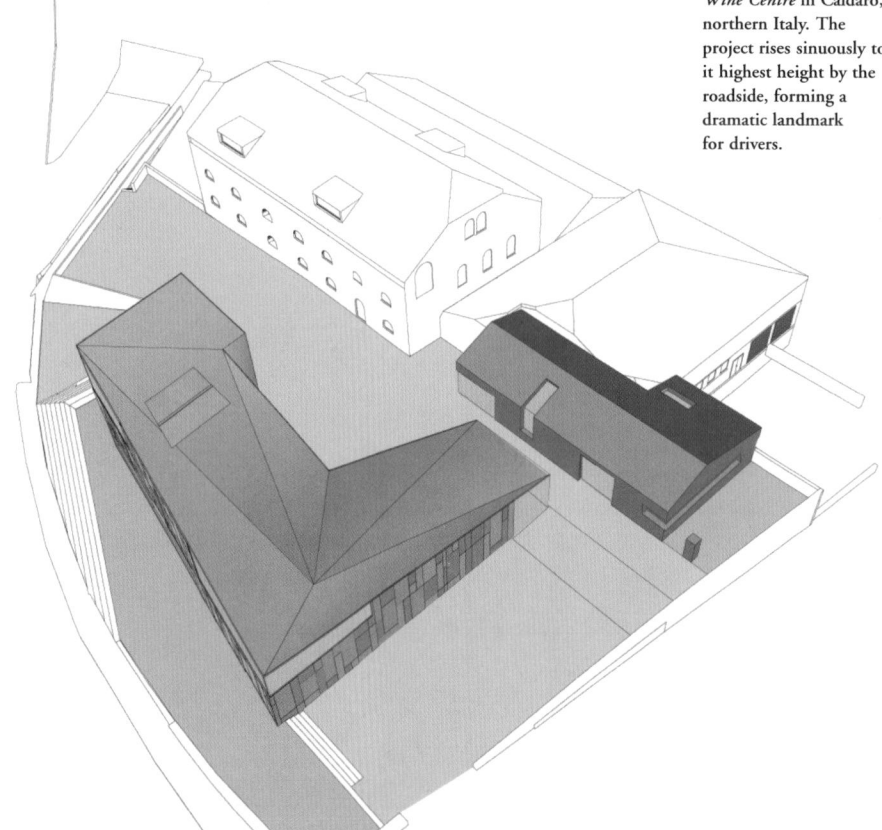

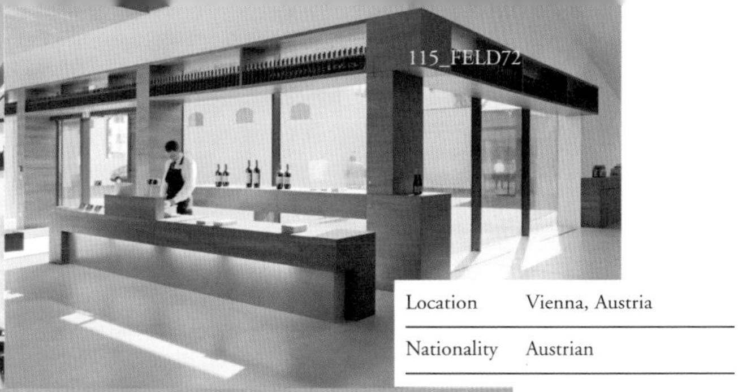

| Location | Vienna, Austria |
|----------|-----------------|
| Nationality | Austrian |

**F**

feld72 is an architecture collective that calls itself 'a laboratory for architecture, engaged in research and finding new strategies for cliché-dominated or underestimated (urban) conditions.' It was founded in 2002 by Anne Catherine Fleith, Michael Obrist, Mario Paintner, Richard Scheich and Peter Zoderer in Vienna. All the partners apart from Fleith studied in the Austrian capital. Built projects include the *Wine Centre* in Caldaro, northern Italy, completed in 2006. In 2002 feld72 won the National Award for Experimental Tendencies in Architecture in Austria, and in 2007 the Chicago Athenaeum International Architecture Award for the *Wine Centre*.

# FNP Architekten

FNP Architekten's project for a showroom in Ramsen in Germany has the clarity of a manifesto. The project, which won an *Architectural Review* award in 2005, takes a well-used approach to historic buildings and makes it disarmingly literal, making clear distinctions between new and old fabric but allowing the historic to define the new. The brief was to make a showroom within a small building that dated from 1780 and that used to be a pigsty. It was, however, in very poor condition, and could not be refurbished economically without a comprehensive reconstruction. The architects decided to leave the building almost as a ruin, and inserted a new timber skin into the pigsty, forming a new interior that simply accepted the openings and dimensions of the historic structure and used them for the new building.

The timber inner skin was craned in, in one prefabricated piece, and glazing was added later. The contract sum for the job was small (around 20,000 euros), and the architects say that what was important about this job was a lack of difficult details. Openings are left as in the original pigsty, no matter how strange an impression that might create. The economy of this approach is described wittily by the architects: 'It is like a cast of the old use of the building. The visitor today might feel irritated, because he will not know why the window is right in the corner, or why it's so small. The pigs never thought about it.'

A new roof protects both the damaged outer skin, and the precious and tactile new interior.

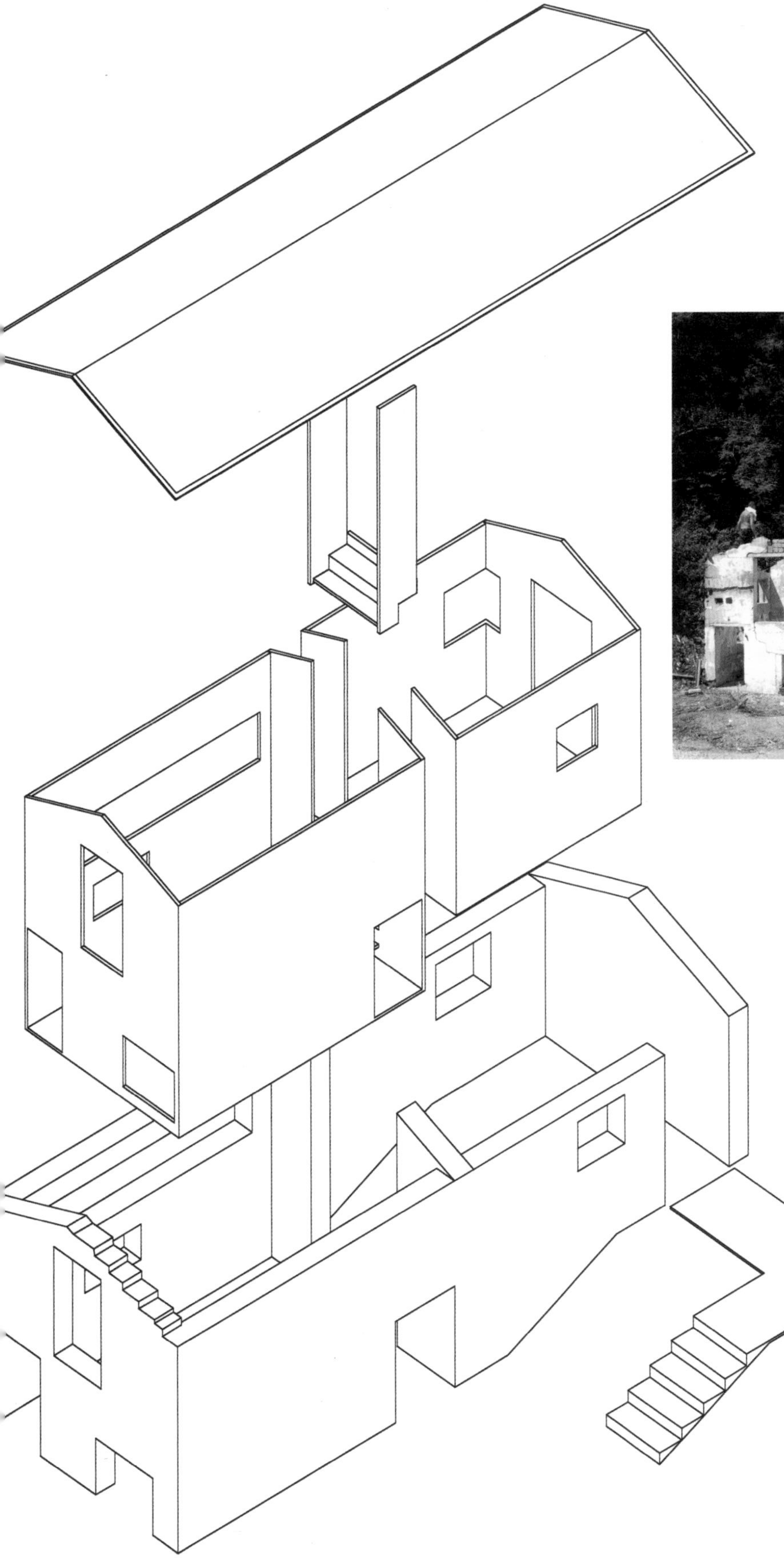

| Location | Stuttgart, Germany |
|---|---|
| Nationality | Swiss<br>German |

FNP Architekten was founded in Stuttgart in 2005 out of the merger of two practices: Fischer and Fischer and Richter Naumann. The four partners are Oliver Fischer, Susanne Fischer, Martin Naumann and Stefanie Naumann. Since 2005 they have won several awards, including a first place in the Rheinland Pfalz Architecture Prize, and an *Architectural Review* award for the showroom in Ramsen in 2005.

This spread: FNP's extraordinary project for a showroom in Ramsen, Germany. As the diagram demonstrates, the strategy was to insert a prefabricated timber box into the ruin of an old farm building.

FNP won an *Architectural Review* award in 2005. Also commended that year were Sou Fujimoto (pp. 122–125) and Pezo von Ellrichshausen (pp. 246–249).

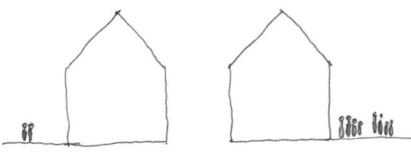

This spread: FNP's *Zweihaus FHS*. Two dwellings are slotted in to a form inspired by a child-like drawing of a house (right). The project is intentionally ambiguous, appearing to be a single house form but in fact containing two dwellings. The house has two entrances and a multitude of window openings that add to the strange feeling of two houses in one. The house has a stepped section that allows windows to appear in irregular places on the gable façades. The materials of the building are super-conventional, and characteristic of supposedly contextual development in Swiss and German villages.

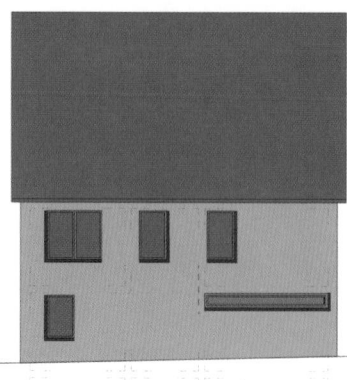

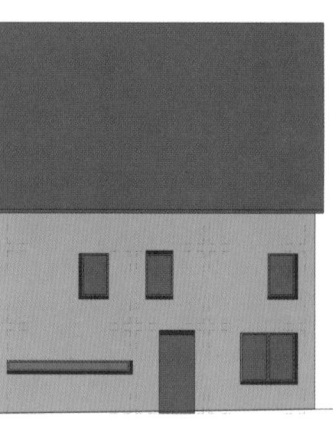

F

# Studio Force4

Studio Force4's flagship project is the *BOASE* sustainable housing concept, which the studio has been developing with the Realdania Foundation, an organization dedicated to funding projects that improve Denmark's built environment. Force4 estimates that there are 14,000 contaminated sites in Denmark, with 148 of them in the capital Copenhagen. The project arose from a desire to improve and build on contaminated land, and will be part of a mixed recreational/housing area planned for the Borgmestervangen on Nørrebro.

Force4's strategy is to use the soil-cleansing properties of certain trees (such as willows) to create urban forests, within which a growing community of prefabricated houses sits, 3m (10ft) above the ground and above the canopy of the forest. The masterplan itself uses the forest as an organizing factor, without being too prescriptive about where the houses develop. The architects write: 'In time the settlement will grow and spread over the ground like the branches of a tree. Its growth is not planned because it is a result of various conditions; the cleaning of the soil, the growth of the plants and the surrounding buildings.'

The houses are industrially fabricated modules that are stacked and clustered around informal communal spaces. The houses are composed of a solar-collecting glazed façade, semi-transparent solar cells and PCM (phase change material) plates, which help to regulate temperature through thermal mass. The inner walls are made of form-moulded plant fibre plates, and the whole unit is recyclable or compostable. The units are small, intended to accommodate a more nomadic lifestyle. Force4 writes: 'The spatial principles build on the duality of the static and the flexible. The private dwelling is the static frame of the settlement. The communal area is the social heart of the settlement. Here social relations are strengthened, even though most inhabitants live alone.'

The first of these forest oases in the city will be built in Copenhagen. There, a more permanent forest of oak and alder grows slowly, while fast-growing willow and poplar cleanse the soil.

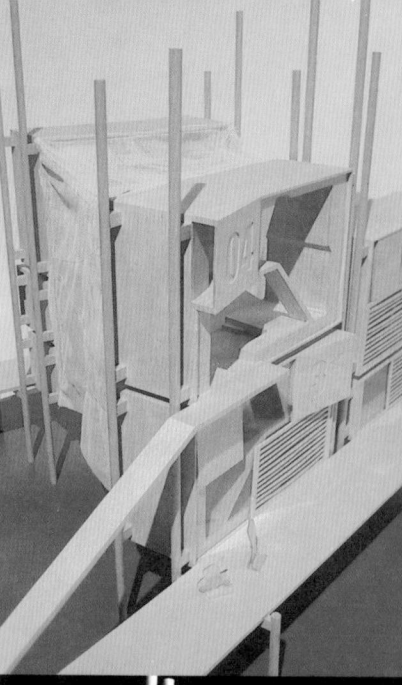

Studio Force4's focus on sustainable architecture is shared by ecoLogic Studio (pp. 90–91) and Jennifer Siegal (pp. 290–291), but by surprisingly few others

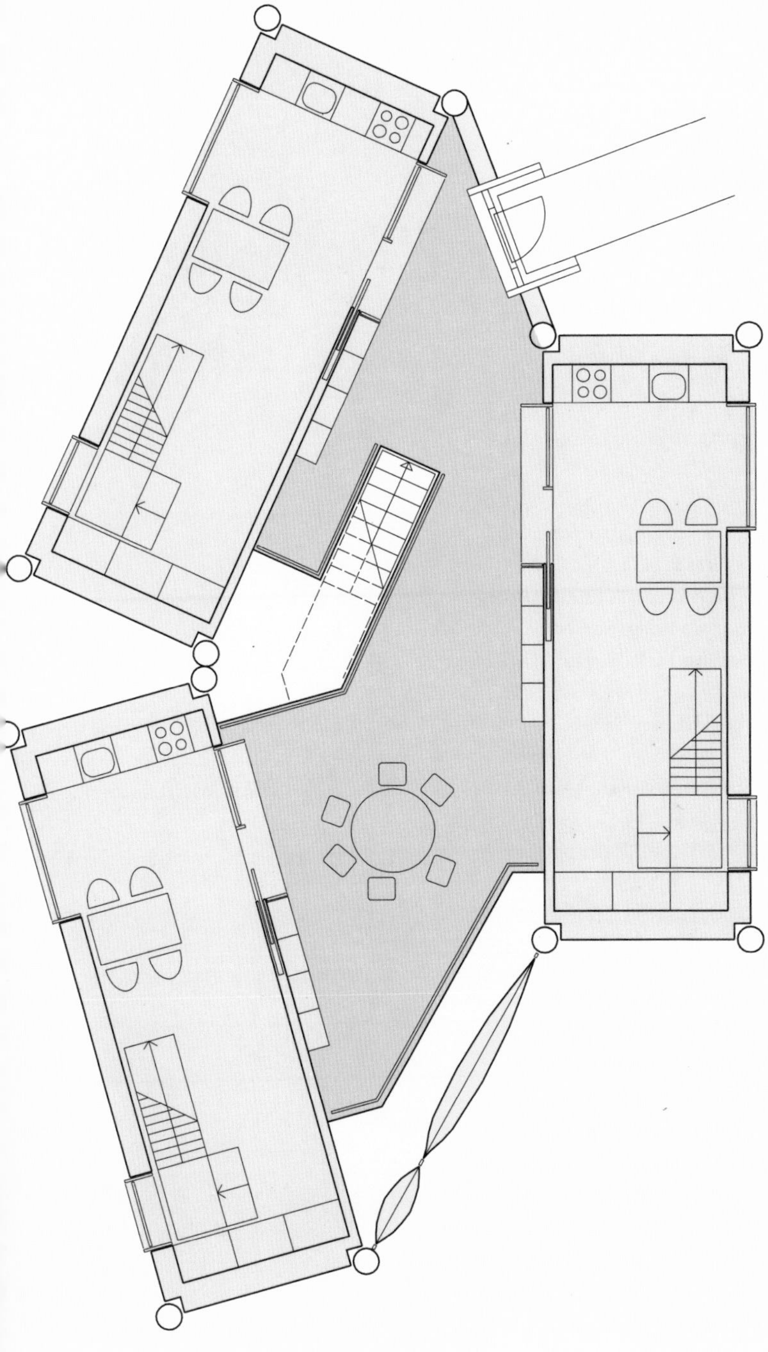

| Location | Nørrebro, Denmark |
|---|---|
| Nationality | Danish |

Studio Force4 is an interdisciplinary studio founded in 2003 in Nørrebro, Denmark. The studio consists of two architects (Andreas Lauesen and Mikala Holme Samsøe) and two designers (Maja Asaa and Christian Dalsdorf). The studio works at every scale from product design to masterplanning. It has developed a specialism in sustainable housing, in projects such as *BOASE* and its 13 houses in Sydhavnen with Arkitema. Force4 is also working on a mixed-use building in Hannemannsparken in Ørestad Syd. The project is in collaboration with the architects 3xNielsen for Nordkranen. The studio received the Danish Design Centre's Visionary Prize in 2001 and Henning Larsen's Prize of Honor in 2005.

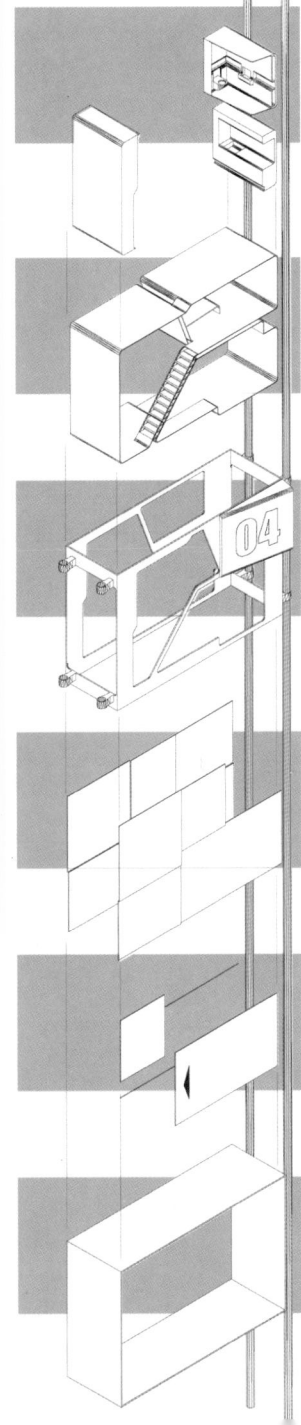

This spread: The *BOASE* project, a sustainable-housing housing concept that will be built in Copenhagen, Denmark. Each house is made out of recyclable materials.

# Sou Fujimoto

Sou Fujimoto's work is concerned with the establishment of new archetypes that can accommodate a very wide range of activities without an overtly imposed order. This libertarianism has led him to propose some radical new kinds of buildings, apparently influenced by some of the older generation of Japanese architects (particularly Kazuyo Sejima and Ryue Nishizawa's SANAA).

Fujimoto's biggest success yet came in 2003 with his polemical project for the Environmental Art Forum in the Japanese new town of Gunma.

The brief for the competition was programmatically vague, and Fujimoto pushed that to an extreme, making a multi-purpose single-storey room of 7,000sq m (75,350sq ft). This single-room strategy was complemented by a meandering plan form that pushed into its surroundings, making an outline particularly tuned to the woods outside, but also creating moments of greater intimacy near the façade.

When Fujimoto was asked to design a centre for emotionally disturbed children in his home town of Hokkaido, he brought some of these lessons to a much more sensitive context. The 2,500sq m (26,700sq ft) building had to accommodate, and help to heal, a community of children with serious emotional and mental problems. The project, from the outside, looks as if it has been planned as an abstracted Italian hilltown, with intersecting concrete boxes recalling the partial

| Location | Tokyo, Japan |
| --- | --- |
| Nationality | Japanese |

Sou Fujimoto began his independent practice in Tokyo in 2000. He studied at the Department of Architecture in the Faculty of Engineering at the University of Tokyo. Fujimoto has worked on a wide range of projects such as houses and medical facilities. High-profile successes include his second place in the Aomori Art Gallery Design Competition in 2000, and his first prize in the competition for the Annaka Environmental Art Forum in 2003. He has won many awards, including the Japan Institute of Architects Best Young Architect Award in 2004 and an *Architectural Review* award in 2006 for his centre for disturbed children in his home town of Hokkaido.

randomness of a vernacular layout. Inside, however, the building's intersecting plan allows the creation of a multiplicity of small alcoves and nooks that individual children can inhabit securely. These are related to much larger, but irregularly shaped, spaces that are filled with natural light. The children can find both security and intimacy, as well as protected places for more social encounters.

Fujimoto describes the spaces as 'vague, unpredictable and filled with unlikelihood'. Taking an almost random approach provides non-dogmatic spaces that he hopes will aid the healing process.

This page: The calm interior of Fujimoto's children's centre helps calm the behaviour of its troubled residents. Opposite: The institution is divided into cube-like forms that give the impression of a small village, rather than a monolithic institution. The section shows how natural light is allowed in through rooflights alternating with solid sections of roof.

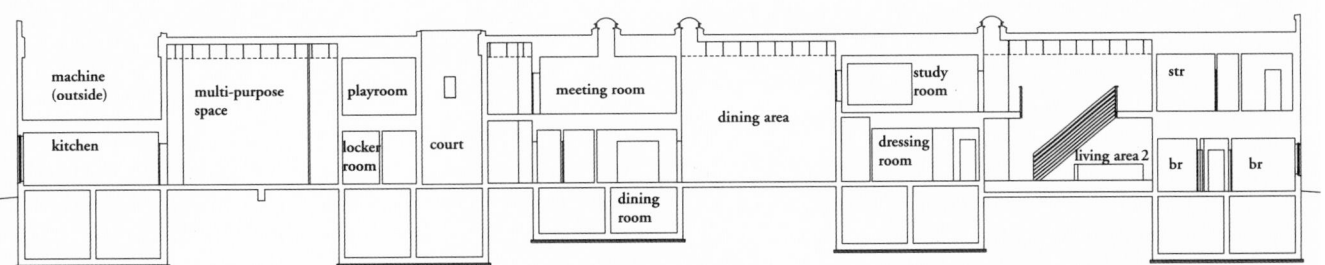

machine
(outside)

kitchen

multi-purpose
space

playroom

locker
room

court

dining
room

meeting room

dining area

study
room

dressing
room

living area 2

str

br

br

**Fujimoto's centre for emotionally disturbed children was included in the book *Parallel Nippon: Contemporary Japanese Architecture 1996–2006*,
as was Sambuichi Architects' Air House (pp. 276–279).**

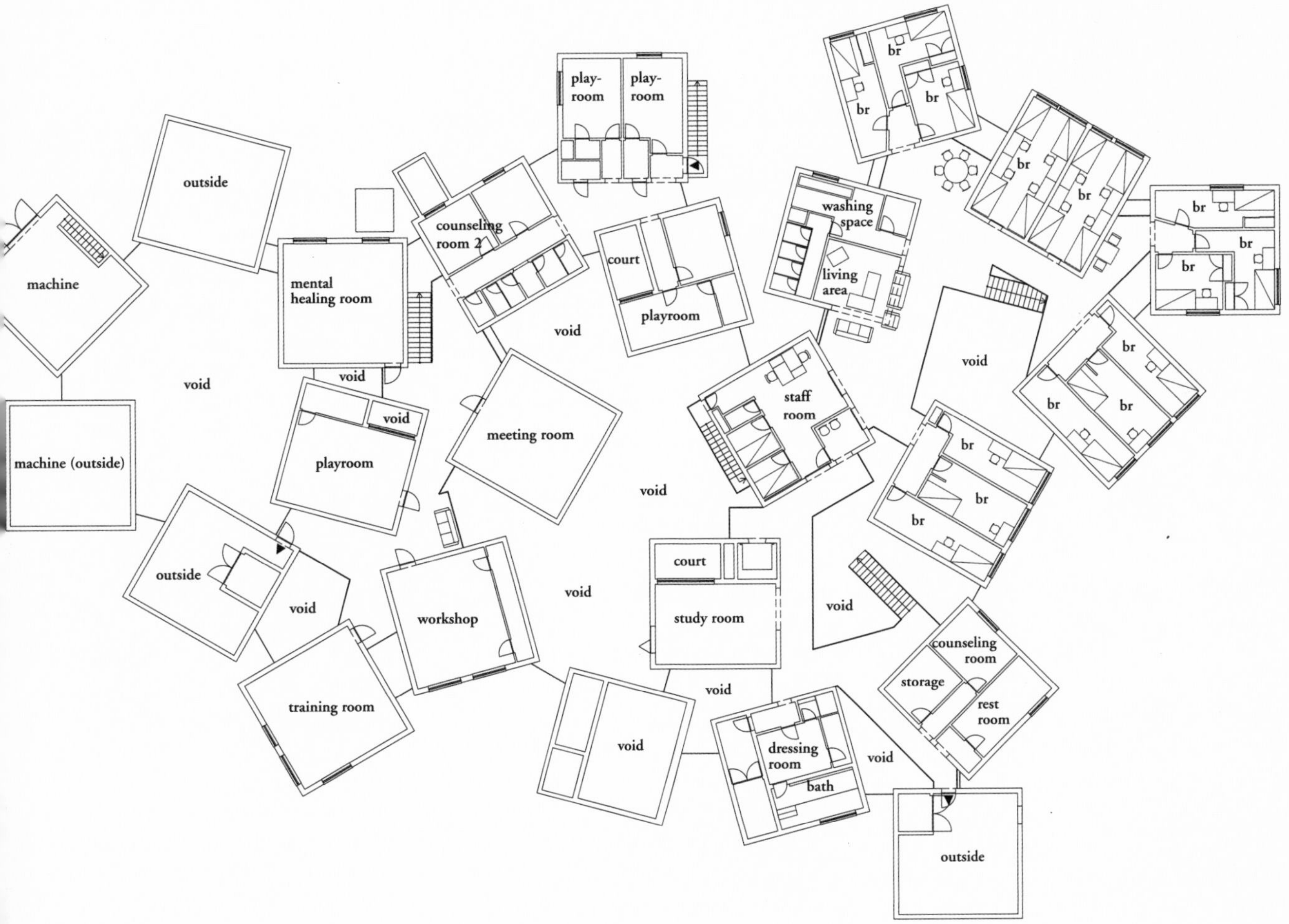

F

playroom

playroom

outside

br

br

br

counseling
room 2

washing
space

machine

court

playroom

living
area

br

br

void

mental
healing room

br

meeting room

staff
room

br

void

machine (outside)

void

void

playroom

void

br

br

outside

br

br

workshop

void

void

court

study room

void

void

counseling
room

training room

storage

rest
room

void

void

dressing
room

void

bath

outside

In this extract from Gadanho's essay *The South Will Rise Again? (On the Emergency of Emergency)*, he tackles two sacred cows: Portuguese aesthetic sensibilities in architecture, and the language of emergence, which has become so current in contemporary architectural culture.

In a scenario in which lack of resources may become critical, it is to be expected that those who always worked within a condition of necessary resourcefulness can offer more sustainable and creative solutions to new everyday problems.

When oil is the object of war, water faces shortage, temperatures rise and energy has to be rethought on alternative sources, one is led to reflect more seriously upon waste and luxurious expenditure. And one may imagine that in a few decades, the values and strategies according to which we build our environment will have to be fundamentally changed.

Although the system of consumption will always serve the conspicuous distinction of a small minority, there may come a time in which the space for inequitable shows of high-technology, expensive materials and shiny starchitecture is increasingly restricted.

Even if justified claims for progress generally lie behind such shows of strength, there may come a time in which its effective evidence has to be devised and enacted in other ways.

The so-called South is already facing this kind of dilemma.

Although integration in a global market and in a global media culture drives entire sections of some Southern countries to seek for a piece of the action within the attractive realm of the more advanced architectural production, the general economic situation of these countries makes inequalities particularly blunt and unacceptable.

Creativity has, thus, to be directed at resourcefulness in the face of adverse conditions.

As it is, it is also true that historically the architectural output of these countries has been frequently singled out precisely on account of the fact that it employs minimal resources, traditional materials and technological scarcity.

Portuguese architecture has been a good example of this predisposition.

It is not only the idea of scarcity that can be identified as a conceptual drive for a long-established way of producing architecture. More recently, the major international recognition of Alvaro Siza Vieira's oeuvre was also interwoven with a particular acknowledgment of his ability to use craftsmanship and a reduced palette of materials and technologies in order to produce an exquisite spatial experience.

Subsequently, however, a tendency arose in Portuguese architecture that turned away from the complexity and resourcefulness of Siza Vieira onto a more generalized minimalist or commercial approach. Albeit at the cost of architectural

Location    Porto, Portugal

Nationality    Portuguese

Pedro Gadanho is an architect, critic and curator in Porto, Portugal. He studied architecture at the University of Porto, and took a Masters at the Kent Institute of Architecture and Design in the UK. He currently teaches at the Porto architecture school, and runs his architecture practice in the same city. Gadanho is the founder and director of the Centre for Contemporary Urban Culture and a former director of the Experimenta design festival in Lisbon. He was the curator of *Metaflux*, Portugal's exhibition at the 2004 Venice Biennale.

**G**

richness and diversity, this has provided a model that still reveals a general pursuit of economical and material restraints.

Unfortunately, these restraints have, in many cases, become something of a straitjacket, rather than an inventive practice that would deal with the economical and social crisis that recently hit the country.

This could mean that in order to reinvent resourcefulness and still enjoy a vibrant and significant architectural practice, Portuguese architects may have to explore new avenues. [...]

If the emergent practitioners that are being portrayed and discussed in recent media are still sprouting from architecture's need to renew itself within a system of autonomous concerns – even if external references are now called upon to instigate and justify a renewal of architecture's established traditions – there are already suggestions that the next step may indeed be taken in the direction of a new type of emergence.

As I was proposing at the somewhat allegorical beginning of this text, a real emergency is becoming tangible just outside the long-established realm of architecture and the practices that are starting to address that emergency are those that, more justly, should be called emergent.

Curiously, if in Portugal this tendency may be sensed – as it is a noticeable rule in some art, design and architecture of most South American countries – it is because this is a country now divided between its European and Southern identity.

It is perhaps from Portugal's closeness to the South and its problems and idiosyncrasies that an explanation may be drawn so as to justify the presence of young practices that, here

and there, are radically evolving from the locally accepted understanding of architecture's social service.

In this sense, architecture is no longer seen only as a self-explanatory and self-sufficient answer to clients and markets, but is seen as a practice that must face up to new problems growing in contemporary societies. [...]

In this sense, and as shown in the emergent – and emergency – deeds of some Southern practices, the resources coming from the by now well-established architectural tradition, the knowledgeable resources of the architect may now be used for something more socially useful than just solidifying a nice career within the ranks of the profession or of the market.

Strategies of self-construction, performative architecture with critical social content, or cooperative models for developing countries fortunately show more concern for sustainable and critical resourcefulness than the mere pursuit of architectural style. Architecture is here shown as a means, rather than an end in itself.

# Gnuform

Gnuform is one of many practices coming out of the flowering of computer-aided formal experimentation that is sweeping architectural education (and, to a lesser degree, practice) in the USA. The partners' skills were honed working for the grandfather and parents of this generation – Peter Eisenman and Reiser & Umemoto. However, the abstract formal experimentation of the East Coast practices wore thin, and Gnuform was drawn to Los Angeles, where the practices associated with SCI-Arc were more interested in making the results of their experiments real.

Partner Jason Payne explains the reasons for the move: 'Part of it is the access to fabrication here, part of it was polemical. In New York, the bandwidth of formal and organizational experimentation seemed to be narrower. I thought it lacked material qualities. Out here it's looser. Sometimes that leads to less rigorous form, but at the same time that bandwidth gets wider.'

The practice is currently working with 3-D printing and other computerized fabrication techniques, and Payne feels that this has made for a more tactile architecture. 'Part of the problem, I felt, with New York, part of my frustration was that because it was not being built, not designed to be built, it was being designed to be looked at,' he says.

The major built manifestation of Gnuform's more sensuous, West Coast work is its interior for risqué television channel No Good TV in Beverly Hills. The project transformed a 2,140sq m (23,000sq ft) building into a headquarters for the network, with a showpiece bar and reception area on the ground floor. The bar uses vacuum forming to make a plastic service with deep folds. The bar itself is decorated with areas of tactile fur and rubber.

Payne says that the sensuous form and materiality of the bar reflects the client's interests. 'A lot of the material at the TV channel borders on the sexually explicit, so we were heading in that direction,' he says. Gnuform not only designed but fabricated and installed much of the project themselves.

Below and right: Gnuform's design for a house in Malibu, California.
Opposite: The practice's sensuous reception area for risqué television station No Good TV.

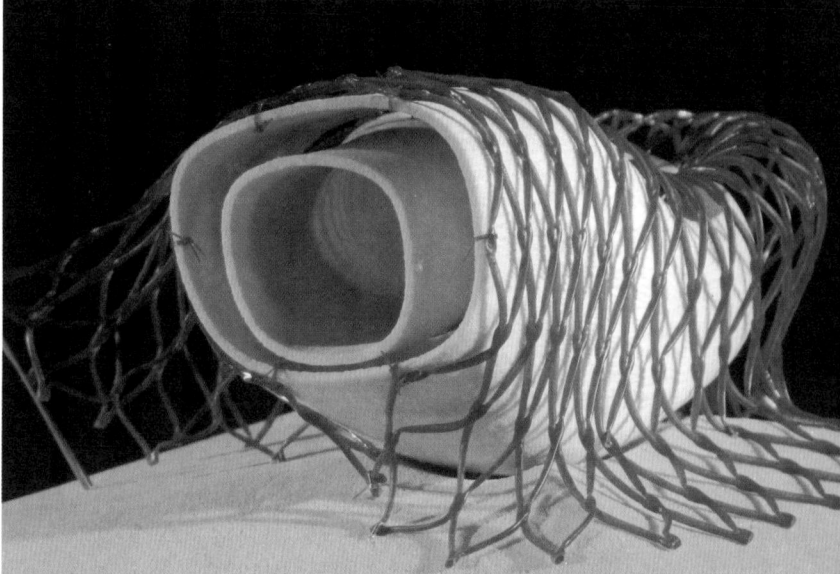

Gnuform was mentioned in an article in 2006 by Chris Hawthorne, architecture critic of the *LA Times*, as one of the 'potential stars' of LA's burgeoning architecture scene, along with Escher GuneWardena (pp. 98–99), Graftlab (pp. 134–135), Xefirotarch (pp. 340–343) and George Yu (pp. 344–347).

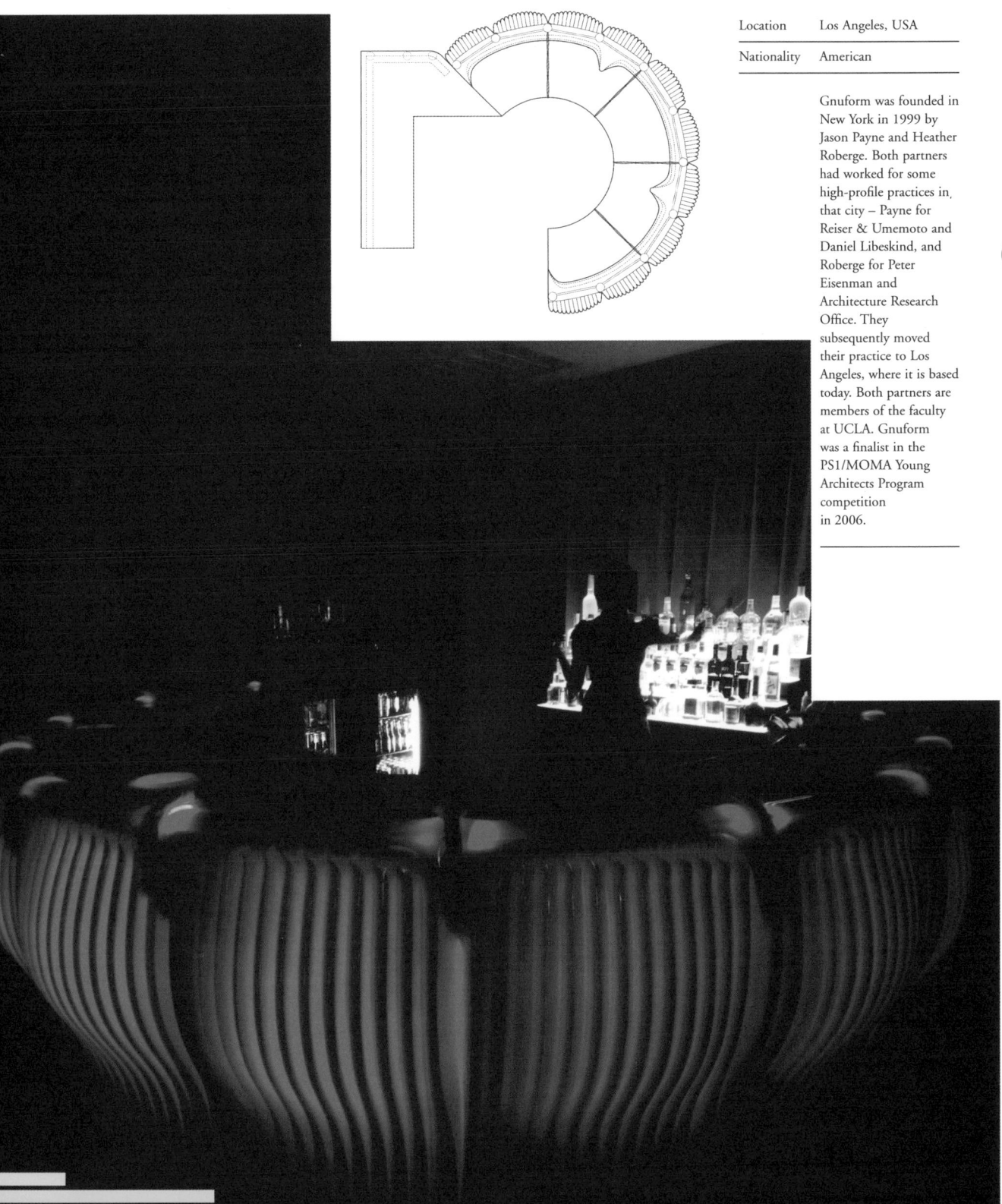

| Location | Los Angeles, USA |
| --- | --- |
| Nationality | American |

Gnuform was founded in New York in 1999 by Jason Payne and Heather Roberge. Both partners had worked for some high-profile practices in that city – Payne for Reiser & Umemoto and Daniel Libeskind, and Roberge for Peter Eisenman and Architecture Research Office. They subsequently moved their practice to Los Angeles, where it is based today. Both partners are members of the faculty at UCLA. Gnuform was a finalist in the PS1/MOMA Young Architects Program competition in 2006.

G

# Oliver Godow

The pictures collected here are an overview of Godow's recent work. All share his particular sensibility of seeing space in the process of becoming. It is appropriate that one of Godow's most 'architectural' commissions was to document the construction of the Camden Arts Centre in London, by Tony Fretton Architects. Godow's work is always interested in the strange and sometimes sterile beauty of places in flux.

**Below: Café Stenerson,
Oslo, 2006.
Opposite: ALEX, Berlin,
2006.**

| Location | UK |
| | Germany |
| Nationality | German |

Oliver Godow is a
photographer based in
the UK and Germany.
He studied at
Bournemouth University
in the UK and later for a
Masters in fine art at the
Glasgow School of Art.
He has exhibited his
work in solo shows in
Scandinavia, Germany
and Switzerland, and in a
number of group shows
including at the
Photographers' Gallery
in London, and galleries
in Germany, the US,
Israel and Russia. Godow
has also carried out
artist-in-residence
programmes at the
Camden Arts Centre in
London and most
recently at Durham
Cathedral. Godow has
lectured widely and his
work resides in a number
of prestigious collections
worldwide.

G

G

# Graftlab

Although Graftlab is now working at a huge scale, including high-rise buildings in Las Vegas, it is with a series of flashy and magazine-friendly interiors that it first made its name. The practice claims that it has no house style, and that 'taste is a lack of appetite', extolling the virtues of a gluttonous approach to architectural culture.

Whether you believe that or not, it is the case that Graftlab's interiors have a very distinct character. From the swooping burgundy forms of its *Hotel Q* in its home city of Berlin, to the canyon-like forms of the *Stack* restaurant interior in Las Vegas, there is a certain aesthetic that recalls what Zaha Hadid might do if she had grown up in Hollywood. One of the best examples of the type is Graftlab's interior for a dental clinic on the Kurfürstendamm in Berlin, completed in 2005. The project attempts to rethink the normally

This spread:
Dental clinic in Kurfürstendamm, Berlin, with diagrams bottom right showing how the surgery is arranged around a diagonal canyon through the floorplate.

| Location | Los Angeles, USA |
| | Berlin, Germany |
| | Beijing, China |
| Nationality | German |

Graftlab was founded in 1998 in Los Angeles by three Germans. All had studied at the Technical University of Braunschweig in Germany. Lars Krückeberg and Wolfram Putz then went on to study at SCI-Arc in Los Angeles, whereas Thomas Willemeit worked for Daniel Libeskind in Berlin. In 2001 they opened offices in Berlin and Beijing. The partners refer to their office not as a practice, but as a 'label for architecture, urban planning, exhibition design, music and the pursuit of happiness'. Early in its life, Graftlab was plucked from relative obscurity to design the house and studio of Hollywood megastar Brad Pitt. Since this success, the practice has grown to become one of the most successful of its generation in Germany.

intimidating environment of the dentist into a futuristic health club with undulating surfaces of lacquered drywall, along with sun terraces and lounges. The clinic is arranged around a dramatic diagonal axis that cuts through the floorplate, decorated in yellow, out of which are carved various treatment and consultation rooms. The architects liken the feeling to being among sand dunes on a beach. They write: 'This creates a space that provides a lush definition of introverted protection without distinct enclosure. "Hills" and "Valleys" are configured, in order to allow privacy and intimacy as well as openness and wide views.'

The lounge waiting area has received the most attention, with relaxing lounge chairs looking across a sun terrace at a view of the city. There is a bar and coffee shop, computer games for kids and wireless Internet access.

This distinctly unmedical atmosphere comes out of Graftlab's vigorous formal expressions, and a view of the world forged on the West Coast of America. This project, and Graftlab's work in general, is camp, glamorous and fun.

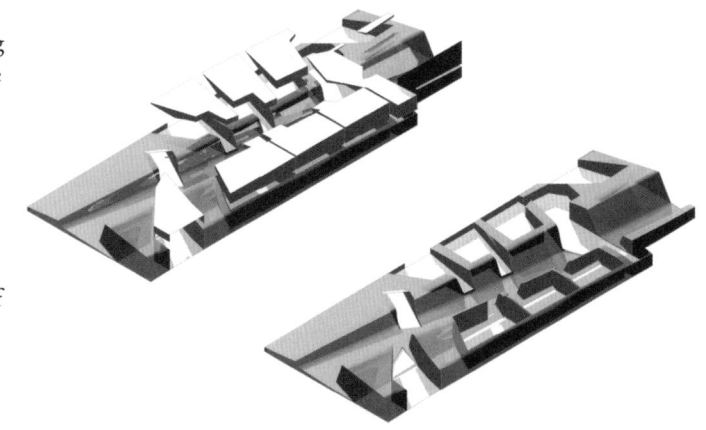

# Griffin Enright

Griffin Enright's work is pleasingly free from the influence of former employers, particularly Thom Mayne's Morphosis, for whom John Enright worked for 12 years. It is surprising that the stridency that characterizes Morphosis has matured with Griffin Enright into a subtle, distinctive and ecologically sound modernism. The practice has completed several private houses that take a somewhat rustic approach to the California landscape, using natural materials and emphasizing a connection with the landscape. Perhaps the most intriguing of these is the *June Lake House* in the alpine climate of the Sierra Mountains. This stocky house is a concrete box wrapped in a standing seam roof form that orientates itself towards the sun. Solar panels power a radiant heating system inside.

Griffin Enright's interest in ecological matters led to its most recent award-winning project, the *Keep Off the Grass* installation at the SCI-Arc Gallery at Southern California Institute. The project was intended to dramatize and critique the use of artificially maintained lawns in Los Angeles, an environment that the partners call 'a veritable desert'.

Both Margaret Griffin and Deborah Richmond of Touraine Richmond (pp. 322–323) appeared at the Femmes Fatales Pecha Kucha lecture night in March 2007 at the LA Forum for Architecture and Design.

They laid a 90sq m (1000sq ft) sod lawn on an undulating surface suspended from the ceiling on wires. A lighting rig suspended 1m (3½ft) above the floor symbolized the amount of water needed to maintain the lawn for a year. However, this lawn was left unwatered for the eight weeks of the exhibition, gradually drying and decomposing. Reflective pools on the floor allowed views of the underside of the dramatic structure. The partners write that, in the installation, 'the inherent dichotomy of the sod's organic and artificial nature is made poignantly clear.'

| Location | Los Angeles, USA |
| --- | --- |
| Nationality | American |

Griffin Enright was founded in Los Angeles in 2000 by Margaret Griffin and John Enright. Both partners studied at Syracuse University before separating for their postgraduate studies, Enright to Columbia and Griffin to Virginia. Enright was an associate at the Pritzker Prize-winning Morphosis for 12 years before starting Griffin Enright. The practice's work ranges from large-scale public buildings to gallery installations, and it was one of the latter (*Keep Off the Grass* at the SCI-Arc Gallery in 2004) that won them a 2006 American Architecture Award from the Chicago Athenaeum. Both partners have long teaching careers behind them, including stints at SCI-Arc, USC, UCLA, Syracuse University and the University of Houston.

This spread: *Keep Off the Grass* at the SCI-Arc Gallery in 2004. The installation gradually decayed to dramatize the ecologically unsound use of artificial irrigation for lawns in California.

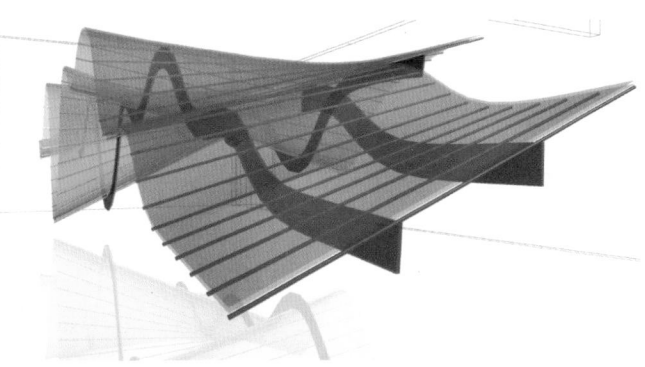

# Joseph Grima

Joseph Grima is the director of the Storefront Gallery in New York, which is shaped like a slice of pizza. Here, he describes how the mediation of the architectural experience through exhibition is a double-edged phenomenon. This piece is called *Notes on a Manifesto for Storefront*.

It's a paradox, but hardly a surprise: despite the absurdities implicit in the concept of exhibiting architecture, recent years have witnessed an almost unbelievable proliferation of architecture galleries. It appears that unlike art, architecture can be legitimately displayed and debated through pictorial placeholders.... Two-dimensional simulacra ...

In a sense there is something supremely liberating about this wilful disregard for authenticity. But there are also concerns. Primarily: in the era of the luxury condo and the boutique hotel, the ideological dimension of spatial planning seems to have gone missing, or at least to have become disconnected from everyday practice. How did we become so disillusioned with the possibilities latent in architecture that we renounced the idea that it could alter our lives for the better? The risk is that the architecture gallery might become the architect's wishful playground, a placebo against greater frustrations in a developer-driven market. The architecture gallery's true potential is as a laboratory for debate, experimentation and research: investigations and ideas for the real world. No event should be an end in itself.

A manifesto is a declaration of intentions, and declarations are inherently verbal. But let's imagine for a minute that a place might itself become a manifesto and venture into the high seas of ideological debate as an active agent.

(Or even as a double agent, an entity that owes allegiances both to the intellectual and professional community but panders to neither. A place where sudden shifts in direction startle the onlooker, then reward their patience

Location    New York, USA

Nationality    British, Italian

Joseph Grima is a
journalist, researcher and
curator based in New
York. Grima studied
architecture at the
Architectural Association
in London, before going
to work for *Domus*
magazine in Milan under
editor Stefano Boeri in
2003. Subsequently,
Grima was appointed
director of the Storefront
architecture gallery in
New York and holds that
post today. He is also a
PhD candidate at the
Centre for Research
Architecture at
Goldsmiths College in
London and contributes
regularly to a wide range
of publications
internationally.

with serendipitous convergences.)
Everything that occurs in this place
could be part of an accumulative script-
in-progress, an improvised but lucid
exploration of our surroundings.

As the disconnect between
architecture as a profession and as a
locus of ideological expression increases,
the gallery must transcend the passive
role of a container for exhibitions and
take on an active role in stimulating
debate. Over the years, the critical
discussion on architecture and the built
environment has fled from universities
into magazines, passing briefly through
the offices of practitioners and from
there into the conference hall … then
where? Maybe onto the web.... The
cultural forces shaping society today are
both more complex and more closely
interwoven than ever before: science,
art, technology, advertising, cinema,
music, literature, geopolitics,
telecommunications.... The gallery must
trawl the globe without preconceptions
in the search for ideas and positions to
examine, compare, bring into collision.
Like the Large Hydron Collider …
trawling universal matter for
microscopic fragments of meaning.... At
times it can be a violent process.

Now let's imagine Storefront as a
biological entity with a metabolism of
its own. It must be an omnivore,
feeding off every possible medium of
expression. Readings, lectures, dinners,
exhibitions, presentations, debates,
meetings, interviews, discussions,
screenings, parties, projections,
installations, reviews, sets, launches,
performances, talks and conflicts must
frictionlessly succeed one another in a
productive, schizophrenic stream of
consciousness, with ideas and ideals as
the only constants.... Equally, the gallery
must feed as diverse an audience as

possible and create opportunities for
convergence. The index of the diversity
of a gallery's program is the diversity of
the audience.

Against nostalgia. The tendency
to measure today's actions against the
past can be fatal, and there are times
when voluntary amnesia can be healthy.
It is acceptable to be faithful to one's
ideals, but not to one's own identity.
Fast Forward: the only limit to what is
possible today is what we can imagine
for tomorrow.

Networks vs. the hegemony of
institutional oligarchies. The peer-to-
peer network is one of the most
devastatingly efficient information
exchange tools ever devised. Why not
imagine a global peer-to-peer network
for physical objects, installations,
exhibition, events.... Or an accumulative
process of discussion and debate....
From passive receptacle to active agent
of change.

# Gross Max

The UK is a country not lacking in architectural talent, but its landscape resources are pretty thin. While there is a stronger agenda than ever towards regenerating public spaces, particularly in inner cities, there is a dearth of practices willing to take it on.

One of the leading lights, though, is Edinburgh-based Gross Max. The practice, despite being based in Scotland, has become prominent in the public spaces of London, most recently completing the park and public space around Norman Foster's *City Hall* near Tower Bridge on the south bank of the Thames. This is combined with an ongoing international focus.

Gross Max's first success in London was its victory in a high-profile Royal Institute of British Architects competition for Hackney Town Hall Square in northeast London. Later, projects like *St John's Square* in

This spread: Images of Gross Max's project for *Potters' Fields*, next to Norman Foster's *City Hall* building near Tower Bridge. One of the most prominent new public spaces in London, the project also connects Tooley Street to the river, with a gateway feeling to its southernmost extent.

Weavers Lane

Potters Fields

Tooley Street

Queen Elizal

Tool

| Location | Edinburgh, UK |
| --- | --- |
| Nationality | British |
| | Dutch |

Gross Max was founded in 1995 in Edinburgh, Scotland, by Eelco Hooftman and Bridget Baines. They were later joined by another partner, Nigel Sampey. The practice's first project was a prize-winning competition entry for the park near the Potsdamer Platz in Berlin. It soon followed this with a prize-winning masterplan for the Hanover Expo in 2000. Gross Max is now probably the UK's most important landscape design practice. It is particularly prominent in the regeneration of London's public spaces, winning several projects. Hooftman has a chair at the Edinburgh College of Art, and the partners have also taught at ETH Zurich, the Academy of Bouwkunst Amsterdam, Royal Academy Copenhagen, Ecole Paysage Versailles and the Architectural Association in London.

G

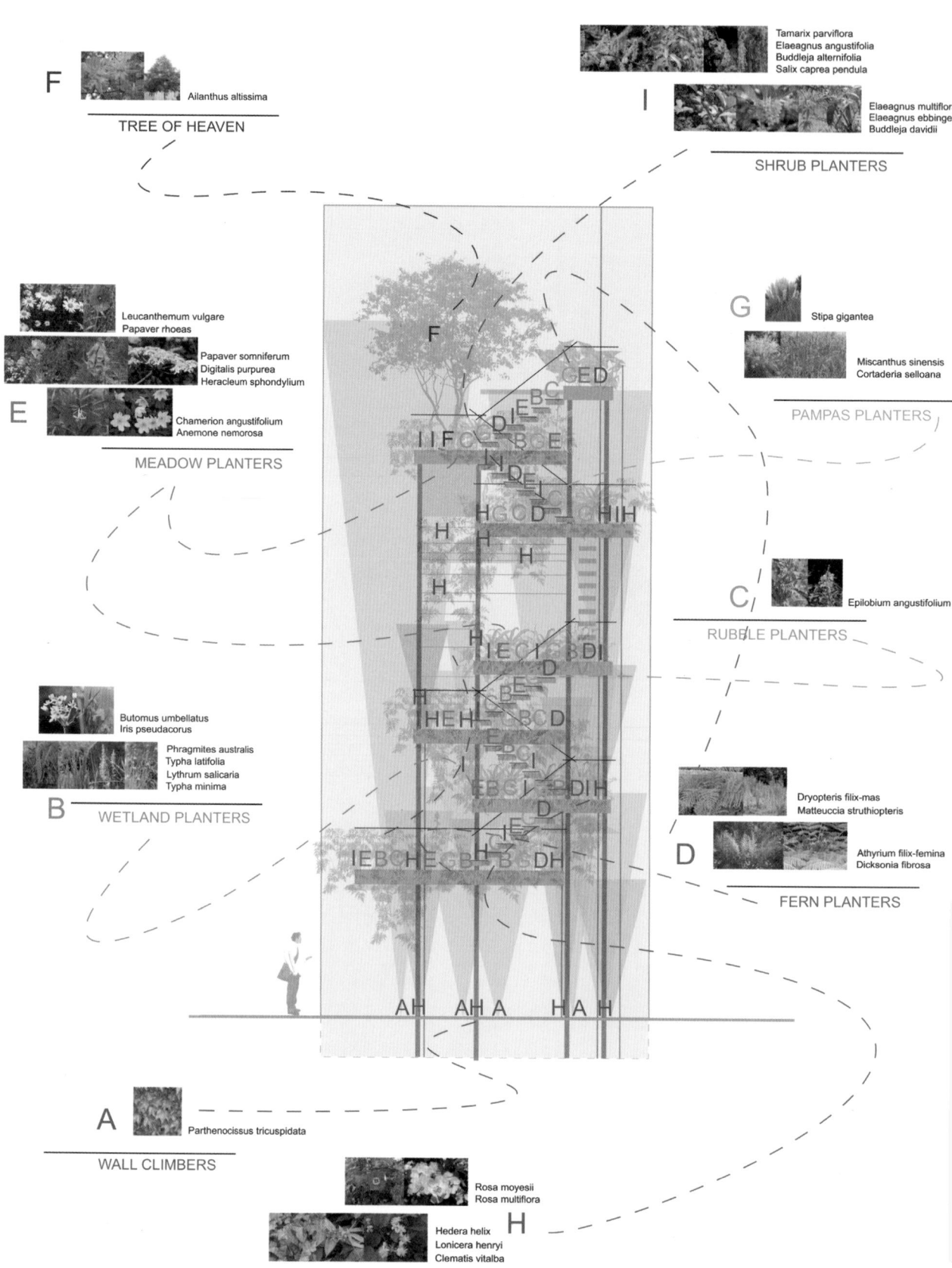

**F** Ailanthus altissima

TREE OF HEAVEN

Tamarix parviflora
Elaeagnus angustifolia
Buddleja alternifolia
Salix caprea pendula

**I** Elaeagnus multiflora
Elaeagnus ebbingei
Buddleja davidii

SHRUB PLANTERS

Leucanthemum vulgare
Papaver rhoeas

Papaver somniferum
Digitalis purpurea
Heracleum sphondylium

**E** Chamerion angustifolium
Anemone nemorosa

MEADOW PLANTERS

**G** Stipa gigantea

Miscanthus sinensis
Cortaderia selloana

PAMPAS PLANTERS

**C** Epilobium angustifolium

RUBBLE PLANTERS

Butomus umbellatus
Iris pseudacorus

Phragmites australis
Typha latifolia
Lythrum salicaria
Typha minima

**B** WETLAND PLANTERS

Dryopteris filix-mas
Matteuccia struthiopteris

Athyrium filix-femina
Dicksonia fibrosa

**D** FERN PLANTERS

**A** Parthenocissus tricuspidata

WALL CLIMBERS

Rosa moyesii
Rosa multiflora

Hedera helix
Lonicera henryi
Clematis vitalba

**H**

STRUCTURAL PLANTERS

Clerkenwell, a project for the public realm outside the Lyric Theatre in Hammersmith, and the hard landscaping on the South Bank outside the Royal Festival Hall proved that Gross Max is one of the major forces shaping London's public spaces. It also meant that the practice was ideally placed to be in the forefront of the London mayor's drive to improve public spaces in the capital.

Gross Max has so far won two projects in the mayor's *100 Public Spaces* scheme: *Potters' Fields*, next to City Hall, and *Brixton Central Square*, a controversial proposal to regenerate a public square in a socially and ethnically diverse area of south London. The design for *Potters' Fields* consists of an intimate neighbourhood park facing residential areas to the south, and a more open space towards the Thames with a series of stepped terraces. The park is planted with a variety of herbaceous plants and grasses designed by planting designer Piet Oudolf. The hard landscape elements include a 20m (65ft) Delftware bench, referring to the site's previous life as a location of potteries. Gross Max's plan also incorporates two pavilions, which were designed by London practice DSDHA.

This spread: Gross Max's theoretical project for a vertical garden.

G

# Tulay <u>Gunes</u>

The architectural consequences of the Israel–Palestine conflict have recently come into sharp focus through the writings of a new generation of academics and journalists. Tulay Gunes' photographic record of mobile architecture in illegal Israeli settlement outposts is attempting the same in the visual realm. While her work is politically charged, Gunes is also fascinated by the latent human drama of these locations. She writes: 'The prefabricated houses awake an impression of resistance, idealism and the hope of initiating a little community while withstanding hard and uncomfortable conditions.'

This spread: Images from Gunes' series on the mobile architecture of Israeli settlements in Palestine.

| Location | Frankfurt, Germany |
| --- | --- |
| Nationality | German |

Tulay Gunes is an architect and photographer from Germany who studied in Frankfurt and at Ball State University in the USA. Gunes has worked for a variety of architecture practices in Frankfurt, but her interest in photography led her to research the role of mobile architecture in Israel's settlements on the West Bank in Gaza. An extended series of these photographs was originally shown in the journal *Polar Inertia* (see pp. 250–251) in 2005.

G

This spread: More of Gunes' views of the mobile architecture of illegal Israeli settlements in Palestine.

Understandably given her interest in mobile architecture, Gunes quotes the work of Santiago Cirugeda (pp. 54–57), Lot-ek (pp. 176–177) and Jennifer Siegal (pp. 290–291) as influences. Her work is also related to Eyal Weizman's (pp. 336–337) writings about the architecture of the Israeli incursions into Palestine.

G

# Heide von Beckerath Alberts

This German practice has the rather odd distinction of having its office on the Kurfürstendamm, the famous shopping street of West Berlin. It is pleasingly quirky to be based there, when most practices prefer fashionably slumming it in the former east. Even more amazingly, Heide von Beckerath Alberts got to build a building on the street – a rare opportunity on the showpiece commercial street of the German capital.

The building is located at Lehniner Platz in Berlin

Charlottenburg, near Erich Mendelsohn's 1928 Lichtspieltheater Universum (now known as the Berlin Schaubühne). The surroundings comprise a mix of nineteenth-century bourgeois housing quarters and buildings from the 1950s and 1960s, a mix characteristic of the heterogeneous West Berlin city centre. The plot has been built upon to the maximum, defined by a free-standing firewall on one side and a massing that creates a tower at the corner. Although the building takes its place as the missing

This spread: The practice's most substantial built project is this apartment building just off the Kurfürstendamm in Berlin.

| Location | Berlin, Germany |
| --- | --- |
| Nationality | German |

Heide von Beckerath Alberts was founded in Berlin in 1996 by Tim Heide, Verena von Beckerath and Andrew Alberts. While Heide studied only architecture, von Beckerath first studied French language and culture at the Sorbonne in Paris, and Alberts biology and the history of art in Cologne. From these beginnings, all three partners ended up at the Technical University in Berlin studying architecture. The practice has completed a wide range of work. It won the Otto Wagner Urbanism Prize in 2001 for its *Wiener Standard* project, and a Baden-Wuerttemberg design prize in 2004. It participated in the German pavilion at the 2004 Venice Biennale.

**H**

part of the Lehniner Platz, it has very much its own character, in its materials (brick and glass), height and massing. There are 13 owner-occupied apartments, and a shop at ground level.

This project is a very elegant apartment building, aided by the cunning massing of the tower at the slimmest part of the site. With the Parisian sunshades like elaborate eyebrows that enliven the otherwise laconic material palette, it's a cut above its surroundings.

The other project shown here is the practice's proposal for a temporary entrance for the iconic KW Gallery in Mitte, Berlin. A steel substructure was proposed to support a passageway of intersecting glass tubes that are lit from within, to create a spectacular glowing threshold to the courtyard behind.

This spread: Heide von Beckerath Alberts collaborated with fellow Berlin practice Barkow Leibinger on this project for a new entrance to the KW Gallery in Berlin's Mitte.

One of Heide von Beckerath Alberts' best-known projects is its house in Wandlitz, which takes a very literal, house-like form in a new direction.

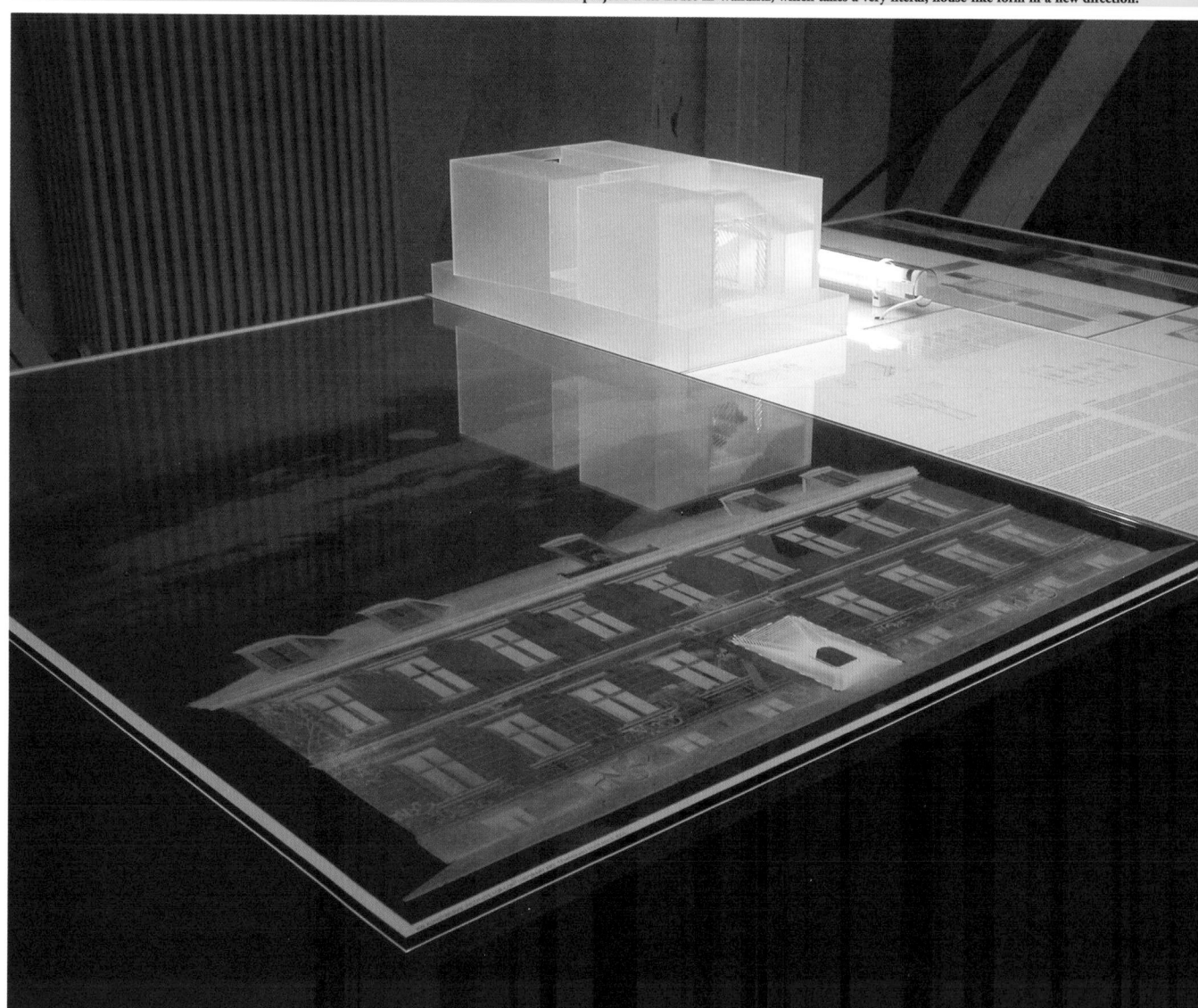

H

This is an abiding theme with many in this book, including Dow Jones (pp. 84–85), FNP Architekten (pp. 116–119) and Jomini Zimmermann (pp. 160–161).

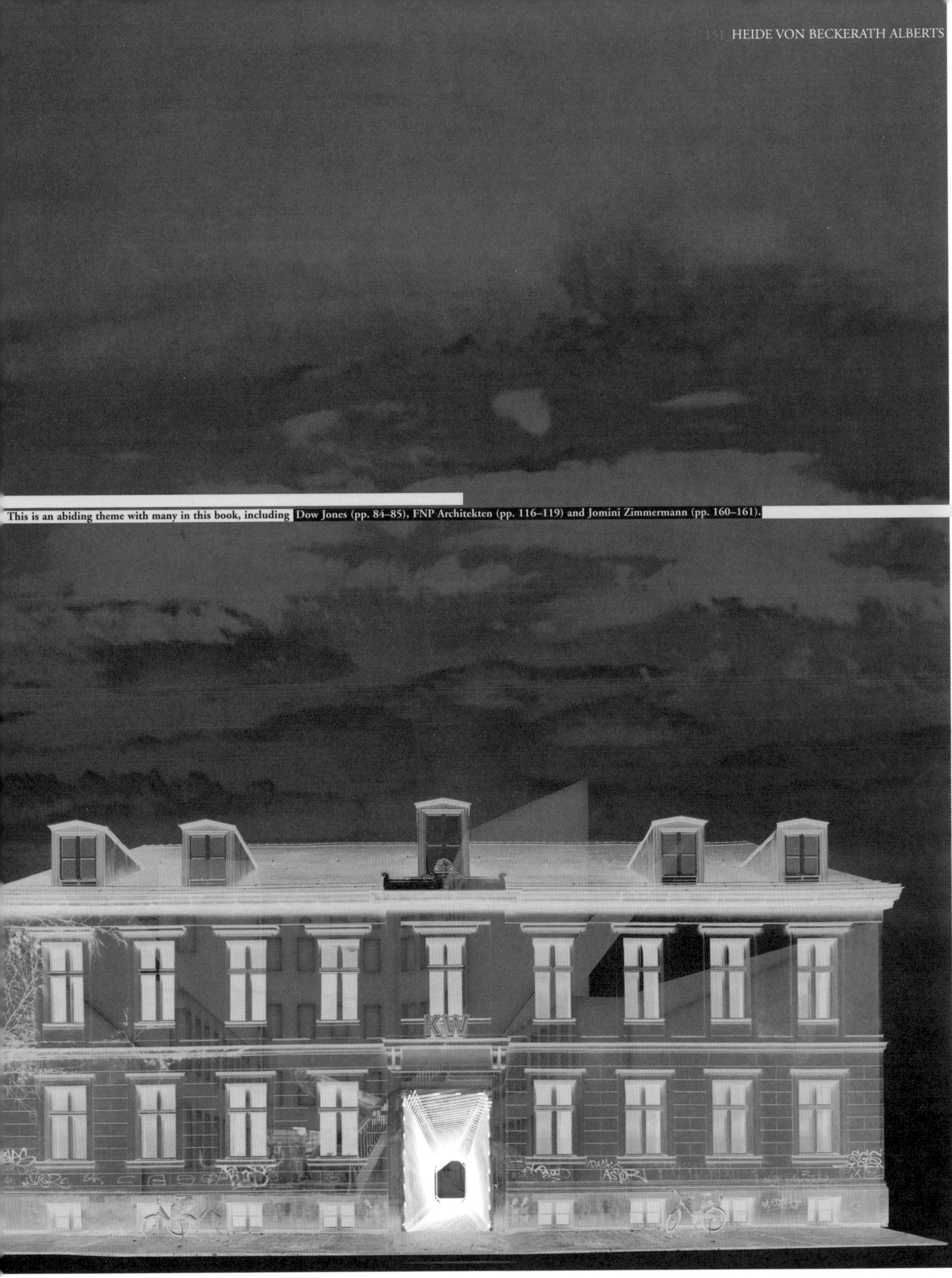

# Instant Architecture

Instant Architecture's work is about the human body, and uses biological processes to generate spatial strategies. These processes are not always unambiguously positive. Their projects have, for example, used diseases to generate architecture (*Sick Space*, a workshop in Zurich in 2004), and have investigated the relationship of hygiene and pollution to the city. Their work takes as one of its starting points the work of the philosopher of science Georges Canguilhem, to 'accept sickness as an integral part of a strong, healthy body'.

The practice's most important built work so far is *Haus Blick* (which Instant translates as 'House Gaze') in 2006. The project was to extend a rather conventional, pitched-roof house from the 1930s in Dusseldorf, Germany. However, the inhabitants had an ambivalent relationship with their new home. Instant partners Hebel and Stollman write: 'While he was looking forward to living in a traditional pitched-roof house, she was terrified of the darkness and narrowness of the house's interiors and was missing a view on the adjacent river Rhine. She had dreamt of a generously glazed modern pavilion.'

Rather than attempting to reconcile this paradox, Instant decided to make it a generating feature of the scheme. The house is conceptualized as a modern pavilion within the pitched-roof house, reconfiguring the

This spread: *Haus Blick*, a house in Dusseldorf, Germany, completed by Instant Architecture in 2006.

ground-floor interior into four principal spaces, connected in an open-plan arrangement. The main external adjustment is an oversized dormer window, behind which sits the so-called 'Rhine Room'. A strange piece of guttering continues the eave line (a planning requirement). Inside, the pattern of a wallpaper from the 1930s is painted on the walls as decoration, in a paint that changes according to the natural light conditions outside.

The bathroom is shared between the children and parents of the family. The two areas are separated only by a curtain and all the elements of the two sides are set out in a mirrored arrangement – what the architects call a 'schizophrenic mirroring'.

| Location | Berlin, Germany |
| | Zurich, Switzerland |
| Nationality | Swiss |

Instant Architecture was founded in 2002 by Dirk Hebel and Jörg Stollman as a laboratory working at 'the intersection of architecture, nature, technology and communication'. Hebel began his studies at the ETH Zurich and Stollman in Berlin, but the two met while studying at Princeton in the USA, where they later went on to teach. They currently hold a teaching position at the ETH, and have offices in Berlin and Zurich. The practice was part of the *Inventioneering Architecture* exhibition of Swiss architecture that toured the US in 2006.

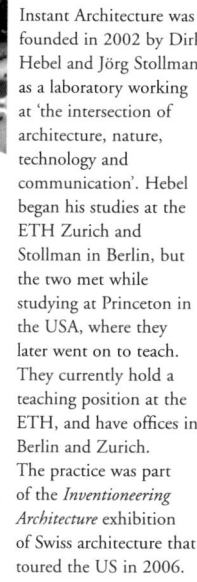

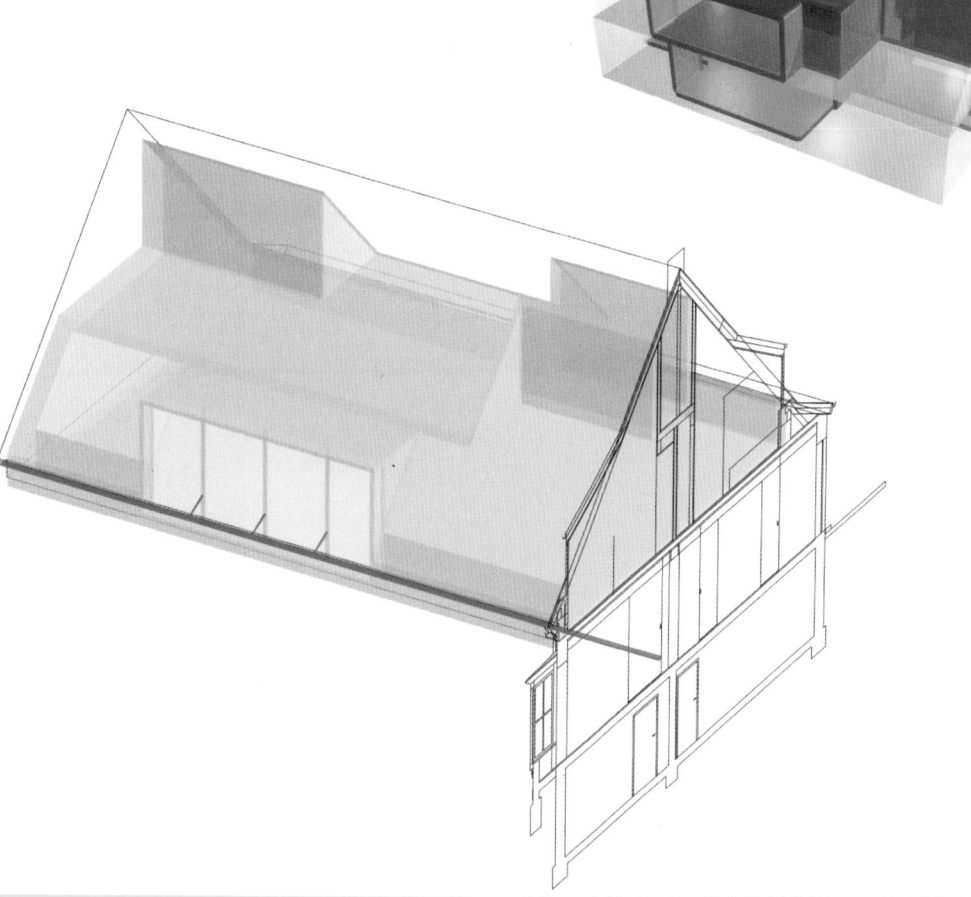

Instant Architecture collaborated with the critics Andreas and Ilka Ruby of Textbild (pp. 312–313) on the *Swiss Bottle* project.

# Andrés Jaque

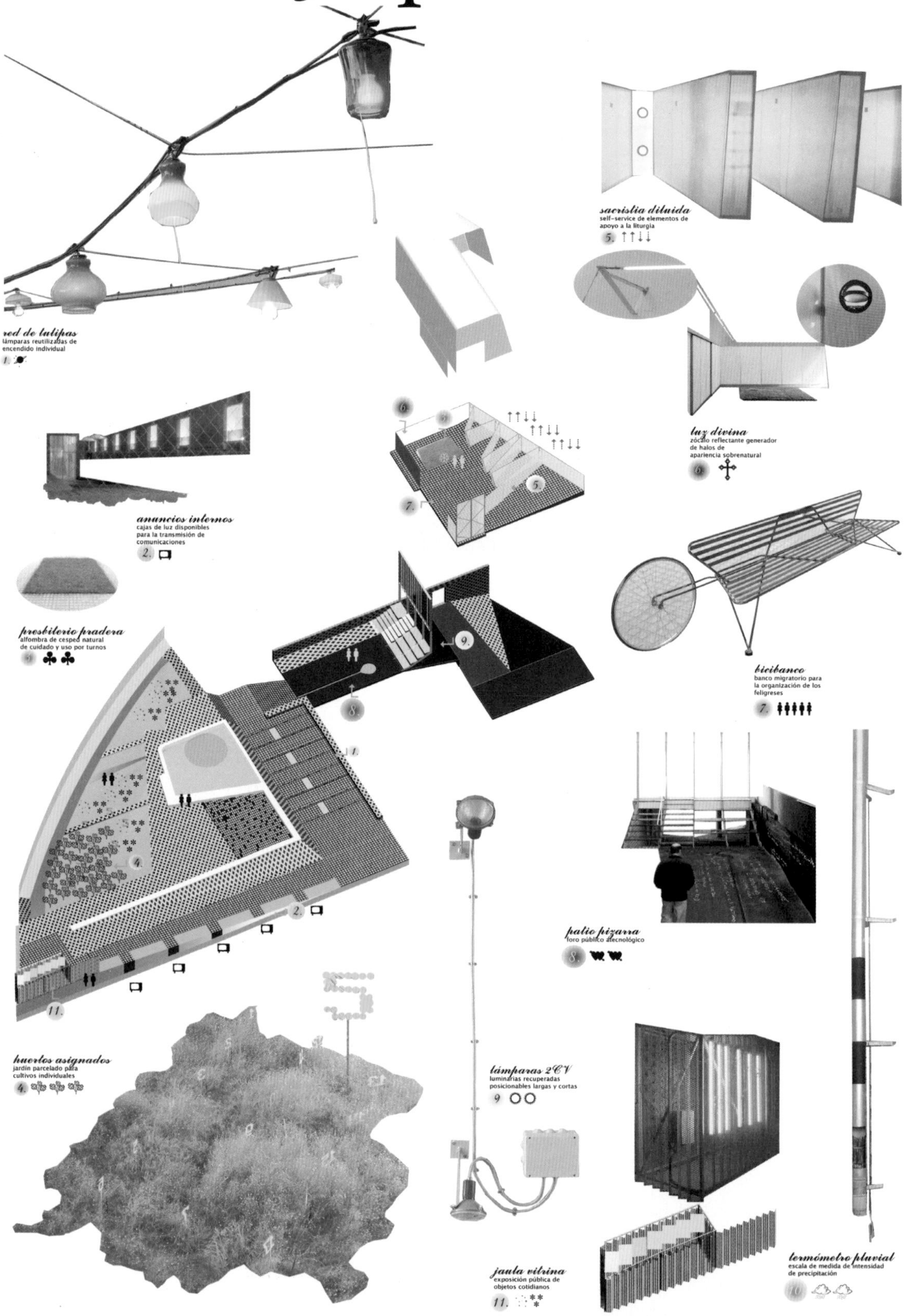

**red de tulipas**
lámparas reutilizadas de
encendido individual
1.

**sacristia diluida**
self-service de elementos de
apoyo a la liturgia
5. ↑↑↓↓

**luz divina**
zócalo reflectante generador
de halos de
apariencia sobrenatural
0.

**anuncios internos**
cajas de luz disponibles
para la transmisión de
comunicaciones
2.

**presbiterio pradera**
alfombra de cesped natural
de cuidado y uso por turnos

**bicibanco**
banco migratorio para
la organización de los
feligreses
7.

**patio pizarra**
foro público atecnológico

**huertos asignados**
jardin parcelado para
cultivos individuales
4.

**lámparas 2CV**
luminarias recuperadas
posicionables largas y cortas
9. ○○

**termómetro pluvial**
escala de medida de intensidad
de precipitación

**jaula vitrina**
exposición pública de
objetos cotidianos
11.

Andrés Jaque was part of the Young European Architects seminar at the NAI in Rotterdam in 2004, along with 6A (pp. 14–15), Santiago Cirugeda (pp. 54–57), Elastik (pp. 92–93) and many others.

Spanish architect Andrés Jaque's project for the conversion of a Catholic seminary in Plasencia, Spain, deals not only with a pressing issue for the Catholic church (the aging clerical population), but also attempts to mediate and understand a new relationship between the church, its ministers and the community of Plasencia.

The project for the *Casa Sacerdotal Diocesana* redevelops a seminary that was originally built in the fifteenth century and was extended in the nineteenth. It occupies a whole city block of the town, and Jaque's brief was to turn the building into a place of care for elderly priests, and provide new public uses such as a convention centre.

The project also attempts to articulate two aspects of the change in priestly life – from the rural and expansive geographical settings of their previous ministries to an urban and concentrated one, and the occupants' passage from individual spiritual leaders of their communities to participants in a smaller, less hierarchized one.

Two strategies were employed. The first creates what Jaque calls 'displacements', concentrating and creating elements that bind the users to the natural world that they were familiar with in their rural parishes. He writes: 'The priestly house contains and intensifies the sensory keys of an extensive territory.' These keys include fragments of pasture, lemon- and cherry-tree groves in the grounds of the seminary, and other specific references to 'banks, books, tents, clouds, lamps, chimneys' and architectural elements and materials such as lime render, paving and shade.

The second strategy was to make the redeveloped seminary full of opportunities for association with the wider community. The chapel, for

| Location | Madrid, Spain |
| --- | --- |
| Nationality | Spanish |

Andrés Jaque founded his office in Madrid in 2000. He is now a prominent architect and commentator on Spanish architecture. His office also goes by the pseudonym Office for Political Enhancement, indicating a politically committed practice. Jaque is a professor at the Escuela Técnica Superior de Arquitectura in Madrid, and his project for the *Casa Sacerdotal Diocesana* in Plasencia was selected as part of the 8th Spanish Architecture Biennale. He has won many awards, including the Grande Area College of Architects Award in 2005 for his *Teddy House* project, and second prize in Europan 7 in Stavanger, Norway.

Opposite: A collection of '*actividades*' – pieces of the interventions in the seminary that are active and changeable.
Below: Plan showing the new garden and other public areas of the redesign.

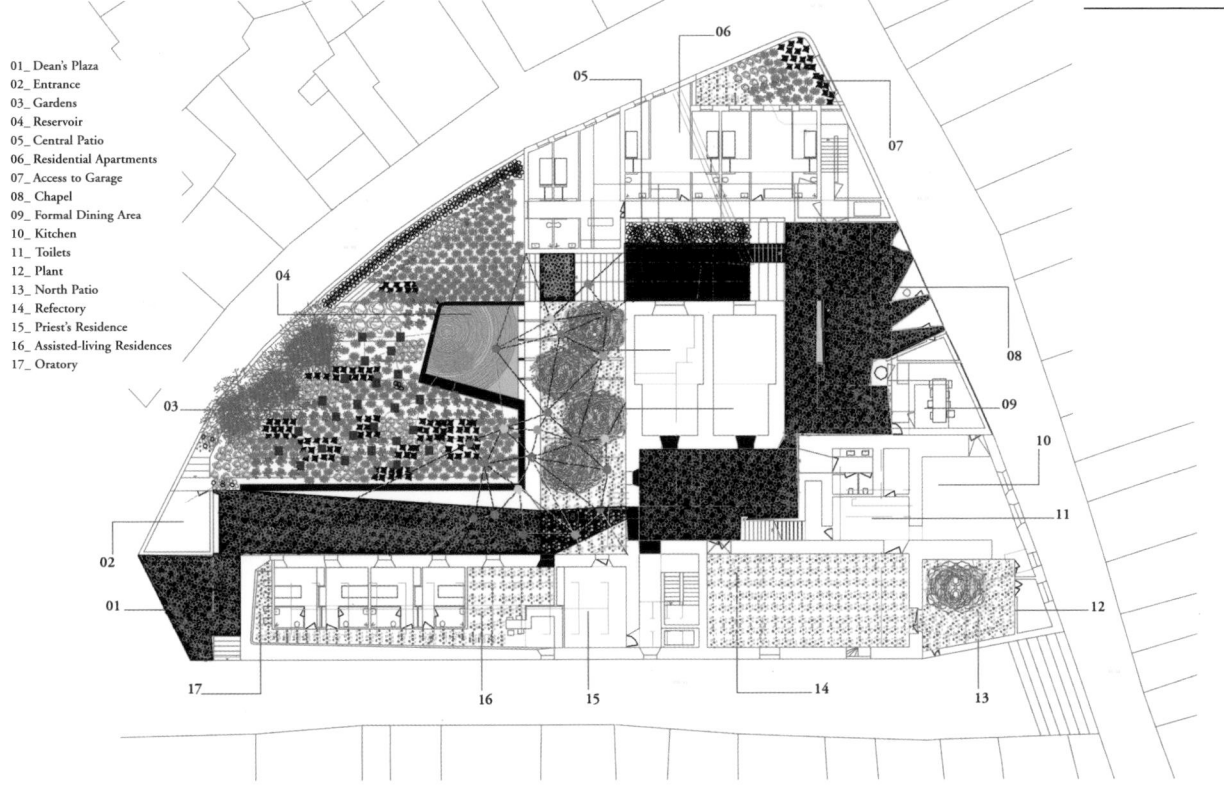

01_ Dean's Plaza
02_ Entrance
03_ Gardens
04_ Reservoir
05_ Central Patio
06_ Residential Apartments
07_ Access to Garage
08_ Chapel
09_ Formal Dining Area
10_ Kitchen
11_ Toilets
12_ Plant
13_ North Patio
14_ Refectory
15_ Priest's Residence
16_ Assisted-living Residences
17_ Oratory

Clockwise from below: Two priests walk through the multi-purpose chapel/community space; The entrance, with a transparent section that gives views from the street into the cloister garden; The view from the street, with the former seminary's new colourful livery on display; The wild garden is intended to be a reminder of the countryside.

Andrés Jaque has lectured at the Institut d'Arquitectura Avançada de Catalunya, as has Enric Ruiz-Geli of Cloud 9 (pp. 62–65

dia Pasquero of ecoLogic Studio (pp. 90–91) and Ilka and Andreas Ruby of Textbild (pp. 312–313), among others.

example, can be transformed for other uses (with the aid of custom-designed, movable pieces of furniture) and the sacristy, normally a closed space, is made light and transparent. The garden is full of things that allow personal engagement on the part of the priests: lights with individual switches, aviaries and movable torches.

The project creates a fantastic world of light and vegetation within the grey walls of the old seminary.

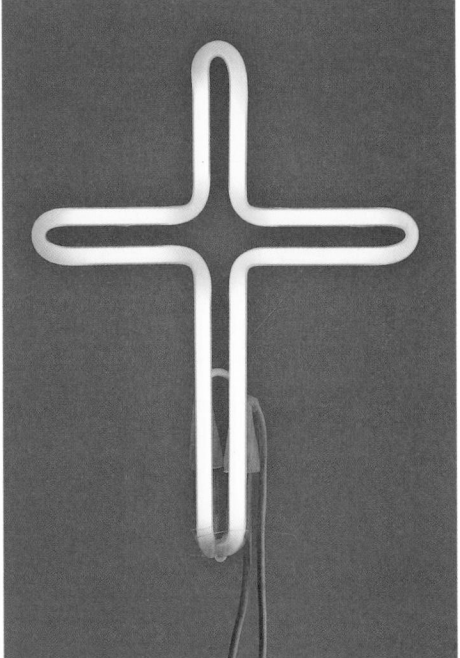

# Johnston Marklee

Johnston Marklee has completed some lyrical and formally distinctive houses, and the *Hill House* is perhaps the best of them. This house, the architects say, is unashamedly in the *California Case Study Houses* tradition, particularly provocative given its close proximity to the canonical *Eames House* in Pacific Palisades, California.

The project is an essay in the historical tradition of modernism on hillsides in California, but also in the much more stringent zoning legislation that now exists to protect the profile of the hillsides. The house was generated by two desires: to provide the maximum possible envelope within the zoning guidelines, and to touch the ground as little as possible. This parlour game has resulted in a strange irregular prism with punched windows deep in the rendered surface of the building.

The structure of the building is a deep concrete foundation with a steel frame above it. The cementitious elastomer outer skin was chosen as it requires no joints, making the monolithic qualities of the building prominent. Although the house can often look white in pictures, it is in fact blue, with a pigment derived from eucalyptus bark giving it an iridescent lavender sheen.

Inside, the only walls and partitions are structural, making for a very open, three-level arrangement, with a sculptural steel and glass stair at its heart. Openings and windows have deep reveals and thresholds, maintaining privacy but maximizing the rooms' openness to views of the Rustic and Sullivan Canyons.

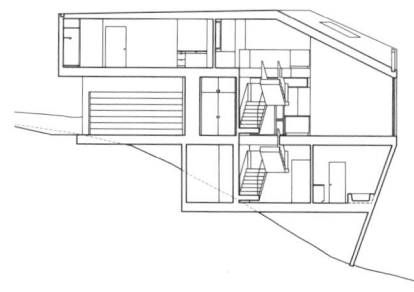

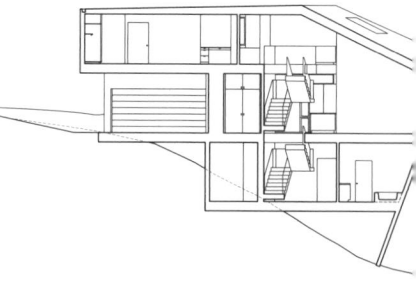

This spread: The *Hill House* in Pacific Palisades, California. The geometry of the house is defined by regulations on the size of the building and maximizing views.

mpetition can be seen on pages 322–323.



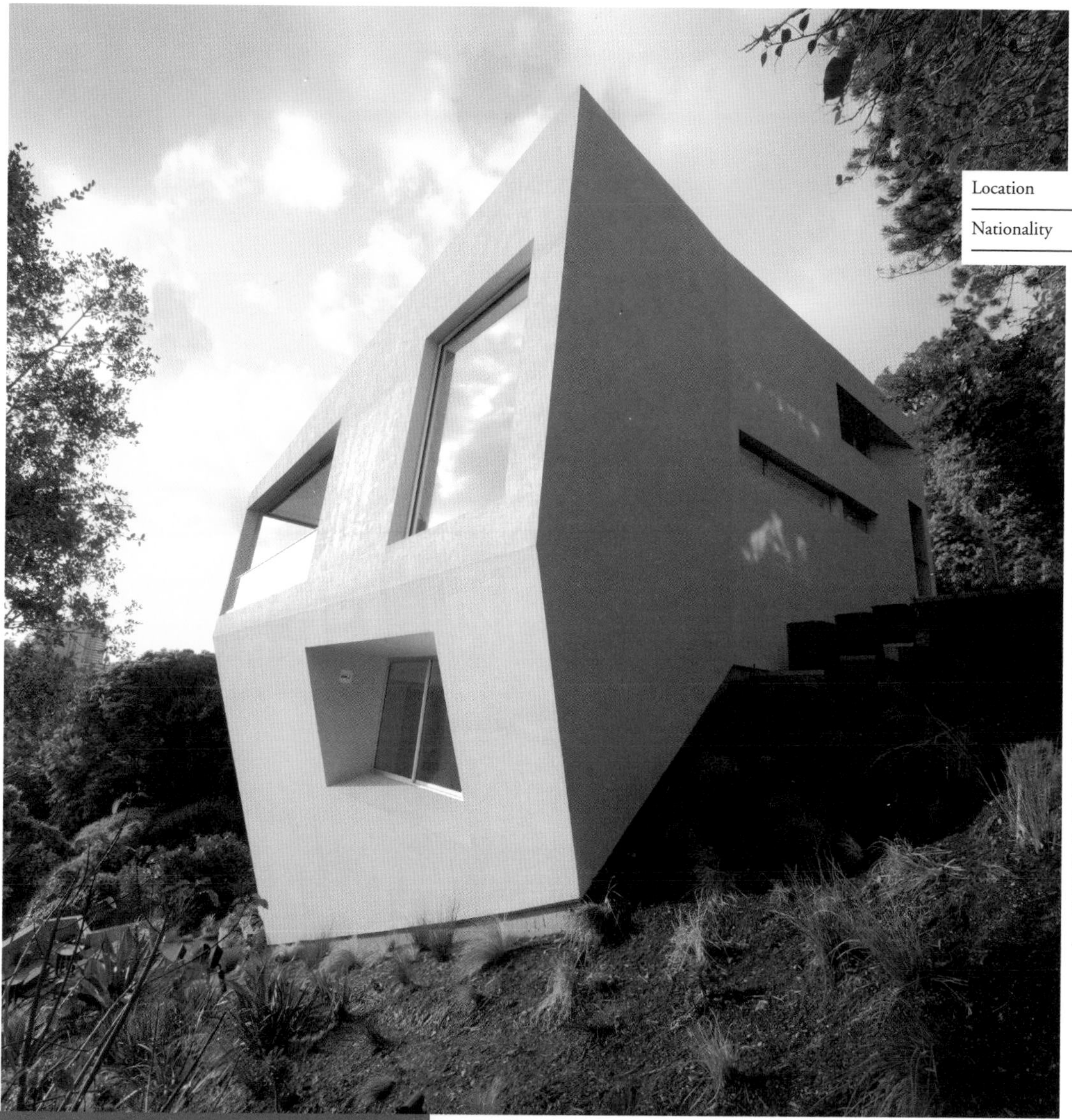

| Location | Los Angeles, USA |
|---|---|
| Nationality | American |

Johnston Marklee was founded in 1998 by Sharon Johnston and Mark Lee. The practice is based in Los Angeles. Lee was educated at the University of Southern California and Johnston at Stanford before they met at the Graduate School of Design at Harvard in 1995. Lee is now vice chair and assistant professor at UCLA, where Johnston is also a lecturer. The practice has completed more projects than many in this book, including a clutch of iconic houses. The *Hill House* in Pacific Palisades in 2004 won an American Institute of Architects award, while the *View House* was honoured with a Next LA Citation award.

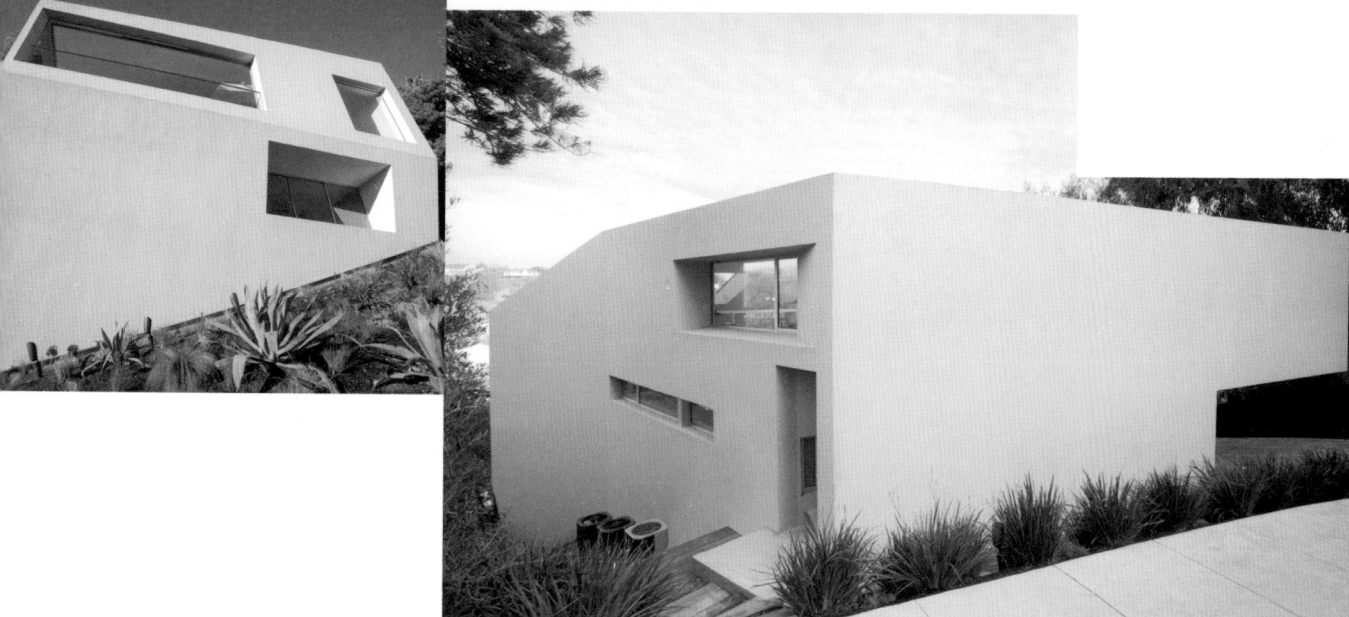

# Jomini Zimmermann

The two partners of Jomini Zimmermann make a point of entering on their CVs the names of their tutors at the ETH in Zurich. You can see why: Valérie Jomini was taught by important British architect Tony Fretton and one of the greatest living historians of architecture, Kenneth Frampton; Stanislas Zimmermann by the Ticinese post-rationalist Luigi Snozzi. It is a fascinating game to try to detect signs of these superstars in their work.

Perhaps the *Haus Faraday* project is the one that unites these sensibilities with an understanding of a Swiss vernacular and a new material sensibility. The project is in Bern, on the Jurastrasse on the banks of the Aare River to the north of the city centre. This edge-of-city site is half rural, with a sheep pasture and wooded slope to one side, and the river and city also in view. The house is for two families to live in, partly communal and partly giving both sets of inhabitants privacy. The house is expressed both as a small tower, and a typical suburban Swiss house with its large pitched roof. It is entirely covered in corrugated copper sheets, which have aged in the years since its completion (2004) to a darker brown colour. Inside, the two dwellings have two floors each. The lower one benefits from the garden and has its entrance directly from the street. The upper dwelling is reached from an external flight of stairs, and has the most impressive space in the house – the attic living space with its 6m (20ft) ceilings, dramatic dormer window facing east and generous south-facing terrace.

The house is a real one-off – absolutely typological, but not as literal as Snozzi, and more charming than the somewhat stark postmodernism of Fretton.

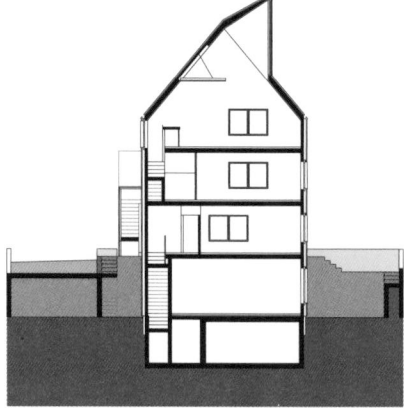

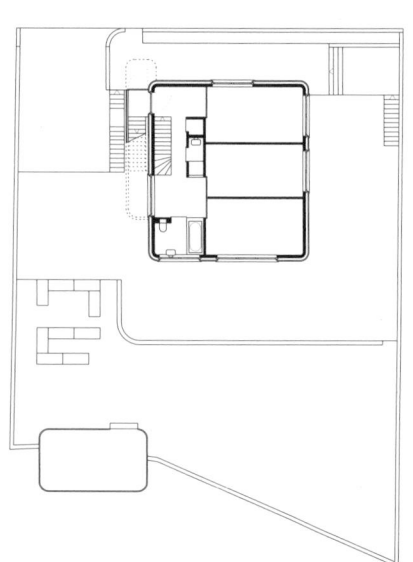

Many of the people in this book have appeared at a Pecha Kucha, the 'architectural karaoke' concept lecture night. Jomini Zimmermann did at Superdeluxe in Tokyo, as did Enric Ruiz-Geli of Cloud 9 (pp. 62–65), Gwenael Nicolas of Curiosity (pp. 72–75), Yusuke Seki (then of FAT, pp. 110–113) and the author.

| Location | Burgdorf, Switzerland |
|---|---|
| Nationality | Swiss |

Valérie Jomini and Stanislas Zimmermann began working together as Jomini Zimmermann in 1997. Both partners studied at the ETH in Zurich until 1996 and started their practice a year later. They also run a furniture label called It Design, designing and manufacturing pieces from their base in Burgdorf, Switzerland. Their work has been published and exhibited widely, including a monographic exhibition at the Youkobo Art Space in Tokyo in 2006.

**This spread:** *Haus Faraday* in Bern contains two homes within its copper envelope.

Haus Faraday bears some resemblance in its two-houses-in-one brief to the *Zweiwohnhaus FHS* by FNP Architekten (pp. 116–119).

# Khosla Associates

Sandeep Khosla worked for the most important Indian modernist architect, Charles Correa, at the beginning of his career, and retains a sensibility in his work that is identifiable from that master's ouevre. Although the scope of Khosla's work reflects the booming Indian economy (large private houses figure prominently), the mix of modernist forms added to a consciousness of climate creates an authentic regionalist architecture.

One of Khosla's finest projects is the *Fernandes Residence* in the centre of Bangalore in the southwest of India. The client wanted a six-bedroom house with underground parking, a swimming pool and a garden. The brief also included the need for adequate air movement through the house and a need for natural light.

The most distinctive features are the sloping tile roofs with large overhangs that deal with the heavy rains of the monsoon season, and the large verandahs and generous entrance court that help to disperse the muggy tropical air. The plan of the house is in an L-shape facing a large garden to the south and west. The entrance court has a shallow reflecting pool clad in turquoise handmade tiles that orientates the visitor towards the main door. The canopy is supported at a single point by a stone pier. The entrance steps to the court are thick pieces of stone stacked one over the other like shifting planes.

On the ground floor are the public and semi-public spaces such as the living room, dining room, kitchen, utility room, study and two guest rooms. A teak staircase rises to the bedrooms and family area on the upper level. The house intentionally looks towards the southwest due to overlooking issues to the north and east. All the bedrooms on the lower and upper level step out into a verandah and overlook the main green space and swimming pool.

The rich use of materials with a modernist sensibility makes the *Fernandes Residence* an exemplar of contemporary Indian luxury.

**Ground Floor Plan**

01_ Driveway
02_ Entrance
03_ Security Cabin
04_ Entrance Courtyard
05_ Entrance Foyer
06_ Living Room
07_ Office/Study
08_ Powder Room
09_ Courtyard
10_ Dining Room
11_ Kitchen
12_ Utility
13_ Store
14_ Bedroom
15_ Toilet
16_ Verandah
17_ Outdoor Dining
18_ Sundeck
19_ Swimming Pool
20_ Landscaped Area
21_ Reflecting Pool
22_ Ramp to Basement
23_ Entrance Courtyard
24_ Master Bedroom
25_ Puja Room
26_ Walk-in Closet
27_ Master Toilet
28_ Family Den
29_ Servants Rooms

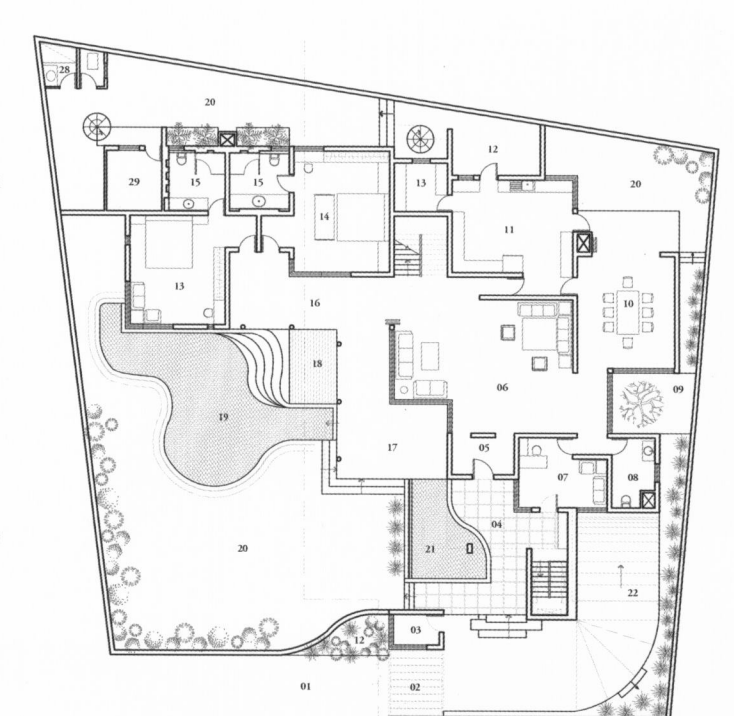

| Location | Bangalore, India |
| --- | --- |
| Nationality | Indian |

Sandeep Khosla set up Khosla Associates in Bangalore in 1995, after studying at the Pratt Institute in New York and working for legendary Indian modernist Charles Correa. The practice has carried out a very broad array of work, including marketing concepts for the likes of Kentucky Fried Chicken and Hard Rock Café, education buildings and some lyrical houses. The practice has won many awards, including the Rajiv Gandhi Shiromani Award in 2006. Khosla was named by *India Today* magazine as one of the 50 men and women under the age of 35 who are poised to be leaders of tomorrow.

K

This spread: Images of the *Fernandes Residence* in Bangalore, India, a project representative of Khosla's climatically adjusted modernism.

# Knesl + Kyncl

Knesl + Kyncl's work, the partners say, is situated 'between the city and the house', at the scale of the public building. It also seems situated between the scales of development that are happening in the Czech Republic: the large-scale and generically western, and the quieter, more distinctive, voice of a nation with a rich modern heritage in architecture.

To look at the practice's rather worryingly strident glass and steel proposal for a university campus at Pardubice, or the early UN Studio posturing of *The Wing* restaurant, one might dismiss them. But there is something extraordinary about the scale of their gestures, such as the stacked volumes of the super-scale proposal for the competition entry for the National Library of the Czech Republic. Of particular interest is the project for a

regional library in Vysocina. This latter project is described by the architects as a 'modest civic monumental form', but looks much more brooding than that. It is symmetrical in two axes and with a scaleless geometric box with one huge, expressionless window looking south. This is mediated by a humane edge to the building, with a ribbon window at ground level and a covered area facing a new public square.

A geometry of squares defines the urban strategy (three squares in plan of 36 x 36m/118 x 118ft) as well as the interior of the library itself (divided in plan into nine squares of 12 x 12m/39 x 39ft). Unfortunately, the project only won third prize in the competition, but it would have been something to see it built – like Morger & Degelo's *Kunstmuseum Liechtenstein*, but with more character.

This spread: Project for a regional library in Vysocina in the Czech Republic.

KRAJSKA KNIHOVNA VYSOČINY

CAFE

Knesl & Kyncl is one of a rising generation from eastern European countries.
See Ofis Arhitekti (pp. 234–235) from Slovenia.

Other entrants in the competition for the National Library in Prague included Emergent (pp. 94–9

| Location | Brno, Czech Republic |
|---|---|
| Nationality | Czech |

Knesl + Kyncl was formed in 2001 by Jiri Knesl and Jakub Kyncl in Brno, Czech Republic. The practice deals with architecture at all scales, from urban planning to interiors. Both partners now teach at the architecture faculty of the VUT Brno, with Kyncl holding the post of vice dean between 1997 and 2000. Kyncl is also the secretary of the Czech branch of Docomomo. The practice was nominated for the Mies van der Rohe Prize in 2007 for its small football ground in Krizanovice.

K

# Krets

Krets is a network of like-minded practitioners pursuing a research method that is gaining in currency in many architecture schools around the world. Working in highly complex models at 1:1 scale, Krets hopes to make installations and components that demonstrate the potential of new technology to make new environments that adjust mechanically to our needs, or adjust themselves according to algorithmic processes.

The *SplineGraft* project, developed by Krets members Pablo Miranda and Jonas Runberger, is one of the group's most advanced realized projects. It is conceived as a moving acoustic panel that can intelligently adjust itself according to the movement of people in the room. The structure of the panel is a dense series of CNC-milled acrylic levers, with integrated actuators, that manipulate a pleated, grey polyurethane curtain. The integrated control system creates the forms in real time, in what the architects describe as 'a continuous form-finding process with emergent patterning effects'.

They continue: 'The behaviour of the *SplineGraft* is controlled by a

This spread: The *SplineGraft* moving acoustic wall by Krets. The polyurethane surface is manipulated by a complicated Perspex armature.

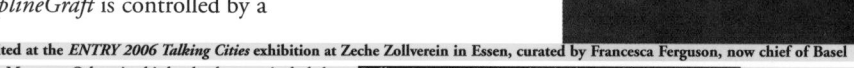

Krets exhibited at the *ENTRY 2006 Talking Cities* exhibition at Zeche Zollverein in Essen, curated by Francesca Ferguson, now chief of Basel Architecture Museum. Others in this book who were included are Stalker (pp. 292–295) and Toh Shimazaki (pp. 318–321).

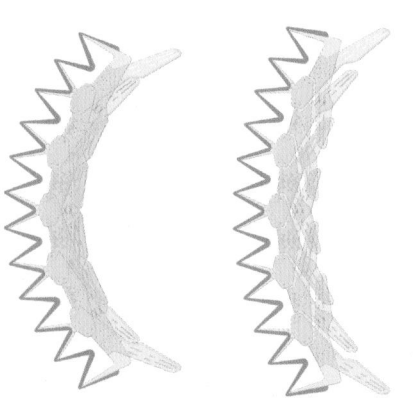
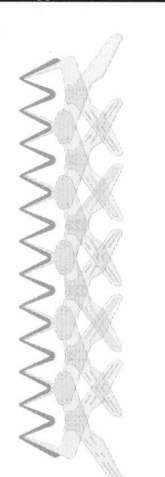

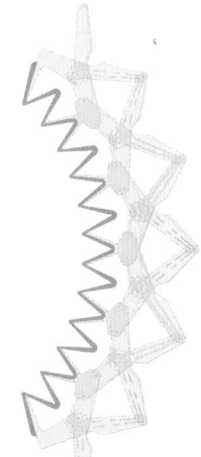

Two members of Krets (Marcelyn Gow and Ulrika Karlsson) are also in Servo (pp. 282–285)

| Location | Stockholm, Sweden |
| | International |
| Nationality | American |
| | Swedish |

Krets (Swedish for 'circle') is a research group founded in 2003 and affiliated with AKAD, the academy for practice-based research in architecture and design, Sweden. The five partners are Marcelyn Gow, Ulrika Karlsson, Pablo Miranda, Daniel Norell and Jonas Runberger. They are variously affiliated with KTH Stockholm, UCLA and the Swiss Federal Institute of Technology in Zurich. The group uses design projects to research the impact of new digital technologies on the built environment. The work of the partners has been widely published and exhibited, including at *Open House: Intelligent Living by Design* at ArtCenter Pasadena and Entry 2006 in Essen.

K

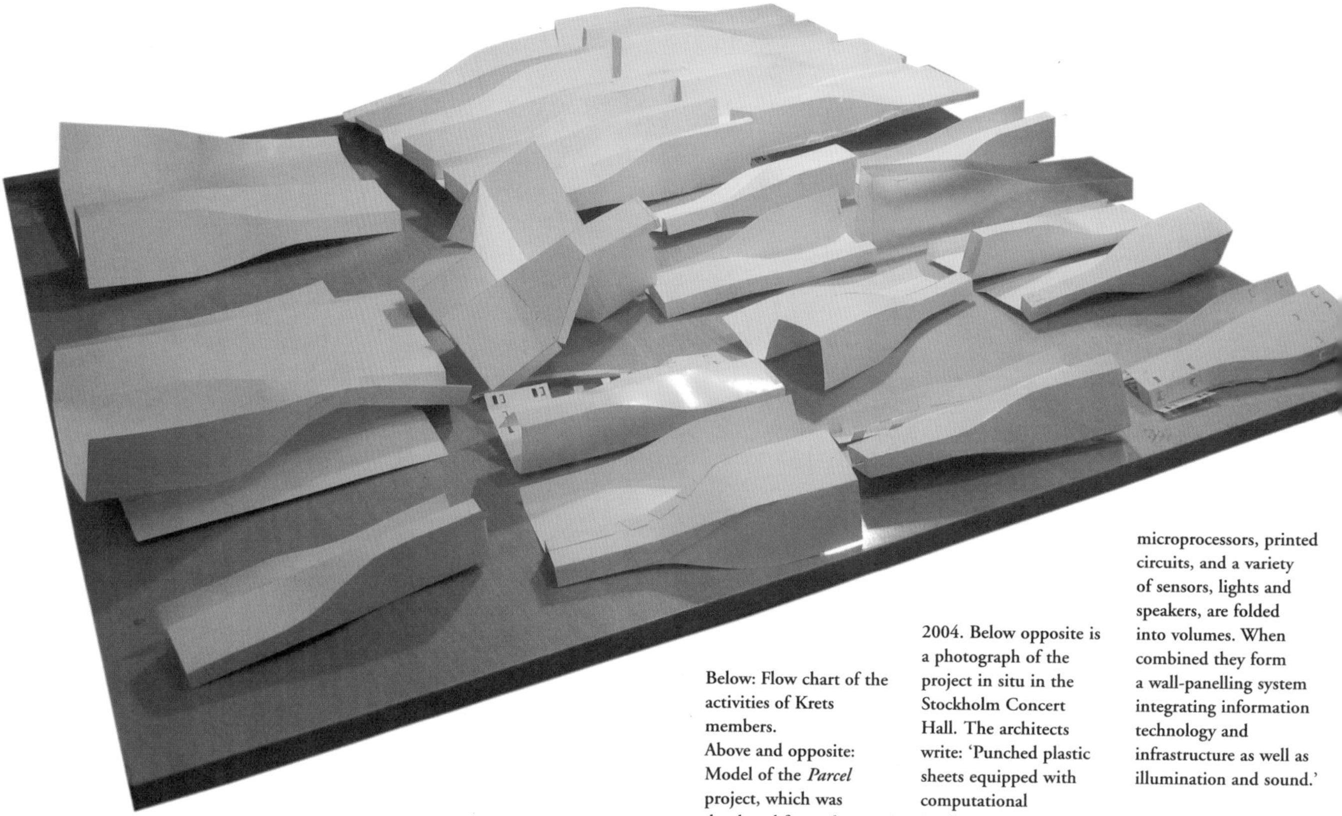

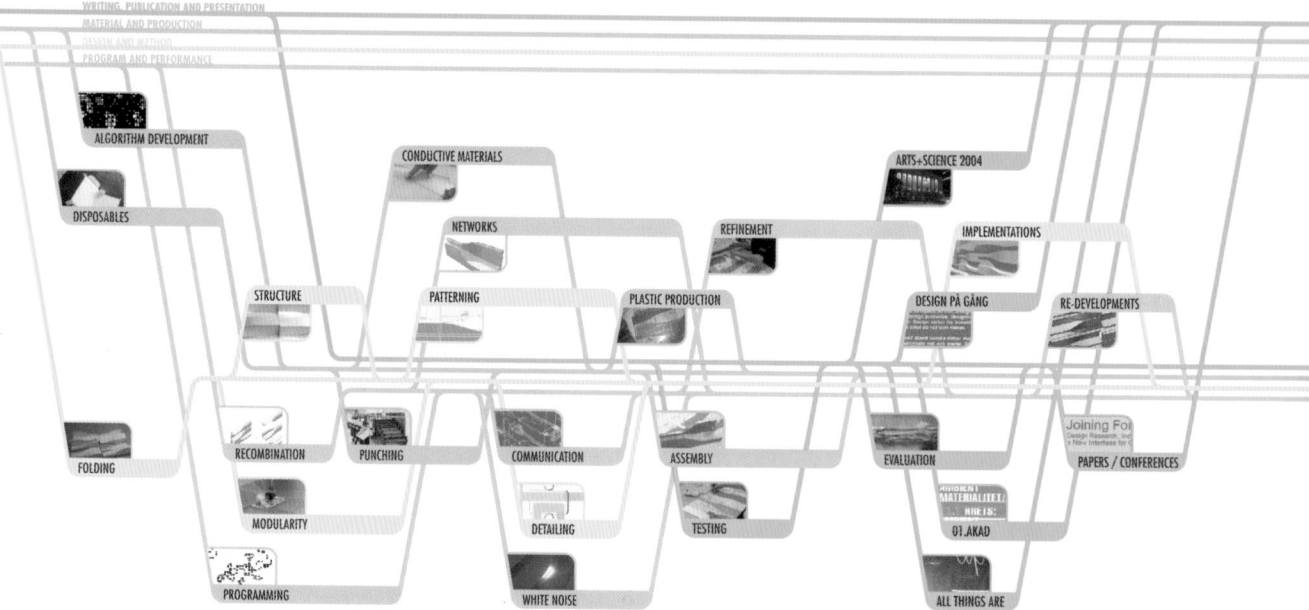

Below: Flow chart of the activities of Krets members.
Above and opposite: Model of the *Parcel* project, which was developed for and shown at Stockholm Arts and Sciences in 2004. Below opposite is a photograph of the project in situ in the Stockholm Concert Hall. The architects write: 'Punched plastic sheets equipped with computational intelligence through microprocessors, printed circuits, and a variety of sensors, lights and speakers, are folded into volumes. When combined they form a wall-panelling system integrating information technology and infrastructure as well as illumination and sound.'

**PARCEL** DEVELOPMENT FLOWCHART

WRITING, PUBLICATION AND PRESENTATION
MATERIAL AND PRODUCTION
DESIGN AND METHOD
PROGRAM AND PERFORMANCE

ALGORITHM DEVELOPMENT

CONDUCTIVE MATERIALS

ARTS+SCIENCE 2004

DISPOSABLES

NETWORKS

REFINEMENT

IMPLEMENTATIONS

STRUCTURE

PATTERNING

PLASTIC PRODUCTION

DESIGN PÅ GÅNG

RE-DEVELOPMENTS

FOLDING

RECOMBINATION

PUNCHING

COMMUNICATION

ASSEMBLY

EVALUATION

Joining For

PAPERS / CONFERENCES

MODULARITY

DETAILING

TESTING

01.AKAD

PROGRAMMING

WHITE NOISE

ALL THINGS ARE

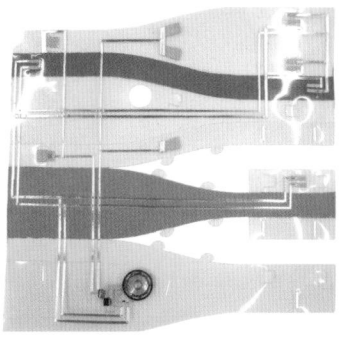

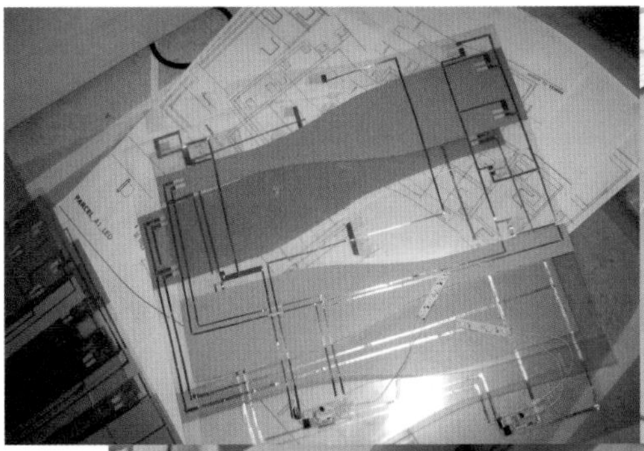

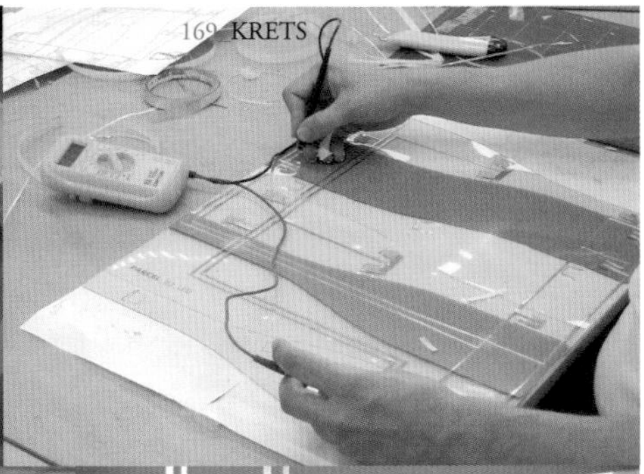

genetic algorithm; a computer program that simulates and compresses the geologically slow processes of natural selection to nanoseconds of computational time, in order to evolve solutions to specific problems. The *SplineGraft* algorithm is in this way trying to emit patterns of movement that stimulate occupation of the space it has been grafted in to.'

The beauty of the fabricated parts and the folded polyurethane material is perhaps not matched by its elegance when moving. The project looks a little bit like someone hiding under a duvet or behind a curtain, but Krets believes that future iterations of this intelligent movement will define interior environments. Also, the sophistication of its fabrication is extreme – each acrylic component integrates wiring and brass conductors, and the actuators are controlled by mini-processors communicating with one another by radio. Like so many of the prototypes of the emergent school, there is a bit of mismatch between technological sophistication and phenomenological effect, but *SplineGraft* is perhaps one step along a very long road.

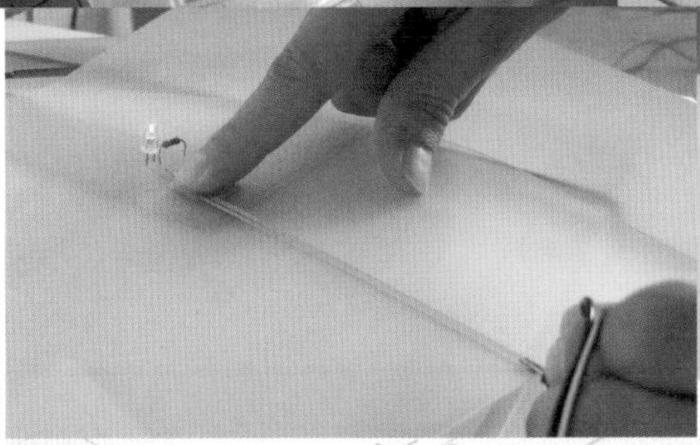

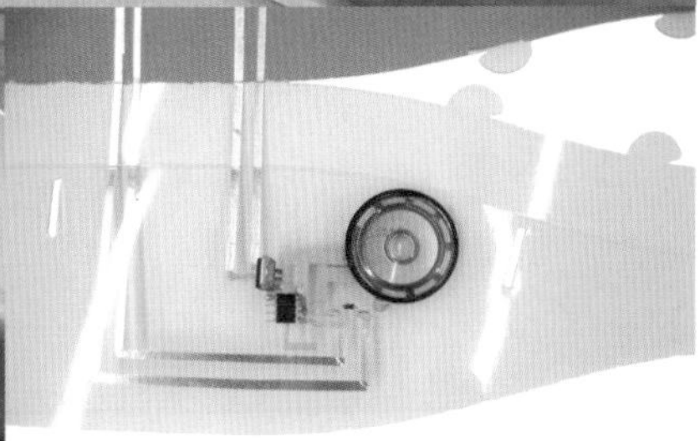

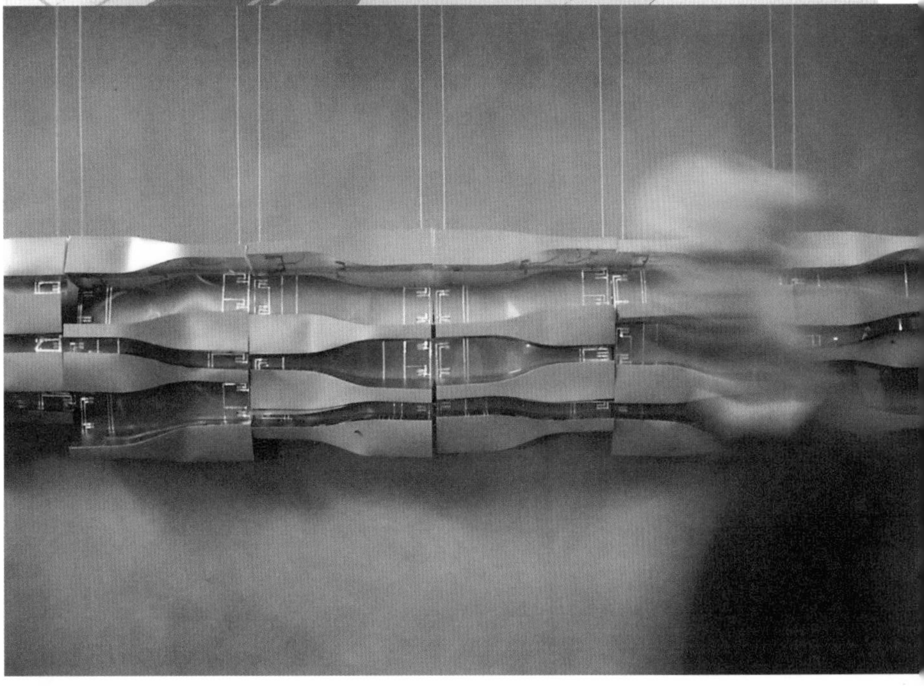

# Lead Pencil Studio

Lead Pencil Studio's work is born out of a conviction that architectural practice is missing something. In an interview for the Architectural League of New York, partner Daniel Mihalyo said: 'We love space. I think there's a sort of gap in professional practice where we've forgotten about the beauty of raw space. It's all about the constraints of codes and programme, so it becomes more about form than space.'

The practice has, nonetheless, made some of the most evocative and seductive forms shown in this book. Lead Pencil's project at the Sand Point Gallery in Seattle in 2003 was perhaps their best. Entitled *Seattle Staircase*, the project created the beginning of a staircase made out of hundreds of pieces of welded wire, which, after a few steps, dissolved into nothing. Across the road, though, was a tower where the top of the stairway miraculously reappeared, but inaccessible.

The project was carried out as a way of linking the history of two buildings facing each other across a road. The top of the staircase was attached to a former fire station, and the bottom to the retaining wall of a building that had earlier burnt down. The piece is elegiac and amusing, as well as very beautiful.

Partner Annie Han says: 'Somebody described it as an accordion that was broken in the middle and I think that's a nice description. We welded these wires together to make it really solid, then it disappears, then it reappears as it gets attached to the tower.' Mihalyo adds: 'You can see it, but you can't access the top, and your mind has to do that work, to make that leap in the gap.'

Although the pair have completed some interesting small architectural projects (their own house – the *4 Parts House* – prominent among them), it is their artistic endeavours that stick in the mind. *Linear Plenum*, their project for the Suyama Space Gallery in Seattle, filled the 280sq m (3,000sq ft) exhibition space with hanging threads of masonry line every 7.5cm (3in). Although a contemplative project in its normal configuration, the threads had a spatial and social effect at the opening. 'It was a wild party,' says Han. 'People were interacting with it, making braids, crocheting things – people would run across the room with their arms out.'

Below: *Minus Space/150 Works of Art*, an installation by Lead Pencil in Seattle in 2005. Opposite: *Seattle Staircase* at the Sand Point Gallery in Seattle in 2003.

| Location | Seattle, USA |
| --- | --- |
| Nationality | Korean American |

Lead Pencil Studio was founded in Seattle in 1997 by Korean Annie Han and American Daniel Mihalyo, after both architects had studied at the University of Oregon and spent time working at Miller Hull. The two began their practice to pursue small architectural projects ('We have no ambition to grow an office,' they say) and artworks in parallel, dividing their practice conceptually into a 'department of architecture' and a 'bureau of spatial enquiry'. They have created a range of artistic projects and installations and have won awards including being chosen by the Architectural League of New York as an Emerging Voice in 2006. The studio was also awarded a visual arts grant from the Creative Capital Foundation in New York, and a Special Projects grant from Arts 4 Culture in Seattle.

L

Left: *Linear Plenum* installation at the Suyama Space Gallery in Seattle. Below: Lead Pencil's *4 Parts House* near downtown Seattle. Opposite: *Maryhill Double,* constructed in 2006. The installation was a full-scale silhouette of the Maryhill Museum of Art made out of scaffolding and construction netting.

The Architectural League of New York's Emerging Voices lecture series in 2006 also included Escher GuneWardena (pp. 98–99) and nArchitects (pp. 212–213).

L

# Workshop Levitas

Workshop Levitas is intended to connote lightness, and the research group's mission statement seems to propose the airily impossible. 'In contrast to conventional architecture based on gravity,' they write, 'The design team wants to manifest precisely the essences of the physical world, which are light, chaos and ephemera. The collaboration explores innovative structures and spatial design, which makes the heaviest material float and exposes the most solid properties of the weakest.'

This paradoxical statement is perhaps manifested best in the group's technologically impressive, and highly romantic, project for a footbridge made entirely of bamboo. The project, which was the one that launched Workshop Levitas, was installed in the courtyard of the Materials & Applications Gallery in Los Angeles in 2006, and was a collaboration with the design and art studio Infranatural.

Infranatural had proposed flooding the courtyard with collected rainwater, and Levitas was given the job of creating a bridge from the street. The bridge was made from 150 individually cut pieces of bamboo from the LA County Arboretum and constructed in 20 days by Levitas and other volunteers. The bamboo pieces are bound together with zip ties. The installation meant that the bridge was often covered in a mysterious fog, adding to the romance of the project.

The bridge is an eroded cylinder, the geometry for which was created using Rhino and GSA, but it was also allowed to distort and flex according to the natural properties of the material. All of this was modelled in the final GSA drawing, including detailing that allowed the structure to deform uniformly without concentrating stresses at the bamboo elements adjacent to the supports at either end of the bridge.

The woven bridge also changed colour during the life of the installation, from the green of the fresh-cut bamboo to a darker colour as it dried out.

This spread: Levitas' bamboo bridge at the Materials & Applications Gallery in Los Angeles, installed in 2006 for the *Here Be Monsters* exhibition.

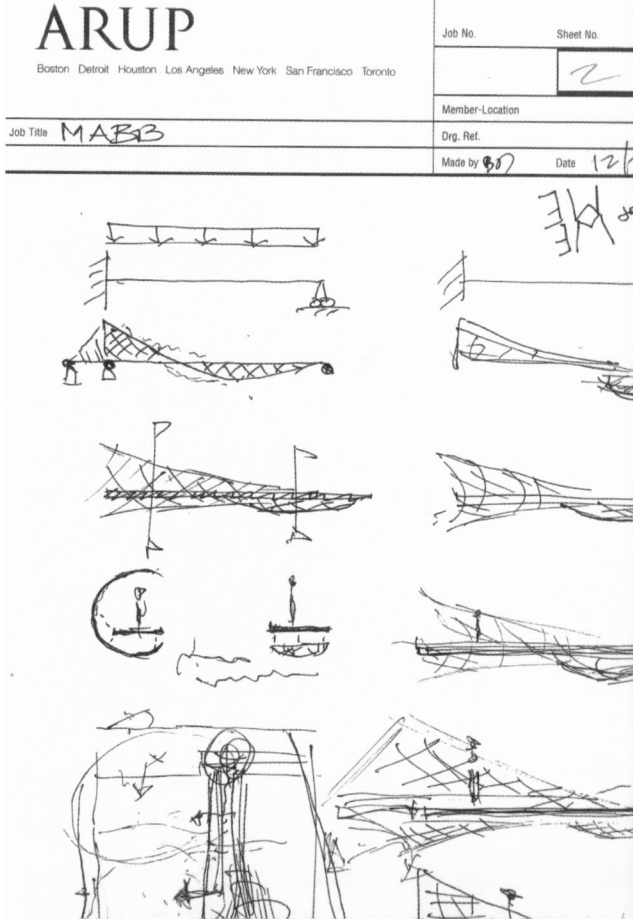

| Location | Los Angeles, USA |
| --- | --- |
| Nationality | German |
| | American |
| | Taiwanese |
| | Hong Kong |

Workshop Levitas is an international, interdisciplinary design collaborative that includes architects, engineers, interactive designers and others. It was founded by structural engineer Bruce Danziger (USA), and interactive designers and emerging architects Shu-Chi Hsu (Taiwan) and Moritz Freund (Germany). Other collaborators include SCI-Arc alumnus and artist Steve Boyer. The group's work consists of architectural interventions, temporary exhibition installations, signage and performance.

**L**

Others to have carried out projects in the courtyard of the Materials & Applications Gallery in LA are Ball Nogues (pp. 38–41) with the *Maximilian's Schell* and Marcelo Spina of Patterns (pp. 242–243) with his *Land Tiles*. The gallery is a non-profit research centre run by Jenna Didier and Oliver Hess.

# Lot-ek

Lot-ek's work has always been about a kind of post-consumer sustainability, interested in reusing what has been left behind, and fascinated by the inhabitation of the infrastructure of commerce and industry. While they became well known for projects reusing cargo containers, recent projects have seen this move to a new level.

Their project for the Sanlitun South retail complex in Beijing is part of a controversial redevelopment of a formerly intricate piece of city, full of seedy bars and characterful corners. A new masterplan, by Hong Kong-based Oval Partnership, attempts to create an ersatz fabric of narrow alleys. Lot-ek was charged with turning the northeast corner of the site into a mall, with retail, restaurants and 'event spaces'.

They write: 'Our concept is centred on the definition of the internal alleys as multi-level, open-air circulation channels. In each alley, a rhythmic system of scaffolding-like metal frames is wedged between the buildings adapting to the varying width of the alley's cross-section. The scaffolding-like frames are connected along the side of the buildings by a random system of horizontal metal rods that function as railing and *brise-soleil*, defining a loggia on the upper levels and generating a tunnel-like perspective within the alleys.'

Their favourite material, the cargo container, provides the dimensions of the structure. Each bay is 2.4m (8ft) wide. Branded containers are inserted into the façades and jut into the internal streets. 'At every level, the containers function as large three-dimensional graphic objects layered with signage and logos,' Lot-ek says. The exterior façades are covered in an orange mesh, punctuated with more containers.

Lot-ek's obsession with containers sometimes leads it to perhaps absurd lengths (the 'inspirotainer', for instance), but it pays off in its project for Metal Management, a metal recycling company in the US. The project consists of one huge wall of customized containers, forming a four-storey façade embellished with supergraphics of the client's logo. Behind this façade are other fingers of containers, which accommodate the diverse functions of the client's organization.

This page and bottom opposite: The Sanlitun retail complex in Beijing is the largest iteration yet of Lot-ek's interest in shipping containers as a construction material. Opposite: Office for Metal Management, a recycling company in the US.

Lot-ek's work was shown in the *Strangely Familiar* exhibition in 2004 (which toured many North American venues), alongside that of fellow container enthusiast Jennifer Siegal (pp. 290–291).

| Location | New York, USA |
| --- | --- |
| Nationality | Italian |

Lot-ek was established in 1993 in New York by Ada Tolla and Giuseppe Lignano. Both partners studied at the University of Naples and Columbia University in New York, where they now teach. The practice's projects concentrate on reusing industrial materials, especially cargo containers, which they have proposed converting into homes, shops and even a mall. Lot-ek (pronounced 'low-tech') published a monograph, *Urban Scan*, in 2003, and was part of the Architectural League, New York Emerging Voices series in 1999. In 2005 they won the Best Interactive Design category in the *ID* magazine awards.

L

# Lynch Architects

Lynch Architects' work attempts to reclaim some of the most fundamental grounds of architecture, using a keen historical knowledge and philosophical grounding to create architecture of phenomenological weight and representational presence.

Patrick Lynch says: 'I'm interested in character in architecture rather than function. I want to think about character as related to place and personae: i.e. the possibility of a house having an ambivalent character – a public face and a specifically private face.'

That the practice's work has so far been realized in a series of private houses is significant. Lynch's work begins with dwelling as a central concern.

The first of these houses, and in a way Lynch Architects' breakthrough

| Location | London, UK |
|---|---|
| Nationality | British German |

Lynch Architects was established by husband-and-wife team Patrick and Claudia Lynch in London in 1997. Patrick studied at Liverpool University before undertaking a Master of Philosophy degree at Cambridge University. Claudia studied in her native Dresden and at the University of North London. The practice is one of the most important emerging practices in the UK, winning *Building Design* magazine's Young Architect of the Year Award in 2005 and being nominated as one of the world's 25 best architects by *Wallpaper** magazine in 2006–07. Lynch Architects have completed several private houses and a community centre in east London. The practice is now working on housing at a larger scale and on a major London office building. The partners are also experienced teachers, and have lectured widely in Europe and America.

project, was a house for an artist in Norfolk, UK, with its extremely flat and beautiful landscape. The project involved rebuilding an existing bungalow, but adding new wings to the original layout, creating a series of charged exterior spaces with very different characters – a terrace looking out across the marsh, an intimate courtyard and a wilder section of garden. Inside, the set piece is the high, timber-lined living room, with an oculus at the top of the roof allowing the client to see the stars at night. The exterior of the building, clad in black-painted timber seemingly leaning against the oversize brick chimney, created an extraordinary landmark on the scale of the landscape, as well as a vertiginous effect within.

A later house, in Hackney, east London, exercised Lynch's interest in

This spread: *Marsh View House*, Norfolk, UK. The tall chimney has an oculus at its summit, through which the client can see the stars at night.

This spread: *Greenwood Road House*, a small timber box of a building on the end of a Georgian terrace in Hackney, east London.

London's historical house types. Set in an end-of-terrace site in a Victorian suburb, Lynch's timber box echoes the window openings of adjacent buildings, but also attempts to create a more gregarious character, with a first-floor balcony (accessed from the living room) that looks down on the street and puts the occupants of the house on display when they appear on it. At its base is a walled garden for the clients' eccentric sculpture collection. The base of the house is also made of brick, signalling a transition from outside to in. The structure of the house is oak, connected with tree nails that expand and contract according to climatic conditions.

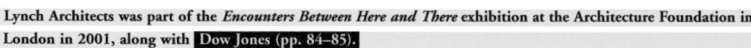

Lynch Architects was part of the *Encounters Between Here and There* exhibition at the Architecture Foundation in London in 2001, along with Dow Jones (pp. 84–85).

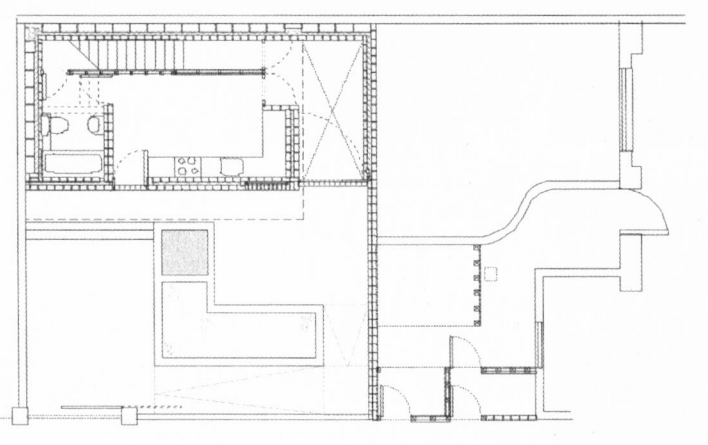

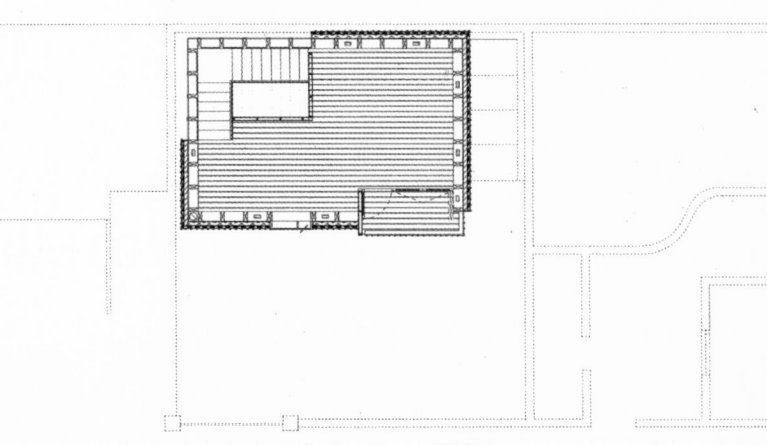

When Lynch Architects won the Young Architect of the Year Award in 2005 DRDH Architects (pp. 86–89) came second.

# MADA s.p.a.m.

Qingyun Ma, the head of MADA s.p.a.m., is a phenomenon. The poster boy of new Chinese architecture, he studied in China and the US, and bridges the two cultures in a way that no other Chinese architect has managed – to the extent that he is now Dean of Architecture at the University of Southern California.

His work oscillates between a sensitive, updated vernacular that recognizes traditions like Chinese courtyard housing and updates them (such as his *Courtyard House* near the Forbidden City in Beijing), and a kind of international super-modernism, clearly influenced by architects such as Rem Koolhaas (with whom Ma worked on the *Harvard Project on Cities*).

An example of the latter mode is MADA's project for the Shanghai Natural History Museum. Its form is a square block, with two canyons seemingly eroded into it. The project's siting is intended as a reaction against many contemporary buildings in

This spread: Building for the truck-making part of Renault, featuring a mix of offices and a visitor centre under a wave-like roof.

In 2007 MADA s.p.a.m. held an exhibition at the Aedes Architecture Gallery in Berlin. Other practices to have exhibited there include AWP (pp. 36–37), Enric Ruiz-Geli of Cloud 9 (pp. 62–65), Graftlab (pp. 134–135) and Urban Think Tank (pp. 328–329).

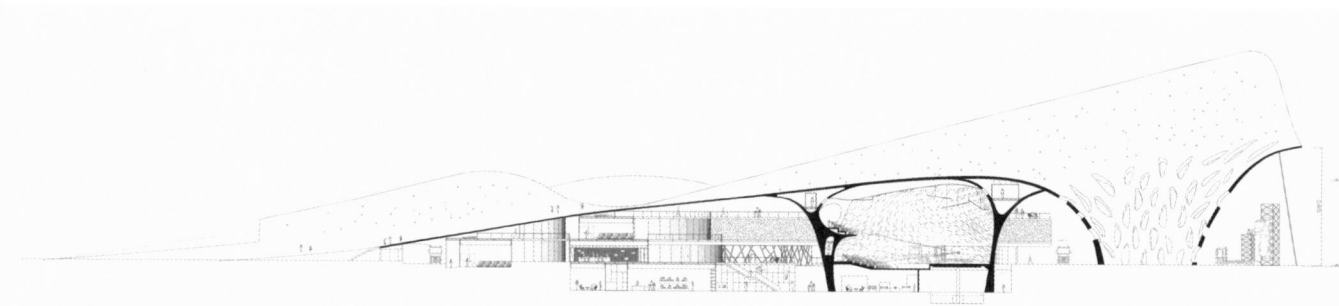

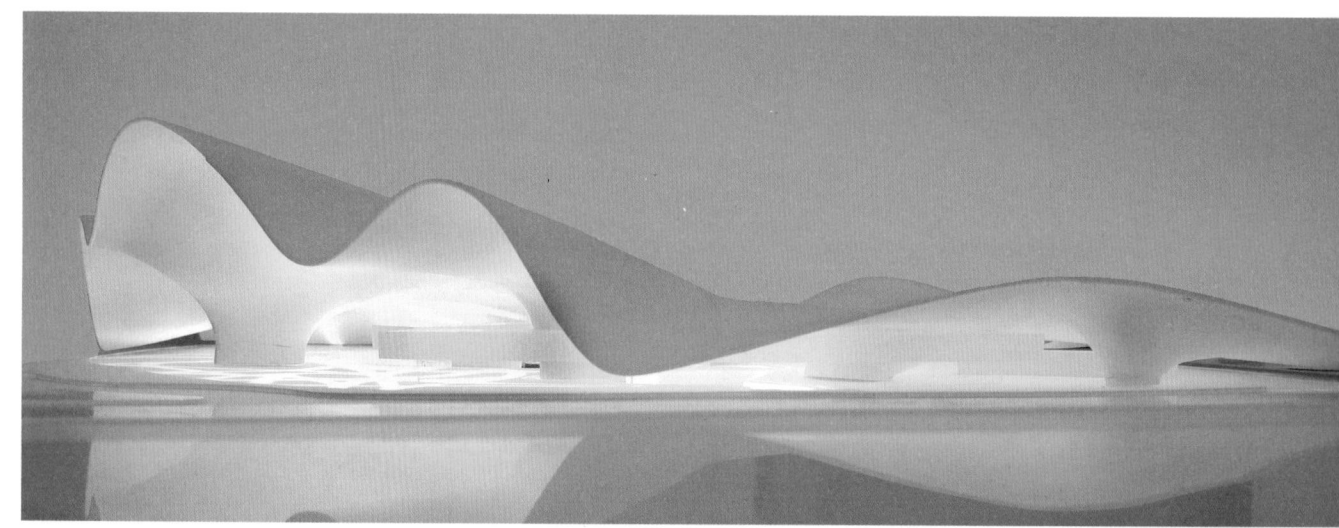

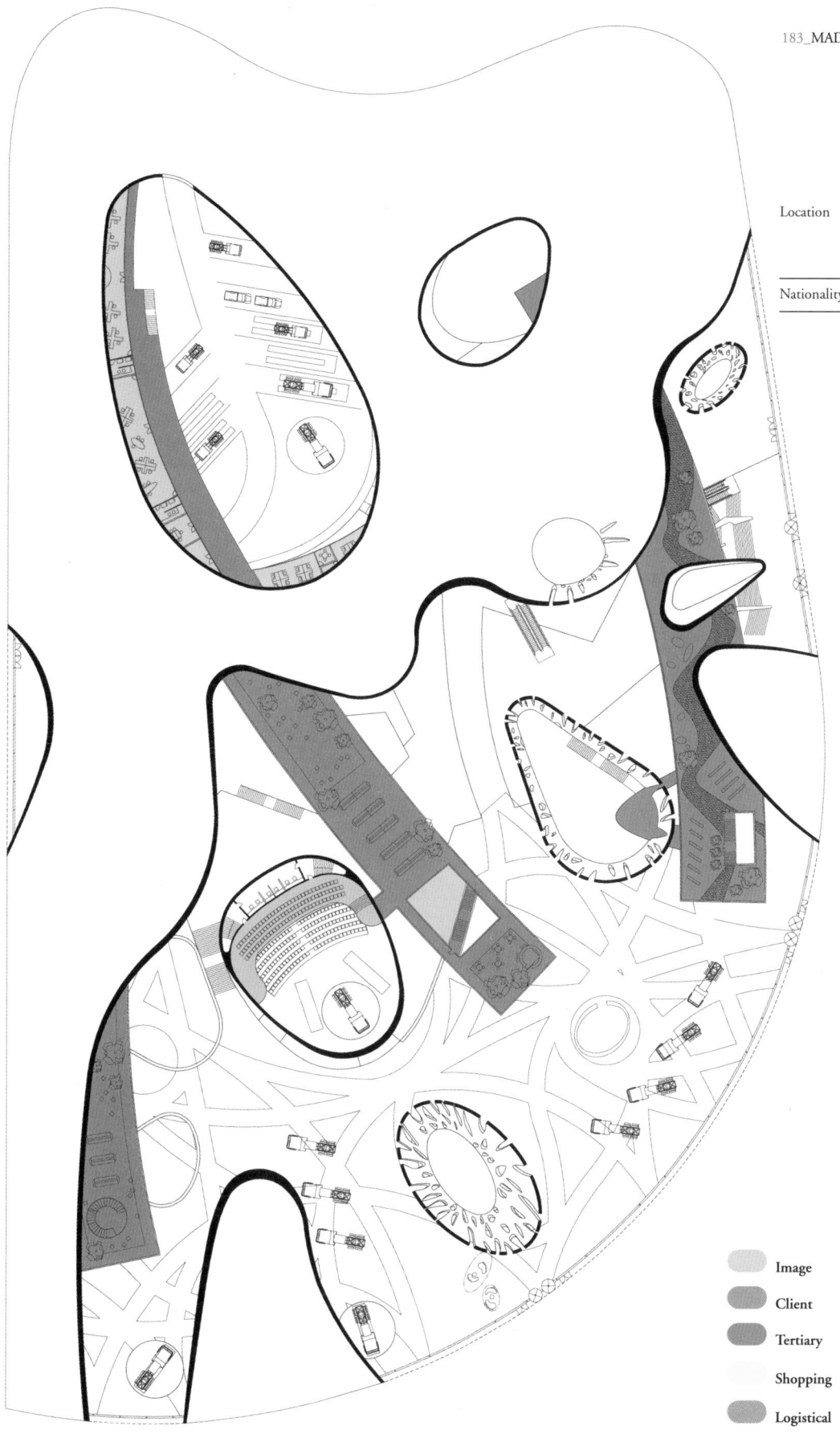

| Location | New York, USA |
| --- | --- |
| | Beijing, China |
| | Shanghai, China |

| Nationality | Chinese |
| --- | --- |

Qingyun Ma studied architecture at Tsinghua University in China, and received his Masters degree at the University of Pennsylvania, the first Chinese to have studied there for 60 years. After graduating he worked as a designer at KPF and in 1995 he established MADA s.p.a.m. in New York, later opening offices in Beijing and Shanghai. Already one of the most important architects in China, Ma has a litany of major projects behind him, including *Qingpu Community Island* in Shanghai, the *Centennial TV and Radio Centre* in Xi'an and *Tianyi City Plaza* in Ningpo. He is Dean of Architecture at the University of Southern California.

Image

Client

Tertiary

Shopping

Logistical

Shanghai that pay scant attention to their contexts. The museum sits in a large garden, which, writes the architect, 'offers green space for the city. At the same time, it helps to dissolve the density of urban life and activity. No doubt the museum will help to improve and try to solve the problem of density.' Despite this urban aspiration, the building has few representational features – it is very much an icon.

However, Ma would not want it categorized in that way. About his project for car-maker Renault, he says that it deliberately avoids making iconic architecture (which, he says ominously, 'as a cruel insertion into the landscape acclaims an era of exploitation and domination') in favour of what he calls

Geo Architecture. While Ma's description is vague, it appears to be a structurally experimental and environmentally efficient architecture that attempts to demonstrate industrial dynamism and innovation. The proposal is very reminiscent of the work of Japanese architect Toyo Ito crossed with the retro-futurism of Felix Candela. It features a white roof that swoops and dips, enclosing the massive truck factory and other facilities.

Ma's work is so extensive that it is impossible to cover all of it here. Suffice to say he is in a unique position as the spokesman of forward-looking Chinese architecture in the West, and of Western architectural and educational influence in his home country.

Opposite: Project for the Shanghai Natural History Museum. This page: ZJJ Administration building.

# Mae

Although Mae's distinctive specialism is probably housing, this project is concentrated on another building type for which there is pressing need in the UK – cemeteries.

After years of research on the subject of burial sites, Mae was commissioned to build a flagship contemporary cemetery on the edge of Letchworth Garden City in Hertfordshire. The project, the architects say, 'hopes to encourage a return to the civic values of the great Victorian burial grounds – when cemeteries were not only places to bury the dead but a central part of the community.'

The landscape is as yet unfinished, but the project centres around a non-denominational chapel, with two lines of mausoleums forming a formal courtyard. The mausoleums are intended for the large Italian community in the area. The chapel itself is a modest composition of two volumes: a generous entrance space with a high pitched roof signalling the entrance, and a generous overhang providing shelter at the edge of the building. The chapel is underneath another pitched roof, toplit, and doubles as a space for meetings and education uses.

A large picture window addresses the landscape beyond, which is the other part of Mae's work on the project. The intention was to make a landscape that people would use for leisure, and this is oriented around a new parkland and woods. The entrance sequence has also been made picturesque, creating a meandering route to the chapel entrance through birch trees – a conscious nod to the great burial landscapes of northern Europe.

The project is a built result of a long period of research for the practice, which has seen them make theoretical proposals for high-density urban burial sites and lecture widely on the subject of cemetery design.

This spread: The chapel and mausoleum of the *Wilbury Hills Cemetery* in Hertfordshire, UK. This picture was taken in early 2007, before the landscape was completed.

The author has taught in collaboration with Mae partner Michael Howe, as well as Daniel Rosbottom of DRDH (pp. 86–89) and Patrick Lynch of Lynch Architects (pp. 178–181). He has been an invited critic with Tom Emerson of 6A (pp. 14–15), Sean Griffiths of FAT (pp. 110–113), Jürgen Mayer H (pp. 194–197) and UFO (pp. 324–327), among others.

| Location | London UK |
| --- | --- |
| Nationality | British |

Mae Architects was founded by Michael Howe and Alex Ely in London, after the two partners met while finishing their studies at the Royal College of Art in London. Howe studied fine art before turning to architecture. Alex Ely was housing adviser at the Commission for Architecture and the Built Environment in the UK, and remains an adviser on housing and planning to agencies and politicians. Mae has undertaken a series of small buildings of note, including its rooftop extension in Hoxton, east London completed in 2006, and the *Wilbury Hills Cemetery* in 2007. The practice is now working on larger-scale work in the housing sector. The partners have lectured widely and taught at Greenwich University.

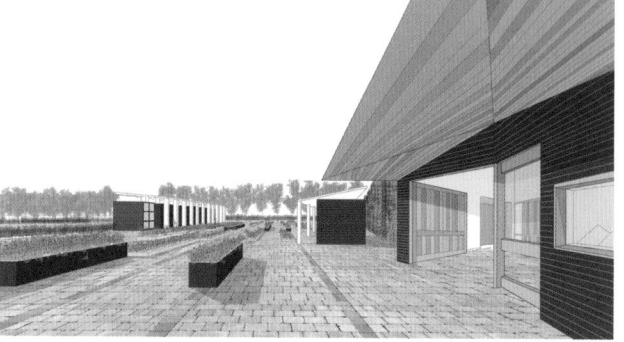

Clockwise from below: The empty niches of the first line of mausoleums to be completed; The colonnade in front of the mausoleum; Two visualizations of how the landscape strategy will look when complete; The chapel building, with the inviting overhang of the roof softening the edge of the building; The view from the back of the chapel. All the buildings use a stack-bonded hard, grey brick for their façades.

# Elena Manferdini

Elena Manferdini says that despite the success of her designs in the field of fashion, her motivation for making clothes is to take lessons learned in that field into architecture. 'I approach the problem of a dress as though it were cladding for a building. I think that my inspiration comes not from external sources, but is a continuous sophistication of geometrical effect that I have always been obsessed with. I consider myself not a designer of ideas, but a designer of forms.'

Her forms are very distinctive. Her dresses are usually laser-cut pieces of fabric, that are then assembled in a very three-dimensional way, creating a conceptual 'cladding' for the body. The cuts themselves are generated using contemporary scripting techniques, such as in the *Bones* collection (Autumn/Winter 2006), where patterns were generated using what Manferdini calls 'flock animations'. Her work pushes the limits of laser-cutting to beautiful effect.

Her most high-profile built work is probably her intricate pavilion for the Beijing Architecture Biennale in 2006 (entitled *Emerging Talents, Emerging Technologies* and curated by theorist Neal Leach). The pavilion, which was called the West Coast Pavilion, was composed of a series of laser-cut steel elements at different scales, creating a three-dimensional structure made of walls that have been described as quilt-like.

**Below and opposite top:** Manferdini's West Coast Pavilion at the Beijing Architecture Biennale in 2006.

**Opposite bottom:** One of Manferdini's dress designs, with characteristic laser-cut decoration.

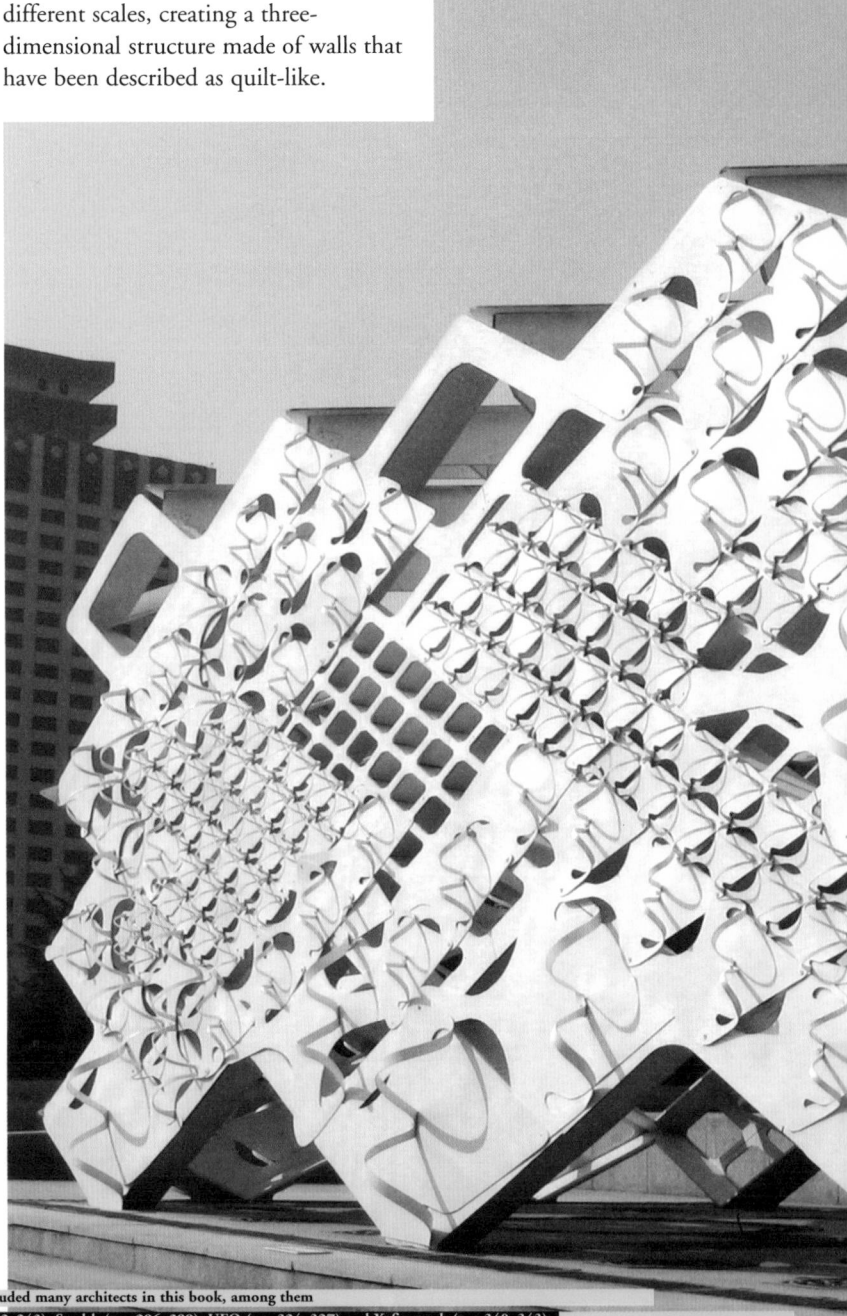

Neil Leach's above-mentioned exhibition in Beijing in 2006 included many architects in this book, among them Biothing (pp. 46–47), Gnuform (pp. 128–129), Patterns (pp. 242–243), Stealth (pp. 296–299), UFO (pp. 324–327) and Xefirotarch (pp. 340–343).

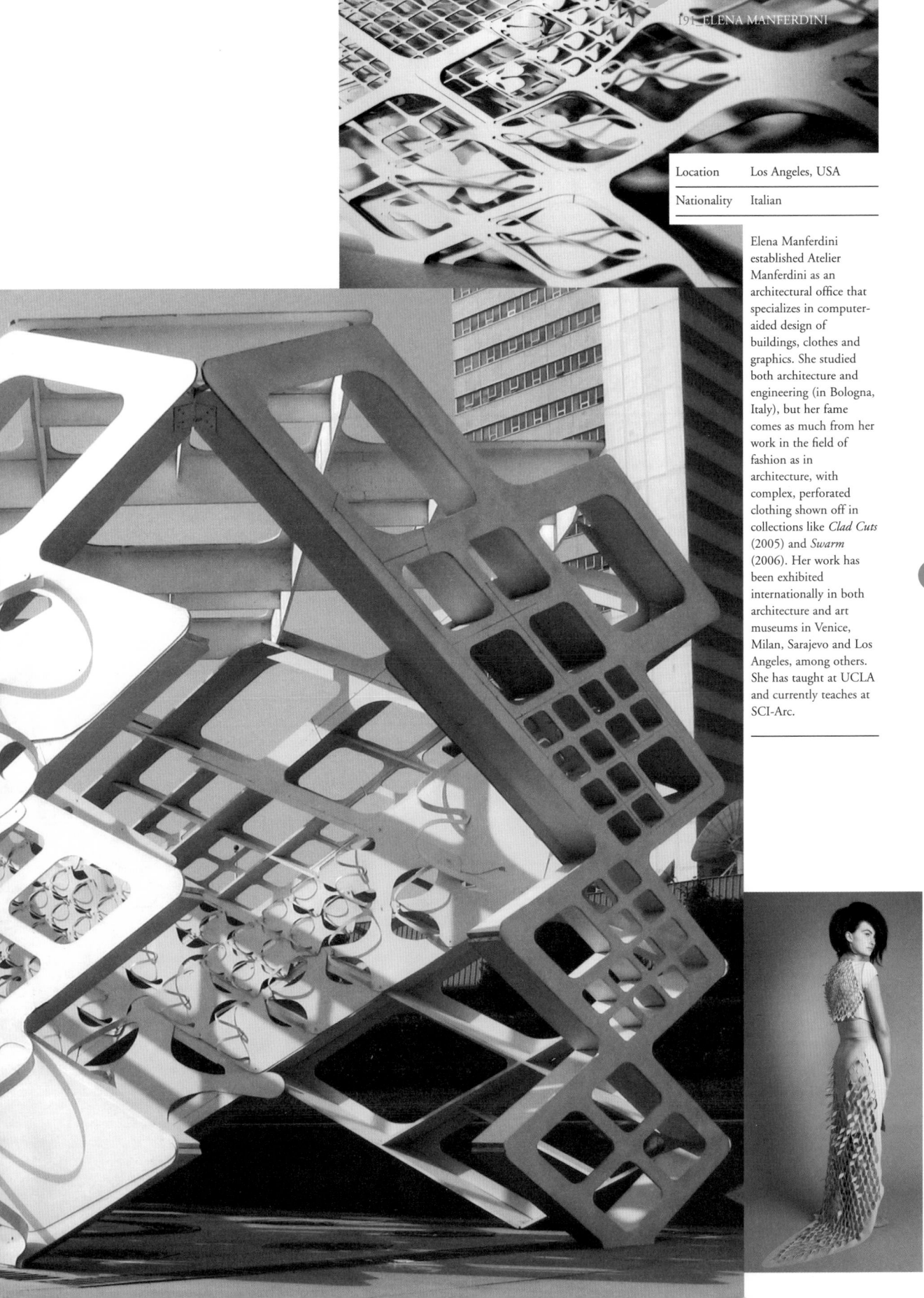

| Location | Los Angeles, USA |
| Nationality | Italian |

Elena Manferdini established Atelier Manferdini as an architectural office that specializes in computer-aided design of buildings, clothes and graphics. She studied both architecture and engineering (in Bologna, Italy), but her fame comes as much from her work in the field of fashion as in architecture, with complex, perforated clothing shown off in collections like *Clad Cuts* (2005) and *Swarm* (2006). Her work has been exhibited internationally in both architecture and art museums in Venice, Milan, Sarajevo and Los Angeles, among others. She has taught at UCLA and currently teaches at SCI-Arc.

**M**

# Matsuokasatoshi Tamurayuki

This Japanese practice is on the up, and will soon be bringing its brand of coolly characterful minimalism to a range of projects in Japan and Southeast Asia. But it is a joyful temporary and rather minor work that we wanted to publish here.

*Balloon Caught* was Matsuokasatoshi Tamurayuki's winning entry in the competition in 2005 to design a temporary installation in Trounce Alley, a shopping street in Vancouver, Canada. Commissioned for a three-day festival designed to focus attention on the future of Vancouver's urban realm, *Balloon Caught* consisted of nine huge, translucent balloons, wedged into the alleyway above street level and illuminated from within. The largest of the balloons was 6m (20ft) across, and the glowing interventions looked as much like distended Chinese lanterns as balloons.

The client for the project, Helena Grdadolnik of Space Agency, described the strengths of the project: 'Instead of trying to impose another space on the alley, the balloons themselves make it seem narrower and tighter, and highlight its interesting features. And balloons are also very festive – they make a party atmosphere. This isn't something that's esoteric and difficult.' The project is just a sketch – a piece of beautiful and provocative scenography – but it bodes well for the future tone of Matsuokasatoshi Tamurayuki's work.

| Location | Tokyo, Japan |
| --- | --- |
| Nationality | Japanese |

Matsuokasatoshi Tamurayuki was founded in Tokyo in 2005 by two principals, Satoshi Matsuoka and Yuki Tamura. Matsuoka studied in Kyoto and Tokyo, before travelling to Columbia University and Delft University in the Netherlands as a Pola Art Foundation Fellow. Tamura studied in Tokyo. Both partners worked for big name practices in Europe (MVRDV, Miralles Tagliabue) before returning to Tokyo to work for SANAA. The practice pursues projects at all scales, from urbanism to product design, and has won many awards, including a first prize in the Seoul Performing Art Center International Ideas Competition in 2005.

M

This spread:
*Balloon Caught*,
an installation in
Trounce Alley,
Vancouver, Canada.

*Balloon Caught* won an honourable mention in the *Architectural Review* Awards in 2005,
when FNP Architekten (pp. 116–119) won, Sou Fujimoto (pp. 122–125) was highly commended and
Pezo von Ellrichshausen (pp. 246–249) was commended.

# Jürgen Mayer H

Jürgen Mayer can no longer really be categorized as an emerging architect. It was as long ago as 2003 that Mayer won a special mention in the Mies van der Rohe Prize for his first completed building – the *Scharnhauser Park Town Hall* in Ostfildern in Germany. Since then he has developed a body of work, including several competition wins for major public buildings, which is one of the most distinct in Europe. You can almost always identify one of Jürgen Mayer's works. They are distinguished by a formal repertoire that has a certain retro-futurism to it, a science-fiction bent that enjoys rounded edges and cartoon organic forms. He has described his formal vocabulary as being influenced by architecture and industrial design of the 1970s, enjoying the optimism about technology of that era,

but also glorying in a certain unfamiliarity, even ugliness. He says: 'The unfamiliar or not-immediately-beautiful building is something that lasts longer and takes more time for appropriation.'

Mayer's project for a dining hall at Karlsruhe University is characteristic, conceived as two planes connected by a forest of columns. Despite the *Star Trek* styling, the building creates a romantic journey through a colonnaded entrance façade into the double-height dining hall, up an almost Schinkel-esque staircase and out on to a roof terrace that overlooks a football pitch and park behind.

Mayer's most impressive competition win, in 2004, is a very unusual project, and promises to be the building that will make his name.

This spread: The *Metropol Parasol* project proposes a huge canopy for a public square in Seville, Spain, composed of six giant mushroom forms 22m (72ft) above the ground. On its roof is a public promenade giving views across the city, accessed by elevators in the mushrooms' shafts. The public plinth houses a museum for archaeological remains and provides a space for a market and concerts above. The timber structure will cover an area 150 x 70m (490 x 230ft) and will be one of the largest timber structures in the world.

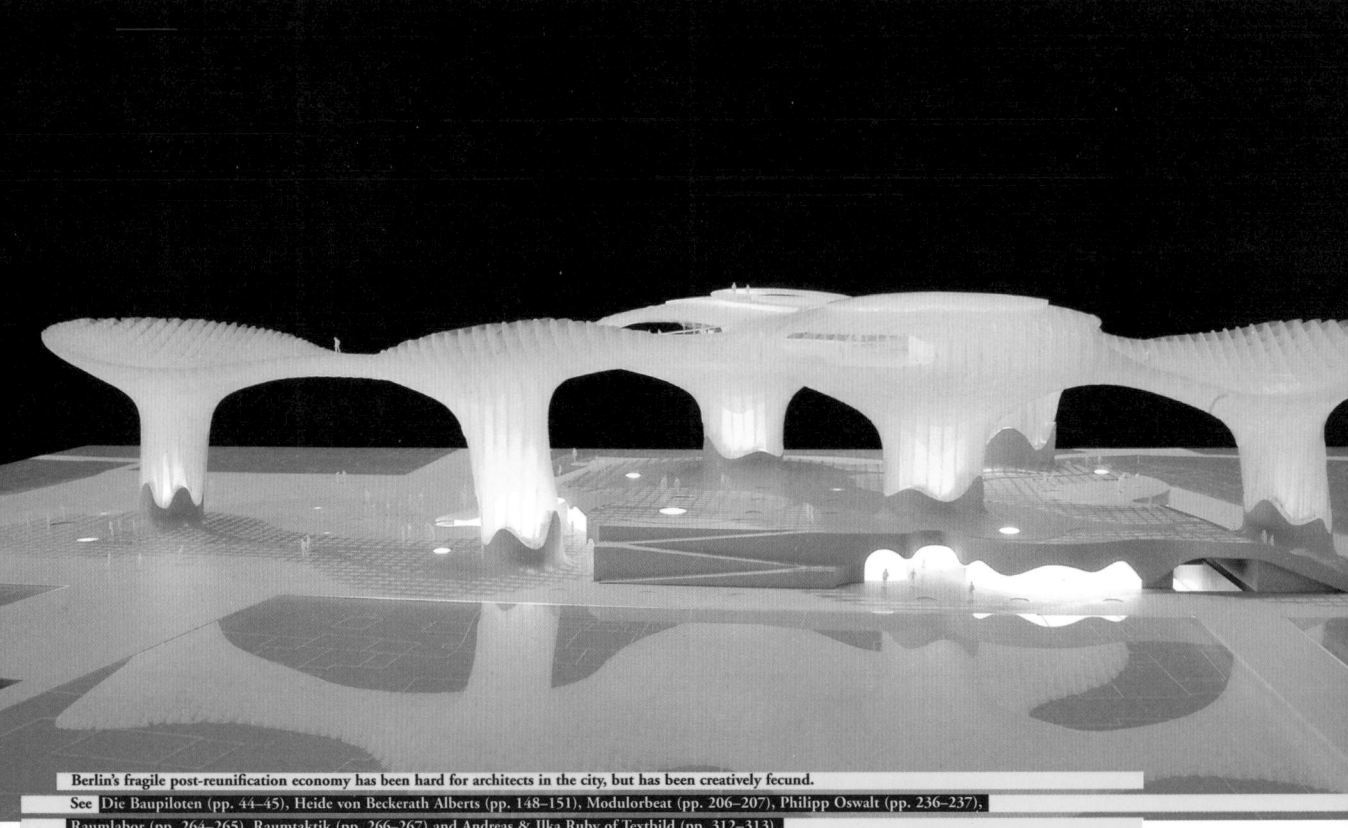

Berlin's fragile post-reunification economy has been hard for architects in the city, but has been creatively fecund.

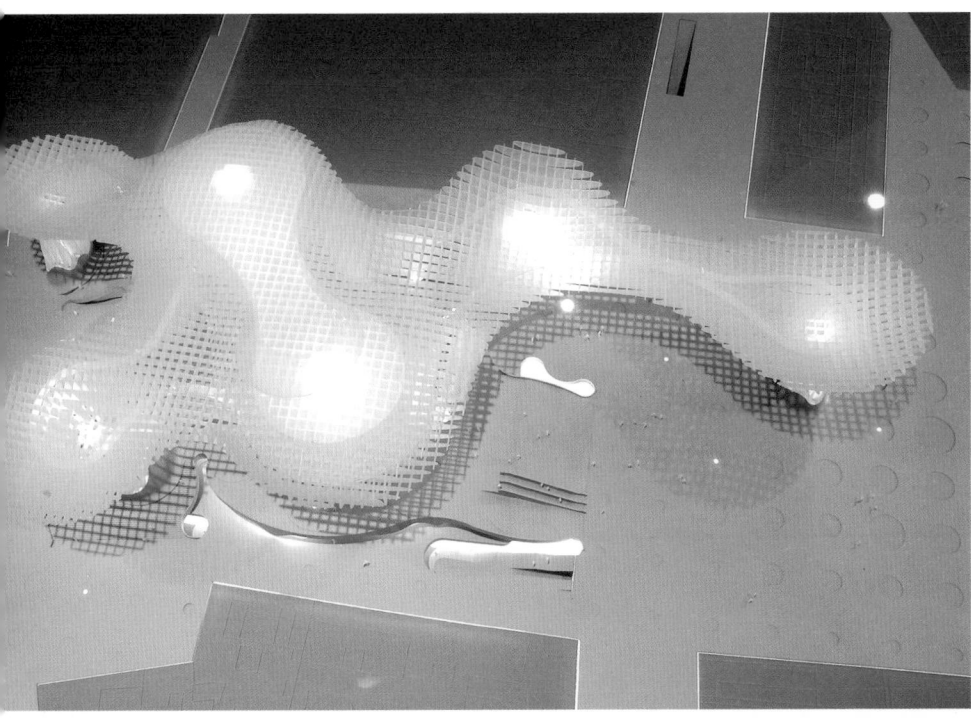

| Location | Berlin, Germany |
| --- | --- |
| Nationality | German |

Jürgen Mayer founded his studio in Berlin in 1996. He studied at Stuttgart University, Cooper Union and Princeton University, and has worked in architecture, masterplanning, furniture design, interior design and art. He now has an office of 14 people, and teaches at universities across Europe and America.

M

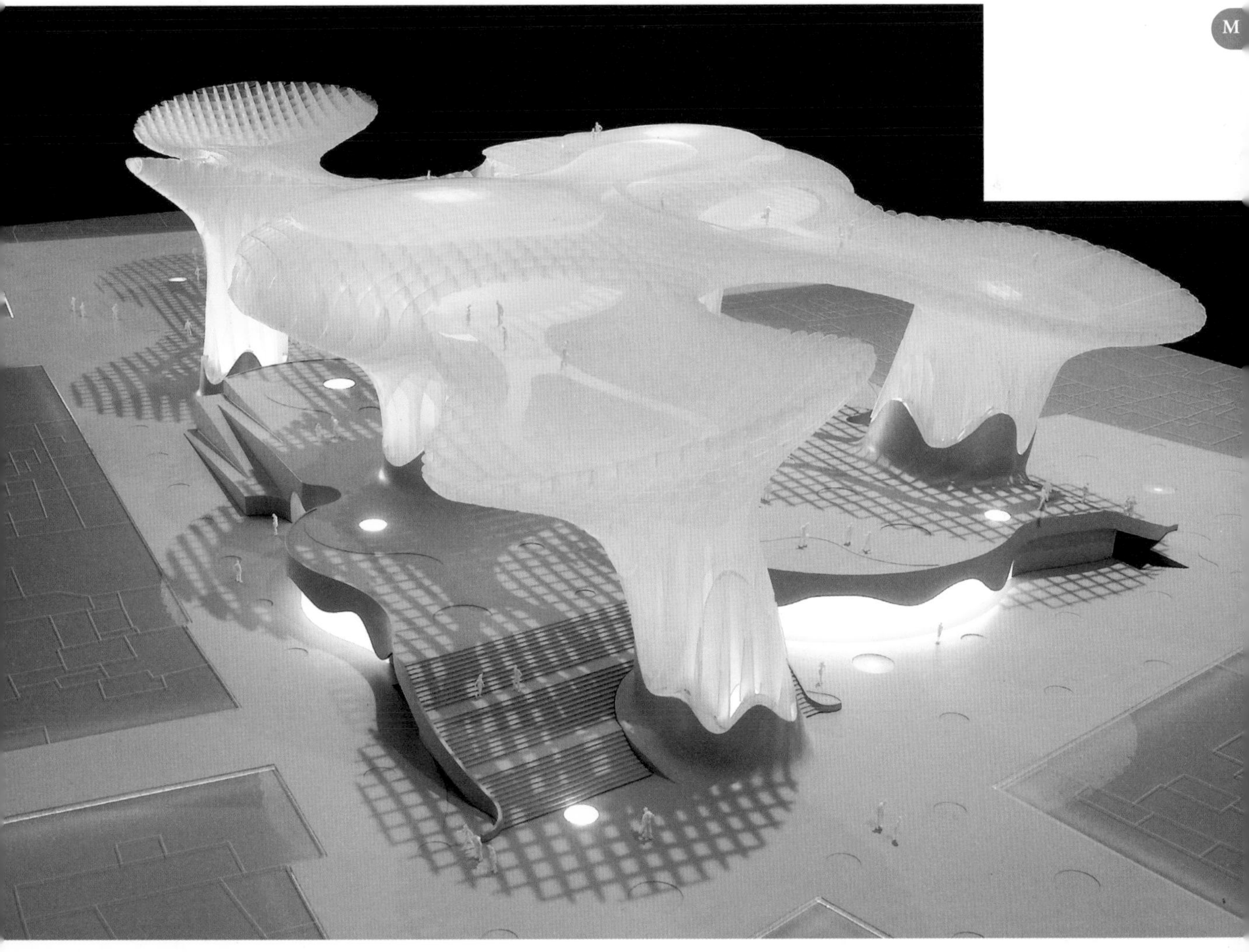

NL Architects (pp. 226–229) were nominated for the Mies van der Rohe Prize two years after Mayer, in 2005.

The competition was for ideas for the Plaza de la Encarnacion in Seville, a square in the very centre of the historic city. Mayer's project proposed erecting a series of umbrella-like forms that will create a venue for a market, concerts and events, as well as a place to experience the city at high level from a walkway on top of the umbrellas. An elevated plinth at ground level provides a way of experiencing archaeological remains uncovered on the site. It is conceived as a piece of infrastructure that creates opportunities for a range of social activities to occur, from sport to commerce.

This spread: The *MENSA Cafeteria* for Karlsruhe University is conceived as two planes with an irregular forest of columns joining them. The section drawing below shows the high percentage of the building dedicated to the huge kitchens and storerooms that allow the café to serve thousands of students per day. The roof terrace sits on top of the kitchen area and gives views to a neighbouring football pitch.

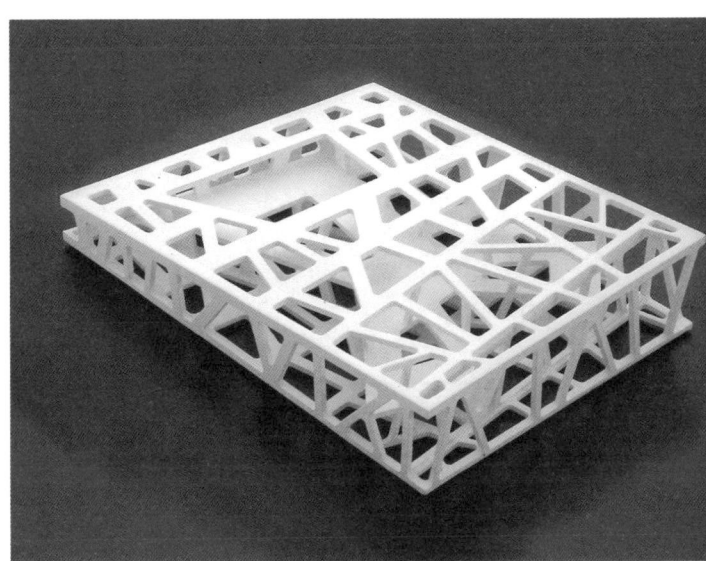

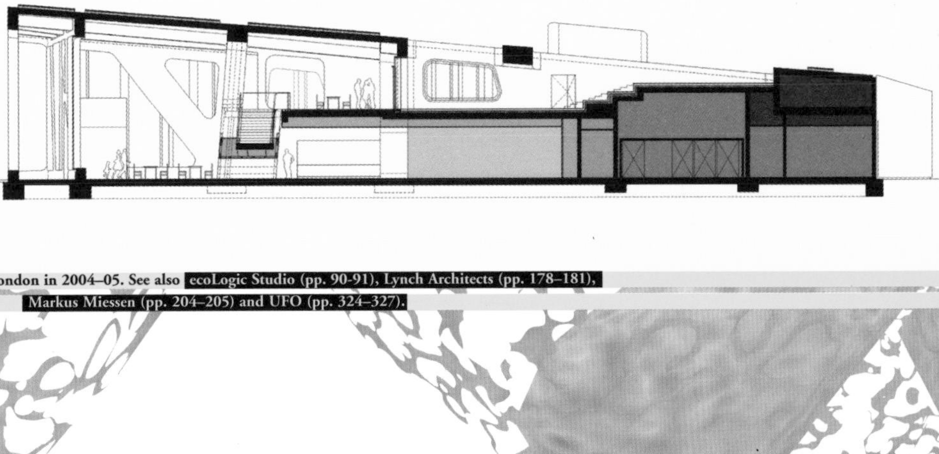

M

Jürgen Mayer H taught at the Architectural Association in London in 2004–05. See also ecoLogic Studio (pp. 90-91), Lynch Architects (pp. 178–181), Markus Miessen (pp. 204–205) and UFO (pp. 324–327).

# Fiona Meadows

Fiona Meadows, architect and curator at the Cité de l'architecture et du patrimoine/Institut Français d'Architecture, takes as the subject of her work the small-scale, using the power of the 1:1 example to make architecture speak across age groups and communities. Here she asks: why small architecture?

From the primal hut made of twigs, leaves and branches to the Japanese pavilion made with perfection, from the suburban, handmade garden shelter to the high-tech capsule of a spaceship, from the simplicity of an igloo to the camping tent, the small scale has been developed in a multitude of ways and its objects compete in invention and poetry.

Small architecture is not just a place of architectural imagination, more free from restrictions than the complex and large scale. It can represent a radical alternative to the standardization of everyday life, to the arbitrariness of the norm. Because of the constraints that the 'small' must satisfy or is fixed by, it

Right: Image from *Small Architecture in Cameroon*, where students travel to Africa to construct buildings using locals' skills and techniques.

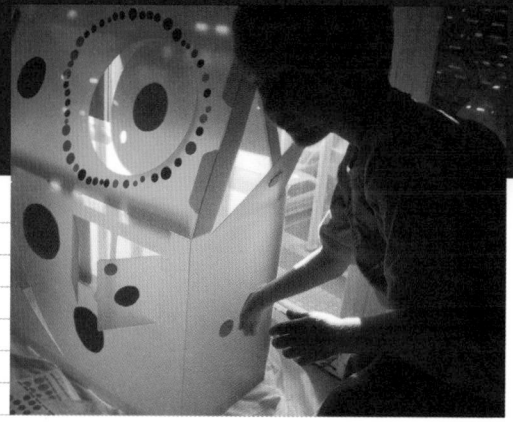

Right: The project *La maison de mon doudou* invites children to work with sculptor François Seigneur.

| Location | Paris, France |
| --- | --- |
| Nationality | French |

Fiona Meadows is an architect and curator and director of the Salon d'Actualité de l'Institut Français d'Architecture since 1999. She grew up in London and Paris, and studied in Paris and Japan before undertaking a PhD at the School of Architecture Paris-La Villette under Jean-Louis Cohen. As an architect, she has collaborated with Frédéric Nantois on a number of successful competition entries, including a second prize in Europan 4 in The Hague. The two have also curated and participated in many exhibitions, including in the French pavilion at the Venice Biennale and at the Architecture Foundation in London.

corresponds often to another economic model, calling for examplars of unskilled construction methods, reuse of materials and the transfer of technologies.

Small architecture develops the kind of creativity nourished, not by established culture, but by contact with a diversity of ways of life, social situations, geographies and human contexts.

The aim of the 'small architecture' program developed at the Institut Français d'Architecture since 1999 is precisely to approach that particular moment that is the 'act of building', collaborating with anyone from qualified architects and students to children and villagers in Africa, Lebanon ... Beyond the evident satisfaction of finalizing a personal project, these experiences are a moment of shared happiness, of building ourselves, together.

Concerning architectural exhibitions, the small, 1:1 scale is also the opportunity for our visitors to experiment physically in an experimental built environment. Our architects are given a project room to try out new ideas at a large scale and not just show small models, drawings or films. For example, the 'lounge' program invites young architects to build an experimental project in the Cité de l'architecture on a human scale, which visitors can live in and come to understand the ideas of the guest architect. The *Mini Maousse* competition is open to French students in architecture, art, landscape, design or engineering schools and offers the five winners the possibility of building a real prototype. The project *La maison de mon doudou* gives children with cancer or AIDS the chance to build a small house at the size of their teddy bear, designed by architect and sculptor François Seigneur in the hospital room. In the *Small Architecture in Cameroon* project, young architects travel to Africa and build a small building (a classroom, a women's social room) with the local villagers using their know-how, their materials, their tools, and bring a little modern comfort with soft technology, solar power that can bring light to the village, energy to the radios or mobile phones. This experience tries to question how to allow progress and economic development without putting the local social equilibrium in peril. How should wealth be redistributed? How should we build a better environment in the Northern and Southern hemispheres? How can we learn from the South?

# Metrogramma

Metrogramma's work is in equal parts a continuation of the thinking of Italian legends like Archizoom and Superstudio, with an added visual touch that makes the majority of its proposals look like something out of *Blade Runner*.

    The megastructures perhaps have something to do with the impressive scale of the Milan-based practice's competition entries, including its project for the new *Lombardy District Offices*, which earned them a third prize in 2004. The building is conceived at the scale of a landmark, or 'sign', as Metrogramma puts it. It aims at, the architects write, 'the definition of a contemporary monument for Milan and Lombardia, of an unedited sign, and of a space generated by the city, which should be both a civic square and a work place, a territorial sign and an urban infrastructure.'

    Three towers create the effect on the skyline, and form generous public spaces at ground level. At the top level is a panoramic terrace. The geometry of

This spread: Proposal for the *Lombardy District Offices* in Milan, for which Metrogramma received a third prize in 2004.

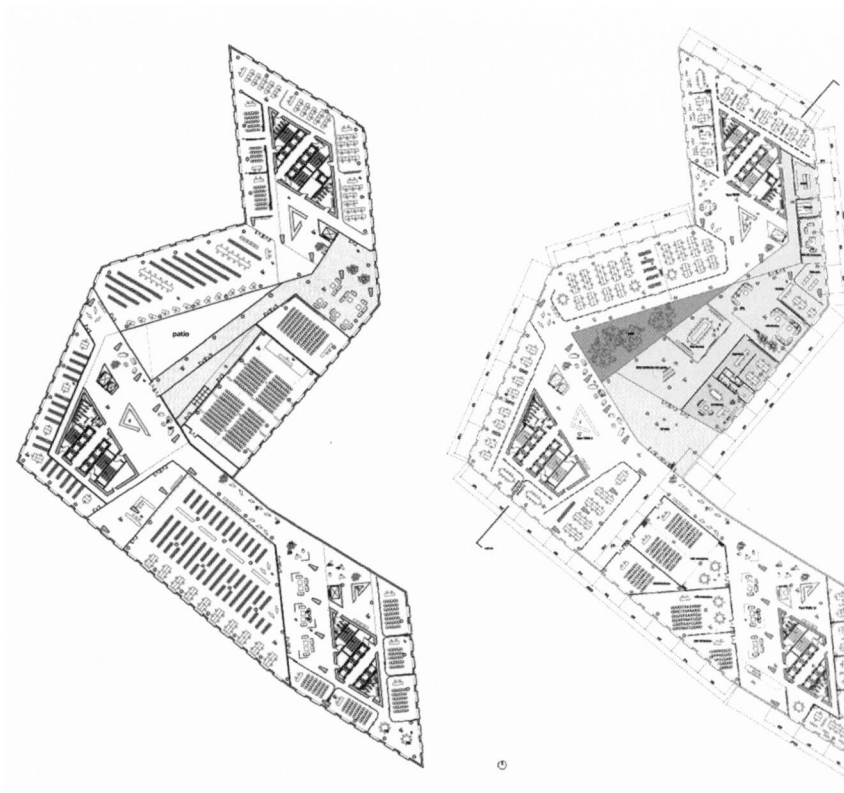

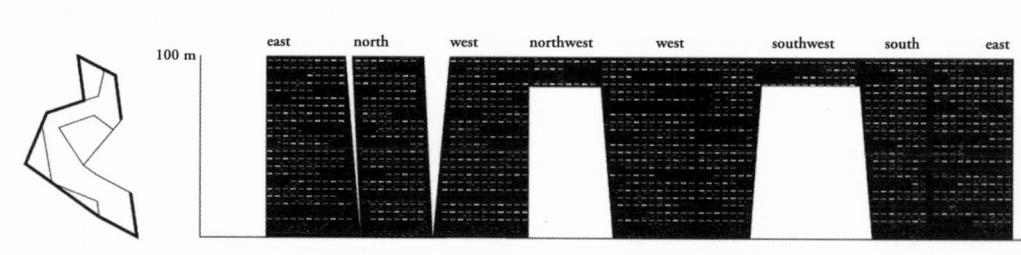

| Location | Milan, Italy |
| --- | --- |
| Nationality | Italian |

Metrogramma is a firm much touted as part of a new wave of Italian architecture, following a barren period for the country's production of quality buildings. Founded by Andrea Boschetti and Alberto Francini in Milan in 1997, Metrogramma pursues a variety of themes concerning the contemporary city. Despite success in several international competitions, the practice is prominent closer to home as a consultant to the city of Bolzano, carrying out several studies and publishing two books. This research received several awards, among them the Gold Medal of Italian Architecture and the Guinigi Award, City of Lucca. In 2002, Metrogramma was nominated for the Mies van der Rohe Prize.

the public spaces responds to the context, but also creates a public park with jewel-like interventions including an auditorium and public hall.

Another competition entry, this time for a new office and factory for Ferrari, contrasts with this strident tower, but is no less of a landmark. This project, emphatically horizontal, creates a floating roof that creates a huge new 'covered square' between several historic buildings around the site. This thick roof is inhabited with new offices.

The other projects we show here are two from Metrogramma's work in Bolzano, Italy: a proposal for a long linear block and a tower that are emblems of the three principles for the town's future – concentrated, linear and diffused development.

Finally, the practice's visionary *Level 17* project proposed a new infrastructure for London, making use of empty parts of the city, creating platforms 17 storeys in the air above the Thames.

Left and below: Images from Metrogramma's work in Bolzano, Italy, entitled *Superinfrastructure.* Bottom: *Level 17* proposal for London, offering a new public space at high level. Opposite: Competition entry for a new office and factory for Ferrari in Maranello, Italy.

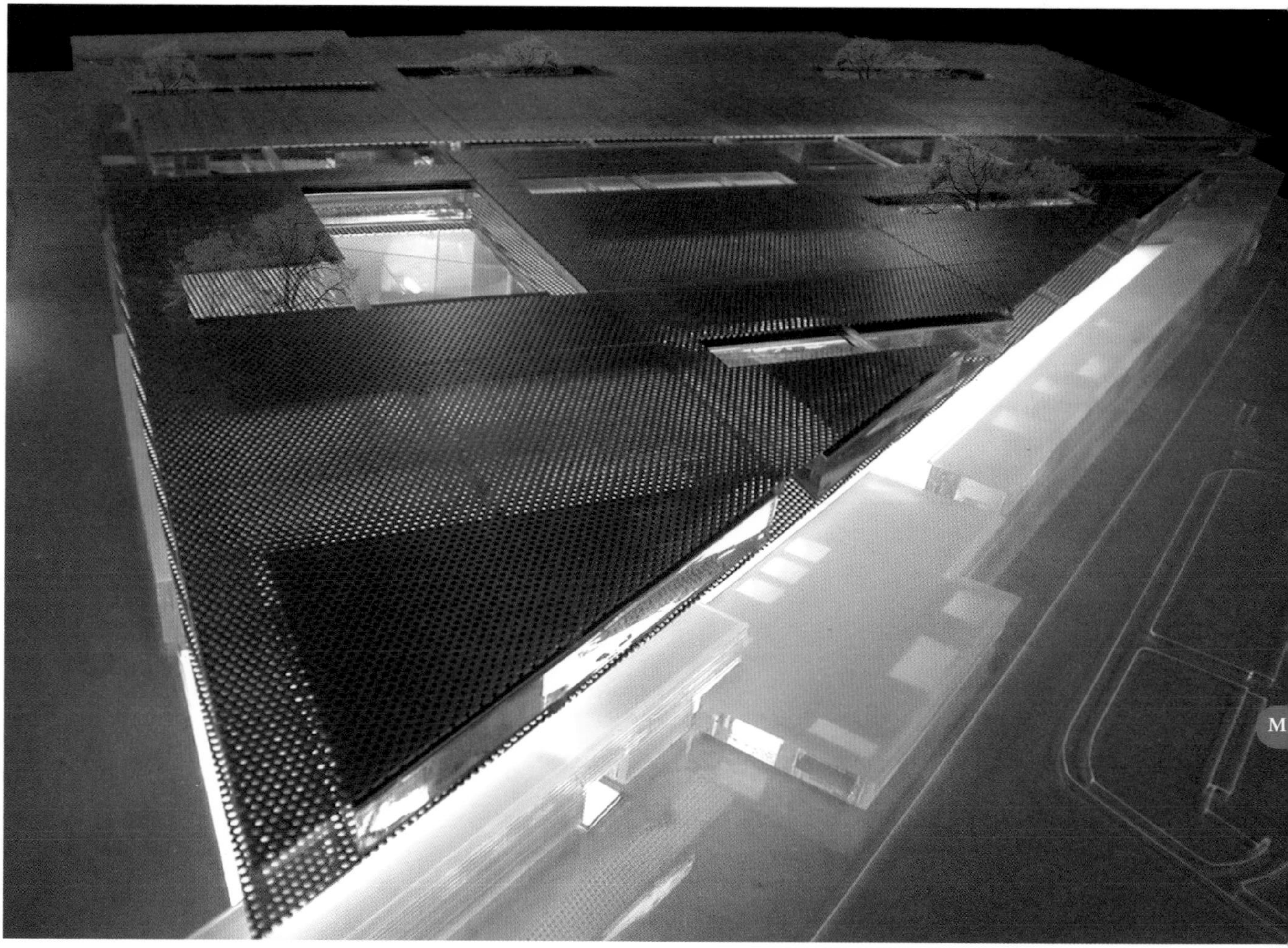

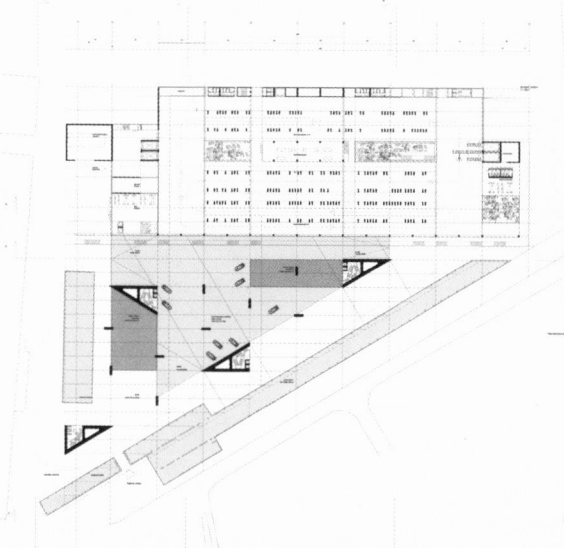

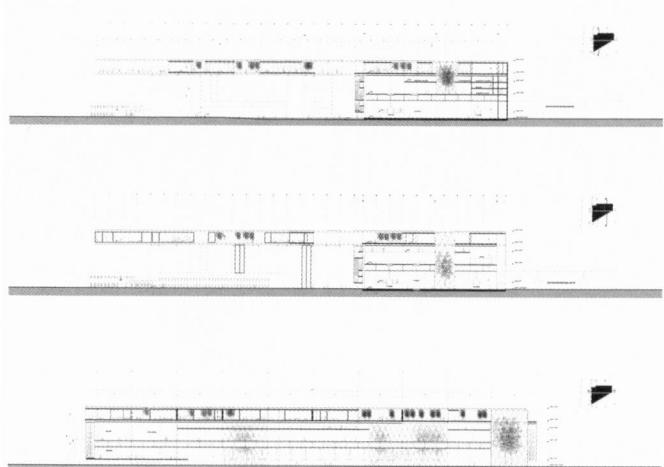

Miessen's work proposes that architectural practice should promote conflict rather than consensus as a means of critically engaging with the city. This extract is from his essay *The Violence of Participation*.

When humans assemble, spatial conflicts arise. Spatial planning is often considered as the management of spatial conflicts. To deal with conflicts, critical decision-making must evolve. The city – and, indeed, the progressive institution – exist as social and spatial conflict zones, renegotiating their limits through constant transformation.

Today, there is an ever-increasing need to consider the breaking of the consensus machine. Taking this notion as a possible starting point, my research attempts to understand and illustrate the importance of critical engagement in alien fields of knowledge – based on spatial conditions as a means of a cultural investigation. It aims to enquire into both the role of the architect and the role of the contemporary institution.

This text presents and discusses today's need for actors operating from outside existing networks, leaving behind conventional boundaries of expertise and overlapping with other fields of knowledge. An alternative model of participation within spatial practice will be proposed, one that begins with an understanding of participation beyond models of consensus. The future spatial practitioner could be understood as an outsider who, instead of trying to set up or sustain consensus, enters existing situations or projects by deliberately instigating conflicts as a form of critical engagement with the environment that he or she operates in. Using the architect's expertise of mapping fields of conflict, the research tries to uncover the relevance of architectural expertise and how, within the remit of institutions, they can facilitate an alternative knowledge production. It seems that today we are in urgent need of a re-evaluation of spatial production beyond traditional definitions, acknowledging the possibility of an 'architecture of knowledge'.

## Participation and Conflict

Participation is war. Any form of participation is already a form of conflict. In war, enemy and adversary usually hold territory, which they can gain or lose, while each has a spokesman or authority that can govern, submit or collapse. In order to participate in any environment or given situation, one needs to understand the forces of conflict that act upon that environment. Participation is often understood as a means of becoming part of something through proactive contribution and the occupation of a particular role. However, it seems that this role is rarely understood as a critical platform of engagement, but rather based on romantic conceptions of harmony and

| Location | London, UK |
|---|---|
| Nationality | German |

Markus Miessen was born in 1978 in Bonn, Germany. He was educated at the Architectural Association in London and is currently studying for a PhD at Goldsmiths College in London. His office, Studio Miessen, is involved in research, criticism, writing, teaching and design. He is the author of many articles and the books *Spaces of Uncertainty* (w. Cupers, Müller+Busmann, 2002), and *Did Someone Say Participate?* (MIT Press/Revolver, 2006, w. Basar).

solidarity. In this context, I would like to promote an understanding of conflictual participation, one that acts as an uninvited irritant.

## Undoing the Innocence of Participation

From the beginning of the TV series *Sex and the City*, Charlotte York is portrayed as the most innocent of the four protagonists. Throughout the series, she is the only one who follows 'dating rules' and expresses a serious desire to marry and have children. In episode 55, Charlotte decides to quit her job as a curator in a Manhattan art gallery. When she reveals her intentions to her disapproving friends, she explains why she wants to stay home. In order to not feel 'bad' about her real motives (wanting to be pregnant and redecorating the house), she justifies her decision by stating that she wants to 'volunteer at Trey's hospital and raise money for the paediatric wing'. In Charlotte's case, volunteering for a social cause is portrayed as what prevents her from being judged for quitting her job.

Isn't this kind of practice precisely the modus operandi that we can find in so many 'socially relevant' practices today? There is an interesting similarity between Charlotte and the way in which some practices have hijacked the notion of participation as a positive, unquestionable means of engagement (while it benefits them economically). But the question is: how is it possible to 'participate' in a given environment or situation without having to compromise one's role as an active agent that is not interested in consensus and 'doing good'?

In architecture, there are frequent examples where critical engagement conflicts with the realities of business interests. In 2006, London-based architect Richard Rogers was summoned to New York by the Empire State Development Corporation (which is overseeing the redesign of New York's $1.7 billion Jacob K. Javits Convention Center that Rogers is designing) to explain Rogers' decision to allow his office to be used by a group of architects connected to Architects and Planners for Justice in Palestine. As a result, several New York officials urged that Rogers be removed from the publicly funded project. This case illustrates how architects are often used by the powerful, but from the perspective of the power structure itself, the architect is not welcome as a participating vector in this force field. He or she is rather understood as a service-provider who delivers a product. As Rem Koolhaas argued in a conversation recently: 'I would say that particularly in America political obliviousness is considered part of the role of the architect.' It is this chasm that I attempt to tackle.

# Modulorbeat

Modulorbeat's work is at the fascinating edge of architecture, curation and party organizing that seems to find so much currency in contemporary Germany. The two projects here are fascinating architectural propositions, but also allowed people to have a decent party.

'Berlin's coolest new club,' as *Newsweek* called it, was designed by Modulorbeat in 2006. *Kubik* was an outdoor club created out of translucent industrial containers separated by steel palettes. These were lit from within with ghostly green light, which pulsed in time to music. The project is one of the defining projects of the new Berlin, occupying vacant land near the Spree River: cheap, semi-legal and innovative. The combination of ready-made elements and sophisticated computer technology takes the potential of this medium into new territory.

On a larger scale was Modulorbeat's *Halle 3b* project in 2004, part of an art festival in the docklands of Muenster. This was a temporary spatial installation in the former Osmo-Hallen, a large industrial shed. In the centre of the hall were created concrete elements, covered in grey felt. A temporary ceiling was hung with 1,000sq m (10,760sq ft) of fabric to create a marquee-like atmosphere. Video projections and sound installations further enhanced the atmosphere. An enlarged thrust stage became a platform for a variety of parties, events, concerts and theatrical performances, and *Halle 3b* became one of the highlights of an otherwise rain-affected festival.

This page: *Halle 3b* installation in Muenster, 2004. Opposite: *Kubik* nightclub, Berlin, 2006.

| Location | Muenster, Germany |
|---|---|
| Nationality | German |

Modulorbeat was founded by two partners, Marc Guennewig and Jan Kampshoff, in Muenster, Germany. Both partners studied in Muenster, and both are now teachers, Guennewig in Berlin and Kampshoff in Muenster. Modulorbeat also has a broad network of collaborators from an interdisciplinary background. The two partners work on a very broad range of projects, but the work is characterized by an engagement with design as event. They have worked on exhibition design (*Switch+* in Muenster), polemical interactive installations (*SFX: PUBLICZNOSC* in the Westfälischer Kunstverein), furniture, and even the setting for a banquet. Modulorbeat's work has been exhibited at the Schweizerischen Architekturmuseum in Basel, Mediengallerie MediaRuimte in Brussels and the Deutsches Architektur Zentrum in Frankfurt.

M

The partners of Modulorbeat were part of the organizing committee for the Freihaus (www.freihaus.ms) project in Muenster. As part of this, they invited feld72 (pp. 114–115), Raumlabor (pp. 264–265) and Realities United (pp. 268–269) to contribute.

# N55

N55's work has the look of being profoundly influenced by the future-gazing of figures like Archigram and Buckminster Fuller, but adds a social and environmental twist that roots it firmly in the twenty-first century.

N55's first significant project was the *Spaceframe* living module in 1999, conceived as a super-lightweight, low-cost and demountable structure that can be placed in any context – even, with the help of the accompanying *Floating Platform* raft, on water.

The project takes its name from its structure – a spaceframe made of small components that are arranged into a truncated tetrahedron with an indoor floor space of 20sq m (215sq ft). Internal floors or other extra modules can be easily added to this flexible infrastructure. The spaceframe is rarely used at a small scale, says N55: 'The building system is configured in what is known as the common space lattice, the octet truss, or the octahedron–tetrahedron complex. The geometry of this space lattice does not depend on gravity for strength or integrity, and therefore is suitable for employment in satellites and space platforms, and in big halls, etc. But it is rarely employed for housing and other small-scale purposes.' All the members in the octet truss (a configuration that was copyrighted by Buckminster Fuller in the 1940s) are of equal length, enabling efficient production. The frame can be assembled by hand with just a screwdriver.

This page: *Small Truck* project, a self-powered vehicle that can carry 'loads of about 300kg [660lb] at slow speeds'. The project was carried out by N55 in collaboration with artist Pelle Brage. The project proposes different modules that could be added to the truck, including the possibility of carrying hens, plants, or even integrating a tiny kitchen.

| Location | Copenhagen, Denmark |
| --- | --- |
| Nationality | Danish |

N55 was established in Copenhagen by Ion Sørvin and Ingvil H. Aarbakke, who both studied at the Royal Danish Academy of Fine Arts between 1991 and 1998. Aarbakke sadly died in 2005, and N55 continues under Sørvin's stewardship. The practice, which is non-commercial and is funded through grants, is fascinated by small-scale solutions to problems, and particularly in creating small, mobile living units called *Micro Dwellings*. The first significant creations were *Floating Platform* and *N55 Spaceframe*, both in Copenhagen in 2000. N55 has exhibited its work in exhibitions across the world, including at the Venice Biennale and the *Talking Cities* exhibition in Essen in 2006.

This page: Various uses of the *Snail Shell System* living unit. The unit is a polyethylene tank, with rubber tracks that help it to roll.

N

The structure can be stabilized by filling plastic canisters with water or sand as a foundation. Insulation can be inserted into the spaceframe cavity, and cladding is steel and polycarbonate.

A later, less elaborate, statement of N55's interests is the *Snail Shell System*, a cylindrical polyethylene tank that can be paddled on water, or rolled down the street by just one person. The tiny living module incorporates cooking equipment as well as a bilge pump, points to ensure secure moorings on water and a mattress that doubles as insulation. 'On water it can be rowed, moved by a kite or hooked up to a vessel,' writes N55, 'for example, a ferry. The unit rests on one flat side and can be anchored in lakes, rivers, harbours or at sea. On land, it can be placed in city spaces, fields, forests, etc. The system takes up very little space and can easily be placed in a discreet way. It can be buried in the ground, exposing only the entrance. It can also function as a comfortable space inside existing buildings.'

N

# nArchitects

Two related and temporary projects serve to demonstrate the breadth of nArchitects' work. The first was their winning and built entry for the annual PS1/MOMA Young Architects Program award in 2004.

Entitled *Canopy*, the structure was a temporary bamboo structure built in the courtyard of the PS1 Gallery. The bamboo lattice was a simple way of providing different territories in the courtyard, and the roof dipped and distorted to form zones of inhabitation. These outdoor rooms all had a different character. One incorporated a wading pool, another created a fine mist, and others were made of sand or gravel. The canopy created different shading effects according to the density of the bamboo members and their orientation according to the sun.

One of the most romantic of the PS1 Young Architects series, *Canopy*'s charm lay in the choice of material: 9,390m (30,800ft) of freshly cut green *Phyllostachys aurea* bamboo was spliced and bound together with 11,280m (37,000 ft) of stainless-steel wire. The initial order of 1,100 bamboo poles was chopped, cleaned and shipped from Georgia in one week, so that it arrived as fresh as possible upon delivery. Once on site, the poles were stored in racks, covered with ultraviolet-resistant tarpaulin and watered twice a day to keep them green and flexible. The construction was carried out by nArchitects and a team of dedicated students. As the installation aged, the bamboo transformed from its initial green and flexible state to a more rigid and browner form.

The second project here is called *Windshape*, and was a 2006 commission from the Savannah College of Art and Design (SCAD) for a temporary meeting space at the top of a castle at its campus in Provence, France. Built in five weeks by nArchitects and SCAD students, the project consisted of two inhabitable pavilions, made of 50km (31 miles) of polypropylene string held together by a vine-like lattice of structural pipes. The installation's name came from its reaction to the mistral which blows in this region. The harder the wind, the more dramatic the deflections in the form of the string, and the louder the hissing noise as the air passed through the lattice. The castle formed an appropriately mysterious background for these ghostly phenomena.

This page: *Windshape*, an installation at the top of a castle in Provence, France, 2006.

| Location | New York, USA |
| --- | --- |
| Nationality | Vietnamese Canadian |

nArchitects was founded in New York by partners Eric Bunge and Mimi Hoang in 1999. Bunge (from Canada) and Hoang (from Vietnam) met at Harvard University, where they both gained Masters degrees. Although we are showing two temporary projects here, they are building on a more permanent scale, including a recently completed apartment building on the Lower East Side of Manhattan. Awards include an American Institute of Architects Design Honor Award (2005); the Canadian Professional Rome Prize (2005); *Architectural Record*'s Design Vanguard (2004); and their victory in the PS1/MOMA Young Architects Program (2004).

N

This page: *Canopy*, nArchitects' installation at the PS1 Gallery in New York, 2004.

nArchitects appeared at the Mixed Media festival of electronic culture in 2006 in Milan, Italy, alongside Lot-ek (pp. 176–177) and Metrogramma (pp. 200–203) as well as a host of more established names.

# Next Architects

Next Architects' bridge over the Glanerbeek in Enschede in the southeast of the Netherlands was the winner of an invited competition run by the municipality of Enschede.

This highly unusual bridge creates a pedestrian route, cycle route and road crossing over a small brook. The simple design strategy was to make a thin surface that is opened up between the pedestrian, cycle and road routes, creating beautiful teardrop openings in the white surface, revealing the brook below. On the surfaces are fences that also integrate seating for pedestrians near trees that grow near and through the voids in the bridge's surface.

Perhaps more remarkable, though, are the piers that support the surface. These piles are made from steel cages containing stones in a gabion-like form. This anti-technological bridge is an idiosyncratic response and is quite unique.

This spread: Pictures of Next's bridge in Enschede, the Netherlands, under construction.

| Location | Amsterdam, The Netherlands |
| --- | --- |
| Nationality | Dutch |

Next Architects is based in Amsterdam, and was founded by John van de Water, Marijn Schenk, Bart Reuser and Michel Schreinemachers in 1999. All four partners studied at Delft, with stints at the offices of Herman Hertzberger, MVRDV, West 8 and NL Architects between them. The partners are prolific teachers, in the Netherlands and abroad. Next was awarded a first prize at Archiprix in 2000 and has won several competitions, including one for a *Water Theatre* in 2005, and the Tour de Belvedere in Leeuwarden in 2003. In 1999, Next Architects set off on a voyage around the world – 26 cities in 125 days – and the resulting images were collected for a publication and an exhibition.

N

This spread: This villa in Almere Overgooi in the Netherlands was the result of five families wanting to make a building as a collective. Five individual houses were created, and then slotted together like Tetris blocks, creating a unified building with shared terraces. The diagrams demonstrate how the five houses were efficiently slotted together.

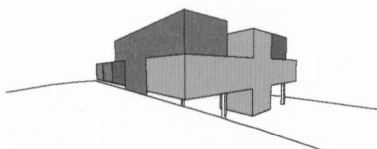

DOEL: accentuering individuele woningen.

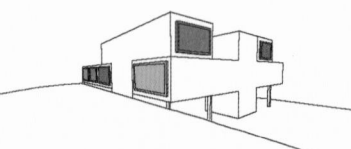

MIDDEL: accentuering kopgevels door middel van opliggende kozijnen.

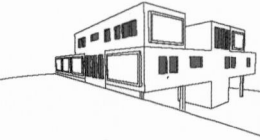

MIDDEL: terugleggen van de raamopgen in de zijgevels.

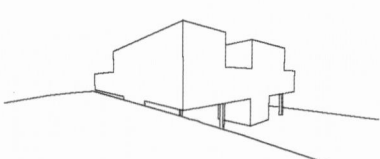

DOEL: uitstraling van één 'villavervangend' gebouw.

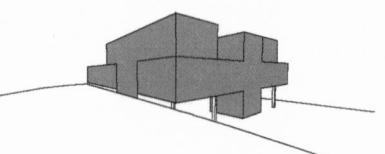

MIDDEL: toepassen van één materiaal voor het gehele gebouw.

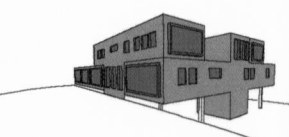

RESULTAAT: één krachtig gebouw w de individuele woning nog leesbaar is

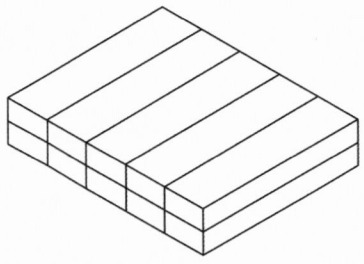

**STAP 1.**
**COMPACT BOUWVOLUME**

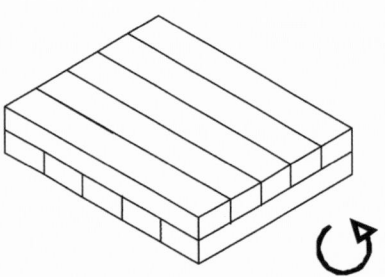

**STAP 2.**
**ORIËNTATIE**

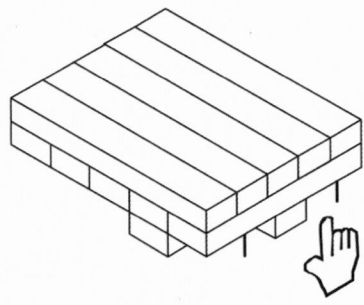

**STAP 3.**
**UITZICHT**

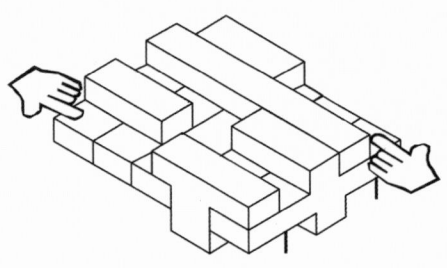

**STAP 4.**
**INDIVIDUELE WENSEN**

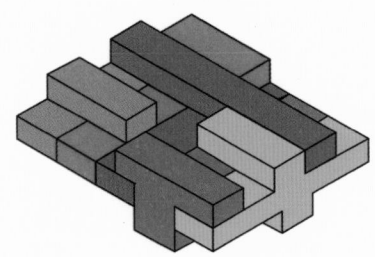

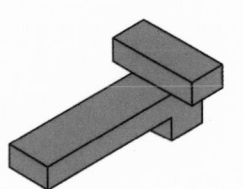
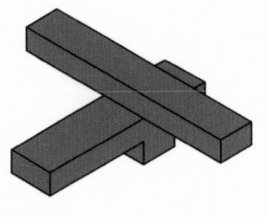
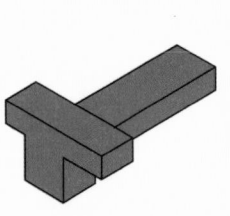
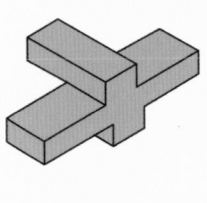

# Next Enterprise Architects

Next Enterprise has been around a little longer than many practices in this book, and was responsible for one of the most delightful projects I have written about in my career as a critic. The *Lakeside* *Bath* at Kaltern is a project that revels in its resort location, giving a sense of spectacle and mystery to the garish world of lakeside tourism in the north of Italy.

The swimming pool was conceived to take up as little space as possible at ground level, so as not to obstruct views from the promenade to the lake. To achieve this, the architect created an elevated sundeck that is joined to the ground at the higher level of the promenade. On this deck are two pools, and two pavilions, one with

Next Enterprise's swimming pool is in Kaltern, Italy, also known as Caldaro and home of feld72's (pp. 114–115) *Wine Centre*.

entrance and ticketing facilities, and another with a café within. In the pools are beautiful, abstract concrete forms that refer to the ruined forts on the dramatic south Tyrolean hills surrounding Kaltern.

A grand staircase/grandstand leads down to the lakeside, and to the world underneath the deck, which has changing rooms, and also a series of

This spread:
The sundeck of Next Enterprise's *Lakeside Bath* in Kaltern, northern Italy.

| Location | Vienna, Austria |
|---|---|
| Nationality | Austrian |

Next Enterprise Architects was founded in 2000 in Vienna by Ernst Fuchs and Marie-Therese Harnoncourt. It grew out of an earlier collaboration, The Poor Boys Enterprise, which ran between 1994 and 2000. Both partners studied at the University of Applied Arts in Vienna. They have won awards including the City of Vienna Award for the Advancement of Architecture in 2003, and the Lower Austria Award for Cultural Achievements in Architecture in 2000. Projects range from experimental interventions such as *Stadtwind* in 2000 and installations such as the *Audiolounge* in 2002, to building commissions like *Haus Zirl* in 1997, and the *Lakeside Bath* in Kaltern, Italy, in 2002.

N

Also commissioned as part of the *Trespassing* exhibition at the Vienna Secession in 2002 was FAT (pp. 110–113).

Above: One of the rooms
contained in the concrete
columns of the swimming
pool. They are lit from
above by skylights.
Right: A view of the
undercroft of the pool
by night.
Below: The swimming
pool, with the café in
the background.

strange and beautiful faceted rooms within the concrete structure. These rooms contain jacuzzis and showers, and are lit from a skylight far above the visitor's head. This area beneath also provides a shady area for children to play in. The faceted concrete of this shady world is spectacular, and the contrasting worlds of the sundeck and the undercroft make this place a special experience.

The second project here shows the range of Next Enterprise's work. What they describe as an 'audio object', the *Olienlöcher* was a means of communicating ten audio interviews without having to resort to headphones. Holes milled in a circular whole encouraged visitors to put their heads inside the object, altering their postures to ensure their attention. The project was made especially for the Secession Gallery in Vienna in 2002 as part of the *Trespassing* exhibition.

This page:
The *Olienlöcher*
'audio object'.
Top: *Olienlöcher* in situ
in the Secession Gallery
in Vienna, 2002.

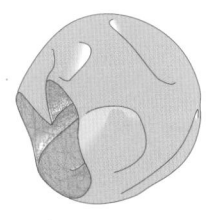
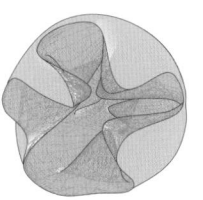

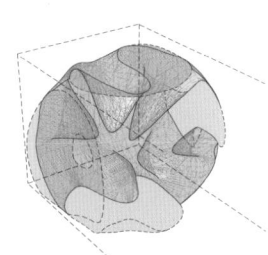
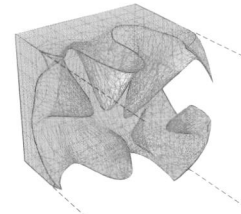
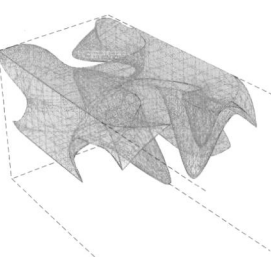

Next Enterprise was involved in MeEtArch, a day conference in Mendrisio, Italy, in 2006 that discussed the new role of the architectural professional. So were Metrogramma (pp. 200–203), Périphériques (pp. 244–245), R&Sie (pp. 258–261), Philippe Rahm (pp. 262–263) and Stalker (pp. 292–295).

# Nio Architecten

Nio's work has taken in those classic projects of the successful young Dutch architect – neat blocks of housing in new development areas. But the work of this practice has something poetic, sinister even, that seems to derive from Maurice Nio's whimsical writings and the translation of that sensibility into built form.

One such project is a cosmetic makeover of an underpass on the VINEX redevelopment site in Tolhek, Pijnacker, the Netherlands, completed in 2004, entitled *Touch of Evil* (in reference to the Orson Welles movie). On the walls and ceiling of the underpass, Nio created a wallcovering in bright red, in an other-worldly and haunting shape. Maurice Nio's own words describe the aspiration to make it look 'as if during the building an unearthly thing got stuck between the formwork. As if the soul of the former landscape, being rooted up by bulldozers, has gone underground. As if the winding pattern of old polder roads, which has made place for rigid urban developments, takes revenge in the tunnel.' This attitude to the disturbed landscape of the VINEX projects, more typically treated as blank canvases by the architects who work there, is like a hysterical outpouring of the previous character of the place. It is, says the architect, 'a tunnel that you will never understand, even though you have been driving through it every day all your life.'

Nio's best-known project, which is christened the *Amazing Whale Jaw*, is

This spread: Bus station in Hoofddorp, the Netherlands, also known as the *Amazing Whale Jaw*. The building is the largest polystyrene foam and polyester object in the world.

| Location | Rotterdam, The Netherlands |
| --- | --- |
| Nationality | Dutch |

Nio Architecten was founded in 2000 by Maurice Nio in Rotterdam, the Netherlands. Nio made his name early with a mercurial graduation project at Delft University for a villa for Michael Jackson. He runs the practice with Joan Almekinders, a partner since 2004. Nio has completed projects at a variety of scales, including 33 houses in Schiedam, completed in 2005, and the much-published bus station at Hoofddorp. Maurice Nio writes that he is currently working on 'the most beautiful shopping centre in the world and the most obscure houseboat in the Netherlands'. He is also a prolific writer, and has published two books: *You Have the Right to Remain Silent* (1998) and *Unseen I Slipped Away* (2004).

N

This spread: *Touch of Evil*, a red wall of an underpass in Pijnacker, the Netherlands.

its bus station outside a hospital in Hoofddorp, the Netherlands, completed in 2003. An expressive shape ('a cross between white modernism and black baroque'), it is made entirely from polystyrene foam and polyester. The architect claims that it is, at 50m (164ft) long, the world's largest structure in synthetic materials. The form is intended to reference a boulder worn away by sight lines or the need for pedestrian access, but Nio also claims it as the result of a very unconventional construction process. Maurice Nio writes: 'It can also be explained as a product of this process, which in this case was somewhat intuitive because of the unfamiliar technical terrain in which everyone had to operate.'

# NL Architects

NL Architects' work has long been inventive with building typologies. Their earliest widely published work was a mysterious, black rubber-clad heat-transfer station that incorporated a climbing wall on one side. And although NL's work also includes much more traditional buildings, the two projects we show here are the best examples of the Amsterdam-based practice's propensity to experiment with type.

The first, their so-called *BasketBar* at the University of Utrecht, mixes a 'grand café', an updated version of a type very common in Dutch cities, with a rooftop basketball court. The project is part of an urban plan by Rem Koolhaas' OMA, which proposes more on-campus housing and intensifies the modernist campus. The café was a key part of giving a nightlife to the place, providing somewhere to meet.

The café is an extension to the ground floor of an existing 21-storey adjacent block. As the ceiling height of that building was not generous, NL excavated the floor to make the required

This spread: Views of *BasketBar* at the University of Utrecht, the Netherlands.

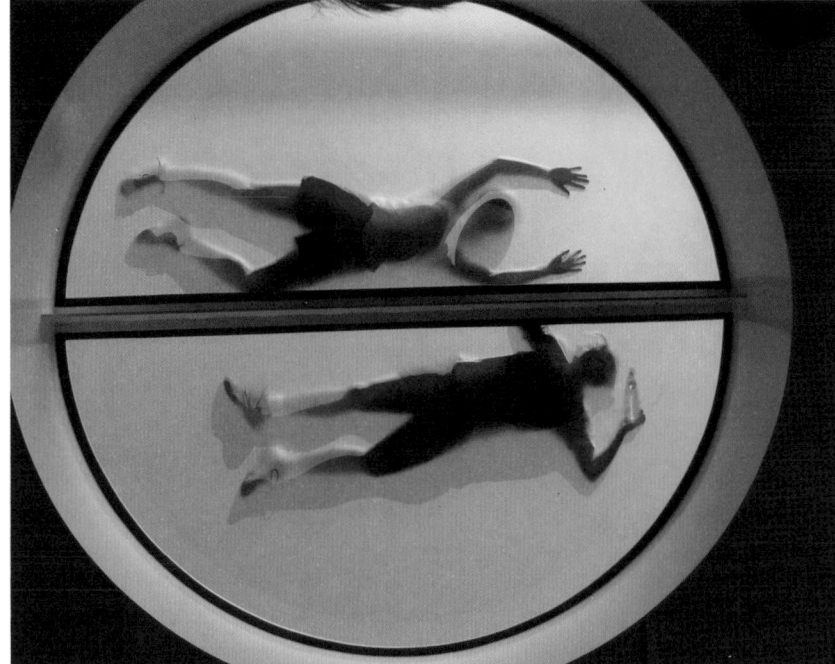

NL Architects has published a small volume of its work with iconic Dutch book publisher Uitgeverij 010, as has Nio Architecten (pp 222–225).

| Location | Amsterdam, The Netherlands |
| --- | --- |
| Nationality | Dutch |

NL Architects was established in Amsterdam by Pieter Bannenberg, Walter van Dijk, Kamiel Klaasse and Mark Linnemann in 1997, but the four had shared workspace together since the early 1990s. Linnemann has since left the partnership. Major projects include *WOS 8* (a rubber-clad heat-transfer station in Utrecht), the *Mandarina Duck Store* in Paris (for/with Droog Design) and the Dutch entry for the Venice Architecture Biennale in 2000 (*NL Lounge*). In 2005, NL won the Emerging Architect Award and the Mies van der Rohe Prize for *BasketBar*, a café with a basketball court on the roof at the university campus of Utrecht. A small book of NL's work, called *NL 98 99 00*, has been published by 010.

N

grand proportion. Thus, the top surface became the perfect height for a basketball court where players could show off their talents. The two uses are linked through skylights, which give coffee-drinkers occasional views of the players above. Outside, a small amphitheatre provides seating and disabled access.

The second project shown here is NL's conversion of an inauspicious undercroft of an elevated road into a skatepark. Called *A8* and located in Zaandam, the Netherlands, the project rethinks the concrete space into a place of urban recreation, using unexpected materials (timber) in such a context.

NL Architects have also created product design (colourful rubber straps that fix to the wall for storage) for Dutch design scions Droog, as have Concrete (pp. 70–71) and Next Enterprise Architects (pp. 218–221).

This spread: The *A8* project, a skatepark underneath a motorway in Zaandam, the Netherlands.

# Obra Architects

Main picture: Obra's
project in the courtyard
of the PS1 Gallery in
New York was a series of
intersecting shells. Pools
of water and steam vents
create a series of micro-
climates themed around
the pools of a Roman
bath house.

Another notable Argentinian architect in this book is Marcelo Spina of Patterns (pp. 242–243).

Gnuform (pp. 128–129) was one of the other practices shortlisted for the PS1/MOMA Young Architects Program in 2006.

Previous winners include Emergent (pp. 94–97), nArchitects (pp. 212–213), SHoP (pp. 286–289) and Xefirotarch (pp. 340–343).

Obra's architecture is somewhat unique among the emerging generation in North America, using an approach influenced by phenomenological philosophy, literature and visual art.

In a lecture in 2004, partner Pablo Castro even went so far as to propose a kind of manifesto for what he calls Architettura Povera, an architectural parody of Arte Povera, the Italian artistic movement of the 1970s. The first of the eight principles is 'We are doomed from the start', going on to quote playwright Samuel Beckett ('To be an artist is to fail, as no other dares to fail'). Despite the Eeyore-like depression of the beginning, Castro goes on to describe how important it is for architecture to use forms that are new but familiar to us, rejecting the idiosyncratic or obscure in favour of a consistency of approach.

| Location | New York, USA |
| --- | --- |
| Nationality | Argentinian American |

Pablo Castro and Jennifer Lee formed Obra Architects in 2000. Castro studied first in San Juan in Argentina, but both partners had Ivy League postgraduate careers. Castro is now a visiting professor at Rhode Island, and Lee at Cooper Union. In 2005, Obra was named as one of the Architectural League of New York's Emerging Voices, and the practice won the PS1/MOMA Young Architects Program competition in 2006.

Level +4.0

Level +0.0

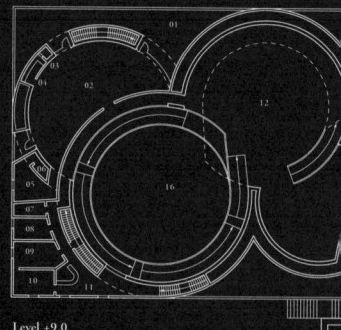

Level +9.0

Castro says: 'We aspire to extend the intentions of our work from project to project, constantly looking for the possibility to address the same problems.... It is precisely because we always try to do the same thing that projects are very different from each other.'

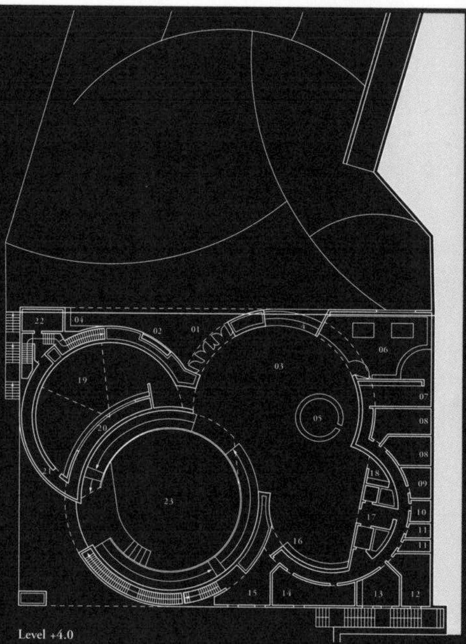

Obra's most significant and high-profile project yet was a temporary installation in the courtyard of the PS1 Gallery in New York in 2006. Every year, PS1 commissions a young architect to make a summer pavilion and the results had become more and more formally hyperactive. Instead of seeing the competition as an opportunity to demonstrate a formal range, Obra made a place for a party. The project is a set of intersecting bubbles, supported by timber arches that span up to 30m (98ft).

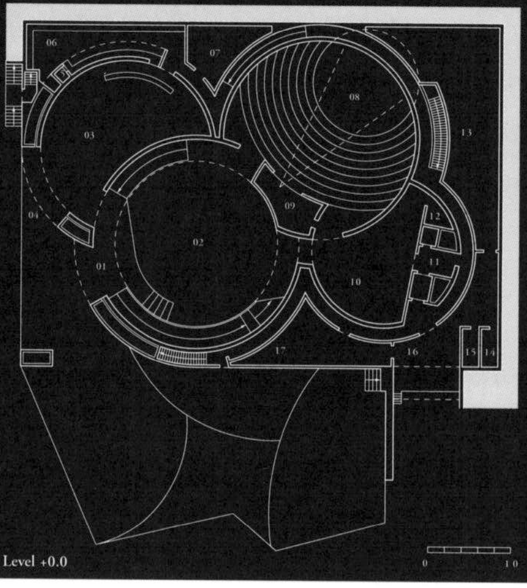

In 2003, Obra won an international design competition for the *Freedom Park and Memorial* in Pretoria, South Africa. Their project, which will be completed in 2009, proposes 30m-high (98ft) beehive-like forms, intended to refer to a tribal African tradition of burying the dead in the trunks of baobab trees.

This spread: Images and model photographs of Obra's competition-winning project for the *Freedom Park and Memorial* in Pretoria, South Africa. The project is a memorial site and museum of apartheid.

Freedom Museum Section

01_ Auditorium
02_ Temporary Exhibits
03_ Restaurant Beyond
04_ Main Entry
05_ Museum Store
06_ Moshate Beyond
07_ Temporary Exhibits
08_ Administration
09_ Pre-Colonial Gallery
10_ AV Gallery Beyond
11_ Pre-Colonial Gallery
12_ Struggle Gallery
13_ Post Apartheid Gallery

# Ofis Arhitekti

This spread: Social housing blocks on the coast of Slovenia at Izola.

| Location | Ljubuljana, Slovenia |
| Nationality | Slovenian |

Ofis Arhitekti was founded in Ljubuljana by Rok Oman and Spela Videcnik in 1996. Both partners studied first in the Slovenian capital and then at the Architectural Association in London, graduating in 2000. They had much early success in competitions, winning first prize for their entry in the Maribor Stadium competition in 1998, and in the competition for the Ljubuljana City Museum in the same year. Their place as one of the most impressive practices of their generation was cemented when they won the *Building Design* Young Architect of the Year Award in 2001. Since then the practice has been nominated for an AR&D award and the Mies van der Rohe Prize. *2G* magazine published a monograph of Ofis' work in July 2006.

Ofis Arhitekti has made its name on the back of the optimism and relative affluence of Slovenia, part of the former Yugoslavia, compared to other transitional eastern European countries. The practice has won projects of a scale that most architects have to wait decades to get close to, including a stadium and large-scale housing projects.

The housing development of 640 units that Ofis completed in 2006 is one of the largest housing projects in Slovenia, and with it came all of the constraints of extremely tight budgets and a draconian schedule of works. The project consisted of four housing blocks containing apartments between 125 and 140m (410–460ft) in length, with 1,200 parking spaces underground, all of which had to be built in 18 months.

The buildings were designed in modular form, with many prefabricated elements and a broader strategy that repeats layouts in different places in the plan. The architects explain: 'Each building is divided into four identical modules, each with its own vertical communications core. There are 42 apartments in each module, varying from small 30sq m [323sq ft] studios to 1.5-bedroom 60sq m [645sq ft] apartments on four identical floors, and larger duplex apartments from 85 to 105sq m [915–1,130sq ft] on the top two floors. The module is repeated four times with slight variations at the far ends of the building.'

The façade does not reveal this repetition, but is broken up by the two-layered approach to cladding the blocks. An inner façade gives every apartment access to a loggia and balcony, and a second skin clads these elements in timber and steel. Ofis writes: 'Like the modules, the façade layer is also repeated four times, but given the different geometry of the elements the repetition passes virtually unnoticed.'

The project graced the cover of the issue of Spanish magazine *2G* dedicated to Ofis' work in 2006.

This article was the introduction to *The Abandoned City*, which was published shortly after Oswalt became interested in the shrinkage of cities. Here he considers the thousands of vacant buildings across Germany as a city in its own right.

Translation: Andrea Scrima

For years already, the Abandoned City has been the most prosperous city in Germany; with its 2.3 million potential inhabitants, it quickly advanced to become Germany's second largest city. It exhibits a building boom the likes of which Europe hasn't seen since the heyday of the Industrial Age at the end of the nineteenth century. For what will soon be more than a decade, growth rates of more than 15% annually have prevailed. Experts' prognoses for the city's development over the coming decades are optimistic, as well: the consensus is that the city will nearly double in size over the next 20 years, reaching over four million potential inhabitants.

To this day, the city's origins remain largely unknown. Its history reaches far back, yet for centuries, apart from brief episodes, it remained modest in size. It first began to exhibit a wave of growth in the 1970s, during which a major city began to take shape and attain national significance.

In 1989, the Abandoned City reached the 900,000 mark of potential inhabitants. Its substance was comprised primarily of pre-industrial districts and areas built around the turn of the century, and included nearly no post-war sections. Even though the city chiefly consisted of quarters in the eastern part of Germany, there were already several important districts in the old Länder of the Federal Republic. Its true prime began in the 1990s. The early phase of the boom was characterized by both a rapid industrialization that encompassed nearly every area of production and a fast growth in cultural institutions, such as cinemas and houses of culture. From the mid-1990s onwards, its growth rate accelerated steadily, now encompassing post-war structures, as well. Along with prefabricated apartment buildings, the number of which became proportionally more significant, contemporary rental dwellings appeared, mostly as the result of tax write-offs. Social facilities such as daycare centres and schools also took on increased meaning. Finally, over the past few years, shopping centres, large-scale movie theatres and numerous automobile businesses joined in. In terms of housing, the Abandoned City lays claim to an above-average number of apartment buildings; contrary to the widespread belief, however, the proportion of prefab structures only comprises around 25%.

A conspicuous feature of the Abandoned City is the diversity in architecture and date and manner of building among the newly arrived buildings and districts. Like no other city, it is marked by a multitude of parts

ipp Oswalt played a large part in the unsuccessful but high-profile campaign to save the communist monument the Palast der Republik in Berlin. Raumlabor's (pp. 264–265) project for a temporary hotel there was also part of this effort.

Also working at OMA when Oswalt was there was Olivier Touraine of Touraine Richmond (pp. 322–323).

| Location | Berlin, Germany |
|---|---|
| Nationality | German |

Philipp Oswalt studied architecture at the Technical University and the University of Fine Arts in Berlin. After working for the German journal *Archplus* and for Rem Koolhaas' OMA, he set up in Berlin, winning the architectural competition for a memorial for the Ravensbrück concentration camp. Perhaps most importantly, Oswalt was the principal curator of the *Shrinking Cities* project, which produced a number of publications and exhibitions about the phenomenon of disintegrating cities in Europe and America. He is a visiting professor at the University of Cottbus, and is the author of *Berlin – City Without Form* (2000).

and facets, considered by many to be one of the essential characteristics and prerequisites of urbanity.

In comparison to other cities, it possesses a greater number of historic buildings. New architectural developments generally turn up with a delay of several decades, yet again and again we see innovative buildings asserting themselves better and more quickly here than anywhere else.

Its collection of simple structures is comparatively large; it also, however, encompasses numerous luxury structures, and no other city can claim such a high number of palaces from various eras and of the highest quality. This is also demonstrated by the fact that far more buildings here have landmark status than in any other major city.

Despite the city's rapid expansion, it has remained little explored due to a lack of source material and interest in the branch. On the one hand, professionals support the thesis that the Abandoned City is characterized by extremes: while it encompasses many buildings of minimal quality, it also has an unusually high ratio of exceptionally good structures. On the other hand, it can hardly be overlooked that broad areas of the city are characterized by average buildings.

Recently, there has been a marked public interest in the Abandoned City. Thus, the federal government settled on an investment programme of 2.5 billion euros last year for the city's urban development. This programme, scheduled to continue for eight years, is primarily designed to compensate for the conflicts between the new-fangled boom town and other existing cities. The proposed redesign will be endangering significant districts

of the Abandoned City in their very substance, much in the manner observed in earlier urban renewal programmes since the post-war era. Approximately one-quarter of its holdings is set to be demolished, of which prefab structures from the time of the GDR (German Democratic Republic) are particularly affected. As problematic as this kind of development will prove to be for the city, and as much as it questions its right to exist, sceptics can nonetheless remain assured that the Abandoned City's excellent growth prognoses will more than compensate for this loss.

The model of the Abandoned City is also spreading outside Germany. In some countries, such as the USA, Great Britain and Belgium, additional examples of this new type of city have already arisen over the past several decades. Regions of other countries, such as the eastern part of Russia, Kazakstan, the north of Finland, or the areas of southern Italy far from the shore show evidence of analogous preconditions. Thus, the Abandoned City could prove to be a prototype that will considerably mark urbanization throughout the coming decades.

Below: The Palast der Republik in Berlin, under demolition. Oswalt was one of the leaders of a campaign to find new uses for the communist landmark.

# Tom de Paor

Tom de Paor's rise to fame was perhaps first aided by his representing Ireland in the Venice Architecture Biennale in 2000, the first time that the country had been represented at the biannual architecture jamboree.

De Paor describes his project, entitled *N3* and consisting of a pavilion made out of bricks of Irish peat, as 'the end of my architectural apprenticeship. It was a masterpiece, in the old sense of the word – the apprentice's final piece of work. Although it was done quickly, it was very, very intense. I was sore after it, sick for a year and a half.'

De Paor's decision to use Irish peat was one that ran the risk of indulging a cliché, but the pavilion had an extraordinary impact. The pavilion had just one route snaking through it, uncomfortably intimate, which plunged the visitor into the smell and texture of the 1,741 stacked briquettes. One of the most talked-about pavilions, *N3* was hard to find, but certainly put de Paor on the map.

Much later came a series of private house projects, from flashy homes on the coast for rich clients to more contingent projects. An example of the latter is a pair of houses in John Dillon Street in Dublin. They are highly unconventional, making an old excavated churchyard into two remarkable, inward-looking and intense dwellings.

Below: *N3*, de Paor's Irish pavilion at the Venice Architecture Biennale in 2000. Above right and opposite: Images of two of de Paor's projects along the A13 motorway in east London, including a field of light masts near Canary Wharf and a decorated concrete monolith (housing a pumping station) in Barking. Opposite bottom: A13 arterial masterplan drawing.

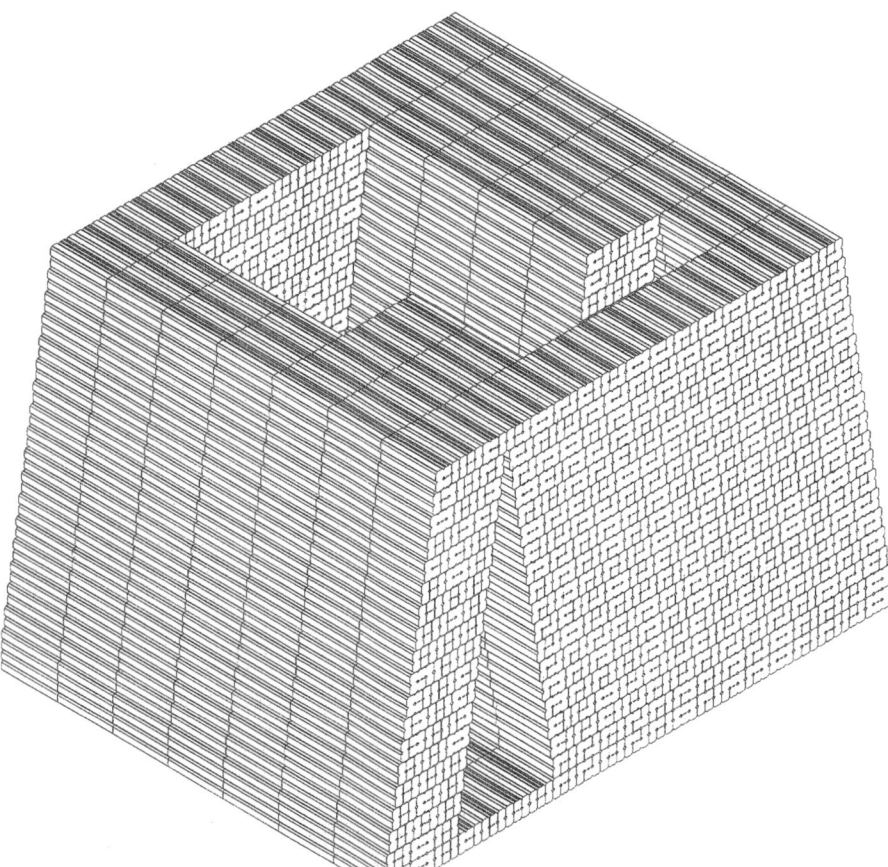

| Location | Dublin, Ireland |
| --- | --- |
| Nationality | Irish |

Tom de Paor is undoubtedly Ireland's most significant young architect. He graduated from the School of Architecture in University College Dublin in 1991, and in that year he won a competition with Emma O'Neill to build a visitor centre at Ballincollig in County Cork. Since then he has completed projects at a range of scales, including a number of private houses and a strategic masterplan of the A13 motorway in east London. He represented Ireland at the Venice Architecture Biennale in 2000, and won *Building Design* magazine's Young Architect of the Year Award in 2003.

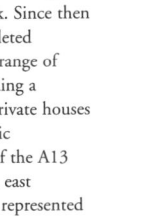

P

Lynch Architects (pp. 178–181), a fellow winner of the Young Architect of the Year Award, has collaborated with Tom de Paor.

Patterns (pp. 242–243) was third in YAYA 2003.

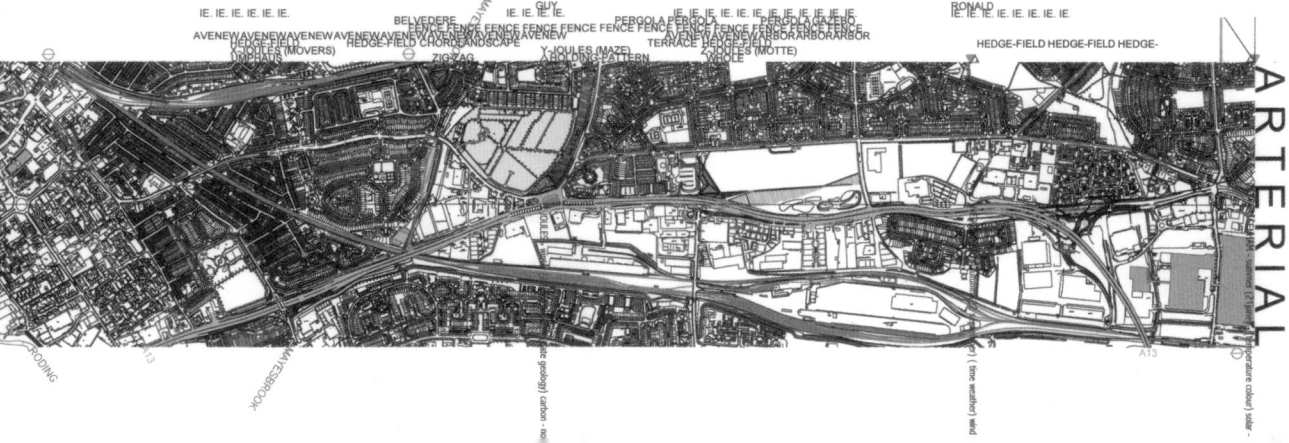

The site was originally part of the precinct of the Church of St Nicholas of Myra, and consisted of a ruined outbuilding, 2m (6ft) lower than the level of the churchyard, accessed from John Dillon Street through a door in the churchyard walls. The houses that replace this ruin have no long views at all, except from concrete rooftop terraces, and are lit from small courtyards. The ground floor accommodates living spaces, and below is the cavern-like bedroom floor. Light is funnelled to the below-ground areas through a two-storey void at the heart of the building.

All the concrete surfaces on the interior are shot-blasted and left exposed, and partitions are glazed, meaning these mysterious houses, while mostly hidden underground, have a high degree of transparency within.

This spread: Images of the two houses in John Dillon Street in Dublin, built behind an old churchyard wall.

# Patterns

Patterns' work, typically of the West-Coast computer-led practices in the US, has substantially existed at the scale of the gallery up to now. But, along with one major building in Rosario, Argentina, completed in 2003, it looks to be the first to build the computerized dream, with commercial and residential projects on the books.

An example of Patterns' gallery work is *The Element*, an installation at the SCI-Arc Gallery in Los Angeles. The project was based on the practice's winning competition entry for a new café and boardroom at the SCI-Arc school, and consists of a monolithic MDF structure clad with a plastic skin, and with embedded plastic seating booths and fibreglass monocoque tables.

The piece is a demonstration of planned library elements that are seamless pieces of furniture, from library bookshelves to seats, benches and desks.

The next generation of Patterns' work is represented here by its project for a 200sq m (2,153sq ft) private house on the edge of Rosario, Argentina's second largest city. The house was conceived as a basic box, which is deformed by the architect according to the topography on which it sits. The house follows dips in the ground, and also develops cuts in its surface that allow light in. The clients have a strong interest in horticulture, and the house integrates a greenhouse at one end of the structure, continuous with a swimming pool and solarium.

| Location | Los Angeles, USA |
| --- | --- |
| Nationality | Argentinian |

Patterns was founded in 1999 by Argentinian Marcelo Spina, and is now based in Hollywood. Spina now has a co-principal – Georgina Huljich. Both partners studied at the University of Rosario in Argentina, before Spina went to Columbia (where he won the William Kinne Fellowship) and Huljich to UCLA. Both partners are prolific teachers, Spina having been a visiting professor at Harvard, Tulane and Berkeley and Huljich as a faculty member at UCLA. Patterns has completed one major project – an apartment building in Rosario, Argentina, in 2003. The practice has also completed several artistic commissions, including *Snake-Rice* in Icheon, Korea, in 2003 and *Land.Tiles* at the Materials & Applications Gallery in Los Angeles in 2003.

P

Opposite: Patterns' installation *The Element* at the SCI-Arc Gallery. This page: Private house in Rosario, Argentina.

Patterns was part of *Architectural Record*'s Design Vanguard in 2003, along with Alejandro Aravena (pp. 26–29) and nArchitects (pp. 212–213).

# Périphériques

In the architecture world, Jussieu in France is most famous for a building that was never built – Rem Koolhaas' seminal library project from 1993. But Périphériques' building for the Université Pierre et Marie Curie (a medical and scientific university) in the town has given it more than a paper landmark

The building, won in competition in 2002 and finished in 2006, completes the 1960s modernist masterplan by Edouard Albert, with a building that conforms to Albert's masterplan, but also subverts it, raising the building on pilotis and creating an extraordinary atrium. Also, two terraces are created (and coloured bright red) that, say the architects, are intended to look 'hollowed out' of the orthogonal mass of the corner building. The impression of mass is further subverted

by the use of the delicate metal cladding system, like tracery. This screen sits over the top of a façade that is intended to be in sympathy with the existing buildings, replicating the rhythm of the glazing.

Périphériques calls the building *L'Atrium*, because the block has a spectacular opening at its heart, rising from the red-coloured ground floors through metallic surfaces with multi-coloured openings. From its escalators can be accessed the floors of the teaching laboratories.

The architects even admit to a little homage: 'At ground-floor level, the existing slab on which the university buildings are built folds up in an origami-like ramp to even up natural and built levels in a fluid movement – an echo of the well-known Jussieu library project designed by Rem Koolhaas some years ago.'

Périphériques was part of the *The Storytellers*, an exhibition at the Beyond Media festival in Florence in 2003, along with FAT (pp. 110–113), ReD Research + Design (pp. 270–271) and Xefirotarch (pp. 340–343).

| Location | Paris, France |
| --- | --- |
| Nationality | French |

Périphériques Architectes was founded as a collaborative practice in 1998 by three Parisian offices – Marin & Trottin, Paillard+Jumeau and Jakob & MacFarlane. While Jakob & MacFarlane is no longer part of the group, the two other offices work sometimes as Périphériques and sometimes independently. As Périphériques, they have won several commissions for public buildings, including 30 experimental houses in Nantes, a médiathèque at l'Ecole Maternelle de Clamart, and others. They also publish books, and a magazine called *IN-EX*. The work of Périphériques has been exhibited widely (including in Paris, Seoul and Tokyo), and the partners teach at architecture schools across France.

P

This spread:
Photographs of the university building in Jussieu, France. It is called *L'Atrium*, due to its spectacular central space (left).

# Pezo von Ellrichshausen

Chile is undergoing something of a renaissance in its architecture scene at the moment, and Pezo von Ellrichshausen is in the vanguard. Educated in Chile, they have established themselves as a powerful voice with work that is the definition of a contemporary regional modernism.

The practice has made its name internationally with a series of one-off houses, perhaps the most prominent among them being the *Casa Poli* in Coliumo, completed in 2005. Located on a cliff edge on a scarcely populated peninsula 550km (340 miles) south of Santiago, the house is a compact cuboid, intended to capture two senses of its eyrie-like site, as the partners explain: 'both the sensation of a natural podium surrounded by vastness and the morbid and unavoidable sight of the foot of the cliffs'.

The house has thick concrete walls, out of which the spaces within are conceptually hollowed. This 'over-dimensioned perimeter' contains storage, circulation, the kitchen and a series of internal balconies commanding

Left and below: *120 Doors*, an artwork in Concepcion, Chile, in 2003.

| Location | Concepcion, Chile |
| --- | --- |
| Nationality | Chilean |

Pezo von Ellrichshausen Architects was founded in Buenos Aires in 2001 by Mauricio Pezo and Sofía von Ellrichshausen. They currently work in Concepcion, southern Chile, on architectural and artistic projects. Pezo was educated at the Universidad Católica de Chile in Santiago and now teaches at Bio-Bio University. He is a visual artist and director of the Movimiento Artista del Sur (MAS). Von Ellrichshausen studied in Buenos Aires and now teaches at the University of Las Americas, Talkca and Andres Bello. The partners have won many awards, including the Architecture Quality Prize at the Biennial of Chilean Architecture in Santiago in 2006, the Young Architects Prize at the 5th Iberoamerican Architecture Biennial (Montevideo, 2006) and were commended in the *Architectural Review* Awards in 2005. Their projects include the *Casa Rivo* in 2003.

P

This page and opposite top: Pezo von Ellrichshausen's elemental *Casa Poli*, a house and arts retreat. The thick concrete provides thermal mass and the deep reveals provide shading.

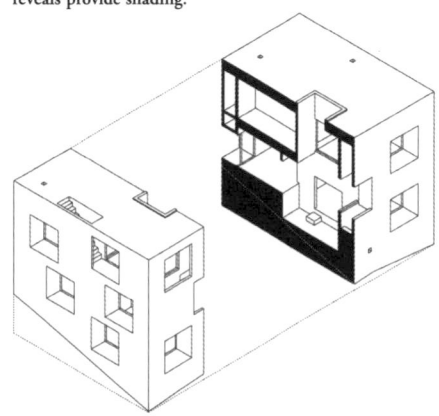

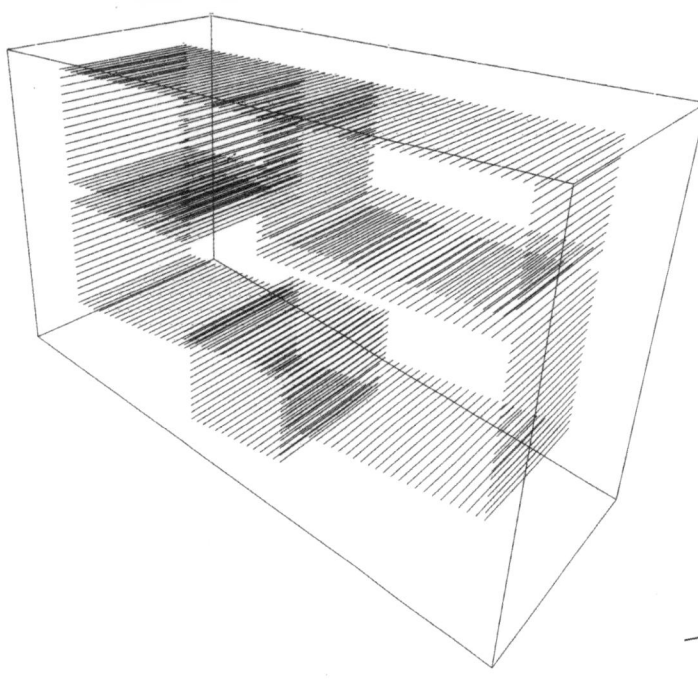

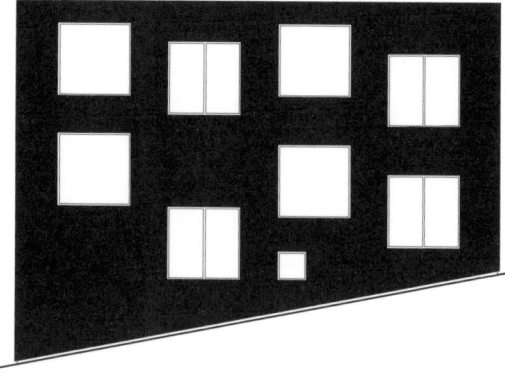

views over the landscape. The building is intended not just as a house, but as a cultural centre, and the thick concrete façade also mediates between a public monumentality and an intimate domestic feeling.

The construction of the house was a modest affair, say the architects: 'All the work was built with handmade concrete, using untreated wooden frames. The work was done with a small mixer and four wheelbarrows, in horizontal strata that matched the height of half a wooden board. We then used the same battered wood of the frames to wrap the interior and to build sliding panels that function both as doors to hide the services of the perimeter and as security shutters that cover the windows when the house is left alone.'

The other side to Pezo von Ellrichshausen's work is its art practice. Projects such as *120 Doors*, a piece of public art in Concepcion in 2003, are intended as investigations of the limits of architecture. In this case, five enclosures made of standard doors were constructed, one within another, to explore 'exploring the points of transmission, or friction, between one place and another.'

This spread: Images of another Pezo von Ellrichshausen house, the *Casa Rivo*, clad in burnt timber.

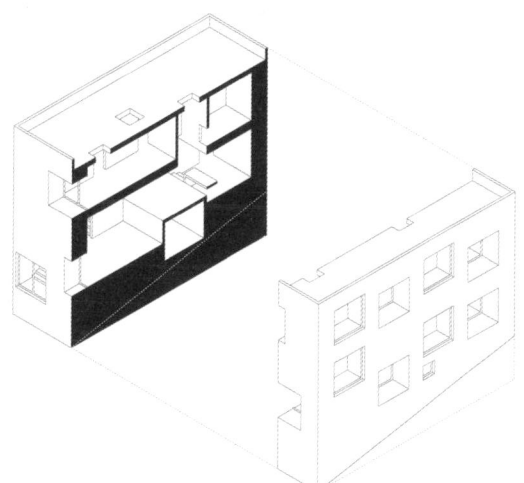

*Polar Inertia* is a journal that keeps alive the spirit of the great English critic Reyner Banham. Banham's fascination with the technology of the American frontiersman is reflected in its pages. But perhaps the technologies have changed somewhat. In this text, called *Taco Trucks: Emergent Urbanism in Los Angeles*, *Polar Inertia*'s editor Mac Kane considers the taco truck as an emblem of West Coast urbanity.

On the streets of LA on any given day are over 4,000 registered and an estimated 2,000 unregistered mobile restaurants, or what the LA county department of health services calls mobile food preparation units (MFPU). The trucks roam the city responding to the daily changes and needs of its citizens, piggybacking on the larger infrastructure of freeways, power and water networks, establishing an unconscious connector of daily life in the city. Each registered taco truck begins its day at one of over 30 commissaries regulated by the county. These commissaries are spread across the region, creating a dispersed network of centres from which a steady flow of restaurants span outwards along independent routes. At the commissaries the taco trucks pay an average of $20 a day for receiving a parking space, cold and hot water hook-ups and drains for cleaning the trucks, as well as access to a market for purchasing food, drink, ice and propane from a wholesale dealer.

The extraordinary competition among the food trucks guarantees, out of economic necessity, that they are drawn to areas where clients are most present. The network of taco trucks follow no central plan or directive, and because of their adaptive nature they are a useful indicator of spaces that cannot be easily categorized by traditional means. The appearance of a taco truck is itself an indication of a certain type of space; most obviously an area underserved by restaurants, or areas that are bettered served by short-term restaurants. Being mobile and largely independently operated, the trucks form distinct patterns of congregation in particular spaces in the city.

Unexpectedly, these spaces occur in a diverse mix of locations in both some of the wealthiest and poorest neighborhoods of the city. For example, you will find the trucks roaming the residential streets of Beverly Hills, Brentwood and Pacific Palisades where they serve the wealthy residents' gardeners, who are isolated from affordable restaurants. The food vans also serve the late-night streets of Hollywood Boulevard where prostitutes congregate, city parks for soccer and softball matches, at day-labour pick-up sites where workers congregate, at construction sites, at east and south LA factories and warehouses, at movie and TV location shoots, and the beachfront

| Location | Los Angeles, USA |
| Nationality | American |

*Polar Inertia* is a bi-monthly journal edited by photographer and architect Mac Kane (above), with Marcel Yarnow as editor at large. The journal has an observational interest in the contemporary city, often publishing photographs and research on phenomena outside the ordinary range of architectural interests – bikes, service stations, escalators, mobile homes, and even a 'hand-dryer world tour'. Although based mainly in Los Angeles, *Polar Inertia* features many contributions from Asia, especially China.

P

streets where surfers and bikers gather. These are spaces peripheral to established commercial districts. The taco trucks occupy the leftover or unattached spaces of the city, reconfiguring them into restaurant zones as the situation warrants.

Following the trucks through the city, one begins to see the city through the eyes of a taco truck, where the spaces of transient density become more apparent. The majority of taco trucks are small business enterprises with the owner also acting as driver. It is common in the business for a beginning driver to start by taking on the route of an experienced driver with an established client base. The established driver will then expand his business by purchasing a second truck, thus becoming both a driver and manager of two routes and through this process will eventually accumulate a fleet of several food vans.

There are two basic types of business model related to taco trucks. The first is a transient business that moves continuously throughout its day, stopping at approximately 20 different locations at 20-minute intervals during an eight-hour shift, typically beginning at 6am and ending at 2pm.

For the transient taco truck, communication is critical to the success of the business, as its route through the city is compiled from connections developed with factory foremen, construction contractors and business owners, culled over many years. Currently the most lucrative routes for a mobile restaurant are among the small industrial factories of east and south LA, where each 30-minute stop can serve several dozen clients. The taco truck owner will work closely with the site supervisors to coincide their stops with breaks.

As an adaptable system interconnected to the transportation and communications networks of the city, the taco trucks adapt to their environment; each van follows its own path on seemingly unrelated routes, but their collective behaviour reveals larger emergent patterns. The taco truck network is only one of the countless systems that combine to recompose the city of Los Angeles each day. Through study of the taco truck we can begin to see how the city evolves not as a static or hierarchical model but as a biological model where emergent systems evolve to create the city. As an adaptable system interconnected to the other networks of the city, the food van is a useful tool for understanding the underlying dynamics of the city, and helps us to understand how the evolving shape of the city emerges from the systems through which the everyday city flows and composes itself.

# Purpur

Purpur may be at home at a variety of scales, but the agency has had most press coverage for an increasingly extraordinary series of interiors, mainly for shops. Perhaps the best is the *Center Apotheke*, a pharmacy in Daniel Gran Straße 13 in St Pölten, Austria.

The site was a retail unit inside a shopping centre, and the strategy of the architects was to draw the customer in by leaving a large circulation space between a display wall and the service desk. The white surfaces of the curving wall are upholstered in white leather, with horizontal slits revealing the products in backlit niches. Because of a lack of space, only a few products are on display. Much of the interior is occupied by a fully automated storeroom connected to the cash register. A mechanized arm retrieves any product ordered from the till, and delivers it down a stainless-steel chute. This astounding mechanism is revealed to customers through a glass pane in the shop's façade, so the curious can see the robot at work. Perhaps most amazingly, this robot can be controlled remotely, meaning the pharmacist can serve customers in the shop from his or her own home, instructing the robot arm over the Internet to deliver medicine to the customer.

This is the kind of shop science-fiction fans were convinced would be ubiquitous by now.

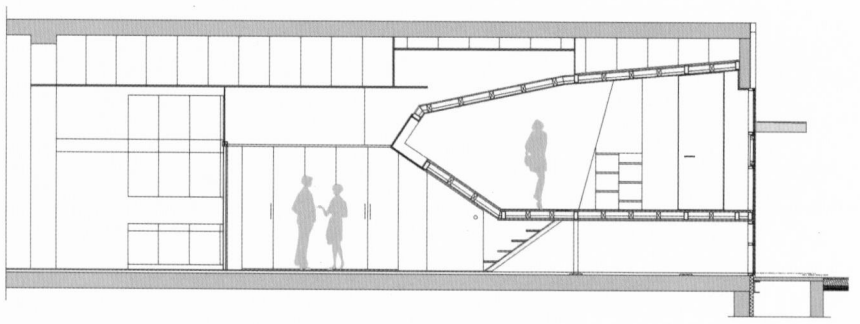

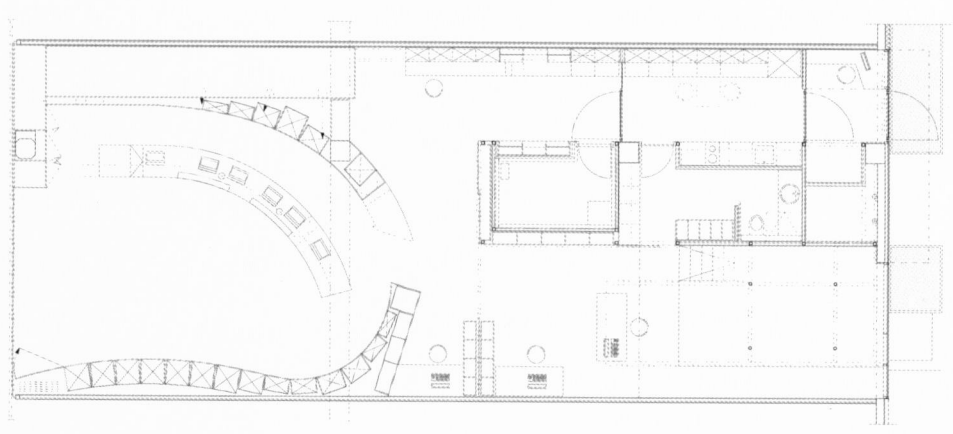

1    5    10 m

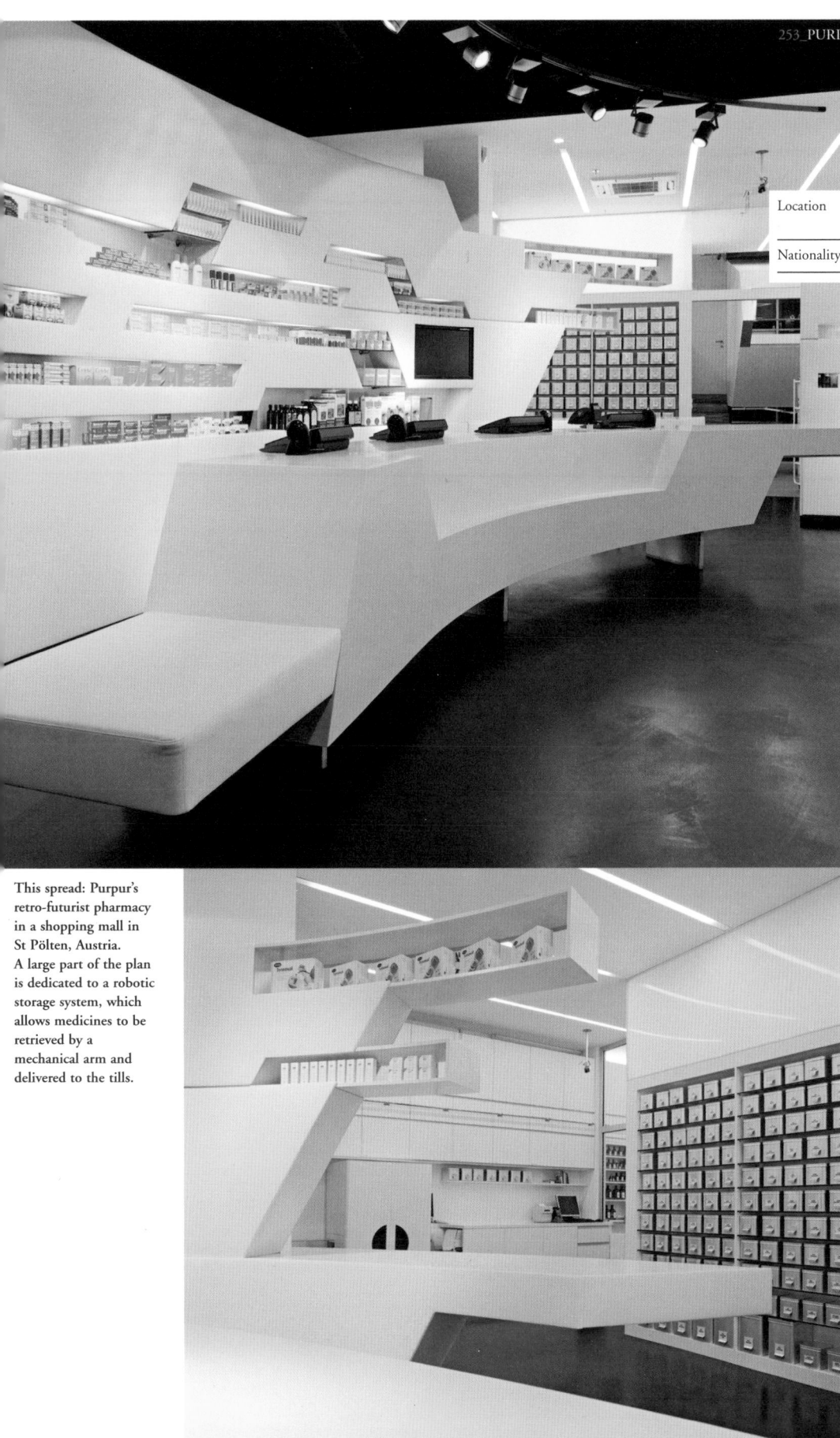

| Location | Graz, Austria |
| | Vienna, Austria |
| Nationality | Austrian |

Purpur was founded in 1999 when Christian Toedtling and Thomas Laengauer set up offices in Graz and Vienna respectively. Alfred Boric joined in 2000, and Alexander Loebel in 2002. The two locations take on different types of projects, from urban planning strategies to interior design. Recent significant projects include a shoe shop in Graz, a pharmacy in St Pölten, a public space design for the Hans-List-Platz/AVL-Forum in Graz in 2005, and their competition-winning scheme for the Lapidarium museum building at the Schloss Eggenberg in Graz, completed in 2004.

P

This spread: Purpur's retro-futurist pharmacy in a shopping mall in St Pölten, Austria. A large part of the plan is dedicated to a robotic storage system, which allows medicines to be retrieved by a mechanical arm and delivered to the tills.

# Qua'Virarch

Qua'Virarch is another member of the ubiquitous SCI-Arc group of small, computer-based practices, ruthlessly promoted by one another and gaining currency while their projects remain at the moment mostly unbuilt. Paul Preissner, the principal of Qua'Virarch, appears to have a pleasingly facetious attitude to the orthodoxies of this group. In an interview, when asked 'What are the hallmarks of your style?' he answered with one word – 'Curvy.'

The interviewer was left speculating that there must be more to it than that, but it is refreshing to see that Preissner admits that his aesthetic predilections define much of his work, making sinuous, quasi-organic forms and atmospheres that he says are inspired by his love of zombie movies.

His most significant project is the award-winning competition entry for the Gyeonggi-do Jeongok Prehistory Museum in South Korea. The project

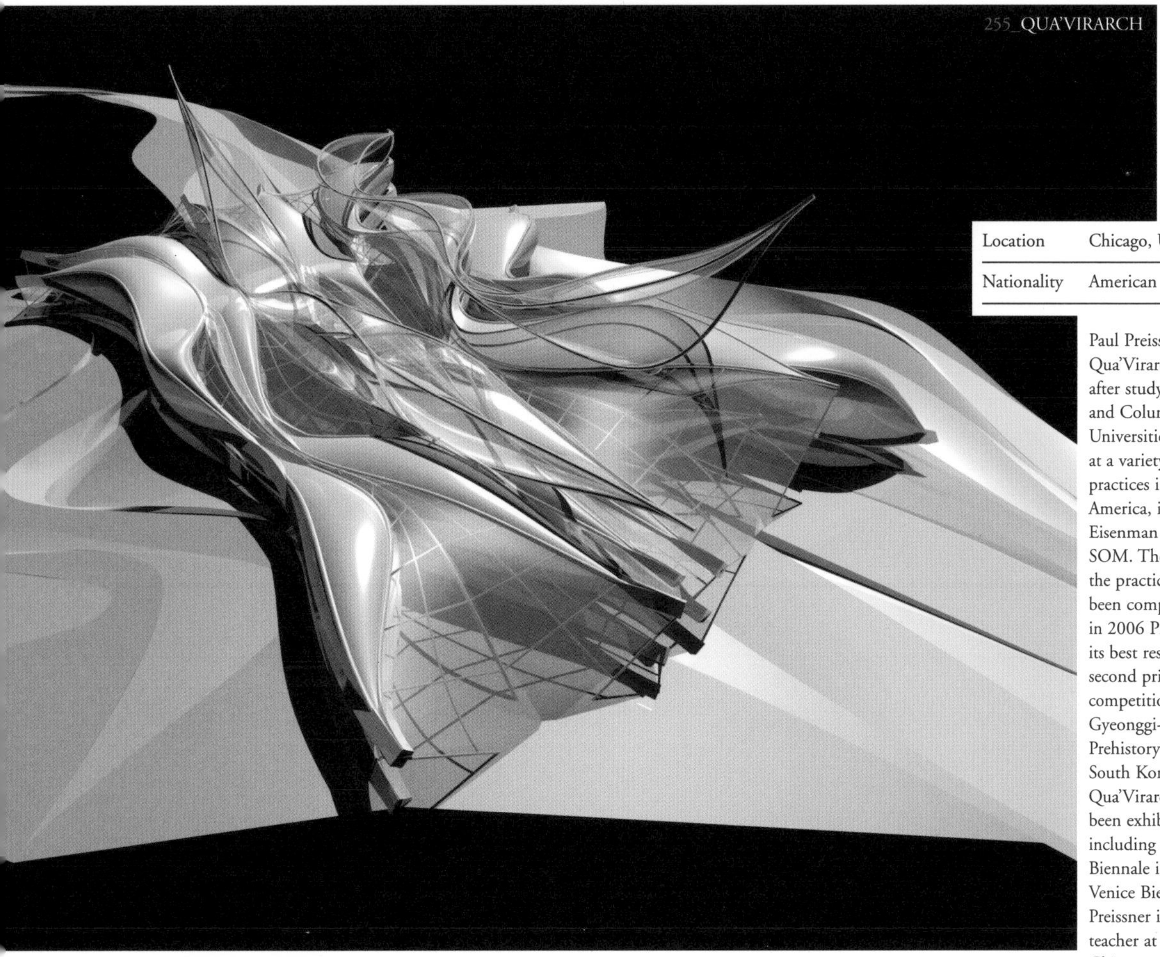

| Location | Chicago, USA |
| --- | --- |
| Nationality | American |

Paul Preissner founded Qua'Virarch in 2003, after studying at Illinois and Columbia Universities and working at a variety of big-name practices in North America, including Eisenman Architects and SOM. The majority of the practice's work has been competitions, and in 2006 Preissner scored its best result yet – a second prize in the competition for the Gyeonggi-do Jeongok Prehistory Museum in South Korea. Qua'Virarch's work has been exhibited widely, including at the Beijing Biennale in 2004 and the Venice Biennale in 2000. Preissner is a prolific teacher at SCI-Arc and Chicago, and currently holds the Visiting Hyde Chair of Excellence at the University of Nebraska-Lincoln.

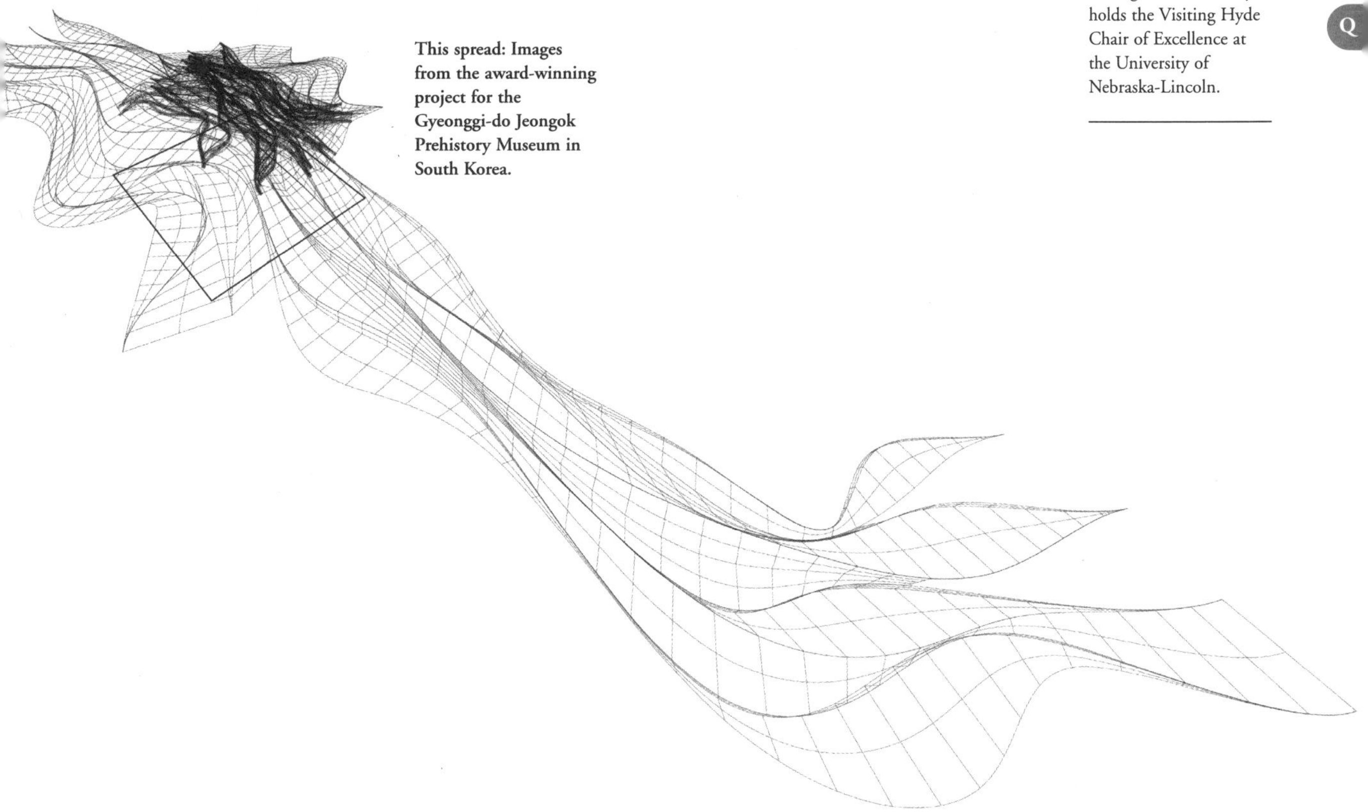

This spread: Images from the award-winning project for the Gyeonggi-do Jeongok Prehistory Museum in South Korea.

creates continuous undulating surfaces within, which Preissner conceptualizes as a rethinking of the role of the museum. 'Every location within the museum is part of the continuous exhibition space,' he writes, 'including the plant room, archival storage, curatorial restoration and basalt precipice.' Dramatic display cases were proposed, which attempt also to propose the historical objects within as part of a living tradition.

The building is made of a system of concrete beams held up by a web of columns. The concrete parts in places to provide skylights, and the whole interior can be lit by indirect sunlight. The thermal mass of the concrete also contributes to the building's aspiration to be zero-carbon – other passive systems are proposed, as well as a photovoltaic array and recycled materials.

Another Qua'Virarch competition entry, for the National Library of the Czech Republic in Prague, bears a remarkable similarity in approach to the Korean project. It proposes another 'fibrous' form, this time transforming what the architect describes as a 'benign' site into an 'organic' and 'somewhat monstrous' form.

This spread: Another competition entry, this time for the competition for the Czech National Library in Prague. The proposal is described as 'somewhat monstrous' by its architect.

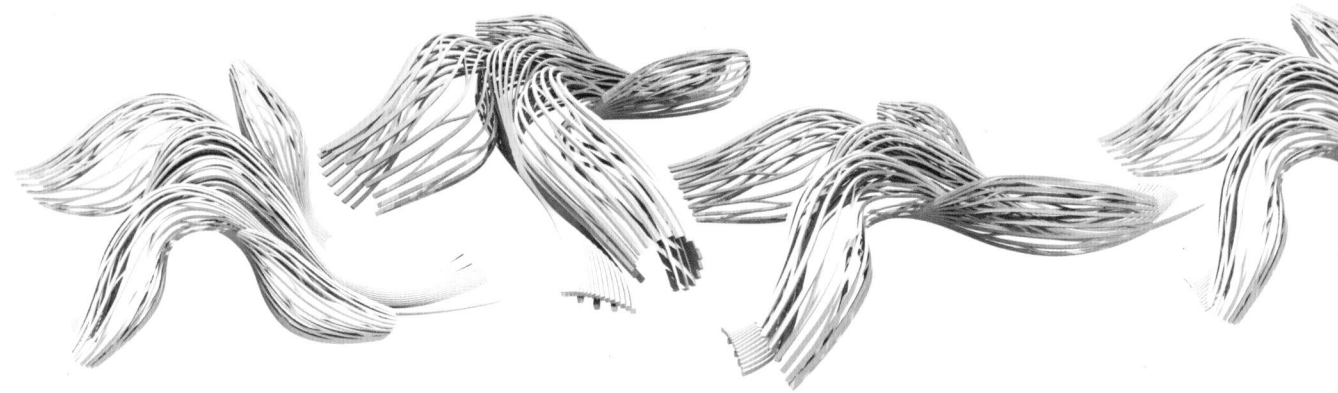

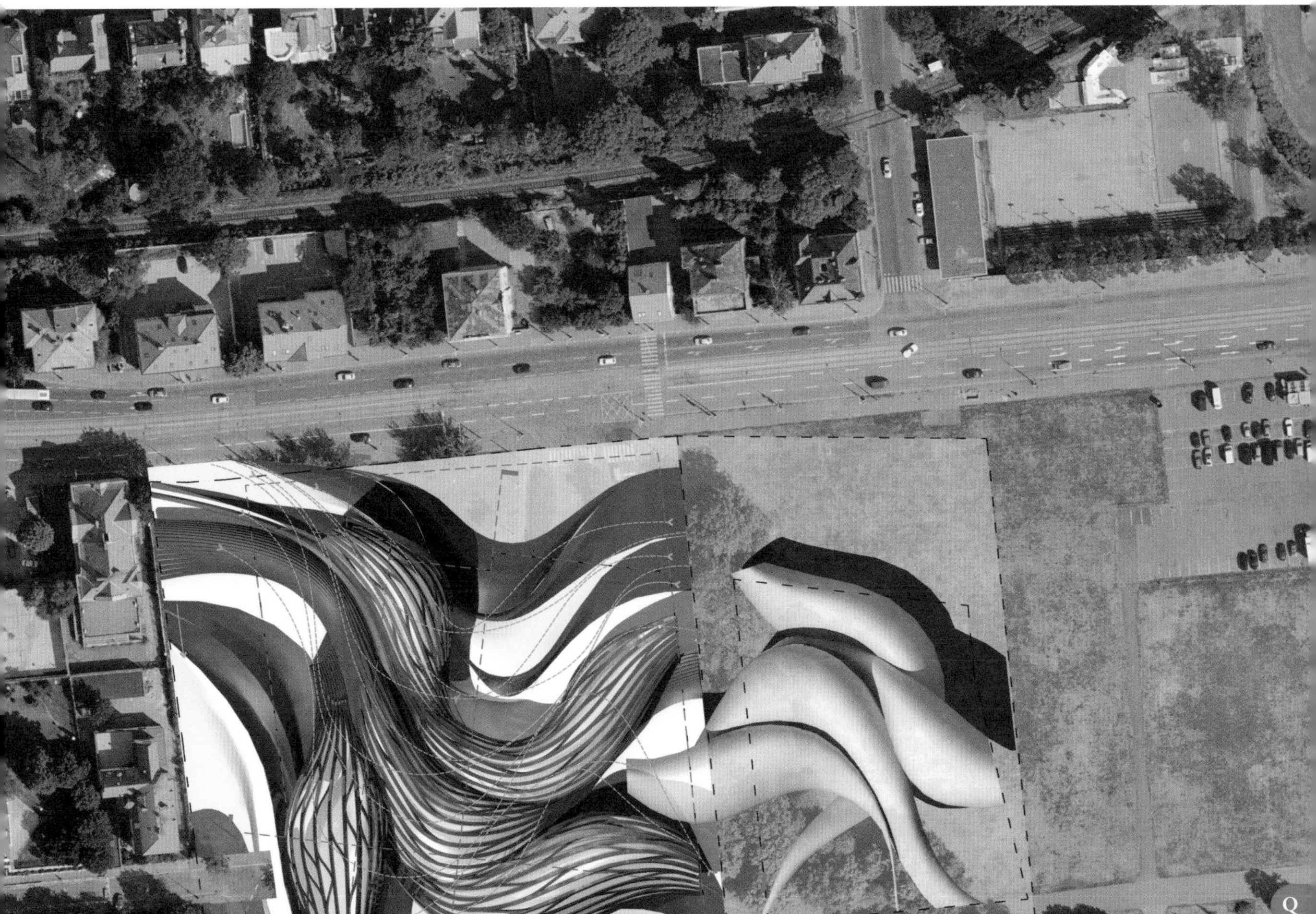

Q

This is another practice irrevocably associated with SCI-Arc, despite its location in
Chicago. Qua'Virarch was part of the team led by Neil Denari as a competition entry for New York's bid
for the 2012 Olympic Games, along with Patterns (pp. 242–243) and Xefirotarch (pp. 340–343).

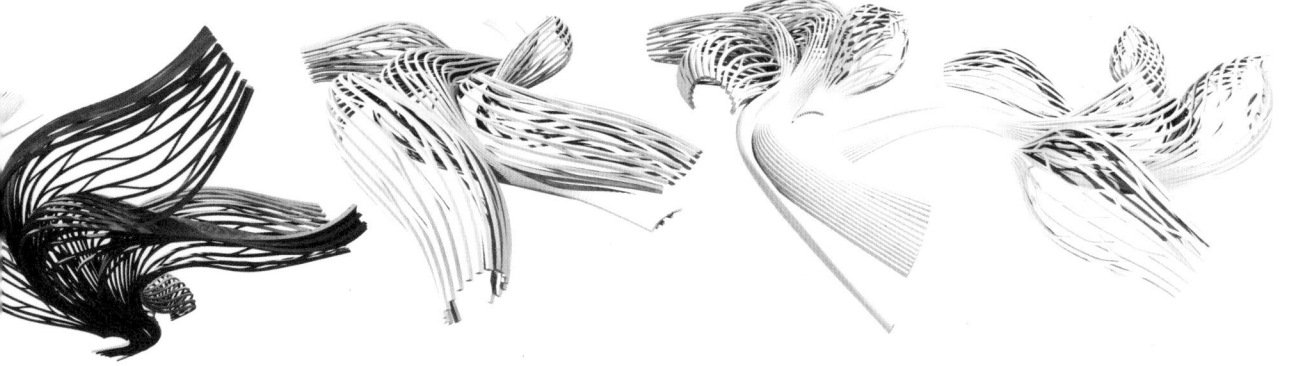

# R&Sie

R&Sie's work has existed often at the scale of the gallery space, and although its work now extends to several buildings, it is appropriate that the projects we show here are some of its installations.

R&Sie's work has appeared in some distinguished settings, and *Terra Incognita*, its collaboration with artist Pierre Huyghe, was one of the most notable. The installation, a honeycomb aluminium landscape, appeared first at the Centre Pompidou in Paris, and later at Tate Modern in London, two of Europe's most prestigious art galleries.

The project was a commentary on global warming and the melting of the polar icecaps. The title comes from a land mass in Antarctica newly revealed due to the receding ice. The aluminium piece was created by R&Sie using a parametric script in a computer, and is unfolded into a landscape. The piece is held up by wires and counterweights, the weights consisting of different volumes of water that represent different volumes of melted Antarctic ice. To finish off the scene, a robotic albino penguin was placed in the space, its only movement an occasional blink.

An installation at the scale of a building, R&Sie's *Hybrid Muscle* was built in Chiang Mai, Thailand, in 2003. The building is an exhibition space, constructed, by hand, out of teak wood, which generates its own electricity. The energy of beasts of burden is used to lift a two-tonne steel counterweight, the potential energy of which is transformed into electrical energy powering ten light bulbs, a laptop computer and mobile phones. The original strategy had been to use an elephant, but its place was taken by an albino buffalo.

The building is naturally ventilated, with breezes coming in through quivering 'leaves' of elastomer. It is significant that the client for this project was the Thai artist Rirkrit Tiravanija, whose work often consists of socially provocative installations – rooms for eating, reading or playing music.

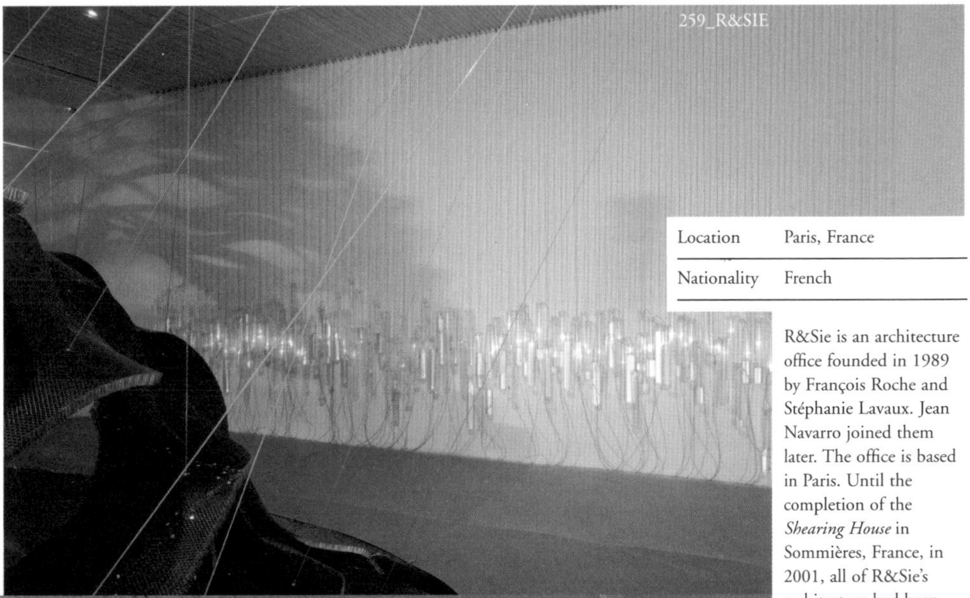

| Location | Paris, France |
| --- | --- |
| Nationality | French |

This spread: images from Pierre Huyghe and R&Sie's *Terra Incognita* artwork, which was shown at Tate Modern in London and the Centre Pompidou in Paris in 2006.
Bottom right: the landscape was generated from a random cut through a mountain in Antarctica.

R&Sie is an architecture office founded in 1989 by François Roche and Stéphanie Lavaux. Jean Navarro joined them later. The office is based in Paris. Until the completion of the *Shearing House* in Sommières, France, in 2001, all of R&Sie's architecture had been theoretical. Since then, the practice has completed other built projects, significantly the astonishing *Asphalt Spot* car park in Tokamashi, Japan. François Roche is an academic in demand, and has held professorships in London (Bartlett), Vienna (TU), Barcelona (ESARQ) and Philadelphia (UPenn). The practice's work has been widely exhibited, including in exhibitions at Tate Modern in London, Mori Art Museum in Tokyo, Centre Pompidou in Paris and many others.

R&Sie's *Terra Incognita* project was included in the book *Did Someone Say Participate?* in 2006, co-edited by Markus Miessen (pp. 204–205) and also including work by Joseph Grima (pp. 138–139) and Eyal Weizman (pp. 336–337).

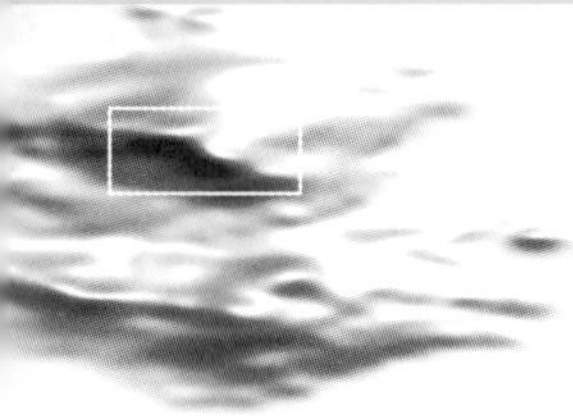

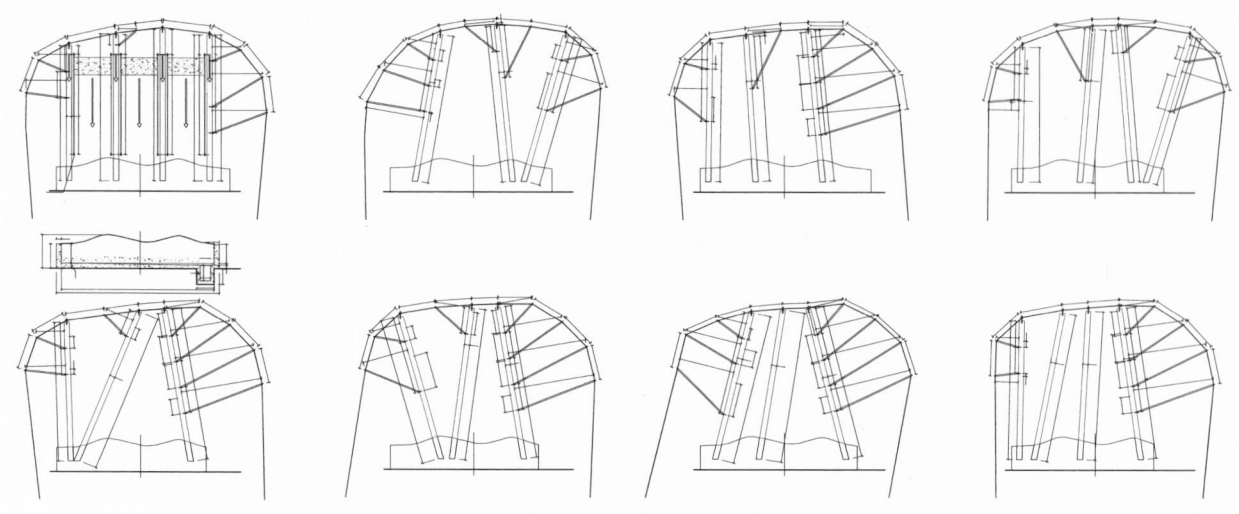

This spread: *Hybrid Muscle*, an artwork built in Chiang Mai, Thailand, in 2003. The client for the project, which translates the power of a beast of burden into electricity, was artist Rirkrit Tiravanija. The original intention had been to use an elephant for the project, but a buffalo proved easier to come by.

# Philippe Rahm

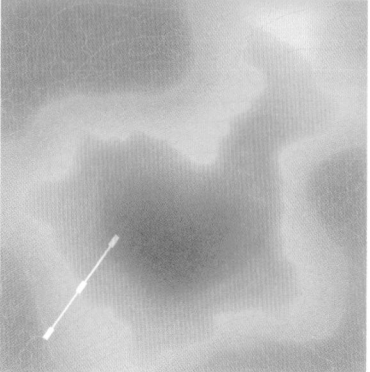

Among the many extraordinary interests refected in the work of Philippe Rahm is his ongoing engagement with diverse climatic conditions that exist or can be created to effect an architectural project.

The most recent demonstration of this idea is his project entitled *House Dilation*, commissioned by Grizedale Arts in Cumbria, UK. The layout of the building is dispersed ('dilated') between three conditions found on the site – the meadow, the border of the field and a forest, and the forest itself. This was inspired by the French writer George Perec. Rahm writes: 'Perec considered the idea of having his living room in the Latin Quarter, his study close to the Champs-Elysées, his bedroom in Montmartre and his bathroom on the Ile de la Cité. The idea is that that an apartment can be disseminated throughout the city of Paris, finding the rooms in various places, according to hours of the day, to the environment of the district, to the desires of the moment and the season.'

*House Dilation* achieves this by choosing locations for rooms according to the qualities of light, humidity and temperature created by the trees. Rahm explains: 'In this situation, architecture removes its outer skin or jacket and it is the environment which then takes on this role, becoming this last skin.' The inhabitant lives according to the scale and rhythms of the landscape, rather than being bounded by the four walls of a conventional house.

Rahm's project for tourist housing in Vassivière in the Limousin region of France takes his interest in humidity and applies it to the problem of creating environmentally efficient buildings. The project generates the form of each space according to the amount of water vapour emitted in typical usage (40g/1.4oz of water vapour per hour while sleeping, 150g/5.3oz per hour when active, 800g/28oz in 20 minutes in the bathroom), and generates a layout according to the route of air renewal in the house. 'Our project refuses to programme the space functionally according to specific activities. It creates spaces that are more or less dry, more or less humid, to be occupied freely, to be appropriated according to the weather and the seasons,' he writes.

T    21°c      18°c      15°c

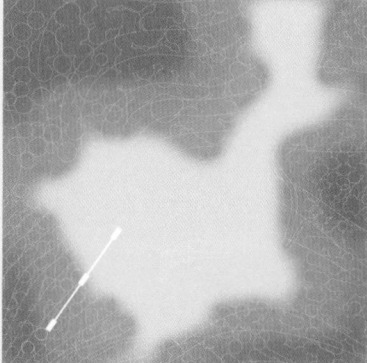

RH    85%   80%   75%    70%    65%

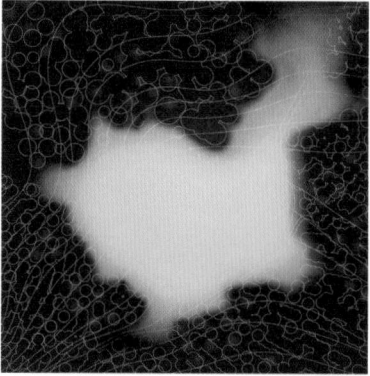

LUX    500 LUX      5000 LUX

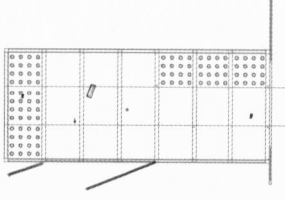

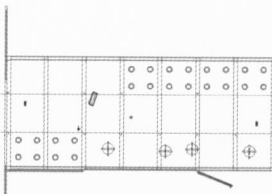

This spread: Images of *House Dilation,* a project that proposes three separate elements of accommodation that respond to different climatic conditions on the site in the Cumbrian countryside in the UK.

| Location | Lausanne, Switzerland Paris, France |
|---|---|
| Nationality | French |

Philippe Rahm studied in Lausanne and Zurich, graduating in 1993 and establishing Décosterd & Rahm with Jean-Gilles Décosterd. They worked together until 2004. Rahm is currently based in Paris, France and Lausanne, Switzerland. Built projects include a winter house for the artist Fabric Hybert and an island garden in Jöss, Austria, but Rahm's work has been far more influential in many exhibitions and publications. To mention just two, Rahm was, in 2002, chosen to represent Switzerland at the Venice Architecture Biennale, and in 2006–07 he had a personal exhibition at the Canadian Centre for Architecture in Montreal. Rahm taught at the Architectural Association in London in 2005–06, and has been a professor at ECAL Lausanne, and the Ecole Nationale Supérieure de Beaux-Arts in Paris. He is currently working on several private and public projects in France, Poland, the UK and Austria.

R

# Raumlabor

Raumlabor's most significant work was part of one of the great pieces of direct-action architecture in recent years. Volkspalast was a campaign to find new uses for the Palast der Republik in Berlin, a communist-era building on the Museums Island, which was slated for demolition. Many thought that the decision to rid Berlin of this concrete and mirror-glass piece of communist modernism was ideologically motivated. They felt an abiding affection for the building (which contained East Berlin's parliament, but also a public ballroom and a bowling alley), and decided to try to save it.

The most strident part of this strategy was Raumlabor's *Gasthof Bergkristall*, a temporary guesthouse right outside the semi-derelict building. It took the form of a crystalline mountain-like form, made out of white tent canvas, that sat outside the front door of the palast. The structure also occupied part of the interior, and appeared to burst from the roof, looking like the architects' description: 'a central massif'.

Of the rooms in the ground-level part of the mountain, Raumlabor writes: 'Each room is individually carved out of the sheer mass of the rock, therefore none of the rooms looks the same. To rest in one of these rooms is a deeply touching experience. You immediately feel the force of the mountain.' These rooms included the 'Schinkel Room' (with a view of Schinkel's Altes Museum across the Lustgarten) and the 'Panorama Room', which offered a view across the Schlossplatz.

The project was at once an elegy and an opening up of a condemned building. '*Gasthof Bergkristall* fills a historical gap and offers the building and its context as a place to stay. Berliners, tourists, the nostalgic, the curious and the say-good-bye-ers mixed as guests in the little hotel. A simple access to history was created that is open to each individual and fits into the life story of many people.' While this poetic project did not save the building, it added a crowning moment to its long and controversial history.

In a more suburban context, Raumlabor's *White Spots* project was a comment on the middle-class dormitory housing areas of Germany's richest city – Munich. Despite the apparently neutral context, Raumlabor became interested in the mix of uses, with housing right next to a large prison, and near a cemetery. These 'historically contaminated' elements constituted a parallel world in Raumlabor's analysis, which demonstrated the 'perfection of separation' at work here. The intervention consisted of choreographing a fleet of silver cars, replicating the most mainstream of vehicles, to arrive mysteriously in the area for a ten-day performance. Raumlabor says: 'The occupation of the area by an everyday object, which is noticed only gradually by its apparent duplication, takes on a threatening character. It is the ordinary interrupted.'

| Location | Berlin, Germany |
|---|---|
| Nationality | German |

Raumlabor consists of Markus Bader, Benjamin Foerster-Baldenius, Andrea Hofmann and Jan Liesegang, and was founded in 1997 in Berlin. They write: 'Various interdisciplinary working teams investigate strategies for urban renewal. Raumlabor does urban and architectural design, buildings, interactive environments and research.' The practice has created many temporary and artistic projects, as well as producing research publications such as *Halle-Neustadt Fuehrer* in 2006, by Markus Bader and Daniel Herrmann, and many other articles and journals. Raumlabor has exhibited at the Venice Architecture Biennale, in 2004, and at the Deutsches Architekturzentrum, Kunstverein Wolfsburg, the BDA Galerie in Berlin and others venues.

Opposite: Images of the *Gasthof Bergkristall*, Raumlabor's temporary hotel at the Palast der Republik, a communist monument slated for demolition in Berlin. This page: *White Spots*, a ten-day performance, with a fleet of silver cars infecting a Munich suburb.

Raumlabor's *White Spots* choreographed cars to artistic effect, as did fellow Berlin practice Deadline's *Space Race* (pp. 76–77).

# Raumtaktik

Like many of the other Berlin practices in this book, Raumtaktik's work has made use of temporary structures and exhibitions to make politically provocative work that extends the definition of what architectural practice might be.

In this idiom is Raumtaktik's *Fanshop of Globalization*, an installation funded by the German Federal Agency for Civic Education that toured Germany during the FIFA World Cup Finals in the country in 2006. 'The *Fanshop of Globalization* was a 12m [40ft] container, redesigned as a mobile fashion store,' writes Raumtaktik. 'In this store, 25 extraordinary outfits made by young German designers were presented. Each outfit is made out of soccer jerseys, representing different teams and different aspects of globalization.' The shopping container also presented 25 stories from the world of soccer, highlighting different 'economic mechanisms, political circumstances and cultural contexts behind the changes in the world economy today.'

This project, a kind of mobile conscience for the otherwise festive sporting event, also had an accompanying catalogue that dealt with the statistics of the football industry as a global phenomenon. Nine German cities hosted the exhibition during the tournament, and the shipping container came to represent 'the basic tool for global exchange of goods for 50 years. Redesigning the container into a glittering fashion store shows the extremes we are actually living in: shiny surfaces on one side, economical and social problems on the other – worldwide, all interconnected.'

**FANSHOP DER GLOBALISIERUNG** **FANSHOP OF GLOBALIZATION**

| Location | Berlin, Germany |
|---|---|
| Nationality | German |

Raumtaktik is a Berlin-based agency run by architects Friedrich von Borries and Matthias Böttger. Both trained as architects and urban planners at the University of Karlsruhe. After that von Borries continued his training in Brussels and Berlin, and Böttger in London. Their activities have ranged towards the less conventional, with Böttger having been part of the theatre group Post Theatre, and claiming to have been the president of the World Dodgeball Association in Berlin for three years. The work of Raumtaktik has existed most often in exhibitions and publications, significantly in von Borries's book *Wer hat Angst vor Niketown?* (*Who's Afraid of Niketown?*), published by Episode in 2005. Exhibitions include *Matchmaker, Matchmaker* at the Jewish Museum Berlin and ArchiLab Orleans (2003–04) and *Shrinking Cities*, Berlin and Leipzig (2004–05).

R

This spread: Images of the *Fanshop of Globalization*, which toured Germany during the World Cup Finals in 2006. For sale were garments made out of football shirts by big-name designers. The intention was to dramatize the relationship of football to global commerce and exploitation.

From 2007 to 2009 Raumtaktik partners Matthias Böttger and Friedrich von Borries are fellows of the Schloss Solitude art academy in Stuttgart, and were nominated for this award by Jürgen Mayer H (pp. 194–197).

# Realities United

Berlin-based studio Realities United has engaged with projects using a range of interactive technologies, from gallery-based installations to furniture, but it is the studio's ground-breaking work with media façades that has gained it a profile. The *BIX* project at Austria's Kunsthaus Graz in 2004 was the breakthrough, a programmable façade that artists could use to create animated artworks at the scale of a building. Rather than making a high-resolution screen, Realities United created a loose and super-low-resolution monochrome grid of 930 fluorescent lamps that could animate at 20 frames per second. The spectacular result was certainly the best thing about the building.

Following this, Realities United was invited to make a large media façade, a project they called *SPOTS*, at Leipziger Platz/Potsdamer Platz, the centre of the reconstructed Berlin. An empty office building was chosen and a screen with a light matrix of 1,800 ordinary fluorescent lamps was installed into its glass façade. The lamps could be individually controlled by a computer and, as a result, sequences of images could be programmed into the façade. A series of artists, including Terry Gilliam, Carsten Nicolai and Jonathan Monk, created various animations for the screen, and its popularity was such that the project's life was extended beyond its projected end, finally being turned off in early 2007.

Realities United write: 'The external shell of the building is transformed into a communicative membrane, which is used primarily for displaying artistic material. With its large grid pattern and low resolution, the matrix of fluorescent tubes harmonizes with the architectural scales of the building and of Potsdamer Platz as a whole. The aim is not to conceal the architecture with a media installation, but rather to implement its logical continuation.'

Left: Realities United designed the *BIX* media façade at the Kunsthaus Graz, Austria, which opened in 2004.

Below: Images from the practice's *BIX* research project.

Opposite: *SPOTS*, which decorated the façade of an empty office building in Potsdamer Platz, Berlin in 2006–07.

| Location | Berlin, Germany |
| --- | --- |
| Nationality | German |

Brothers Jan and Tim Edler founded Realities United in 2000 as a studio for art, architecture and technology. Before that, they had been the co-founders of Berlin art group Kunst und Technik. Jan Edler studied in Aachen and then at the Bartlett in London, while Tim studied in Berlin. Their projects have included interactive technologies for museums such as the Paul Klee Centre in Bern, Switzerland (2005) and Kunsthaus Graz (2004), and many media façade projects. The most famous of these was its façade for the Kunsthaus Graz, a building designed by Peter Cook and Colin Fournier. This pixelated screen won a host of awards, including the 50,000-euro Inspire! Award by German Telekom (2005), the 'Goldener Nagel' (Golden Nail) at the Art Director Club Awards in Germany (2004), the Hans Schaefers Award by the German Architects Association Berlin (2004) and a Design distinction at the New York ID Annual Design Review (2004). The brothers have taught and lectured widely, and Tim Edler currently holds a visiting professorship at the art school in Bremen.

# ReD Research + Design

ReD's *M-City* project for the Kunsthaus Graz, Austria, could lay claim to being a successful interior design in the most difficult interior in contemporary architecture. What ReD euphemistically calls the 'singularity' of the space could be translated as 'nightmare,' with its tricky lighting conditions, non-orthogonal surfaces, and wide-open spaces punctuated by escalators. Peter Cook and Colin Fournier's so-called 'Friendly Alien' is a tricky site.

The practice writes: 'Previous exhibitions deployed two dominant design approaches: the use of standard modular walls to subdivide the space and organize visitor circulations, or the construction of completely autonomous installations with an inherent structure and morphology. However, both (either anonymous or self-referent) lacked a direct relationship with the building.' ReD's intention was to use the building to help generate the exhibition design, and create what the practice calls an 'interface' between the building and the exhibition contents. The exhibition, curated by Marco De Michelis, concentrated on cities, with work from 30 artists in a wide range of media, with film prominent among them.

ReD's project treated the two exhibition floors separately. The first floor, which is a large, open space lit by fluorescent lights, was given a ceiling hung with white flags hanging at different lengths. ReD calls this 'inverted topography' *FLUOsoft*, and used a computer script to define the depth of this undulating surface. ReD hoped that it would 'suggest "areas" and "circulation paths" without using traditional walls or corridors.' On the top floor was the *CONEPlex*, a series of giant nozzles hanging from the ceiling that provided localized areas for the exhibition of film and other animated media that were dark but not completely closed off to the rest of the floor.

Below: *CONEPlex*, the installation on the upper floor of the Kunsthaus Graz, Austria, for the exhibition *M-City*. Opposite top: *FLUOsoft*, an undulating series of flags mounted on the ceiling. Opposite bottom: The space before the exhibition was installed.

| Location | Barcelona, Spain |
| | Porto, Portugal |
| Nationality | Spanish |
| | Portuguese |

ReD Research + Design was founded by architects Marta Malé-Alemany and José Pedro Sousa, and operates from Barcelona, Spain and Porto, Portugal. Malé-Alemany studied in Barcelona and at Columbia University, and has taught widely in the US and Europe. Pedro Sousa studied in Porto, and holds a Master in Genetic Architectures from the ESARQ-UIC school in Barcelona. ReD has built projects in Austria, Spain, the USA and Portugal, and has lectured and published widely. In 2005, ReD won the prestigious and lucrative Far Eastern International Digital Architectural Design Award.

The Kunsthaus Graz links ReD with three of our emerging architects:
Philippe Rahm (pp. 262–263), who exhibited in the *Protections* show there in 2006, Realities United (pp. 268–269), who designed the *BIX* media façade, and ReD.

# Lindy <u>Roy</u>

Lindy Roy has maintained a high profile in the popular press, and her name is associated with some of the great press-generating stories in architecture in recent years. The projects we show here are two of them.

The first is Roy's project for a house on Long Island. This commission wasn't the average. It was part of the *Houses at Sagaponac* project, initiated by the late Harry J Brown (a property developer) and legendary New York architect Richard Meier. The project as a whole was for 34 summer houses, each by a different architect, in the picturesque setting of the Hamptons, that well-known summer retreat for urban New Yorkers. Contributors to the project include Zaha Hadid, Richard Rogers, Eric Owen Moss and Michael Graves, among a galaxy of others. The project promised to be one of the great architectural zoos of our time – a case-study house programme for the twenty-first century East Coast.

Roy was invited to contribute a project to the development, and came up with the *Pool House*. It looks heavily influenced by her former mentors Ricardo Scofidio and Elizabeth Diller, and revolves around the use of eight S-shaped structural elements, wrapped in glazing and timber louvres. The

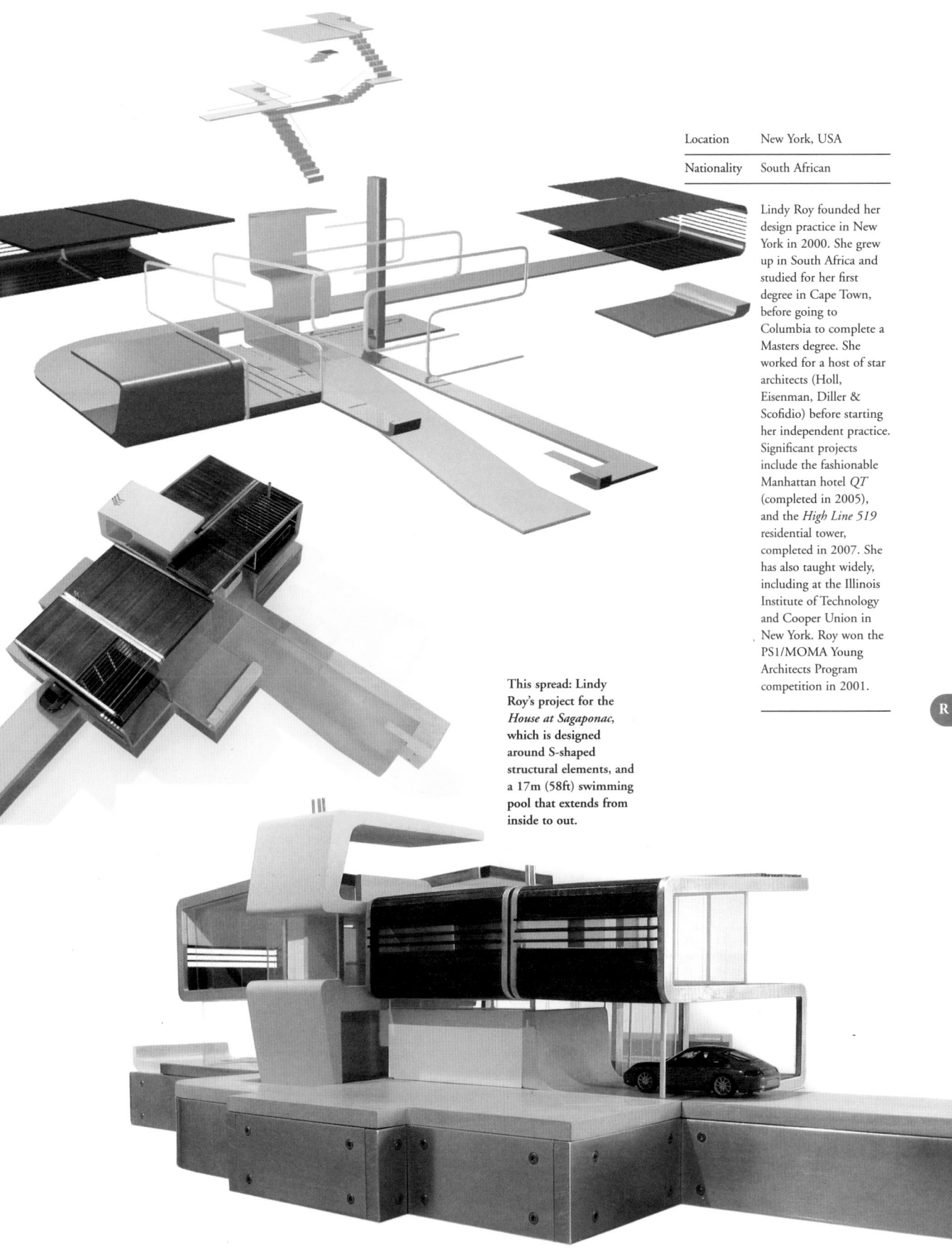

| Location | New York, USA |
| --- | --- |
| Nationality | South African |

Lindy Roy founded her design practice in New York in 2000. She grew up in South Africa and studied for her first degree in Cape Town, before going to Columbia to complete a Masters degree. She worked for a host of star architects (Holl, Eisenman, Diller & Scofidio) before starting her independent practice. Significant projects include the fashionable Manhattan hotel *QT* (completed in 2005), and the *High Line 519* residential tower, completed in 2007. She has also taught widely, including at the Illinois Institute of Technology and Cooper Union in New York. Roy won the PS1/MOMA Young Architects Program competition in 2001.

This spread: Lindy Roy's project for the *House at Sagaponac*, which is designed around S-shaped structural elements, and a 17m (58ft) swimming pool that extends from inside to out.

R

Right: Speculative proposal for a residential tower on West Street, Manhattan, commissioned by the *New York Times* in the wake of the 11 September terrorist attacks in 2001.

house has three bedrooms on the upper floor (two with terraces) and the ground floor has an open-plan configuration, with a double-height dining area. The intention has been to attempt to make the house very open to the exterior. Perhaps the most obvious way this has happened is with the swimming pool, which is 17m (58ft) long, and extends from exterior to interior, culminating in a 'wet bar', steam room and bathrooms.

The other high-profile project shown here is Roy's speculative proposal for a tower on West Street. The 28-storey design was part of the *New York Times'* proposal for Lower Manhattan after the terrorist attacks of 11 September, 2001. The form of the tower came from the idea to take the Westside Highway and extend it upwards, taking four ribbons up and over the height of the tower. On the other side, the ribbons are curled to form balconies and terraces. At its base, the tower has mixed uses, and above is residential.

Furniture manufacturer Vitra considered a number of architects to design its New York showroom in 2001, including SHoP (pp. 286–289). It ended up being Lindy Roy's first built project.

R

# Sambuichi Architects

Sambuichi Architects' dental clinic in Hiroshima, Japan, is not a typical medical building. Eschewing the image of a white, hygienic future, Hiroshi Sambuichi has made an extraordinary retreat in rich, dark timber, hidden behind a series of hedges on artificial berms and beneath grass roofs that make this building almost invisible in its urban context.

Constructed from earth in metal cages, the berms shield the building from view, but allow a great deal of glass in the façades. The feeling is of being on a terrace, with decking extending from inside to out, and curving soffits swooping and opening up to the sky. Treatment rooms are behind huge sliding doors of rich timber. Waiting areas are serene, with Jasper Morrison furniture facing a large north window with its cool light and a view of trees.

Sambuichi is also known for a series of remarkable houses. The *Sloping North House* proposed a building dug into the side of a mountain with a dramatically sloping roof. The building took full advantage of the ecologically efficient passive cooling properties of the

ground, and a later, related project, the *Stone House*, takes this theme much further.

The *Stone House* is in the west of Japan, where the difference between summer and winter temperatures can be extreme ranging from subtropical heat to deep snow. Sambuichi oriented a massive translucent roof to the south to get maximum heat in the winter,

while good cross-ventilation keeps the house cool in summer. The name of the project comes from its base, a giant gabion wall that looks almost like a pile of stones in a quarry. The thermal mass of this stone also helps to keep the house cool in summer. The contrast between the heavy gabions and the lightweight roof and timber structure makes for a unique and strange project.

| Location | Hiroshima, Japan |
| --- | --- |
| Nationality | Japanese |

Hiroshi Sambuichi established Sambuichi Architects in Hiroshima, Japan in 1997. Sambuichi trained at the Tokyo University of Science, and worked for Shinichi Ogawa before starting his own practice. The office now employs seven people. Significant projects include the *Sloping North House* in 2002, the *Air House* in 2003 and a dental clinic in Hiroshima in 2005. In 2003 Sambuichi was commended in the AR+D Awards, and he won the Detail Prize in 2005. He lectures at Yamaguchi University.

Opposite top: The car park and entrance to Sambuichi's dental clinic in Hiroshima.

Opposite bottom: The interior of the clinic is not classically clinical, and is intended to embrace the patient with its curving walls and dark timber surfaces.

Below: Another interior of the clinic. The waiting rooms are shielded from the dense city context by artificial berms.

Right: The clinic in context.

S

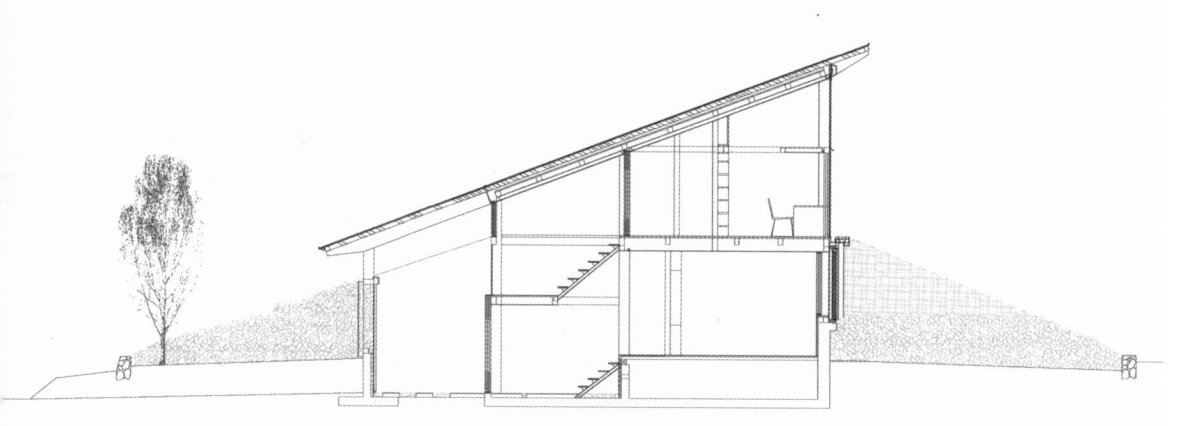

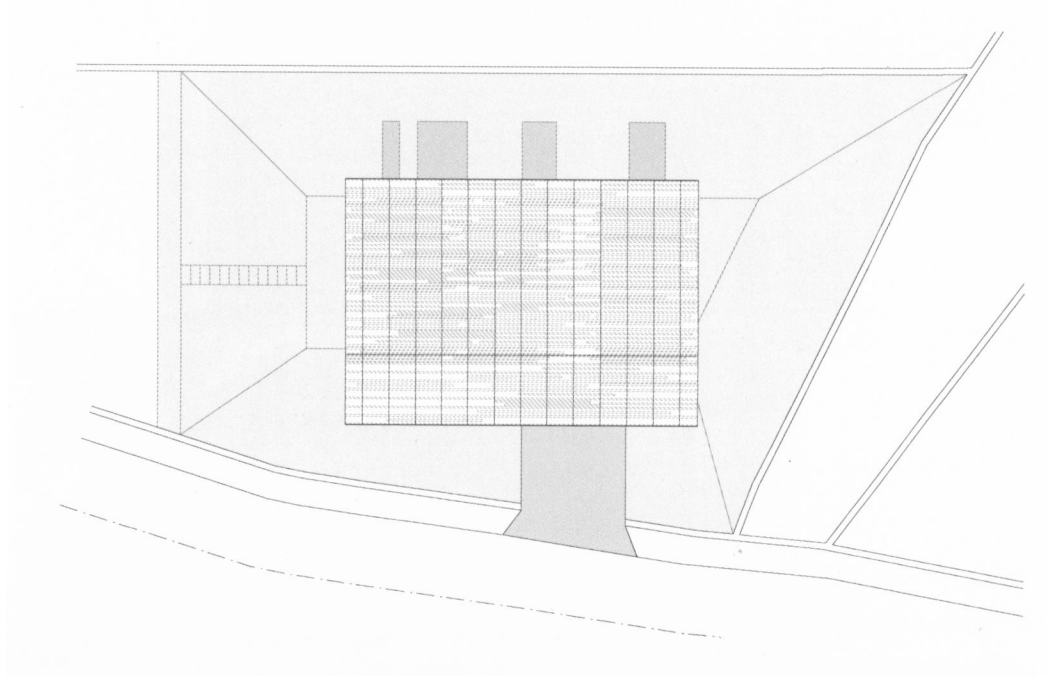

Left: Drawings of the
*Stone House.* The house
is surrounded on three
sides by a gabion-like
arrangement of stones
in cages, which help
with the passive cooling
of the building in
summer.
Above: The roof is
transparent to maximize
solar gain in winter, but
still provides shade.
Opposite top: The
façade facing the
mountain range beyond.
Opposite bottom: The
entrance façade.

S

# Regina Schineis

Regina Schineis' work is characterized by bold and colourful forms with scaleless, luxurious exteriors.

Her building for a music rehearsal room in the small German town of Thannhausen must be a project close to her heart, given her past as an organ scholar in Bayreuth. The building was built into a music society's existing premises on land owned by a school. The whole building had to be constructed during the school's holidays.

The exterior is in copper, which Schineis describes as a material still connoting 'permanence and wealth' in this part of the country. This was provided in prefabricated panels, and hung on to the innovative timber structure. The timber, also largely prefabricated, was used to create a self-supporting shell of a building, folded for stiffness and created out of 10cm-thick (4in) timber elements.

The room was intended for a wind ensemble, and the proportions were generated by its requirements. 10m wide and 16m long (33 by 52ft), the room has a slight off-set towards the rear to create an entrance area. The inner form has proven to be excellent acoustically. The sawtooth soffit and timber lining help the acoustic properties, 'causing the room to resound, making the room itself into an instrument,' writes Schineis.

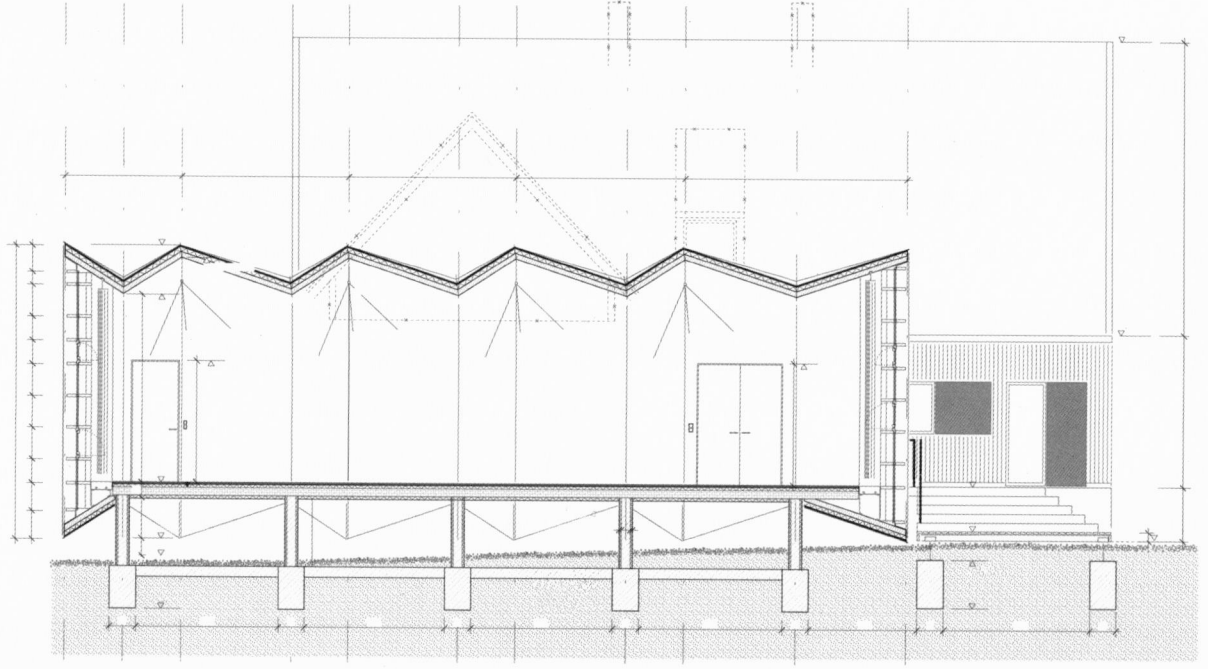

| Location | Augsburg, Germany |
| --- | --- |
| Nationality | German |

Regina Schineis founded her office for architecture and urbanism in Augsburg, Germany, in 1998. She studied music before turning to architecture. After studying in Darmstadt, she attended Tulane University in New Orleans on a Fulbright scholarship. Early projects include the *Haus Jenuwein*, Schönberg, in 1999 and the passenger waiting system (bus stops) in Augsburg, completed in 2001. In 2003 Schineis was commended in the German Architecture Prizes for her rehearsal room at the Musikverein Thannhausen, and in 2000 she won the City of Augsburg Award for the promotion of the arts. She has taught in Augsburg, and has lectured in Germany and the US.

*Haus Karg* is a house built on a very restricted site, and made into a 140sq m (1,500sq ft) dwelling on a 7 by 7m (23 x 23ft) floorplate. The almost seamless timber façade of the building is an unfamiliar exterior expression, but Schineis describes the effect as giving 'the impression of a piece of furniture' to the building.

Inside, the building is flooded with light from one entirely glazed façade. There is a rather sad footnote to the building, however. A disagreement with the owners of the house meant that they never paid the architect's fee, and although the house is complete, the 'architect's role is unrecognized'.

Opposite: Music practice room in Thannhausen, Germany. The section shows its unusual timber shell construction.
This page: *Haus Karg*, from 2004. Schineis and the clients subsequently fell out.

# Servo

Servo's work is some of the most alluring of the interface-obsessed generation of architects of which it is part, integrating high technology with a certain space-age gothic glamour.

The most astonishing of the practice's works so far is the *Dark Places* installation at the Santa Monica Museum of Art in Los Angeles in collaboration with the curator Joshua Decter. The exhibition was on the subject of enigmatic or ambiguous social spaces in urban and suburban contexts, and showed a range of pieces of art, from paintings to films, all collected into eight curatorial sequences presented in digital form.

Servo's project created an armature to show these eight sequences, consisting of eight strands, suspended from a reconfigurable ceiling structure and woven together to create

unexpected adjacencies. Each strand had at its end a vitrine with a projector and display, showing the sequences of artworks. The visitor could interact with the display through interactive workstations that revealed more about the works on display. The whole structure was ethereally lit by fibre optics, which pulsed according to the viewer's activity, shedding more or less light according to the intensity of the visitor's interaction.

Servo writes that its installation was not only responsive to the works on display, but was itself a physical evocation of perhaps the ultimate contemporary 'dark place': the Internet. 'In the twentieth-century metropolis, it was the residual openings or dark places within the city, spaces that were underused and thus held the potential for new forms of use to emerge, which became sites of creative and enigmatic agency,' they write. 'These dark places were sometimes physical and spatial, but they could also take the form of political, economic and legal openings in the city's infrastructure. In the twenty-first century, the Internet has generated a whole new urbanism of potentially productive dark places.'

At the MAK Center in Los Angeles in 2006, Servo created its *Spoorg* design concept for an exhibition about information technologies and genetics called *Gen(h)ome*. Spoorgs are semi-porous operable organisms, micro-organisms that are capable of fusing with other spores and creating new forms that are often unlike either parent. Servo designed cell-like objects in green vacuum-formed plastic that exist both inside and outside of a glazed façade. Each cell integrates sensors, speakers and wireless radio so that each cell can communicate with the others, and the network can respond with sound and light to changes in its local environment. Servo calls it a 'demonstration project', and writes: 'The *Spoorg* system revises the conventional notion of cellularity in architecture as a material aggregate and proposes a composite information aggregate where information cells take on material attributes in the architectural environment.'

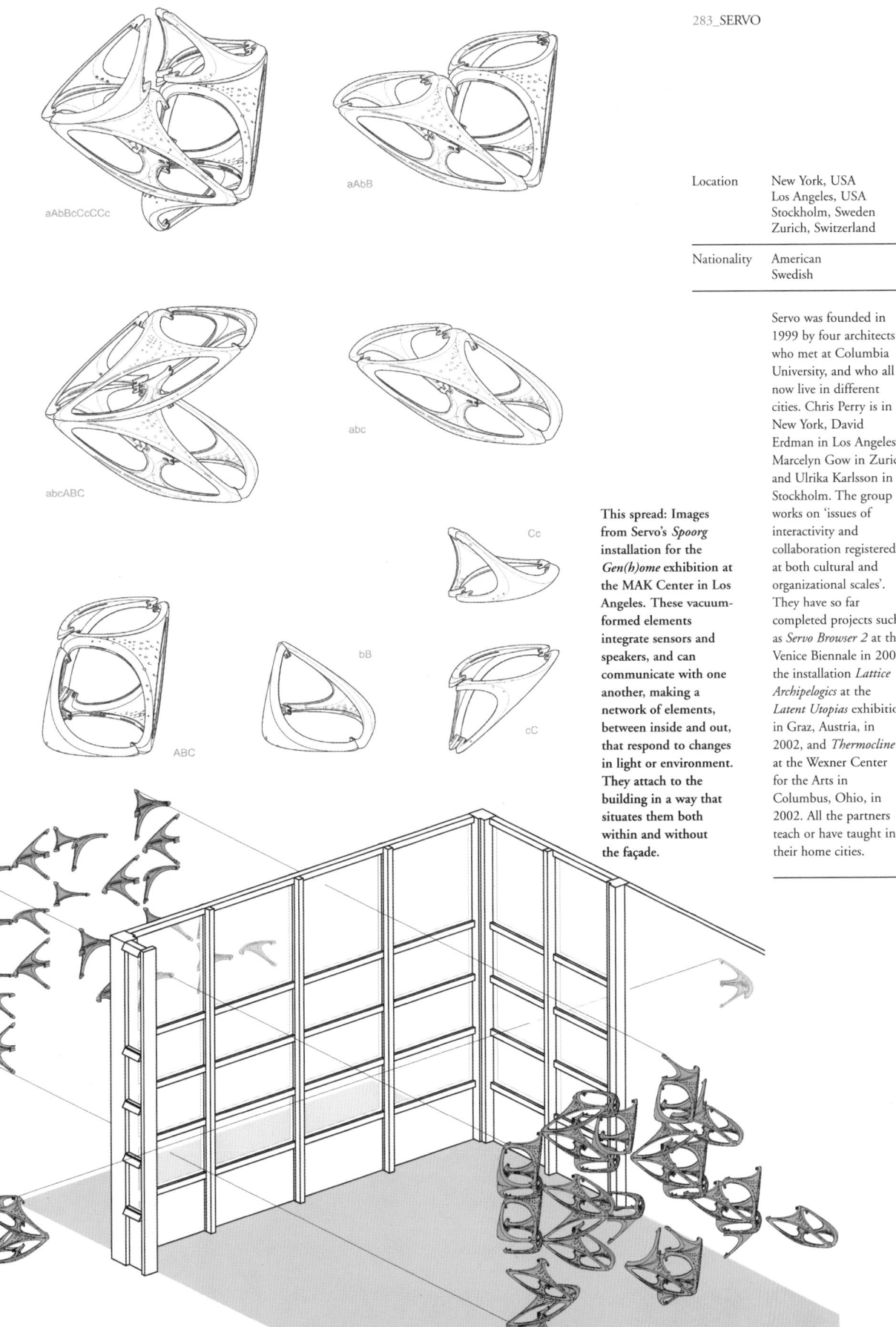

aAbBcCcCCc

aAbB

abcABC

abc

ABC

bB

Cc

cC

| Location | New York, USA |
| --- | --- |
| | Los Angeles, USA |
| | Stockholm, Sweden |
| | Zurich, Switzerland |
| Nationality | American |
| | Swedish |

Servo was founded in 1999 by four architects who met at Columbia University, and who all now live in different cities. Chris Perry is in New York, David Erdman in Los Angeles, Marcelyn Gow in Zurich and Ulrika Karlsson in Stockholm. The group works on 'issues of interactivity and collaboration registered at both cultural and organizational scales'. They have so far completed projects such as *Servo Browser 2* at the Venice Biennale in 2003, the installation *Lattice Archipelogics* at the *Latent Utopias* exhibition in Graz, Austria, in 2002, and *Thermocline* at the Wexner Center for the Arts in Columbus, Ohio, in 2002. All the partners teach or have taught in their home cities.

This spread: Images from Servo's *Spoorg* installation for the *Gen(h)ome* exhibition at the MAK Center in Los Angeles. These vacuum-formed elements integrate sensors and speakers, and can communicate with one another, making a network of elements, between inside and out, that respond to changes in light or environment. They attach to the building in a way that situates them both within and without the façade.

S

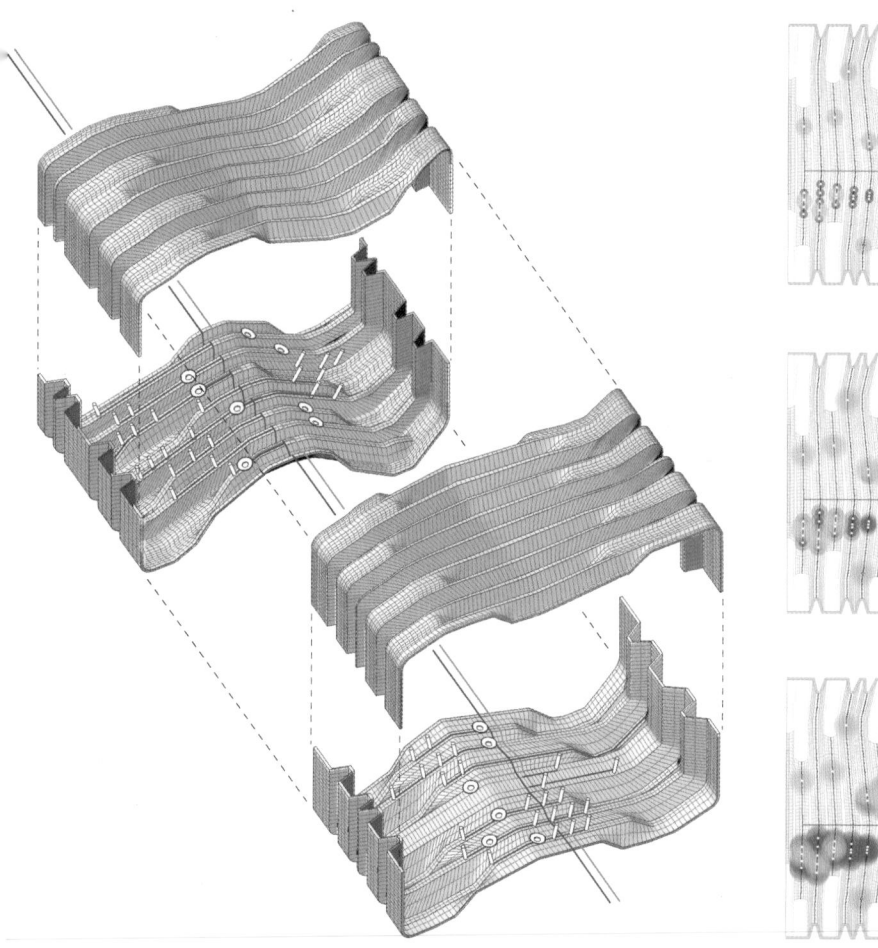
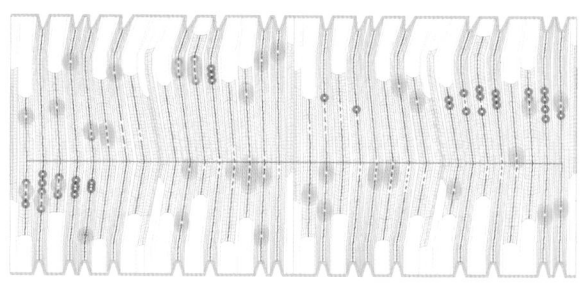
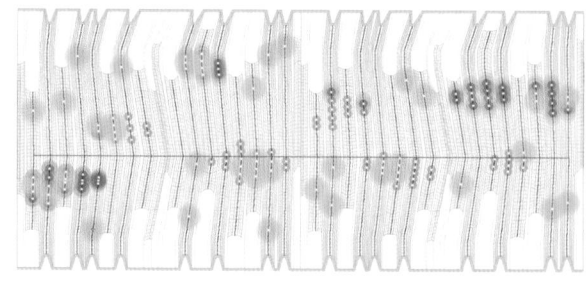
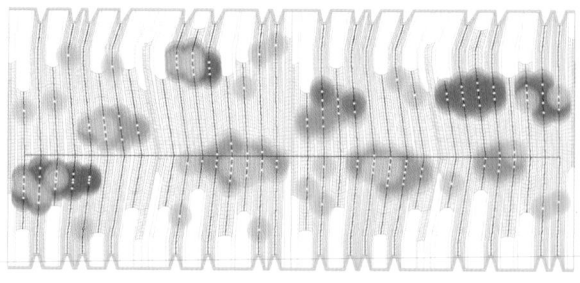

Opposite: *Thermocline*, made for the Wexner Center for the Arts in 2002. It is a piece of furniture, manufactured using digital prototyping methods, that integrates light, sound and sensors.

This page: *Dark Places*, an installation at the Santa Monica Museum of Art in Los Angeles in 2006. Each projector presented a series of images of artworks created by curator Joshua Decter.

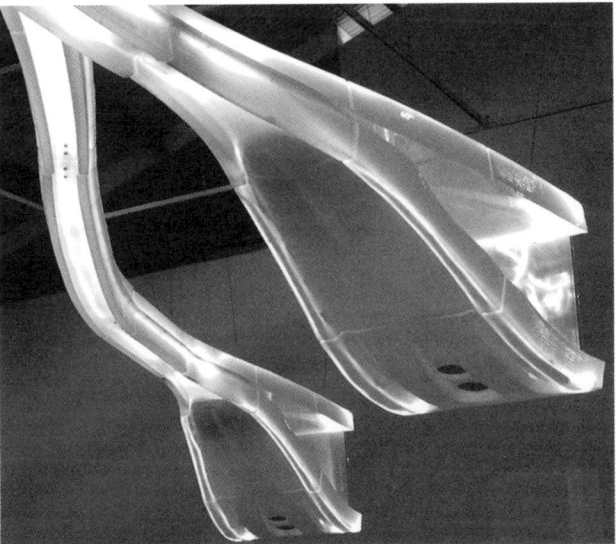

Servo partners Marcelyn Gow and Ulrika Karlsson are part of the Krets (pp. 166–169) collaborative.

S

# SHoP

This spread: The
*Hangil Book House* at
Heyri Art Valley near
Seoul in South Korea.

| Location | New York, USA |
| --- | --- |
| Nationality | American |

SHoP (Sharples Holden Pasquarelli) was founded in New York in 1996 by five partners: Christopher Sharples, Coren Sharples, William Sharples, Kimberly Holden and Gregg Pasquarelli. All studied for their postgraduate degrees at Columbia. The office is the biggest in this book, at 50 strong. Early successes included victory in the PS1/MOMA Young Architects Program competition in 2000 with the *Dunescape* project, and an unbuilt project for a Museum of Sex in New York. The practice followed this with work all over the world from single-family residences to urban plans. SHoP has been published and exhibited internationally, and the model of *Dunescape* is in the permanent collection of MOMA New York. Most of the partners are teachers; Christopher Sharples teaches at Columbia, while Pasquarelli is a visiting professor at Yale.

SHoP (Sharples Holden Pasquarelli) is, in a way, too big for this book, but it stands as a fascinating counterpoint to much of the American architecture included. Here is a practice that is genuinely interested in building for commercial clients on a large scale.

Perhaps the best example of this could lay claim to being the most significant piece of non-public architecture built in Manhattan in the last decade or more. The *Porter House* is a 22-unit luxury housing development in the Meatpacking District on the corner of Ninth Avenue and 15th Street, completed in 2003. Part of the project was the refurbishment of a fine warehouse dating from 1905, but the main visible part of the work is a new box, seemingly hanging off one corner of the old warehouse, clad in black and dotted with slivers of light, which give it a coolly glamorous profile at night. The project is now very much part of the atmosphere of this district of the city, and presaged a mini-revival in contemporary architecture for housing in New York, particularly in the Lower West Side.

Another recent built project from SHoP is its building at the architectural zoo that is Heyri Art Valley, near Seoul in South Korea.

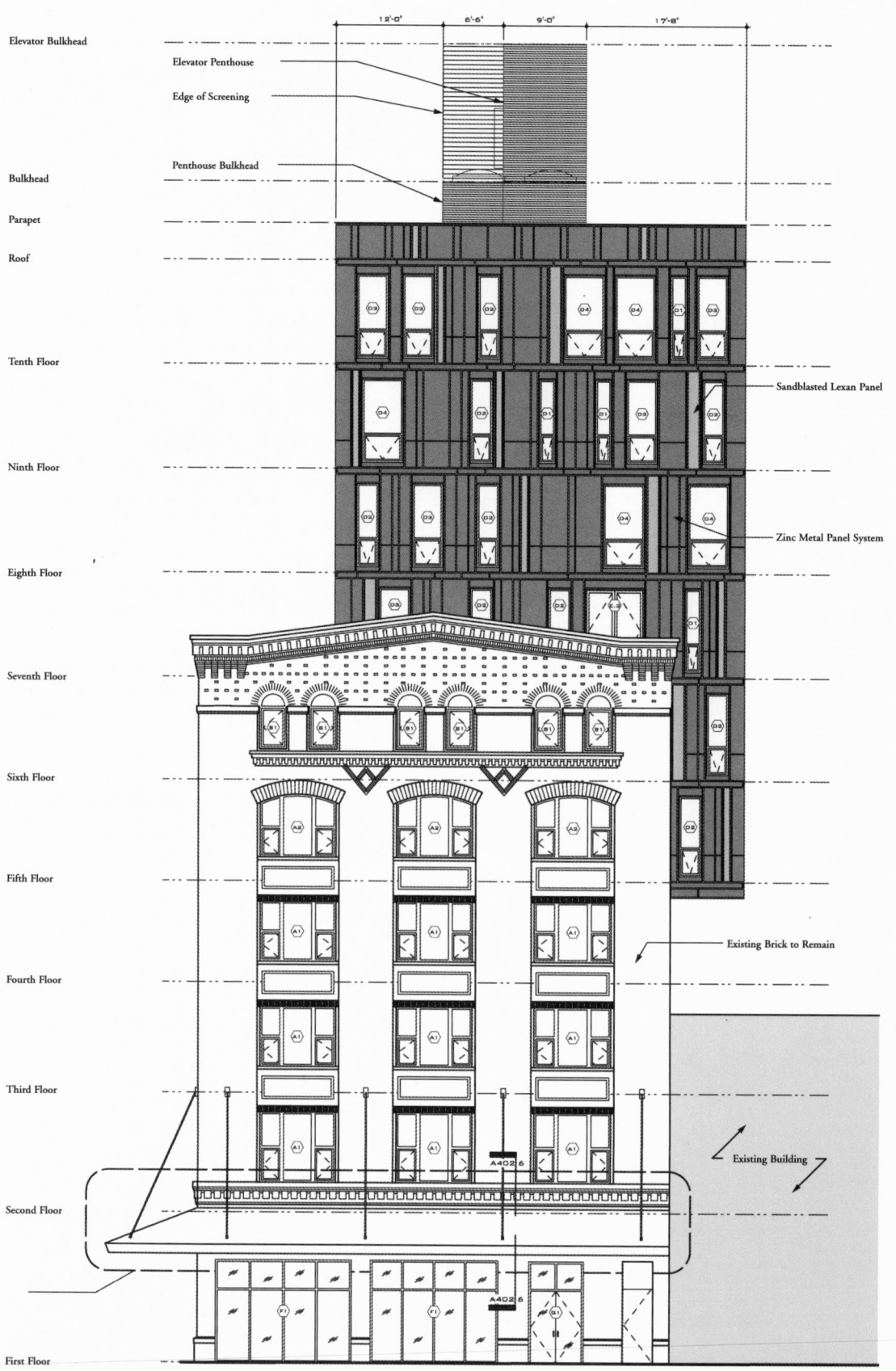

Elevator Bulkhead

Elevator Penthouse

Edge of Screening

Penthouse Bulkhead

Bulkhead

Parapet

Roof

Tenth Floor

Sandblasted Lexan Panel

Ninth Floor

Eighth Floor

Zinc Metal Panel System

Seventh Floor

Sixth Floor

Fifth Floor

Existing Brick to Remain

Fourth Floor

Third Floor

Existing Building

Second Floor

First Floor

12'-0"   6'-6"   9'-0"   17'-8"

This spread: SHoP's
*Porter House* residen
building in New Yo
Meatpacking Distri
completed in 2003.

Gregg Pasquarelli spent time at the office of Frank Gehry, as did the partners of Ball Nogues (pp. 38–41).

The area has buildings from a variety of architects, both Korean and international. It hopes to become a 24-hour piece of city with a variety of arts venues being built in the next few years. The *Hangil Book House* was completed in 2004 for a publishing company, and accommodates many uses, from bookstores, a café and outdoor reading locations, to performance and exhibition spaces. The building is conceived as a built landscape, sitting as it does at the foot of a hill. The architects write: 'The house is in two distinct zones: a vertical bar connected to the outdoor reading space on the hillside, and a large hall housing the mixed-use programs.' The entire building is clad in an ipe wood skin, with a formal colonnade at ground floor deforming to a much freer form at roof level. Inside, a ramped route takes the visitor up and through the building, past the spectacular three-storey book wall. At each landing of the ramp is a different reading space.

# Jennifer Siegal

Jennifer Siegal is fascinated by the potential of mobile architecture – trailers, caravans and other infrastructures that can help us to live in a more ecologically sustainable way. She takes her inspiration in part from Antonia Sant'Elia's *Futurist Manifesto*, dating from 1914. 'We no longer believe in the monumental, the heavy and the static,' he wrote. Siegal's work follows this, proposing a series of mobile and adapted dwellings.

One of Siegal's earlier mobile projects was the *Ecolab*, built in 1998 in collaboration with the Hollywood Beautification Team agency. The trailer was conceived as a mobile classroom and exhibition space, constructed within a donated cargo-truck trailer measuring 2.4 x 10.7m (8 x 35ft). Materials used included cast-offs from Hollywood movie sets. The trailer now travels around Los Angeles, educating children about ecological matters. Siegal writes: 'Like a circus tent, this mobile icon arrives at the schoolyard where elevated walkways fold down and slide out of the trailer's body. It is immediately recognizable as a place for interaction, discovery and fun.'

A later project, the *Portable Construction Training Centre* (*PCTC*) is a mobile education facility for the Venice Community Housing Corporation, intended to be a place for local people to learn skills associated with the construction industry. The trailer, which measures 4.2 x 19.8m (14 x 65ft), is fully demountable but also has serious architectural intent. A threshold is created along one of the long sides of the trailer, in the form of a covered terrace that invites potential trainees in, while a central meeting room also makes the place accessible.

Four trades are taught in the trailer: plumbing, painting and plastering, and carpentry and electrics. These areas are on display for all to observe. The *PCTC* tries to be an exemplar of innovative construction techniques; it uses cross-ventilation and passive shading, and has an attractive timber roof structure revealed within.

Opposite: *Ecolab*, a trailer created in 1998 as a mobile education centre for ecological issues. It was made out of a donated cargo-truck trailer and old sets from Hollywood film studios. This page: *PCTC*, a mobile education facility that teaches construction skills.

| Location | Venice, USA |
| --- | --- |
| Nationality | American |

Jennifer Siegal founded her practice, the Office of Mobile Design, in 1998 after studying at SCI-Arc in Los Angeles for her Masters. She became a Loeb Fellow at the Harvard Graduate School of Design in 2003, and is still a professor. She is based in Venice, California. As well as authoring books such as *Mobile: The Art of Portable Architecture*, Siegal has something of a mainstream media profile, with appearances on the TV show *What's With That House?* and others. She won an America's Best and Brightest Award from *Esquire* magazine in 2003, and in the same year was nominated in the New York Architecture League's Emerging Voices Awards, showing how she straddles architectural and popular culture.

**Siegal was honoured by US men's magazine *Esquire* in 2003.**

**Patrick Lynch of Lynch Architects (pp. 178–181) was UK *Arena* magazine's Creative Man of the Year in 2005.**

S

# Stalker

Campo Boario is an area of Rome that used to be a slaughterhouse, but since 1975 has had no specific use and has lain derelict. At least that is the categorization that many architects, planners or city officials might give it. In fact, it has become home to thousands of travelling communities, particularly a Kurdish population of refugees that has found asylum in the city. They have occupied this territory and made it their own.

This has also become exactly the kind of territory that Stalker finds fascinating, and the Italian art/architecture collective has carried out a series of works there since 1999. Francesco Careri and Lorenzo Romito of Stalker describe the place as 'an urban area produced by the globalization process as many others in different cities and countries of the world. These are areas that seem extraneous to our culture even though they are part of it by now.... In these places, the city forgets all its masks and becomes naked, showing what the city itself doesn't know. No traditional projects are accepted, the energies and the intelligence to redefine itself are found in its ability of self-organizing ....'

Stalker's engagement began in 1999 with the appropriation and renovation of the former veterinary building of the slaughterhouse. The place was renamed Ararat, and became a place for the Kurdish community to gather, and a space for artists and architects to work. The approach from then on has been to create in Campo Boario what Stalker calls a series of 'games', making interventions that are always temporary, but that allow a sense of community to develop and create a new contemporary history for the place. Stalker describes elements of its three years of activity at Campo Boario: 'The large asphalt space became the playground for collective games: the *Carta di non identità* ('non-ID card'), which was distributed to all the inhabitants on the occasion of Clandestino Day; the *Pranzo Boario* (*Boario Lunch*), a big circular dining table where Kurdish food, gypsy goulash and Japanese seaweed (cooked by Asako Iwama, Japanese artist and architect) were served together; the *Global Game*, during which residents were encouraged to write stories of Campo Boario on one of 2,000 soccer balls; the *Transborderline*, a spiral space that symbolically represented a permeable and inhabitable border, which was then illegally installed on the Italian/ Slovenian borderline; the *Tappeto Volante* (*Flying Carpet*), an itinerant ceiling that traces the *muqarnas* [decorative, stalactite-like ceiling] of the Palatine Chapel in Palermo using ropes and copper.'

While the projects have left no physical traces, the project moves ideas of participation and community engagement forwards from top-down strategies of creating fictional identities, towards an engagement with uncertainty and opposition in the city. Stalker writes: 'Campo Boario needs neither artworks nor public architecture to define its clear identity. Its characteristics are the uncertainty, the indefiniteness and the self-organization of its own physical and relational spaces. The challenge is to produce a public space starting from these premises.'

Above and opposite top: Fake passport (*Carta di non identità*) created to commemorate Clandestino Day on 24 September.
Opposite below: Stalker's projects at Campo Boario in Rome have consisted of various artistic and temporary interventions designed to help the immigrant Kurdish community that lives on the site semi-legally.

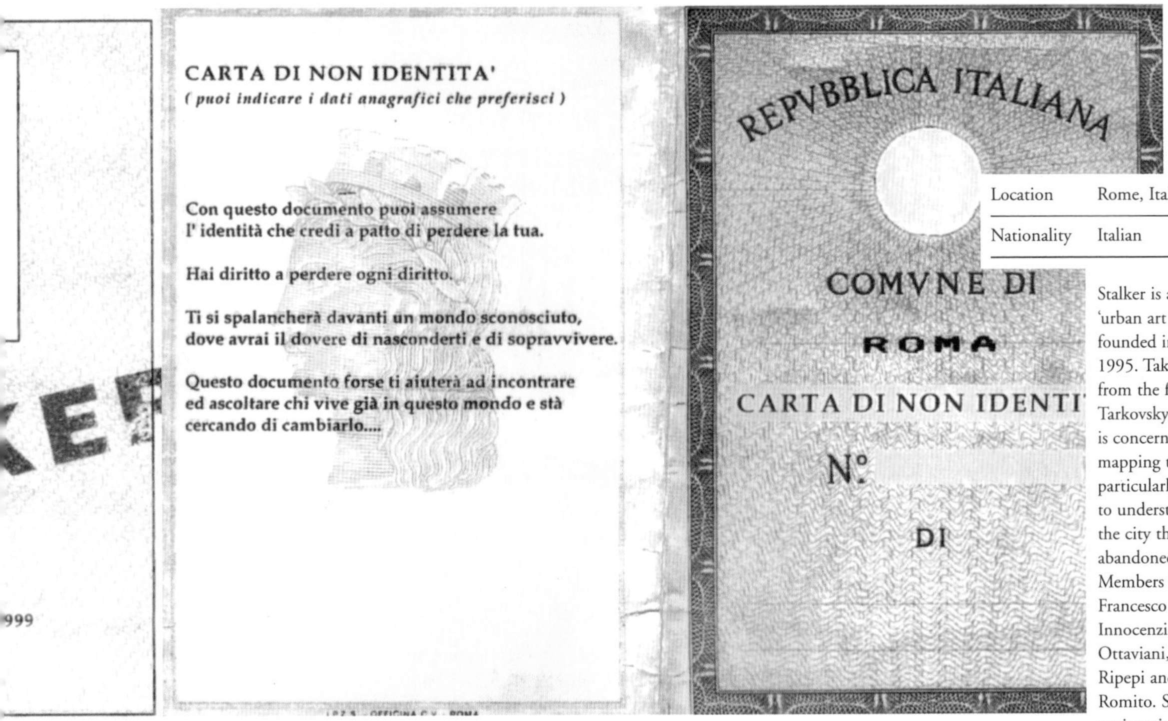

**CARTA DI NON IDENTITA'**
*( puoi indicare i dati anagrafici che preferisci )*

Con questo documento puoi assumere
l' identità che credi a patto di perdere la tua.

Hai diritto a perdere ogni diritto.

Ti si spalancherà davanti un mondo sconosciuto,
dove avrai il dovere di nasconderti e di sopravvivere.

Questo documento forse ti aiuterà ad incontrare
ed ascoltare chi vive già in questo mondo e stà
cercando di cambiarlo....

REPVBBLICA ITALIANA

COMVNE DI

ROMA

CARTA DI NON IDENTIT

N°

DI

| Location | Rome, Italy |
|----------|-------------|
| Nationality | Italian |

Stalker is a collective, or 'urban art laboratory', founded in Rome in 1995. Taking its name from the film by Andrei Tarkovsky, Stalker's work is concerned with mapping the city, particularly Rome, trying to understand linkages in the city through abandoned zones. Members include Francesco Careri, Aldo Innocenzi, Romolo Ottaviani, Giovanna Ripepi and Valerio Romito. Significant projects include *Transborderline*, a habitable structure shown at the Venice Biennale in 2000, and Stalker's ongoing engagement with Campo Boario in Rome, a former slaughterhouse site that has been home to many of the group's interventions. Stalker has also instituted the transdisciplinary and international research network called Osservatorio Nomade.

This spread: More
images from the Campo
Boario project. Nothing
permanent was created,
but events such as this
meal (*Pranzo Boario*,
with cooking from
Japanese, Hungarian
and Kurdish chefs) were
an attempt to begin a
public space in a place
of illegal occupation.

Stalker participated in the Camp for Oppositional Architecture, along with
Joseph Grima (pp. 138–139), Mac Kane of *Polar Inertia* (pp. 250–251), Raumlabor (pp. 264–265) and Raumtaktik (pp. 266–267).

# Stealth

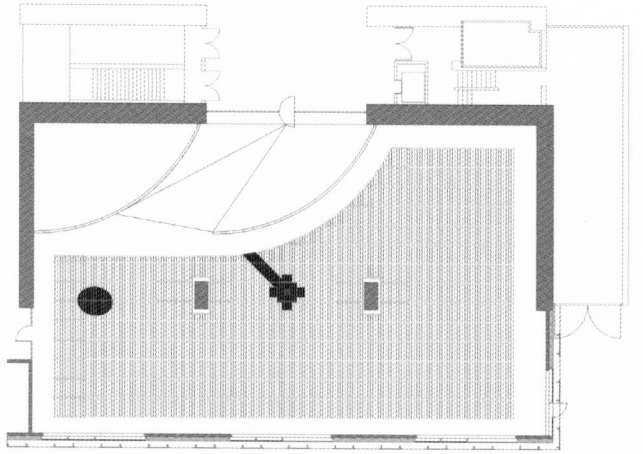

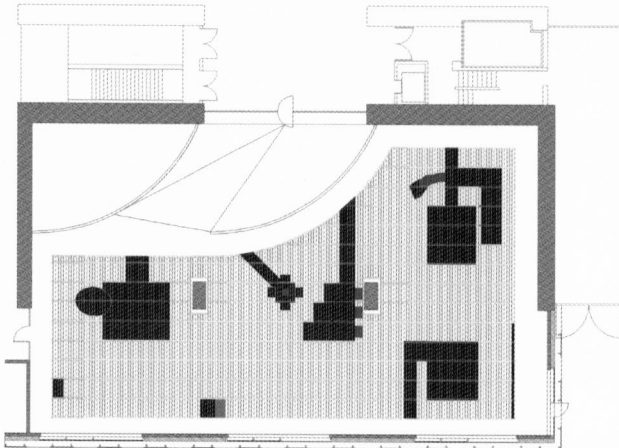

Stealth's work is in the strange territory between urbanism and interface design, attempting to find new ways of accessing, managing and presenting information about the city that gets ever more complex and inaccessible.

Often Stealth's work takes the form of computer models or proposals that exist within the digital realm. But in 2006, Stealth was commissioned by the Boijmans van Beuningen Museum in Rotterdam to undertake a participatory work of art at the scale of a gallery space. Stealth designed a structure consisting of 2,000 cardboard sheets, covering 1,100 cubic m (1,438 cubic yd) of the gallery, and held in place by MDF 'combs' at 15cm (6in) intervals. Stealth called this installation 'a device; a testing tool on a 1:1 scale that invites a line of activities to respond spatially and programmatically.'

To occupy this field, Stealth invited a number of people to come and excavate spaces for themselves to use, cutting away the cardboard into rooms and passageways. There were more than 15 interventions, cutting out 'an office space for a writer, residency space for an

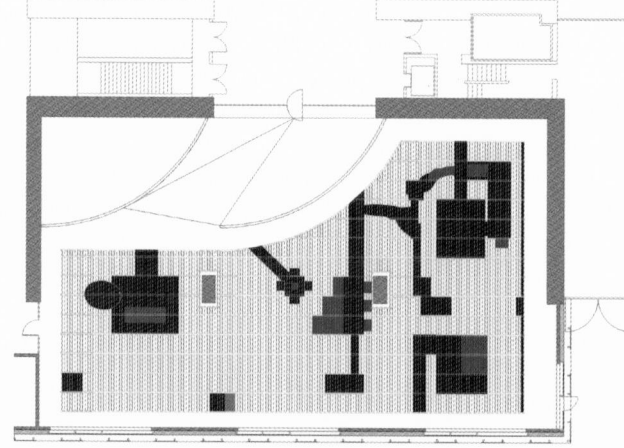

This spread: Stealth's project at the Boijmans van Beuningen Museum in Rotterdam in 2006, entitled *Cut for Purpose*. Groups were invited to cut rooms out of a field of cardboard for a variety of purposes.

| Location | Amsterdam, The Netherlands |
| --- | --- |
| Nationality | Serbian Dutch Brazilian |

Stealth started from a collaboration on the project *Wild City*, by Ana Dzokic, Milica Topalovic, Marc Neelen and Ivan Kucina. In 2004, the group transformed to Stealth Unlimited, which consists of Dzokic, Neelen and Mario Campanella. Dzokic studied in Belgrade and at the Berlage in Rotterdam; Neelen at the Technical University in Delft, the Netherlands; and Campanella at the Instituto Militar de Engenharia, Brazil. The practice's work is concentrated on cities, and the unseen power relations that define contemporary urbanism. Its work attempts to reveal the temporary forces acting on sites, and it makes (often digital) prototypes that encourage interaction with them. The practice's work has been exhibited and published widely, including at the Architecture Biennale in Beijing in 2006, at the Museum Boijmans van Beuningen in Rotterdam in 2006, at ArchiLab 2004 in Orleans, and at Urban Drift in 2003 in Berlin. Significant projects include the *AmsterdamNoord.tmp*, a plan for the redevelopment of the Ij embankment in Amsterdam, and *ProcessMatter*, a computer simulator of urban systems (2002–04).

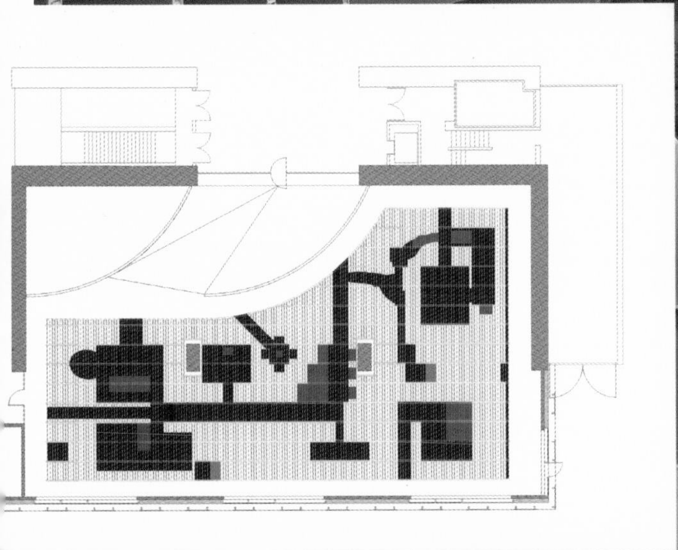

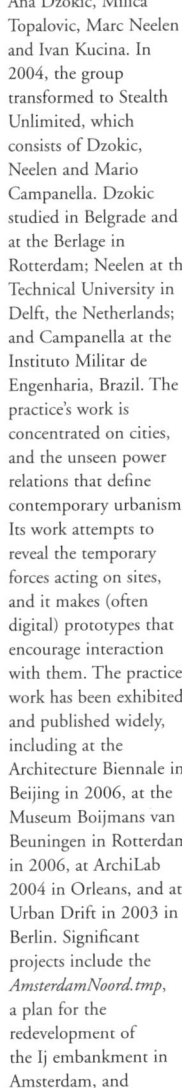

S

This spread: Images from Stealth's *Street/Appropriation/Struggle* project, a simulation of users of the public space on Witte de With Street in Rotterdam, the Netherlands (shown bottom on this page). The simulation was shown at the V2 Gallery in Rotterdam in 2005.

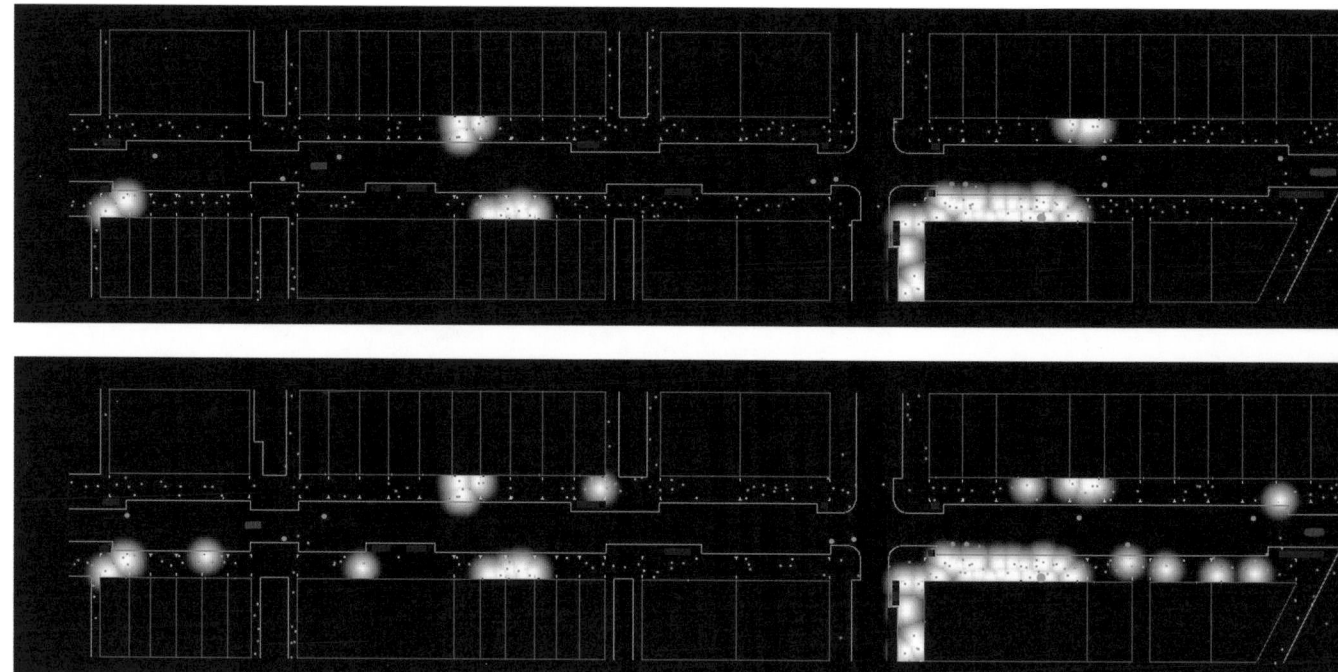

for this an empty one? Or is it something we have to cut, carve and claim?'

The second project here is Stealth's *Street/Appropriation/Struggle*, which was devised for the *Infractures* exhibition at the V2 Gallery in Rotterdam in 2005. The project is a digital simulation of pedestrian movement on Witte de With Street in Rotterdam, projected 12m wide and 3m high (39 by 10ft) in the V2 Gallery. The simulation looks in detail at how boundaries affect movement, according to the numbers or direction of the people in the space. The intention was to question and dramatize some of the discussion emerging from new legislation in the Netherlands giving police the power to ban public assembly (and protest) in 'high-risk' areas.

art collective, a workshop for a product designer, a video room, a sound room, a meeting space, a garden, a set-up for a DJ battle/film, and radio space.' The project attempted to ask a question of the kinds of places that encourage social interaction: 'Is the field of play necessary

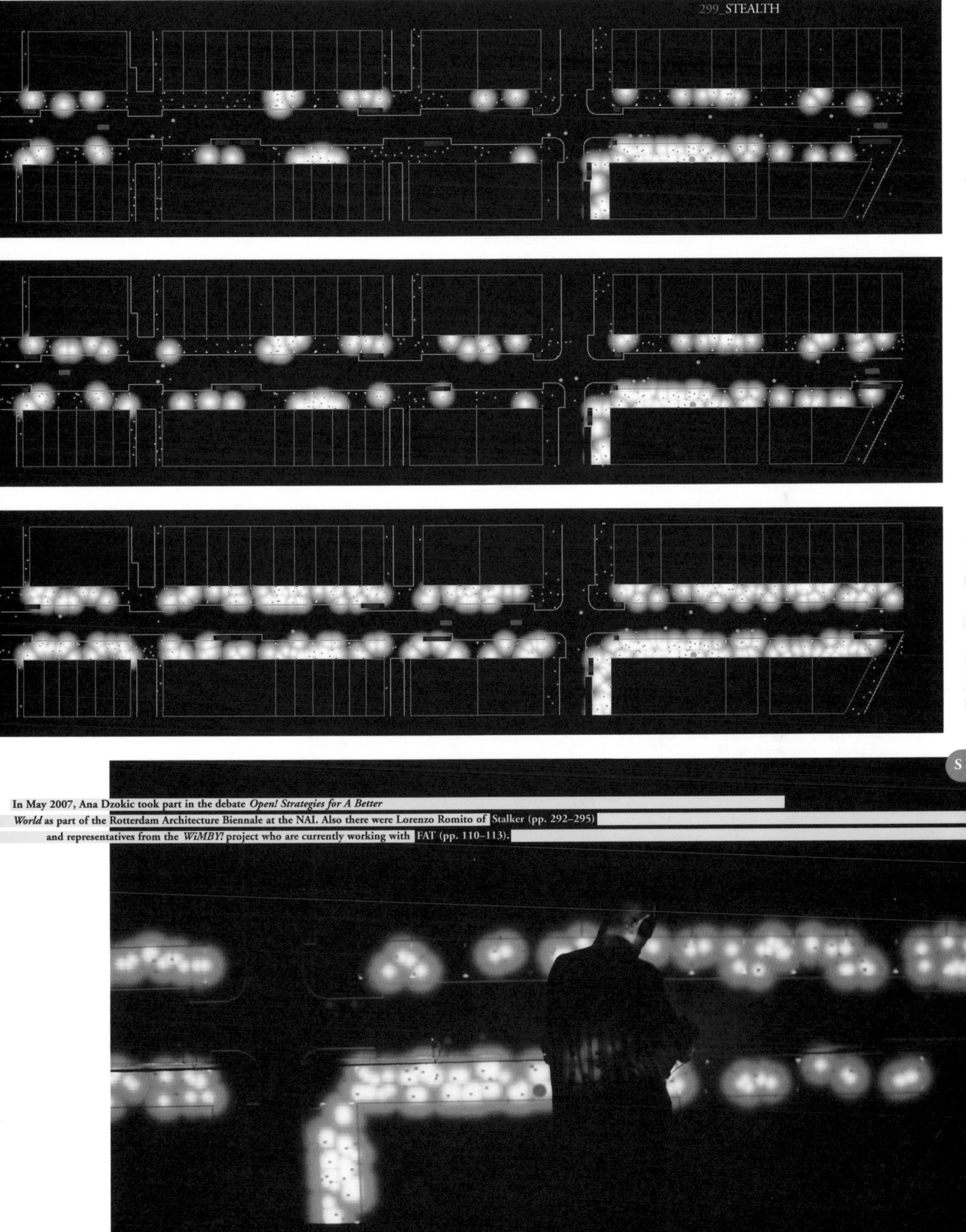

In May 2007, Ana Dzokic took part in the debate *Open! Strategies for A Better World* as part of the Rotterdam Architecture Biennale at the NAI. Also there were Lorenzo Romito of Stalker (pp. 292–295) and representatives from the *WiMBY!* project who are currently working with FAT (pp. 110–113).

# Atelier Tekuto

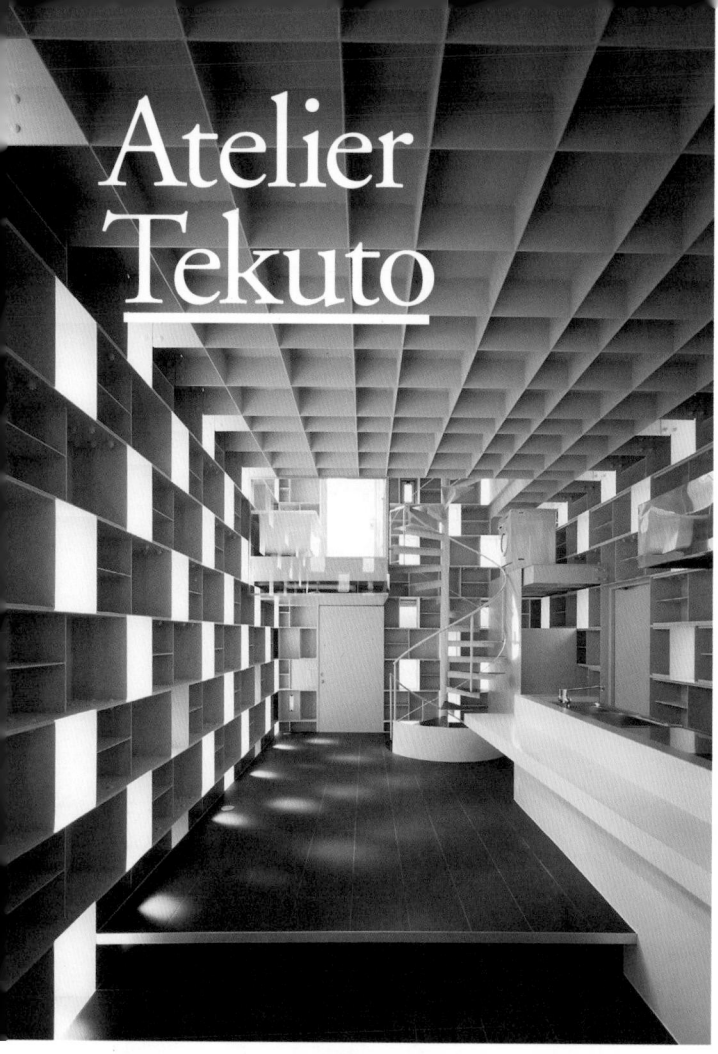

Yasuhiro Yamashita seems to have a voracious and always varied appetite for one-off house commissions. With a series of projects (56 at the last count), he has taken the slivers of land available in Japanese cities and made a wildly varied collection of residential buildings, from Corbusian plays of mass and void in the early days, to spectacular structural feats (the cantilevered *Wafers House*, 2004) and deconstructivist confections (*Ref-Ring*, Kanagawa, 2005) latterly. Although it is impossible to generalize about this oeuvre (eg. the boat-like roof structure of the *Lucky Drop* house, 2005), recent projects have tended towards a more elemental, prismatic formal vocabulary, using the material of the surfaces to achieve the desired effects. To Western eyes, these houses look extraordinary – one wonders what building regulations in Japan say about insulation and thermal bridging.

This spread: *Cell Brick House* in Tokyo. It is constructed out of prefabricated modules of five or six steel boxes, alternating with glazing.

The boxes (a technique that Yamashita calls 'void masonry') form storage on the inside.

| Location | Tokyo, Japan |
| Nationality | Japanese |

Atelier Tekuto was established in 1991 by Yasuhiro Yamashita in Tokyo as Yamashita Kai. He changed the name to Atelier Tekuto in 1995. Yamashita studied at Shibaura Institute of Technology, where he teaches today. He has won awards from *Wallpaper\** and *Architectural Review* magazines, and has been honoured several times in the INAX design competition. The majority of Atelier Tekuto's work is domestic, one-off houses, of which Yamashita has completed 56. Significant among these are *Layers House*, *Lucky Drop* and *Magritte's House*, all in Tokyo, and *Aluminium House* in Kanagawa, all completed in 2005. In 2007, the practice completed the *Busan Eco Centre* in Korea.

T

This spread: The *Crystal Brick House*, in Bunkyo, Tokyo.

In any case, the first of the two remarkable houses here was built for a woman in her 50s who lives with her two children, both in their 20s. The site, on a corner in a quiet Tokyo housing area, is only 33sq m (355sq ft), and the house in total, over its three floors, is 85sq m (915sq ft). The project's name, the *Cell Brick House*, comes from the system used for the walls. Yamashita calls the construction of these hit-and-miss walls 'void masonry', alternating steel boxes with voids to create a *brise-soleil* wall. The boxes, each of which measure 90 x 45 x 30cm (35 x 17 x 12in), also function as storage inside the house. The building was constructed using modules of five or six steel boxes, stacked on top of one another. The lighting effect inside, says Yamashita, is intended to evoke the dappled light of the sun shining through trees in a forest.

The *Crystal Brick House*, in the Bunkyo district of Tokyo and completed in 2004, is an extension of an existing steel-frame building. The client's request was that the house should provide a living area on the first floor for the parents, and on the ground floor for a younger couple. The building is a three-storey structure, entirely clad in glass blocks which are also the structural walls of the extension. This innovative structural arrangement was achieved in collaboration with the manufacturer, engineer and a university department. This glass block wall is given variation and depth by three different treatments on the interior, as the architect explains: 'The transparent layer for view lines, the semi-transparent layer for perception of the light, and the non-transparent layer for the perception of the distance and boundary.' This glowing, crystalline house was inspired by the client's collection of minerals.

In 2004, the *Cell Brick House* won an AR+D award. In the same year, Die Baupiloten (pp. 44–45), Manuel Clavel Rojo (pp. 58–61), Ofis Arhitekti (pp. 234–235) and Theskyisbeautiful (pp. 316–317) were mentioned or commended.

T

# Testbedstudio

Testbedstudio's projects take the kind of earnest urban activism typical of emerging practices in Berlin or Vienna and give it a light-hearted Nordic twist, making mini-urbanism with a healthily developed sense of the absurd.

*The Book of Ideas: 100 Ideas for Urban Improvement* was published for the Urban Planning Biennale in Copenhagen, Denmark, in 2005 and later exhibited in Stockholm. Conceived as '100 ready-to-use ideas for urban improvement', the 100 ideas were small and playful, influenced by what the practice calls 'Mega Trends' – huge-scale concepts such as globalization, environmentalism and demography that are the most pressing concerns of modern Western cities. Each of the 100 ideas was categorized under one of these trends, despite their tiny size. For example, under welfare/wellbeing was a proposal for a tree of basketball hoops. Under the theme of 'environment' was a

**Right:** The main illustration from *The Book of Ideas: 100 Ideas for Urban Improvement.*

proposal for 'Lose Some Win Some', a box where people can leave unwanted items, and pick out things they do need. Other proposals took the form of tiny planters or communal skateboards.

This strategy of micro-intervention was continued with the project *100 Crown Arkitektur*, a project for the SOC Gallery in Stockholm. The exhibition called for projects about funding, and how money was spent on culture and architecture. Testbedstudio's

argument was: 'Everyone can do something for their environment, the public places and spaces that you do not exactly own, or even for those spaces someone else owns. Architecture doesn't have to be expensive. Ten euros can be enough.'

They continue: 'A footbridge over a brook could be made of a board for ten euros, whereas the Årsta bridge commands a price of 150,000,000 euros."

| Location | Malmö, Sweden |
| | Stockholm, Sweden |
| Nationality | Swedish |

Testbedstudio was founded in Malmö, Sweden, in 2000 by Fredrik Magnusson and Jonas Olsson. Today the practice has offices in both Malmö and Stockholm. Current members are Fredrik Magnusson, Katarina Rundgren, Anders Johansson, Erik Wingquist and Helena Mattsson. The practice began with an exhibit in Gammel Dok in Copenhagen about urban development in Malmö, quickly followed by several pavilions and work for the *Bo01* housing exhibition in Malmö.

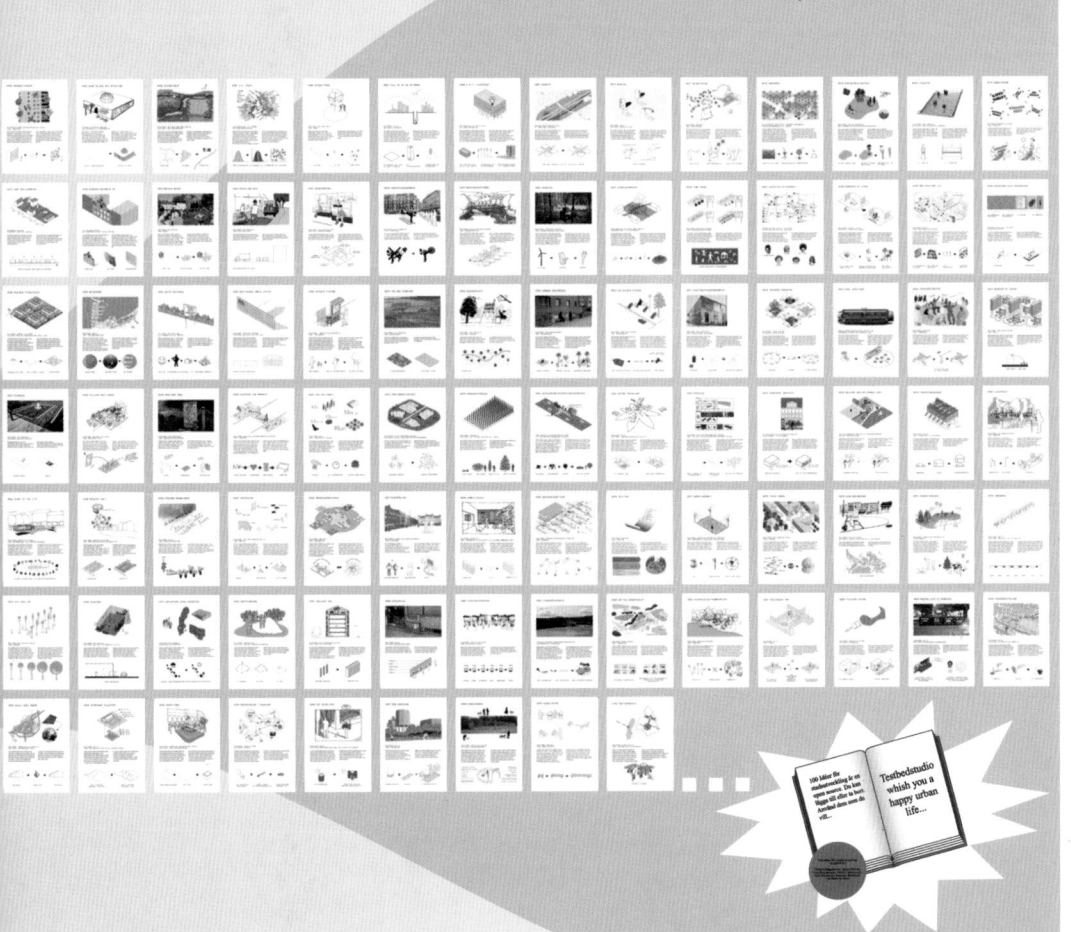

The project asked questions about how we place monetary value on interventions in the city, and speculated about how architecture might manipulate this 'economy of interchangeability'. Provocatively, particularly in a highly centralized state like Sweden, they wrote: 'Some qualities in the city are more easily valued than others. What can't be sold can easily be conceived as having no value, and therefore regarded as not necessary. Which qualities are we prepared to pay for?'

Opposite: Some of the objects inserted into the physical environment of Stockholm as part of Testbedstudio's *100 Crown Arkitektur* exhibition in 2005. Below: Axonometric of the practice's proposal for a multi-use sports centre in an old underground car park in the poor Stockholm satellite of Tensta. It is an example of what Testbedstudio have referred to as 'activity-oriented architecture', presenting a place of seething and intense activity.

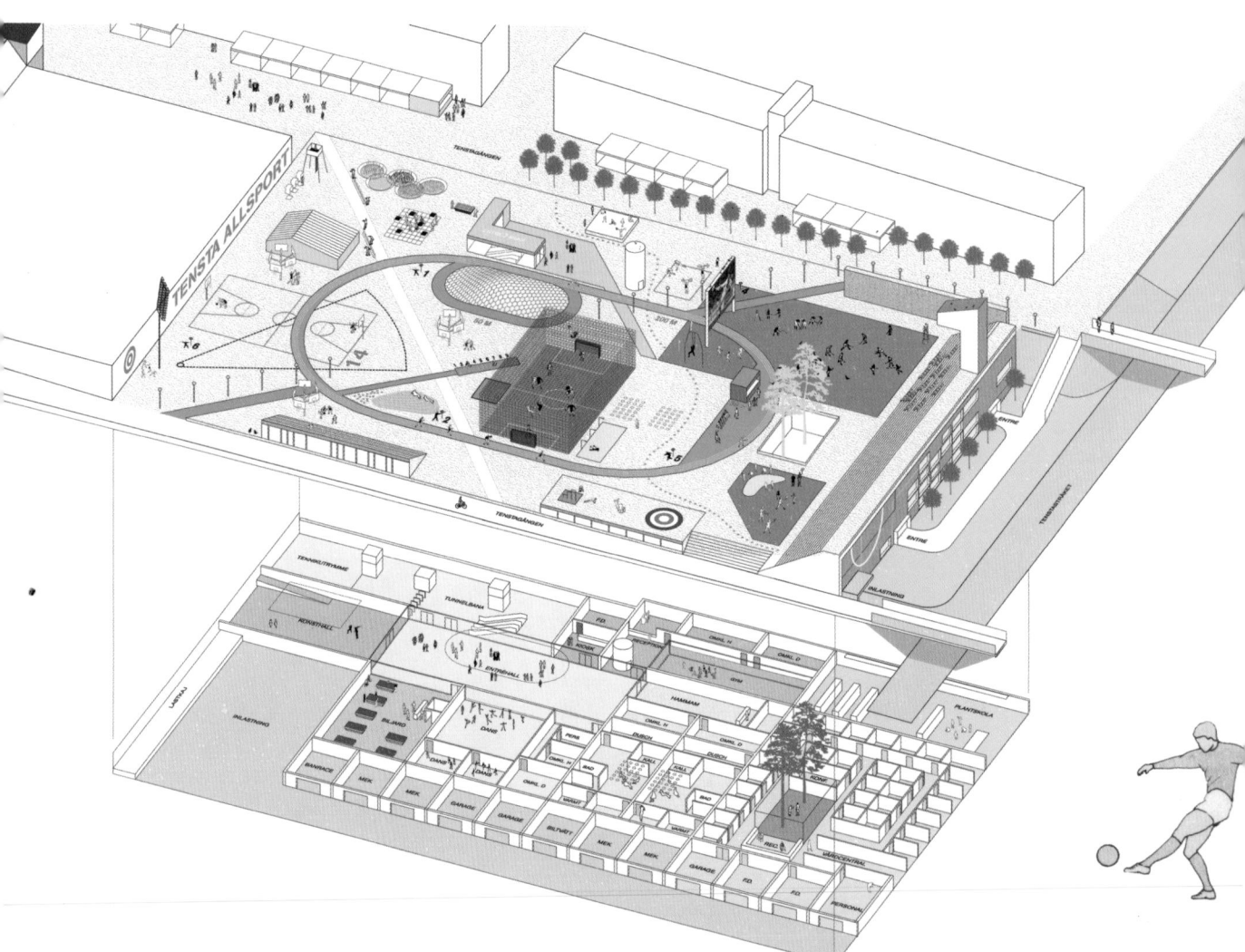

In 2005, Testbedstudio took part in the 6th Town Planning Biennial in the Öresund Region, organized by the Danish town-planning institute. Also there was Studio Force4 (pp. 120–121).

**TRANSPORT**

**NATUR**

**SPORT**

**SERVICE**

**MÖBLER**

**HEM**

**INFRASTRUKTUR**

**DIALOG**

**KOMMERS**

T

# Joël Tettamanti

Photographer Joël Tettamanti has an uncanny eye for the strange coexistence of everyday human needs and timeless landscapes. He is fascinated by the infrastructures of inhabitation, from satellite towers to road bridges, piles of slag or timber to dirt tracks and power lines. This selection of images is taken from series taken in Japan, Greenland and Denmark.

Below: *Untitled* from the series *Niseko*, Okaido Island, Japan, 2004. Opposite, both images: *Untitled* from the series *Qaqortoq*, Greenland, 2004. Tettamanti says: '[this is] one of my main series. I went to the south of Greenland to visit my Danish family, to the city of Qaqortoq. This is the third largest city in Greenland, which is actually not that big. It has about 2,000 inhabitants. The people there almost fight the nature and climate. Houses need to have very elementary architecture. Greenland is nearly an impossible place to live. In the winter it is incredibly cold and summer might be even worse with all the mosquitoes. I was impressed by the obsession of people staying in a place that is so clearly not made for humans.'

| Location | Lausanne, Switzerland |
|----------|----------------------|
| Nationality | Swiss |

Joël Tettamanti is a photographer in Switzerland. He studied at Lausanne Art School before beginning his career as a fine-art photographer. The subject matter of his work is often the interaction between man's built works and the landscapes that accommodate them. He travels widely and has made photographs in Mexico, Japan, Greenland and other places, as well as in his native Switzerland. Significant exhibitions include *Lux at Mudam* (Musée d'Art Moderne Grand – Duc Jean) in Luxembourg in 2006, and *Stadtlandschweiz* at the Centre Culturel Suisse in Paris in 2005. His work has been widely published, and a book of *Stadtlandschweiz* was published by Birkhäuser in 2003 (available in English as *Urbanscape Switzerland*).

T

Below: *Untitled* from the series *Danzigman*, Laesö Island, Denmark, 2006. Tettamanti says: 'Half of my family is Danish. I went to visit them in Laesö Island, a tiny island maybe 12km [7 miles] long between Jutland and Sweden. That series is a continuation of my analysis of the northern countries. It continues my study of the light of the north that fascinates me.'

Opposite: *Untitled* from the series *Qaqortoq*, Greenland, 2004.

# Textbild

In this piece, which they call *Beware of Design*, Ilka and Andreas Ruby say that contemporary architecture's interest in form is just an opiate, distracting us from more disturbing truths. This article is a call for architecture to be a mirror held up in front of reality, rather than an escape from it. It is also, perhaps, an indictment of some of the architecture in this book…

Design is worthless if it does not make us want to engage with the world. A perfectly beautiful object in particular does not necessitate nor encourage any interaction on our part. In fact, all we could do would be possibly harmful to its perfect beauty. However, an object with flaws (from light crudeness to outright ugliness) appeals to our empathy. As most of us are not flawless either, we can identify with the object and start to care for it. An object or space with flaws can produce an aura of strangeness that can help to discharge the behavioural codes that are embedded in any given typology or programme. Discreetly we are pushed to rethink the modes of our interaction with a given object or space. If a museum building does not confirm the rhetorical clichés of its programme, we are forced to define the terms of our relationship with the museum. How can we interact with it? What other use could we make of it that is not part of its premeditated programmatic script? What would we assume the building to be if we didn't know its raison d'être? Strangeness is hence not just a quirky concept to make things look strange, or, even worse, 'interesting'. Rather, it is a tool to stimulate our imagination to transform a familiar situation by appropriating it with different scenarios, which will ultimately enable us to relate differently to the world around us.

This was the ambition of the '*Verfremdungseffekt*' (V-Effect), which Bertolt Brecht explained in his 'Theory of Epic Theatre' in the late 1920s. He introduced the concept of estrangement (*Verfremdung*) as a means to counter the effects of alienation (*Entfremdung*) that according to Marx characterizes the relationships of the late-capitalist individual to its physical and social environment. According to Brecht '*Verfremdung*' first and foremost means 'to strip an action or a character of anything that appears evident, familiar and understandable about it and to arouse curiosity and astonishment about it instead.' This estrangement will cause a critical reflectivity in the viewer towards what he sees on the stage. 'With regard to the representatives of mankind on the stage', Brecht continues, 'he will take the same attitude that he as a modern subject has with regard to nature…. And the theatre does no longer try to make him drunk, to fill him up

with illusions, to make him forget the world and reconcile him with his fate. The Theatre lays the world out in front of him to take hold of it.'

This concept of '*Verfremdung*' poses a powerful challenge to the fetishization of design in the contemporary architectural avant-garde and its one-dimensional use of form. While the aesthetical capital of form is excessively exploited, its content potential is blatantly abandoned. Instead of questioning how architecture might engage with our uncertain future(s), a substantial part of contemporary design withdraws to the safe haven of retro-futurism. To take the design of our childhoods as a mere stylistic formula deeply misses the cultural and ideological function that 1970s design had with regard to its own historical period, which was a profoundly dystopian one. What to us today may appear as a happy cocktail of amazing colours, sensual materials and dynamic shapes was back in its time more often than not used as a spatial tranquillizer to soothe the trauma of the failed revolution of 1968. It is no coincidence that 1970s design provides the scenic background of major dystopian films such as *Rollerball* (1975). The film features a world controlled by a handful of private corporations (the nation-states having disappeared in the last war), which manipulate the population to best serve the interests of the corporate world. To keep the masses obedient, 'Rollerball' was installed, a cruel and deadly game 'whose social purpose is to show the futility of any individual effort'; in addition, people are constantly given tranquillizer pills. What makes this disturbing scenario even more disturbing is the fact that it takes place in strikingly beautiful, elegant and flamboyant interior designs. Speechless, we have to witness how 'good' design is (ab)used as the expression of an evil power. Verner Panton's *Fantasy Landscape*, produced for the design exhibition *Visiona 2* held in Cologne in 1970, became the primitive hut diagram of a society that created interior worlds of design in order to escape confronting itself with exponentially aggravating problems of the exterior world: energy crisis, terrorism of fundamentalist ideologies (RAF, IRA, Brigate Rosse, etc), the 'Limits to Growth' detected by the Club of Rome in 1972, etc. Interestingly enough, the challenges that our world is facing today are shockingly similar: again we have an energy crisis (oil), which is furthermore related to the confrontation of fundamentalist ideologies (Islamism vs. Neo-Liberalism), and likewise we witness a rapid population growth coupled with an increasingly unsurpassable divide between the rich and the poor. And finally we also have a current mainstream of 'avant-garde' architecture with an increasing aesthetic convergence towards a new *Gesamtkunstwerk* that wraps our lives in 100% design. This leaves room to speculate whether our design isn't as deeply immersed in escapism as was the design of the 1970s. But if we look at some emergent tendencies in contemporary architecture, we can detect a growing awareness that while design may confine itself to give comfort, architecture has to make the world present to us, as 'if our eyelids were cut away' (Heinrich von Kleist), and give us an anticipation of the breathtaking sensation of how it feels to rip the tubes off our backs that both feed and chain us to the Matrix.

For ultimately, the real is the sweetest drug.

| Location | Berlin, Germany |
|---|---|
| Nationality | German |

Textbild was established in 2001 by Ilka and Andreas Ruby. The Rubys write books and articles, design books, curate exhibitions and organize symposia. Ilka Ruby studied in Aachen, Germany, and Vienna, Austria, before working in practice. She has taught at Cornell University, Ithaca and the University of the Arts in Berlin. Andreas Ruby studied history of art in Cologne and history of architecture in Paris and at Columbia, New York. They have published their work in journals, specialist magazines and national newspapers in Germany (*Die Zeit*, *Frankfurter Allgemeine Zeitung*). They have written books on architects as diverse as Dominique Perrault, Hans Scharoun and Decq & Cornette, and have published many other books. They have also curated exhibitions, including as co-curators of ArchiLab in Orléans, France.

T

# Tham & Videgård Hansson

Tham & Videgård Hansson's *Villa K* in Stocklund, a suburb to the north of the Swedish capital, can look quite foreboding in photographs. The lapped black-painted plywood façade stretches on and on, filling your field of vision in the half-light of a Stockholm summer night.

But the very wide and slim house is not just there to maximize daylight. The architects write: 'Using the full width of the property, [the house] separates the front yard facing east from the garden in the southwest. Through its position on the site, the house is experienced almost exclusively at a frontal angle, and appears as if it is just a line, a wall with a certain depth to fit in space for living.' This is a rather spooky effect, but there is detail in this scaleless façade. The main structure is in-situ concrete, exposed in the very thin cantilevered entrance canopy. The black plywood panels are mounted on a pine frame.

Inside, the materials are much more characteristic of Scandinavian modernism, with white render and white ash timber, and the arrangement of two double-height areas allows light and views across the space.

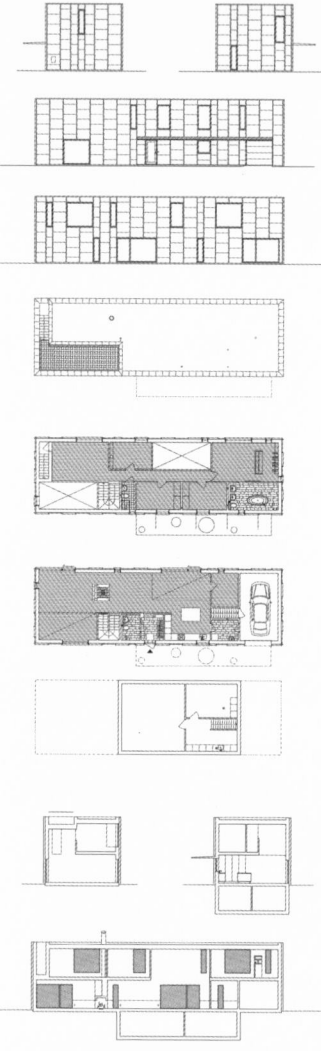

Other Stockholm architects in this book are members of Servo (pp. 282–285) and Testbedstudio (pp. 304–307).

| Location | Stockholm, Sweden |
| --- | --- |
| Nationality | Swedish |

Tham & Videgård Hansson was founded in 1999 by Bolle Tham and Martin Videgård Hansson in Stockholm, Sweden. The practice first came to real prominence with its victory in the international competition to design Kalmar Art Museum in 2004. The practice has since been named architects of the year by *Residence* magazine, in 2005, and their *Villa K* in Stocklund was given an award by Scandinavian architecture magazine *Forum*. Most recently, the practice won the commission to redesign the Östasiatiska Museet in Stockholm.

T

**This spread:** *Villa K* in Stocklund, a suburb to the north of Stockholm.

# Theskyisbeautiful

Theskyisbeautiful's project for a school near Nha Trang, Vietnam, is one of the most inspiring projects in this book. Conceived with both the social and physical context in mind, the project used locally sourced materials and local labour, while creating a place of inspired architectural content for a rural community.

The client for the project was the charity École Sauvage, which was set up at the end of the nineteenth century to help educate underprivileged children in this part of Vietnam. Along with the Vietnamese education ministry, they came up with the 15,000 euros needed to build the project.

The frame of the building is in concrete, but the rest of it is made from bamboo. Theskyisbeautiful's attitude to this material was key to the project. Fed up with seeing it used just as decoration in rich people's houses, they decided to use its inherent properties (strength and lightness) to structural effect. Working with local craftspeople, the architects created simple details that could be built quickly and easily. More than 5,000 stems of bamboo were used, for roof structures (holding up sheet metal), soffits, blinds and sections of façade, which allowed for cross-ventilation. The other benefit of the material was its propensity to bend in the heavy Vietnamese storms, but not break.

In the first phase, three schoolrooms were made (which were used in shifts), along with a generous colonnaded space, which was used for parking bicycles and as a play area when the weather was wet. However, after just two years the school had become a victim of its own success, and demanded extension. As the architects write: 'The three classrooms were constantly used, and the large colonnade had become a little too anarchic. Also, there weren't enough classrooms, so some primary students could not get a place in the senior school.' The school was effectively doubled in size, in collaboration with Vietnamese architect Nguyen Vu Hop, and is now able to provide for six classes of 36 students in a pleasant environment. Also, the school has had an urban effect: a road has been created, and houses have begun to spring up around it.

This project was undertaken in the most idealistic frame of mind, and seems to be a heartening success.

This spread: Images of the school in Nha Trang, Vietnam, completed in 2003 and extended in 2005. Left: Plan drawing showing the extension. Opposite: The school under construction and completed. The construction of the building used more than 5,000 stems of bamboo.

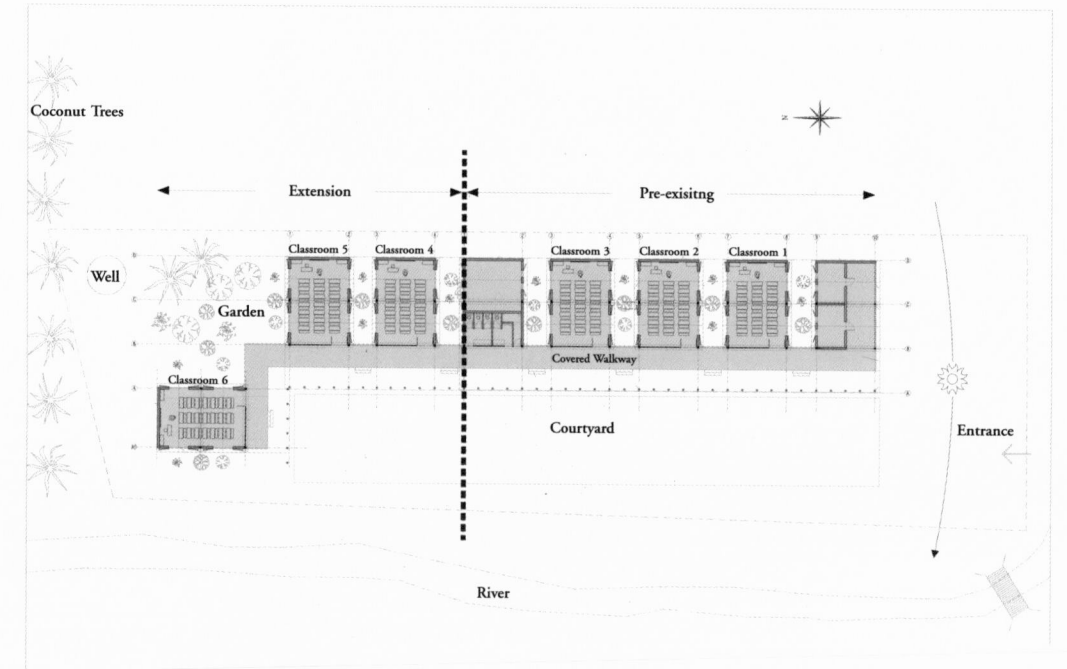

Coconut Trees

Extension | Pre-exisitng

Well

Garden

Classroom 5 | Classroom 4 | Classroom 3 | Classroom 2 | Classroom 1

Classroom 6

Covered Walkway

Courtyard

Entrance

River

| Location | Paris, France |
|---|---|
| Nationality | Vietnamese French |

Theskyisbeautiful was founded by Nguyen Chi Tam and Charlotte Juillard-Dupinet in 2000, with the intention of making ecologically and socially sustainable projects in Southeast Asia, and particularly in Tam's native Vietnam. Tam emigrated as a political dissident in 1976 and graduated as an architect in 1996, winning the Marcel Bleustein-Blanchet Foundation Prize. He formerly worked for Renzo Piano Building Workshop. Theskyisbeautiful's projects have included video and gallery works, but its most significant work is the *Bamboo School* in Nha Trang, Vietnam, completed in two phases in 2003 and 2005. It won an Environmental Award from Cityscape/ *Architectural Review* and a commendation in the AR+D Awards in 2004.

**Theskyisbeautiful was featured in the book** *Design Like You Give a Damn*, **by Cameron Sinclair, head of Architecture for Humanity.**
**Also included was the** *Shrinking Cities* **project (led by** Philipp Oswalt pp. 236–237), Rafi Siegal
and Eyal Weizman (pp. 336–337) **and the Elemental housing initiative by** Alejandro Aravena (pp. 26–29).

# Toh Shimazaki

Toh Shimazaki kept under the radar for a long time in London, quietly assembling one of the most diverse but artistically coherent portfolios of any young architect in the city. The practice's rise to broader attention began with its participation in the high-profile *Talking Cities* exhibition at the Zeche Zollverein in Essen, Germany, in 2006, and with the publication of the remarkable *OSh House* (*Open and Shut House*).

The dwelling is from an architectural genre increasingly rare in the UK – the country house set in acres of unspoilt landscape. This one is quite idiosyncratic, somehow not exactly

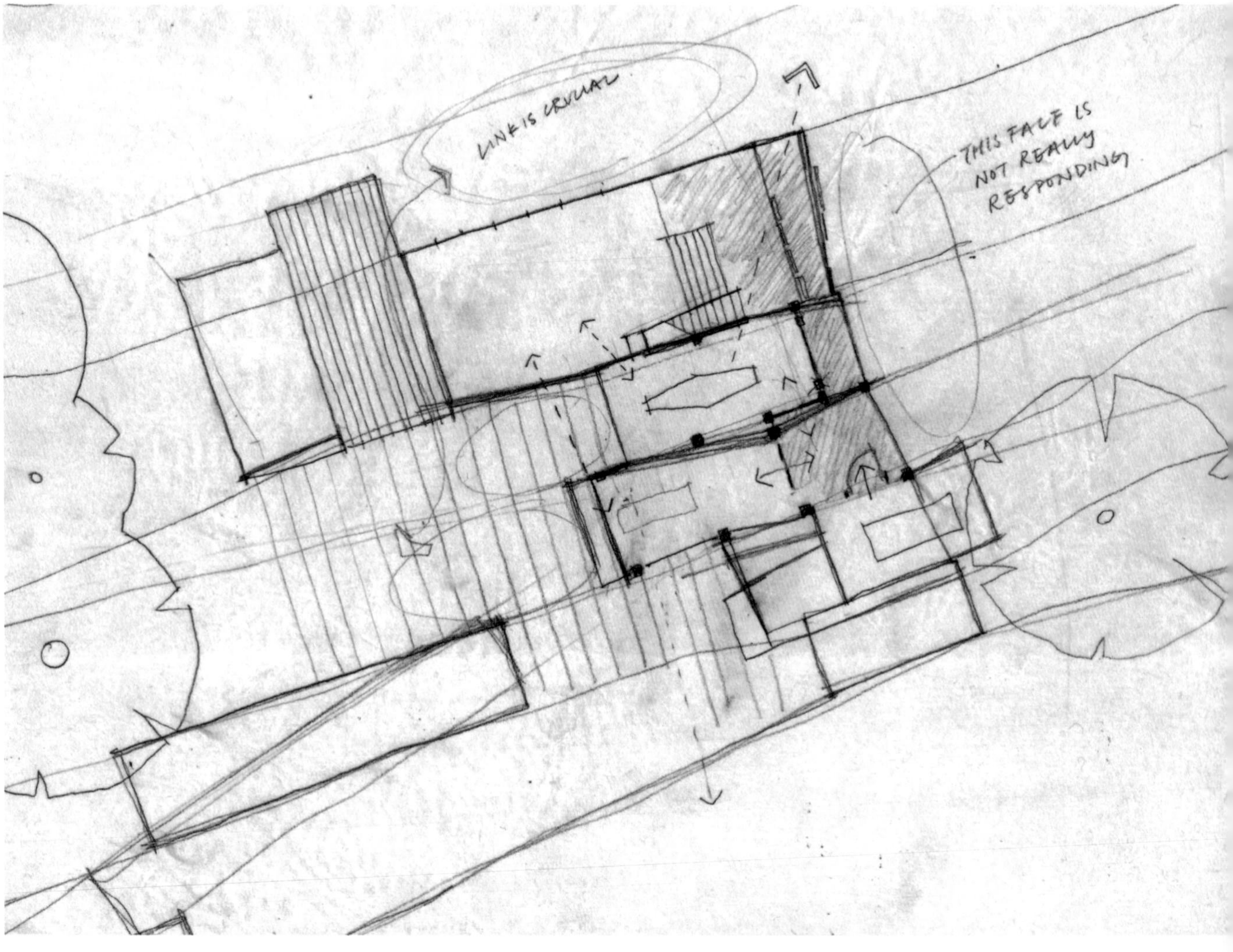

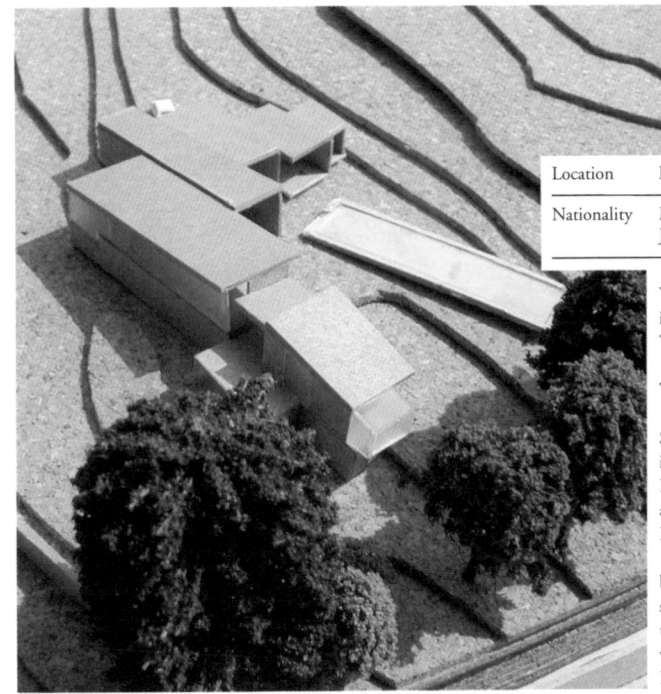

| Location | London, UK |
| --- | --- |
| Nationality | Malaysian Japanese |

modern, and betraying debts to the late work of Peter Smithson (for whom the architects briefly worked), and through that to a Scandinavian twentieth-century municipal idiom that makes this a real one-off.

The project was conceived in its landscape, and the entrance façade responds to the approach. A large canopy above a void signals the front door, and a glazed corner, with the house's characteristic ladder-like (iroko timber) mullions, looks out across the landscape. The use of brick for the house was inspired by the long walls surrounding the site, relics of the country estate that once annexed this

Yuli Toh founded her independent practice TOH in London in 1995, and was joined by Takero Shimazaki in 1998 to form Toh Shimazaki. Toh was born in Malaysia, studied in Bristol and Edinburgh, and worked for Richard Rogers Partnership until 1995. Shimazaki was born in Tokyo, and studied in Cardiff and at the Bartlett, London, working for Itsuko Hasegawa and Richard Rogers until 1998. He is currently visiting lecturer at universities in Oxford and east London in the UK, and in Graz, Austria. Toh Shimazaki's work is diverse, taking in interiors of restaurants (including one of Britain's finest, the Fat Duck in Bray), healthcare buildings (York Hospital entrance building, Birmingham Heartlands Hospital), houses and extensions and gallery installations.

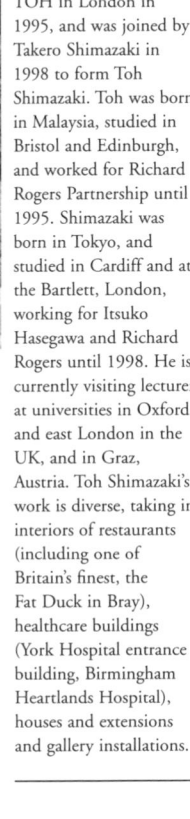

This spread: Sketches, drawings and working models of the *OSh House*, Toh Shimazaki's breakthrough project for a house in the English countryside.

T

Takero Shimazaki teaches at the Technical University in Graz, where Caramel (pp. 52–53) and feld72 (pp. 114–115), among many others, have taught.

This spread: Views
of the *OSh House*,
in Surrey, UK. The
house is oriented around
choreographed views of
the landscape.

land. The house has two storeys, but
the emphasis is horizontal, with a
composition of generous spaces,
variously lit by full-height glazing, and
arranged in an L-shape around a
courtyard containing a swimming pool.
The architects describe this as the
house 'unfolding into its surrounding',
and it also responds to the client's
desire to have a place that is friendly
to children.

The architects explain: 'The
irregular and rhythmic character of the

site has been translated into the
arrangement of living spaces as an
assemblage of four distinct blocks. Each
part rests at its own angle and level,
defining, opening and shutting views and
connections to the landscape.' Inside,
these spaces are joined in a shifting open
plan, which directs views out towards the
landscape. The materials are white-
rendered walls and a brown resin floor,
with some areas of floorboards made of
timber reclaimed from buildings
demolished to make way for the house.

# Touraine Richmond

Although Touraine Richmond have completed one or two wonderful houses, it is pleasing to see them give us here an unbuilt project at a slightly larger scale. The Ford Calumet Environmental Center competition, for an education centre in a nature reserve near to Chicago, attracted entries from

Deborah Touraine contributed an essay to the Actar book *Los Angeles, Infrastructural City*, edited by Kazys Varnelis (pp. 330–331).

a number of very interesting young US practices, being won by Chicago practice Studio Gang. But Touraine Richmond's project was one of the exhibited schemes, and deserves its place here.

The proposal was for a 'Sod Raft', a building that existed conceptually between the dirt of the ground and the blue of the sky, disguised against the prairie grasses that grow on the Hegewisch Marsh. The structure is a floating concrete slab and precast concrete south façade, with rammed earth used for other walls and concrete for the roof. The whole is covered in grass and vegetation in different densities according to the orientation of each façade. The project is considered to have six façades (including the top and bottom), and each has its own focus: 'south: deciduous *brise-soleil*, sun in winter, shade in summer; north: concrete wall with openings, soft light year-round, protection against harshest winter weather; east: thick concrete wall with vegetation; west: glazed wall with overhang, panoramic views; bottom:

concrete slab provides thermal mass, radiant heating and perimeter convection heating; top: planted with native grasses, provides insulation, eliminates heat-island effect.'

Inside, the building is relatively open plan, with enclosed areas for laboratories, offices, storage and services punctuating the space. These 'cores' are also constructed from rammed earth.

For Touraine Richmond, the project provides a new conception of how modernism and sustainability might work together. The partners wrote in their competition document: 'Modernity since Mies van der Rohe built in Chicago has splintered into many rich avenues of expression. The work of environmental artists, in particular Richard Long, Robert Smithson, Andrew Goldsworthy and James Turrell, inspires architects to reconsider their relationship to nature neither as "conquest" nor as "simile", but as system. By elucidating the systemic properties of site and climate, we achieve a technological poetry of correspondence between site forces, form, space and function.'

**This spread: Images from the practice's competition entry for the Ford Calumet Environmental Center near Chicago, USA.**

| Location | Venice, USA |
| --- | --- |
| Nationality | French American |

Touraine Richmond is based in Venice, California, and was established in 1998 by Frenchman Olivier Touraine and American Deborah Richmond. Touraine worked for a host of star architects (Renzo Piano, Rem Koolhaas, Jean Nouvel) and Richmond for Koolhaas before they began their practice together. The practice has carried out projects at many scales (including designing furniture for film director Wim Wenders), but probably its best-known built work is the *One Window House* in Venice, USA, in 2005. Touraine Richmond has had some success in competitions, including a notable mention in the Ford Calumet Environmental Center competition. Touraine was made a Chevalier des Arts et Lettres by the French Ministry of Culture in 2005. Both partners have taught at a variety of American schools, including Columbia, UCLA and SCI-Arc, and Deborah Richmond has published some entertaining essays in the academic journal *Log*.

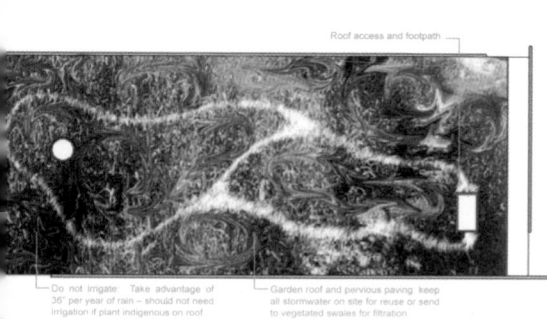

Roof access and footpath

Do not irrigate. Take advantage of 36" per year of rain – should not need irrigation if plant indigenous on roof.

Garden roof and pervious paving keep all stormwater on site for reuse or send to vegetated swales for filtration.

1/32" =1'-0"

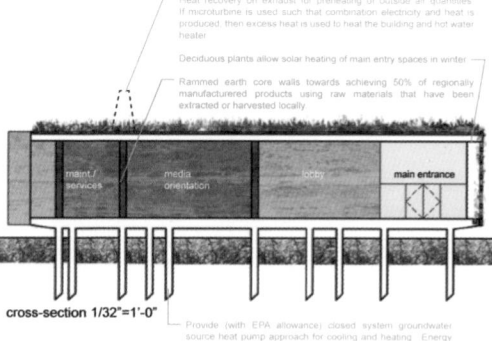

Heat recovery on exhaust for preheating of outside air quantities. If microturbine is used such that combination electricity and heat is produced, then excess heat is used to heat the building and hot water heater.

Deciduous plants allow solar heating of main entry spaces in winter.

Rammed earth core walls towards achieving 50% of regionally manufacturered products using raw materials that have been extracted or harvested locally.

maint./services    media orientation    lobby    main entrance

cross-section 1/32"=1'-0"

Provide (with EPA allowance) closed system groundwater source heat pump approach for cooling and heating. Energy piles for heat transfer into ground water, which is an average temp of 56F per ASHRAE.

oints for obtaining a minimum LEED
ing (see worksheet at end of document)
oints for general green
practices + LEED

T

# UFO

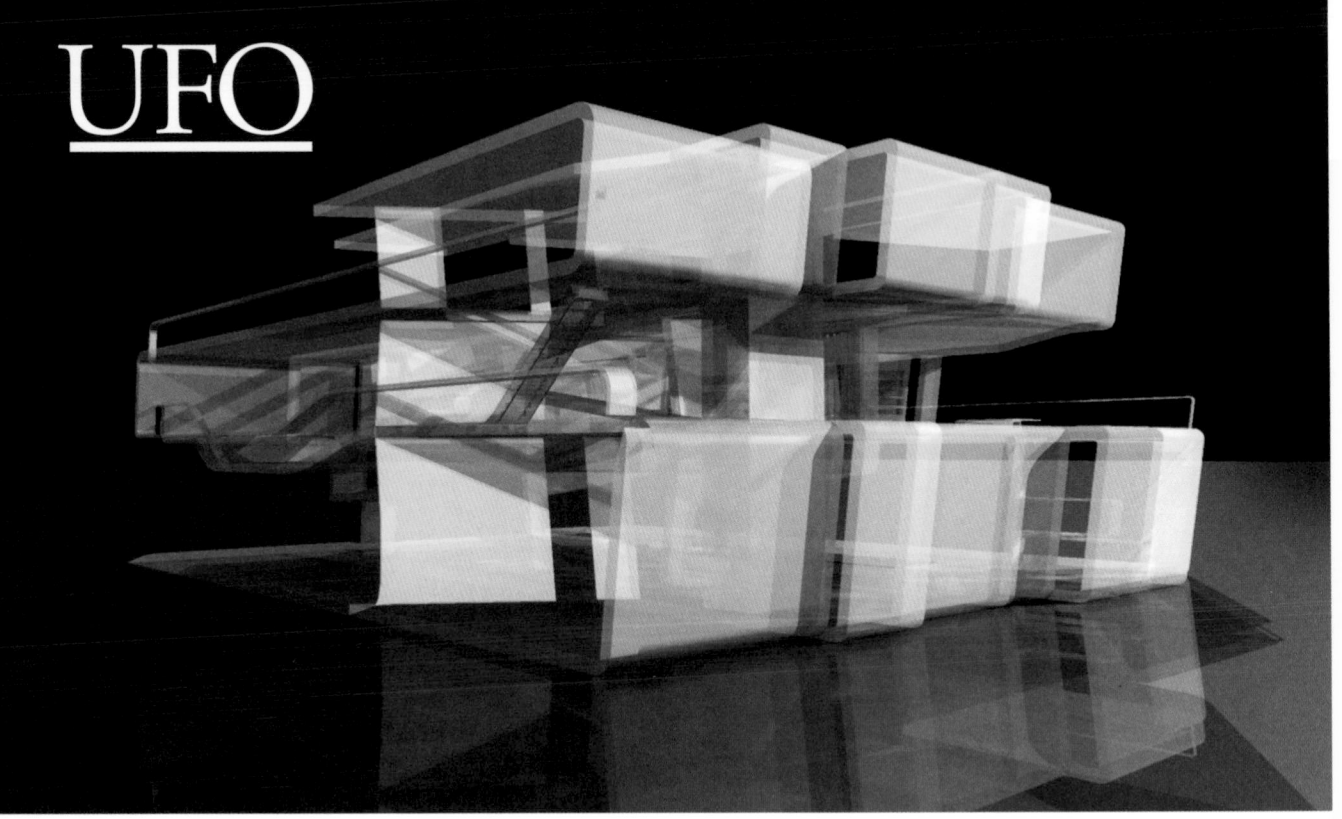

Because of UFO (Urban Future Organization)'s distributed network of collaborators, it has a diverse portfolio that seems to move at different speeds according to location. In London, the office is still completing an interior of a private house for one of its partners, whereas in Italy, it has several medium-sized projects under way, including an arts centre and a recently completed private house.

In the latter category is the *Simone Gatto Lemon Factory* in Messina, Italy. Simone Gatto is a company that makes products associated with citrus fruits, and this project was commissioned to expand the factory floor to double its current size, and provide a new office, crèche and other accommodation. The project provides ribbons of circulation in an attempt to 'smooth the conflicts' between the old and new. The architects write: 'The project folds the complex organizational diagram into a continuous wrapping and warping space where shortcuts and quick links make connections from one space to the other more effective and efficient.'

Meanwhile in London, the practice is completing a private house in de Beauvoir town, in the northeast of the city. The exterior is hardly touched, but inside the Georgian terraced house is radically reconfigured. The name of the house (*Nested House*) comes from the two bedrooms, conceived as 'nests' and set on slightly differing levels. The section of the house is kept as free and uninterrupted as possible, to emphasize vertical connections, particularly with the split-level roof garden.

The project uses innovative techniques in the management of its construction. UFO writes: 'The digital 3-D model is the single source of all the project information, ranging from the early stages of design to the manufacturing and construction of the project.' The model was used in a parametric way at the beginning, to work out the optimum size and arrangement of spaces given the 45sq m (485sq ft) Georgian envelope. The model is maintained, and whenever it is altered, the rest of the design can change around it.

| Location | Worldwide |
|---|---|
| Nationality | Various |

Urban Future Organization was founded in 1996 as a network of individuals, who sometimes work independently or pool their resources when required to tackle larger and more complex projects. UFO has affiliated offices in Italy, the Netherlands, Greece, Spain and the UK. The network has scored two major competition wins, first in the competition for a vast new underground concert hall in Sarajevo, Bosnia (still under development) and for an art gallery in Castelmola in Sicily, Italy. The practice has also completed private houses and is currently working on the *Simone Gatto Lemon Factory* in Messina, Italy. In London, the partners are prolific teachers, teaching in almost every London architecture school.

**This spread: The extension to the *Simone Gatto Lemon Factory* in Messina, Italy, which is under construction.**

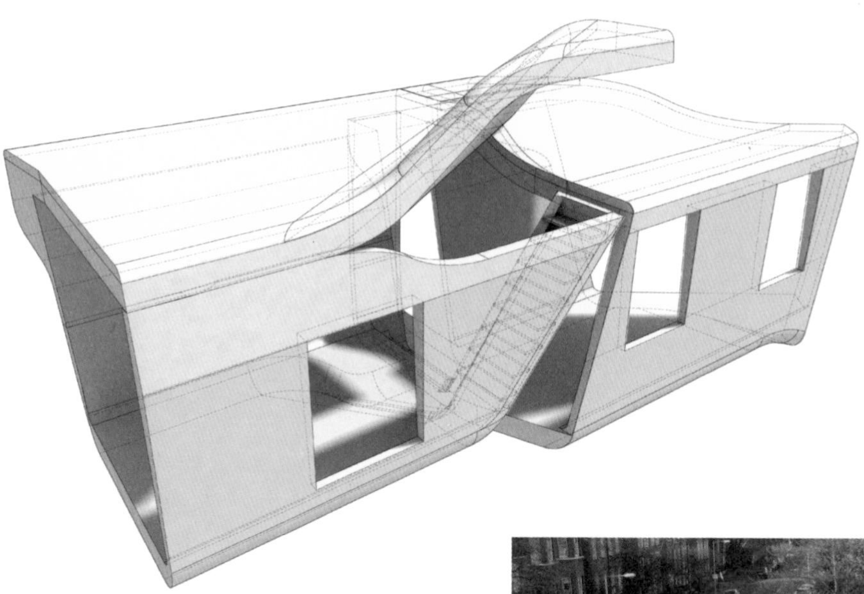

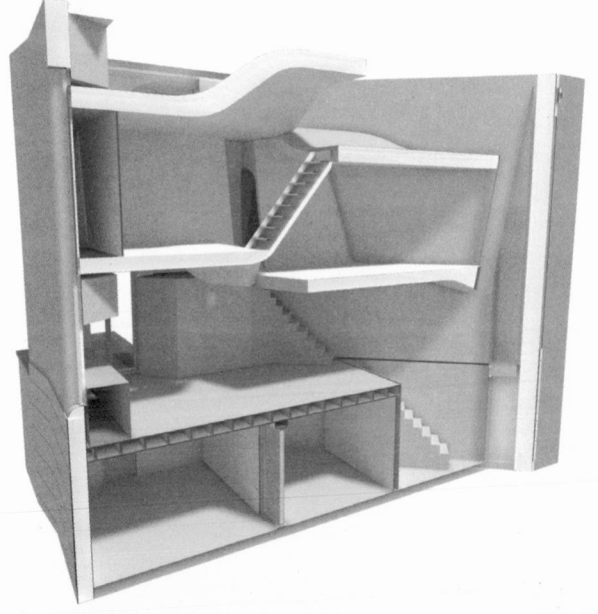

This spread: *Nested House*, a project for the refurbishment of a terraced house in London.

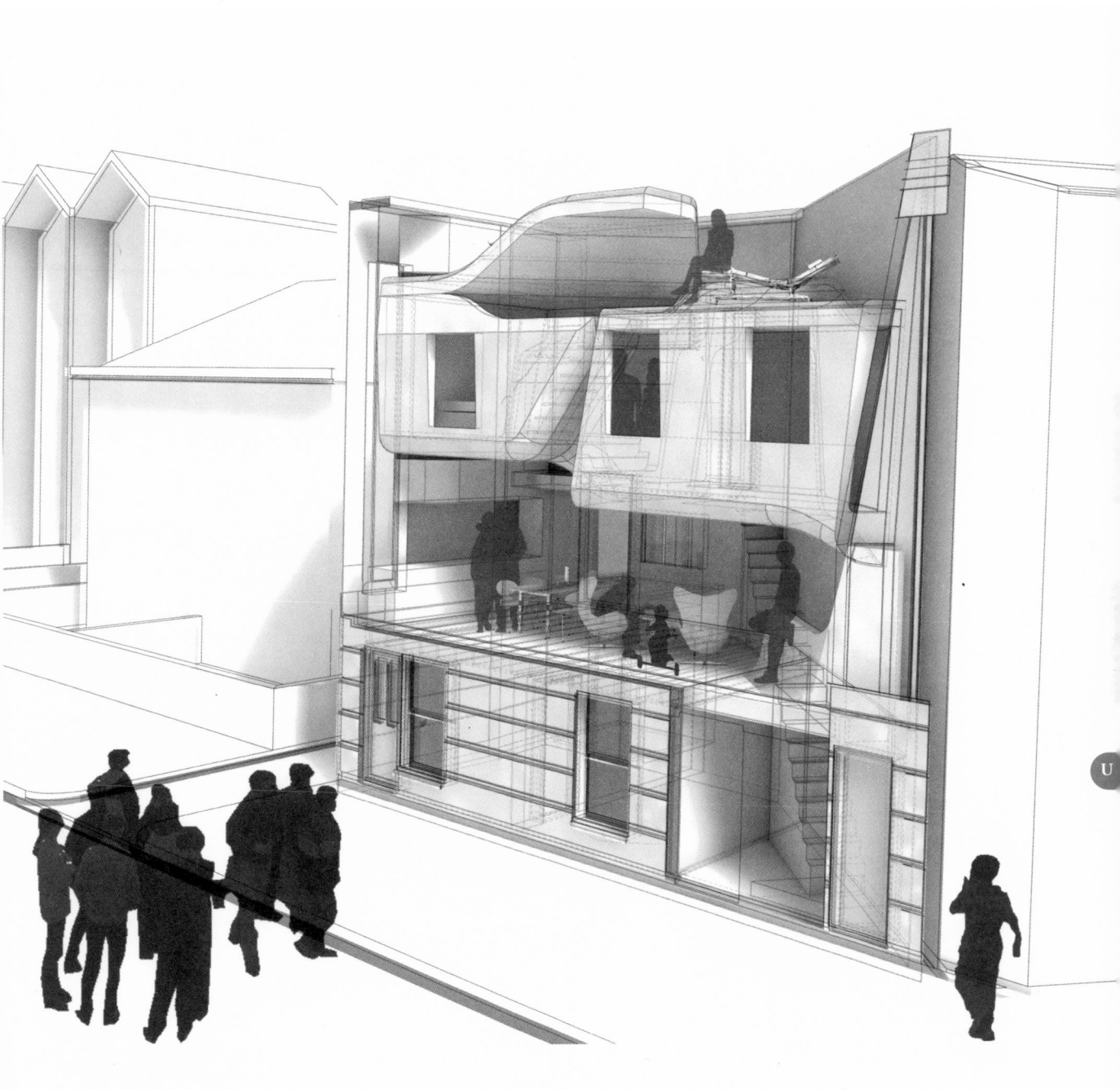

U

# Urban Think Tank

Urban Think Tank's *Vertical Gymnasium* in Caracas, Venezuela, has become an emblematic project, both for the practice itself, and for all those researching the slums of the world's fastest-growing cities. The project sums up an interest that has been growing for some time within the architecture community, distilled by the Venice Architecture Biennale of 2006, in the urbanizing populations of South America, Africa and Asia. The exhibition, which was curated by Richard Burdett, showed endless images of shantytowns, *barrios* and *favelas*, from Cairo to Rio, Bogota to Shanghai, and, of course, Caracas.

Urban Think Tank was in charge of the submission for Caracas, but despite the breadth of its research, it was the *Vertical Gymnasium* that people remembered. The project is a multi-storey sports facility in the heart of the Bello Campo neighbourhood in the city. Created from prefabricated elements, and constructed on an existing but run-down sports field, the gym offers a multitude of activities, in an attempt to keep kids off the streets and away from crime. Murder is the number-one cause of death for adolescents in Caracas, and sports and recreation facilities are vanishingly rare. In order to compensate for the lack of space, the gym divides spaces for volleyball, martial arts, a running track, weightlifting area, basketball and other sports across three floors, accommodating up to 200 people at any one time. The gym is free of charge.

The gym's success in Bello Campo needs no more demonstration than the 17,000 monthly visitors to the facility. Its success in Venice and among the international community may have been due to Richard Burdett's claim that the gym 'succeeded in reducing the murder rate by an astounding 35% in a six-block radius around it.'

It seems clear that Urban Think Tank would not want the project presented as so unambiguous a panacea, but partners Brillembourg and Klumpner have copyrighted the idea and are hoping to propagate more gyms around the world in troubled districts of cities. The next stop is London, where Urban Think Tank is collaborating with UK engineer Battle McCarthy on a version using entirely sustainable materials. Another gym is already planned for Caracas, in the *barrio* of Santa Cruz del Este.

Below and below right: The context of the *Vertical Gymnasium* is the dense *barrio* in the Bello Campo district in Caracas. The project has had a remarkable effect on crime.
Opposite: The gym stacks leisure uses that are open to everybody. There is a running track, indoor gym and a basketball court on the roof, among other facilities.

| Location | Caracas, Venezuela<br>New York, USA |
| --- | --- |
| Nationality | Venezuelan<br>Austrian |

Urban Think Tank was founded in 1993 by Alfredo Brillembourg, and in 1998 he was joined by Hubert Klumpner as co-principal. The office now employs ten people in Caracas, and has a secondary office in New York. Both partners studied at Columbia University. Brillembourg has been a guest professor at the University José Maria Vargas, the University Simon Bolivar and at the Central University in Venezuela, while Klumpner is a guest professor at the Central University. Urban Think Tank is a research office, and the partners work with organizations such as UNESCO, the World Bank, national governments and city authorities on projects. The office also has several buildings behind it, including an Anglican church (2005), a branch office for the Bank of Venezuela (2003) and the *Vertical Gymnasium* (2004), all in Caracas. The office has won several awards and grants from the Architectural League of New York and the German Culture Foundation, among others. Urban Think Tank has also published a book called *Informal City: Caracas Case*.

U

Other practices represented in the main exhibition of the 2006 Venice Biennale included Gross Max (pp. 140–143), MADA s.p.a.m. (pp. 182–185), SHoP (pp. 286–289) and others.

In this extract from Varnelis' forthcoming book *Blue Monday* (co-authored with Robert Sumrell), he argues that *One Wilshire*, a skyscraper in Los Angeles that houses only computers, is an example of what he calls 'Immaterial Culture' – the lived dream of a world without objects.

The dream of a world without objects, brought into Ether with the blessing of the computer and the network, is merely an elaborate fiction. Far from disappearing, physical objects proliferate endlessly. And yet, that is their annihilation. Consumer goods lose their natural meaning and become empty forms, ready to be filled with whatever provisional meanings we assign them. Objects are wild signs, free-floating signifiers unable to represent anything specific themselves, only the mechanism of circulation, which becomes a goal in and of itself. For a month, a Beanie Baby is worth $1,000. The next month it is valueless. What order exists comes from the function of objects within an internally coherent system. Like tech stocks, the emptiness of their promise is precisely what gives them vitality. The case of the dot-com boom is instructive: it was not that we all hoped to take our profits and get out before it failed; it was that we wanted to be part of its failure and to feel its destruction. Like the Bomb, the greatest tragedy of the dot-com crash of 2000 was its failure to bring about its greatest promise: the end of all things, the liberation of objects into pure energy, the conversion of economy into information.

So it is that there is no release from the need to own. We purchase goods to validate our identity, to affirm ourselves as individuals. But in maintaining these objects, we submit ourselves to them as willing slaves. Our own existence is as purposeless as theirs. All that is left is desire and the craving for its impossible satisfaction. If we cannot join their world, we dream of a new equality: to be as ethereal and meaningless to them as they are to us. We pray for dispensation, to leave the material world and dissipate in Ether. And yet, as conflicted beings, we also hope that one day our objects will invest in us the same animistic beliefs with which we invest them. This is not our nightmare, it is the achievement of a utopian dream. Both people and objects become members of a giant stock exchange, not as investors on the floor, but as flickering numbers running across a banner, some rising, some falling, always moving up and down.

Built by Skidmore, Owings, and Merrill in 1966, *One Wilshire* is a nondescript 39-storey skyscraper in downtown Los Angeles. In the early 1990s, made obsolete by a culture that valued the flexible horizontality of the office park over the congestion of the city core, *One Wilshire* was retrofitted as a telecom hotel. Today, it is a key hub on the informatic gird, a 'carrier hotel' packed full of telecommunications equipment, connected to the world

| Location | New York, USA |
| --- | --- |
| Nationality | American |

Kazys Varnelis is an
architect, academic and
writer based in New
York. He is currently
director of the Network
Architecture Lab at the
School of Architecture at
Columbia University,
and holds a post at the
University of Limerick,
Ireland. He studied at
Cornell University,
attaining a PhD in the
history of architecture
and urbanism in 1994.
Varnelis has published
widely in books, journals
and magazines, and is
the co-author of the
book *Blue Monday* with
Robert Sumrell,
published by Actar in
2007. With Sumrell he
also founded the new
media collaborative
AUDC in 2000, and
through this organization
has curated a number of
exhibitions, including
*One Wilshire* at the
CLUI Los Angeles
Facility Exhibit Space
in 2002.

through dozens of major fibre-optic conduits that spill into the building's below-grade parking garage.

Just as *One Wilshire* was recycled into a citadel for immaterial culture, all we can do is recycle old things in phases to make them newly desirable commodities again. Supply and demand emerge out of what is already lying around. At *One Wilshire*, architecture, like all other objects, enters into a pure system of exchange. Through symbol libraries and the magic of the .dxf import command, it has become possible for architectural plans to reproduce at will. The restrooms from the Guggenheim Museum at Bilbao can be copied onto a Flash drive by an intern to endlessly reappear in schools of architecture worldwide, their first role in life irrelevant and forgotten. In this light, the prevalence of the computation-intensive blob in the academy is revealed as the product of

fear, a desperate attempt to reintroduce the hand and slow down architectural production just at the moment that it threatens to proliferate wildly, becoming pure Ether.

*One Wilshire* has no such fear. Created before the dawn of computer-aided design, it transcends architecture as pure diagram and pure idea. Endlessly repeatable, there is no limit to its potent reach. It is the architectural realization of Hegel's spirit itself. *One Wilshire* is an architecture of pure self-negation, simultaneously real and virtual, visible and unseen. An unimportant building without any physical presence or ability to signify its function, *One Wilshire* is nevertheless crucial. *One Wilshire* is the unreal exposing and making real of the unreal. *One Wilshire* is the palace for the empire of Ether.

Left: A model of *One Wilshire* standing in the desert. The real building is a server farm in Los Angeles.

# Guilherme Machado V<u>a</u>z

Despite this being a book full of young architects, Guilherme Machado Vaz is one of the youngest. Born in 1974, his work is still in formation, but this has not stopped him from building a remarkable and idiosyncratic private house, as well as working on a host of public projects in his role in the city design department in Porto, Portugal.

Vaz took on the *Valley House* project while he was still a student, and the client, his psychiatrist father, proved an ideal one for the young architect. 'He wasn't really very interested. I would say to him: "I'm thinking of maybe four rooms instead of five." And he would say: "Oh, ok".' The long gestation of the project also meant that Vaz could work through his influences – he admits to having one version of the house that was a homage to Australian architect Glen Murcutt, and a wide variety of strategies that would have placed the house in

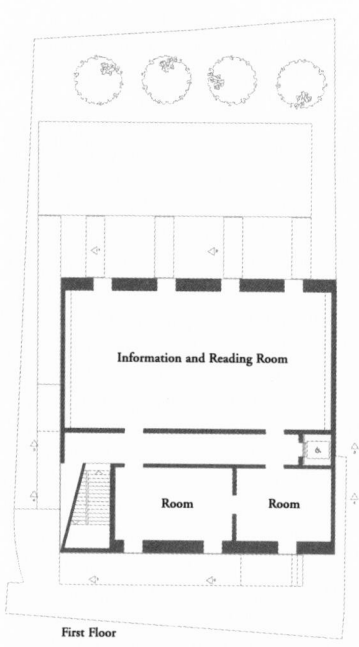

First Floor

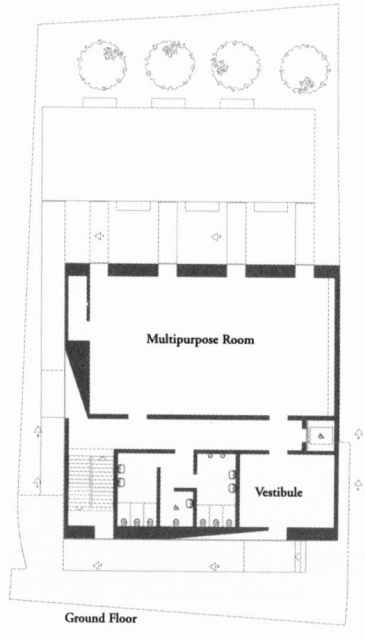

Ground Floor

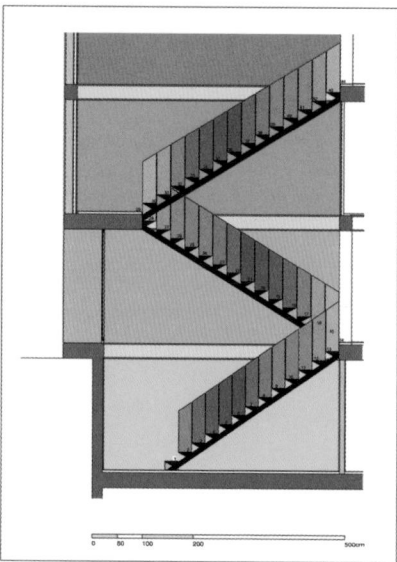

This spread: Images of *Matosinhos Town Hall* in Portugal, completed by Vaz in 2006. The drawing above is of the colour scheme for the bright staircase within.

| Location | Porto, Portugal |
| --- | --- |
| Nationality | Portuguese |

Guilherme Machado Vaz combines work on his own personal architectural projects with a design role for the city authority of Porto, Portugal. Vaz studied in Porto and in Paris, and spent a year in the office of legendary Portuguese architect Eduardo Souto de Moura in Porto before starting his own practice. He has completed one significant public project – *Matosinhos Town Hall* (2006) – and in 2006 was a finalist for the Iberian Architecture Prize for the *Valley House*. Vaz came second in the international competition for a new Faculty for Education for Coimbra University in 2003 (in collaboration with Nuno Graça Moura), and recently completed four houses at the Bom Sucesso resort in Óbidos, Portugal.

V

different locations on the site. But the success of this project is in its choice of site, occupying the northern side of a large area that was once orchards but has long since lain fallow. This side of the site is also characterized by retaining walls, holding the side of the valley back. The house is conceived as another retaining wall, dug into the side of the valley, long and low, forming an elongated shoebox that contains all accommodation on one level. This concrete tube points towards the spectacular mountain range to the east at the end of the valley.

The concrete exterior of the house is very, very rough, partly due to the inexperience of the local builder, and partly deliberately. But this gives it an infrastructural presence in the landscape, as if the house itself is holding back the steep hill. The plan is highly unconventional. Vaz says that the

house went through several versions before he realized that the vernacular farmhouses of the region shared one characteristic that he could use: a verandah. This is usually an outdoor space at first-floor level from which all the rooms of the house can be accessed. Vaz translated this into a generous corridor along the south façade of the house, glazed in full-height windows that can slide away completely to leave a letterbox opening.

The depth of the south-facing verandah is such that the low winter sun can shine in (through the leaves of several trees) and warm the space, whereas the high summer sun does not encroach. It is the heart of the house, and the other rooms are all accessible from it. Four bedrooms are arranged in two self-sufficient modules behind doors on the north wall of the verandah, and at the western end you find the kitchen.

This spread: The *Valley House*, in the north of Portugal. This long, low house is intended to take its place among the retaining walls of the steep valley side. All the accommodation is on one level.
Right: The picture window frames a spectacular view of mountains.
Below: Plan showing how all the spaces are accessible from a generous, south-facing verandah (numbered 7 on this drawing).

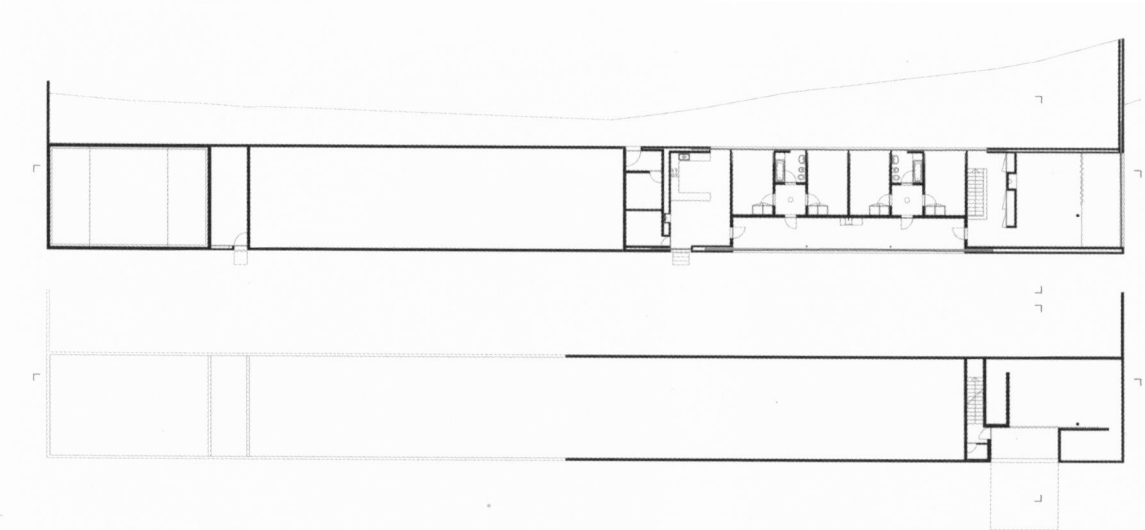

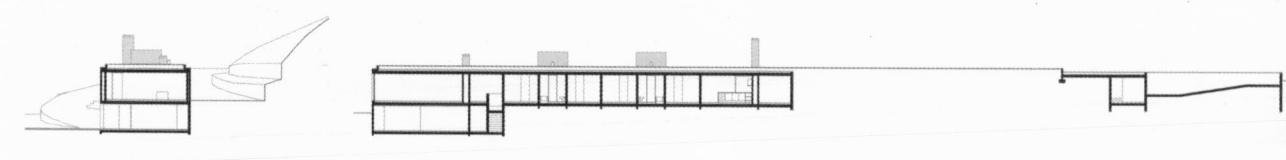

V

Weizman's work has begun an explosion of interest in the architectural intent behind many military strategies, particularly in the context of Israel and Palestine. Here he reveals how architecture theory became the inspiration behind military strategies of the Israeli army, in an extract from his 2007 book *Hollow Land: the Architecture of Israeli Occupation.*

There is a considerable overlap among the theoretical texts considered essential by military academies and architectural schools. Indeed, the reading lists of contemporary military institutions include works from around 1968 (with a special emphasis on the writings of Gilles Deleuze, Félix Guattari and Guy Debord), as well as more contemporary writings on urbanism, psychology, cybernetics, post-colonial and post-structuralist theory. If, as some writers claim, the space for criticality withered away in late-twentieth-century capitalist culture, it seems now to have found a place to flourish in the military.

Shimon Naveh, one of the directors of Israel's Defence College, summed up the mission of his institute, which was founded in 1996: 'We are like the Jesuit Order. We attempt to teach and train soldiers to think. We read Christopher Alexander, can you imagine? We read John Forester, and other architects. We are reading Gregory Bateson; we are reading Clifford Geertz. Not myself, but our soldiers, our generals are reflecting on these kinds of materials.' Naveh recently translated Bernard Tschumi's *Architecture and Disjunction* to Hebrew. 'We have established a school and developed a curriculum that trains "operational architects".'[1] In a lecture, Naveh showed a diagram resembling a 'square of opposition' that plots a set of logical relationships between certain propositions referring to military and guerilla operations. Labelled with phrases such as 'Difference and Repetition – The Dialectics of Structuring and Structure', 'Formless Rival Entities', 'Fractal Manoeuvre', 'Velocity vs. Rhythms', 'The Wahabi War Machine', 'Postmodern Anarchists' and 'Nomadic Terrorists', they often reference the work of Deleuze and Guattari. War machines, according to Deleuze and Guattari, are polymorphous; diffuse organizations characterized by their capacity for metamorphosis, made up of small groups that split up or merge with one another, depending on contingency and circumstances. (Deleuze and Guattari were aware that the state can willingly transform itself into a war machine. Similarly, in their discussion of 'smooth space' it is implied that this conception may lead to domination.)

I asked Naveh why Deleuze and Guattari were so popular with the Israeli military. He replied that 'several of the concepts in *A Thousand Plateaus* became

| | |
|---|---|
| Location | London, UK |
| Nationality | Israeli |

instrumental for us allowing us to explain contemporary situations in a way that we could not have otherwise. It problematized our own paradigms. Most important was the distinction Deleuze and Guattari have pointed out between the concepts of "smooth" and "striated" space [which accordingly reflect] the organizational concepts of the "war machine" and the "state apparatus". In the IDF we now often use the term "to smooth out space" when we want to refer to operation in a space as if it had no borders. Palestinian areas could indeed be thought of as "striated" in the sense that they are enclosed by fences, walls, ditches, roadblocks and so on.'[2] When I asked him if moving through walls was part of it, he explained that, 'In Nablus, the IDF understood urban fighting as a spatial problem. Travelling through walls is a simple mechanical solution that connects theory and practice.'[3]

Although you do not need Deleuze to attack Nablus, theory helped the military reorganize by providing a new language in which to speak to itself and to others. A 'smart weapon' theory has both a practical and a discursive function in redefining urban warfare. The practical or tactical function, the extent to which Deleuzian theory influences military tactics and manoeuvres, raises questions about the relation between theory and practice. Theory obviously has the power to stimulate new sensibilities, but it may also help to explain, develop or even justify ideas that emerged independently within disparate fields of knowledge and with quite different ethical bases. When the military talks theory to itself, it seems to be about changing its organizational structure and hierarchies. When it invokes theory in

communications with the public – in lectures, broadcasts and publications – it seems to be about projecting an image of a civilized and sophisticated military. And, when the military 'talks' (as every military does) to the enemy, theory could be understood as a particularly intimidating weapon of 'shock and awe,' the message being: 'You will never even understand that which kills you.'

1   There are different modes of humanitarian intervention in the occupied Palestinian territories: neutral intervention (international committee of Red Cross, UNRWA); humanitarian action combining intervention with witnessing (MSF, Oxfam); and the new form of popular activism for the protection of the population under occupation (civil missions, the International Solidarity Movement, Ta'aush). In the context of its work in Palestinian areas, MSF has surprisingly adopted a stance of neutrality rather than that of witnessing. See: Sari Hanafi & Linda Tabar, 'The Intifada and the Aid Industry: The Impact of the New Liberal Agenda on the Palestinian NGOs', *Comparative Studies of South Asia, Africa and the Middle East* 23.1-2 (2003), pp. 205–214.

2   On the impossibility to bear witness, and the structural lacuna contained within it. See: Giorgio Agamben, 'Remnants of Auschwitz', *The Witness and the Archive*, New York (Zone Books) 2002.

3   Furthermore, the humanitarian must reserve for her/himself the possibility to withdraw from participation in a situation when the consequences of complicity with power may become counter-productive. There are no rules to define when complicity may turn against the interest of the victims; a degree of complicity with power is almost always inevitable, and must be defined in each situation anew by applying a good measure of common sense. In any case, it is by 'remaining in a relation of tension to power' Brauman insisted, that one can limit the danger of political instrumentalization. Rony Brauman, 'From Philanthropy to Humanitarianism', *South Atlantic Quarterly* no. 2/3 (Spring 2004), pp. 397–417 especially pp. 399, 406.

Eyal Weizman is an architect, writer and curator based in London. He studied architecture at the Architectural Association in London and completed his PhD at the London Consortium. Despite winning prizes in architectural competitions, it is for his academic work that he is best known. He has written extensively about the architectural intent of the Israel–Palestine conflict, and has worked with a variety of NGOs and human rights groups in Israel and Palestine. Weizman has taught, lectured and organized conferences in many institutions worldwide. His books include *Hollow Land* (2007, Verso Press), *A Civilian Occupation, Territories 1,2 and 3* and *Yellow Rhythms*. He has also written many articles. He is a contributing editor for *Domus* magazine and for *Cabinet* magazine, and is the founding director of the Centre for Research Architecture at Goldsmiths College in London.

W

# Gus Wüstemann

Gus Wüstemann's entry to the competition for a new Museum of Beaux-Arts (nMBA) in Lausanne, Switzerland, in 2005 tries to mediate its lakeside location with a powerful and elemental form composed of solids and glazed voids.

The site is next to a shipyard and near a pleasure garden, on Bellerive on the banks of Lac Leman. Wüstemann's strategy was to make a powerful attractor to bring people to the banks of the lake, but not to privilege the museum's ownership of the extraordinary location, allowing address of the waterfront to be laconic and subtle (in stark contrast to the project that won the competition, interestingly).

The form, says Wüstemann, is generated by the conditions around the site: 'Physically, the building takes its form from the tension created by the flow of the city, the constraints imposed by the museum [programme] and its situation at the edge of the lake.' The impression the proposal gives on the city and lake façades is very different, with the more civic face towards the city conceived as a massive, rockface-like façade. On the lake side, a glowing, transparent platform is created, floating on the lake itself. This is conceived as a sculpture park, and is the first, ethereal view that visitors arriving by boat would see; the visitor has the opportunity to 'walk on water'.

The theme of an ambiguous space with a function between the display of art and more general public uses continues inside, and is characteristic of Wüstemann's interest in spaces of non-typological, undefined and free character. He writes: 'The space of the museum results from the competing gravitational fields of the public art space and the public space in general.' The sculpture garden and the 'polyvalent room' of the entrance are strongly connected, allowing the uses of one to affect the other. The large entrance lobby allows two accesses to exhibition areas, which are deliberately kept flexible. Part of the interior is underground, and effectively below the level of the lake. This is dramatized with a glazed brick string course signalling the level of the water.

Below: The models of Wüstemann's entry to the nMBA competition in Lausanne, for a new museum on the banks of the Lac Leman. Opposite: *Swiss Lounge* – a VIP airport lounge for Swiss airlines.

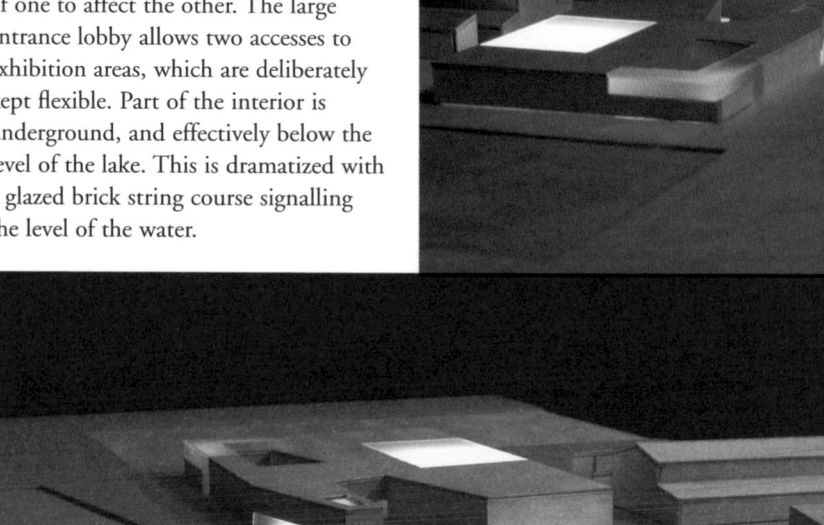

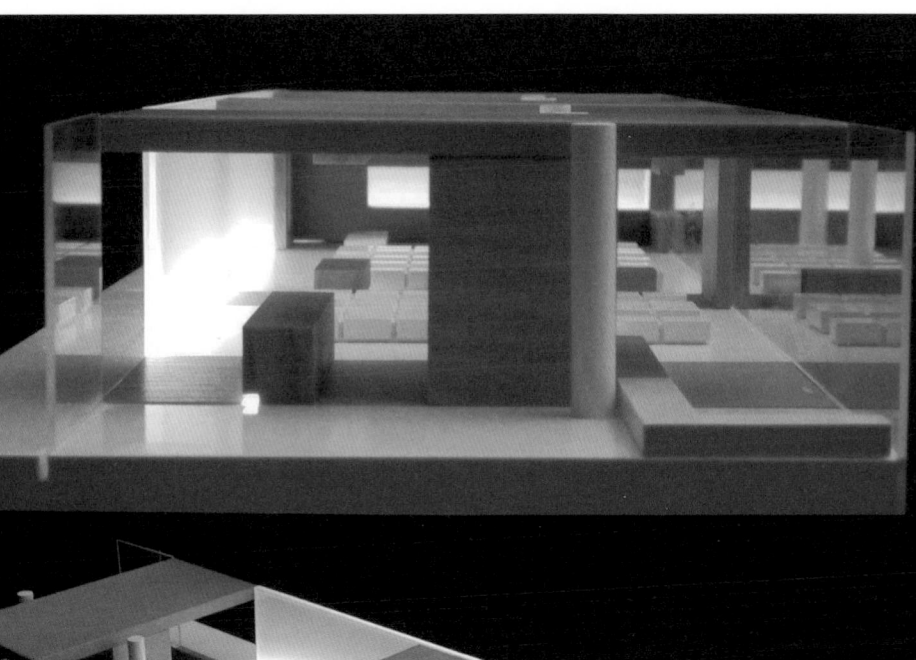

| Location | Zurich, Switzerland |
| | Barcelona, Spain |
| Nationality | Swiss |

Gus Wüstemann was born in Zurich and worked as a professional snowboarder and model before studying architecture at the ETH in Zurich with an exchange semester in Ahmadabad, India. After work experience with architects such as Santiago Calatrava, he founded his own office in 1997. He now has offices in Zurich and Barcelona. Important projects include a long series of private houses, among which is the much-published *Glacier* interior for an apartment in Lucerne, Switzerland, completed in 2005. He has also had some success in competitions and is now working on a block of student residences in Barcelona.

Other entrants in the nMBA competition in Lausanne included R&Sie (pp. 258–261), who won 6th prize.

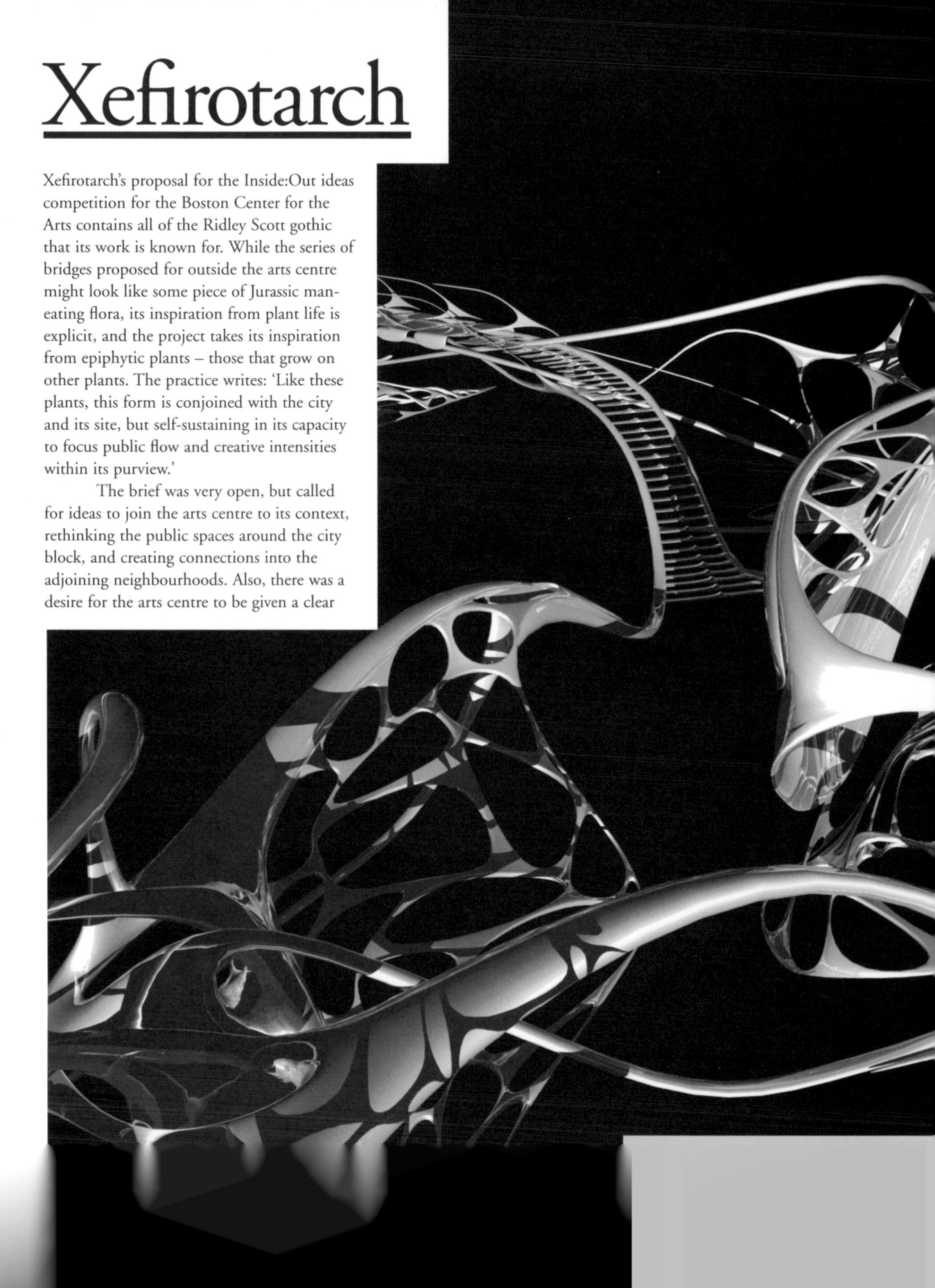

# Xefirotarch

Xefirotarch's proposal for the Inside:Out ideas competition for the Boston Center for the Arts contains all of the Ridley Scott gothic that its work is known for. While the series of bridges proposed for outside the arts centre might look like some piece of Jurassic man-eating flora, its inspiration from plant life is explicit, and the project takes its inspiration from epiphytic plants – those that grow on other plants. The practice writes: 'Like these plants, this form is conjoined with the city and its site, but self-sustaining in its capacity to focus public flow and creative intensities within its purview.'

The brief was very open, but called for ideas to join the arts centre to its context, rethinking the public spaces around the city block, and creating connections into the adjoining neighbourhoods. Also, there was a desire for the arts centre to be given a clear

| Location | Los Angeles, USA |
| --- | --- |
| Nationality | Argentinian |

Xefirotarch is the practice of Hernan Diaz-Alonso. He began his architectural education at the University of Rosario in his native Argentina before moving to the US to enroll in the Advanced Architectural Design program at Columbia University. After that he worked for legendary Catalan architect Enric Miralles in Barcelona and for Peter Eisenman in New York. He teaches at SCI-Arc in Los Angeles and has been a visiting professor at the University of Illinois in Chicago and at Columbia. His major works include his competition-winning project for the PS1/MOMA Young Architects Program in 2005, and prize-winning projects in competitions including the high-profile U2 Landmark Tower competition in Dublin. In 2006 Xefirotarch was the subject of a solo exhibition at the San Francisco Museum of Modern Art, and a monograph was produced to coincide with it.

X

In 2007, the Koplin Del Rio Gallery in LA held an exhibition called *Entropy: the Art in Architects*, which included work from many SCI-Arc alumni, among them Xefirotarch, Elena Manferdini (pp. 190–191), Marcelo Spina of Patterns (pp. 242–243), id Erdman of Servo (pp. 282–285), Jennifer Siegal (pp. 290–291) and George Yu (pp. 344–347).

This spread: Visualization of Xefirotarch's proposal for a series of bridges connecting Boston Center for the Arts to its context.

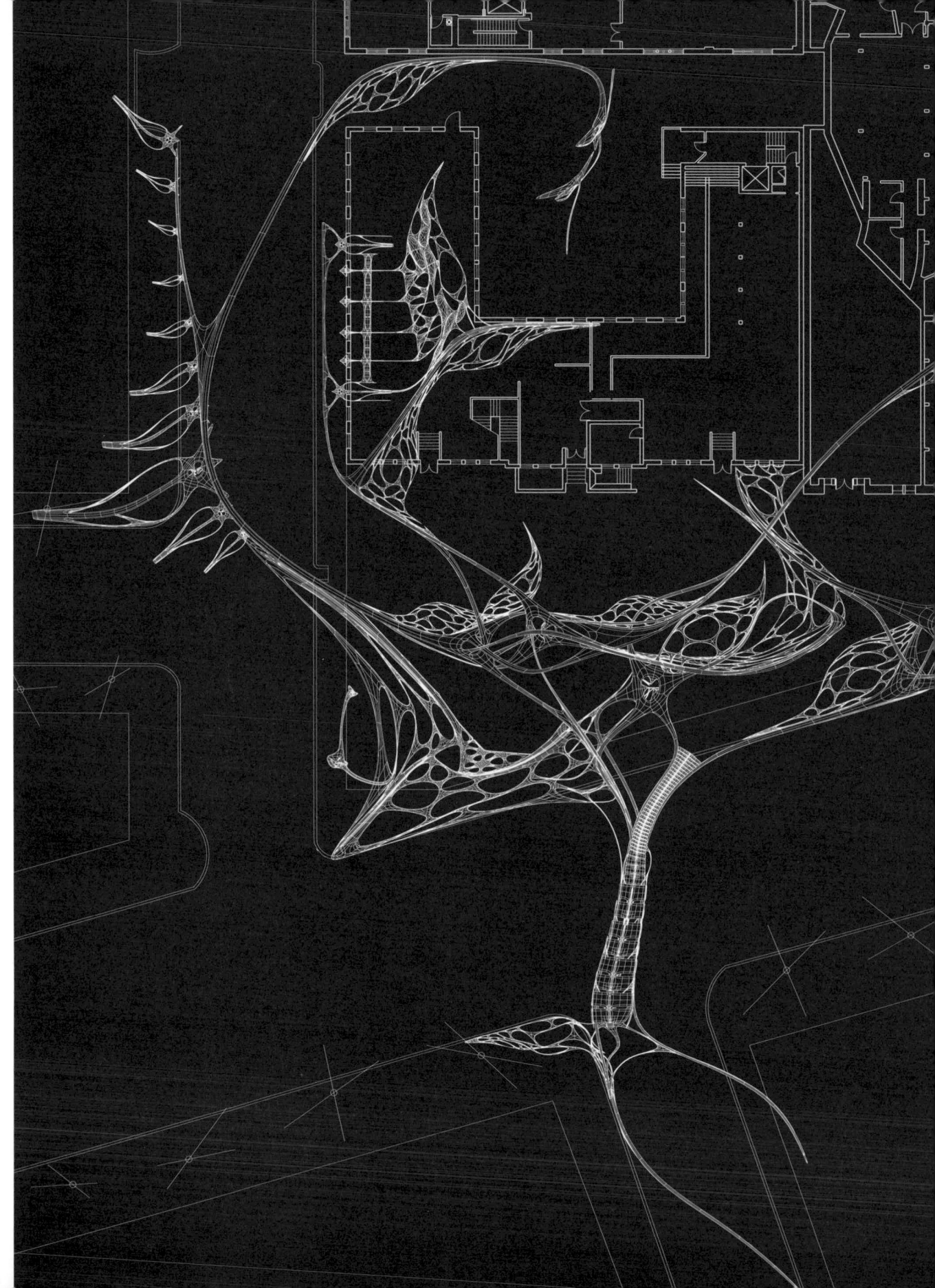

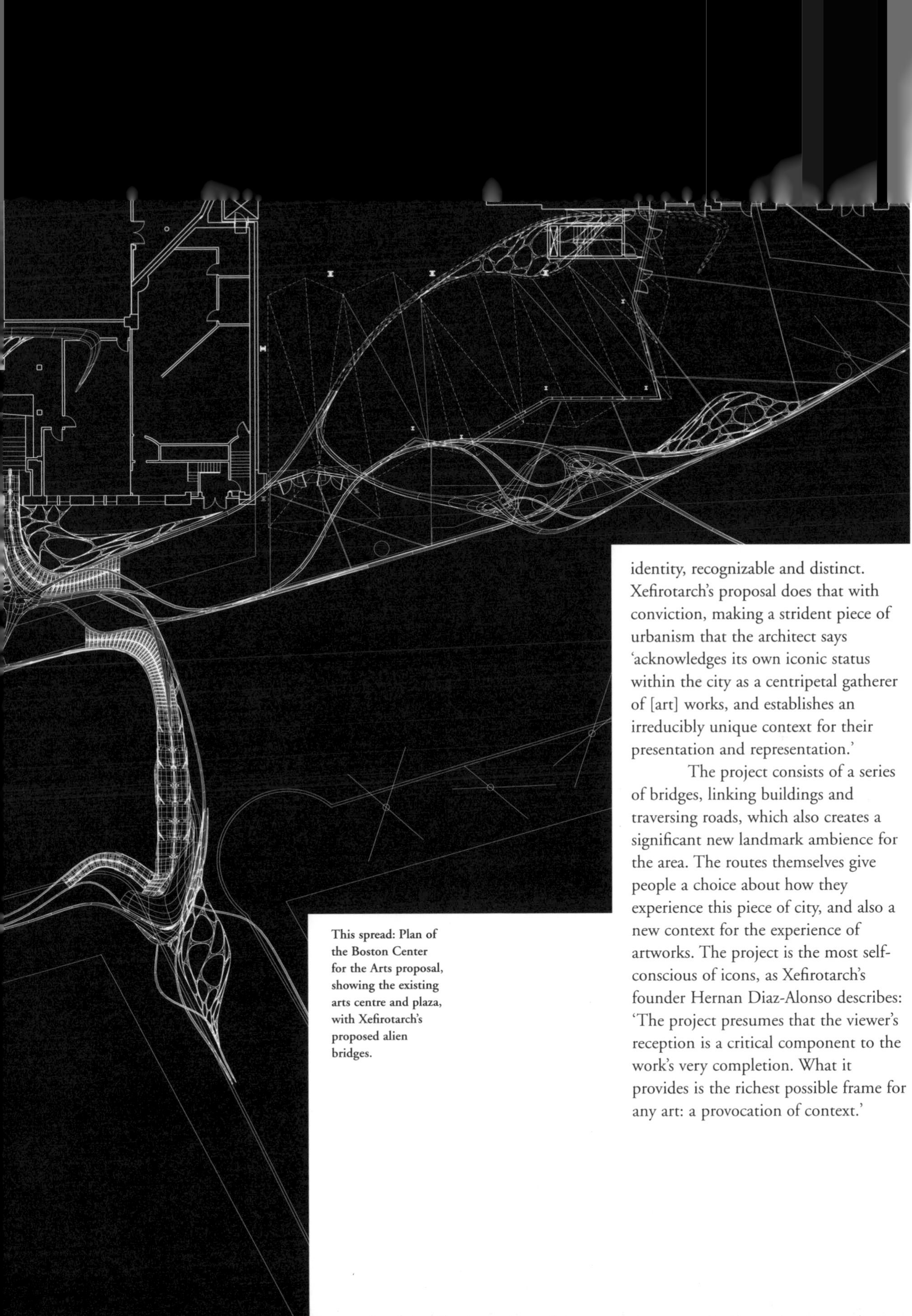

identity, recognizable and distinct. Xefirotarch's proposal does that with conviction, making a strident piece of urbanism that the architect says 'acknowledges its own iconic status within the city as a centripetal gatherer of [art] works, and establishes an irreducibly unique context for their presentation and representation.'

The project consists of a series of bridges, linking buildings and traversing roads, which also creates a significant new landmark ambience for the area. The routes themselves give people a choice about how they experience this piece of city, and also a new context for the experience of artworks. The project is the most self-conscious of icons, as Xefirotarch's founder Hernan Diaz-Alonso describes: 'The project presumes that the viewer's reception is a critical component to the work's very completion. What it provides is the richest possible frame for any art: a provocation of context.'

This spread: Plan of the Boston Center for the Arts proposal, showing the existing arts centre and plaza, with Xefirotarch's proposed alien bridges.

# George <u>Yu</u>

The project shown here is George Yu's entry into the *Gardens by the Bay* competition in Singapore, for which he was shortlisted to the final ten. The major international competition was held in 2006 to find plans for the redevelopment of three major new parks in Marina Bay, downtown in the island city-state, on 94 ha (232.2a) of land. The project will create Singapore's second botanical garden and a new conservatory, both of which were part of Yu's entry. The practice collaborated on the project with fellow West Coast firm Ah'bé Landscape Architects.

The project consisted of a complex series of canopy-like proposals, made of a series of 'patches' in a variety of categories: transparent, open, concrete, green, water and planter. These patches were alternated and added together to create a variegated landscape that was in some places very green, and in others filled with more commercial or public uses. Yu called this infrastructure of canopies and paths 'the Manifold', and speculated that it could become a new way of making landscape in Singapore. 'We propose an architectural form unique to Singapore – the Manifold – that creates a new relationship between building and nature. The Manifold represents a new and shuffled order based on interconnection, close-knit patterns of association, and possibilities for growth over time allowing for different approaches to phasing construction. It is an intelligent, dynamic, breathing and ecologically sustainable architecture that emerges with the larger site design strategies and the changing needs of the park and botanical garden program.'

Complex sections were created for buildings such as the visitor centre,

**This spread:**
Visualizations of George Yu's shortlisted proposal for the *Gardens by the Bay* competition for Marina Bay in Singapore.

| Location | Los Angeles, USA |
|---|---|
| Nationality | Hong Kong/Canadian |

George Yu founded George Yu Architects in 1992 in Los Angeles. Yu was born in Hong Kong, but grew up in Canada, receiving his first degree in urban geography from the University of British Columbia before going to the University of California for his Masters. The practice has completed more than 65 projects, from small interiors to major shopping centres, including the headquarters for Nettwerk records in Vancouver, workplaces for IBM in Chicago and the Daido Jusco shopping centre in Nagoya, Japan. Yu was an adjunct professor at British Columbia between 1995 and 1998, and taught at SCI-Arc in Los Angeles from 1998. The practice's work has been widely exhibited and published, and has won two *ID* design awards and the Prix de Rome from the Canada Council. As this book was going to press, Yu died of cancer at the age of 43.

At the time of writing, Yu's installation in collaboration with the Honda Advanced Design Center was showing in the SCI-Arc library. At the same time, Emergent (pp. 94–97) and Buro Happold's *Dragonfly* was showing in the college's gallery.

Y

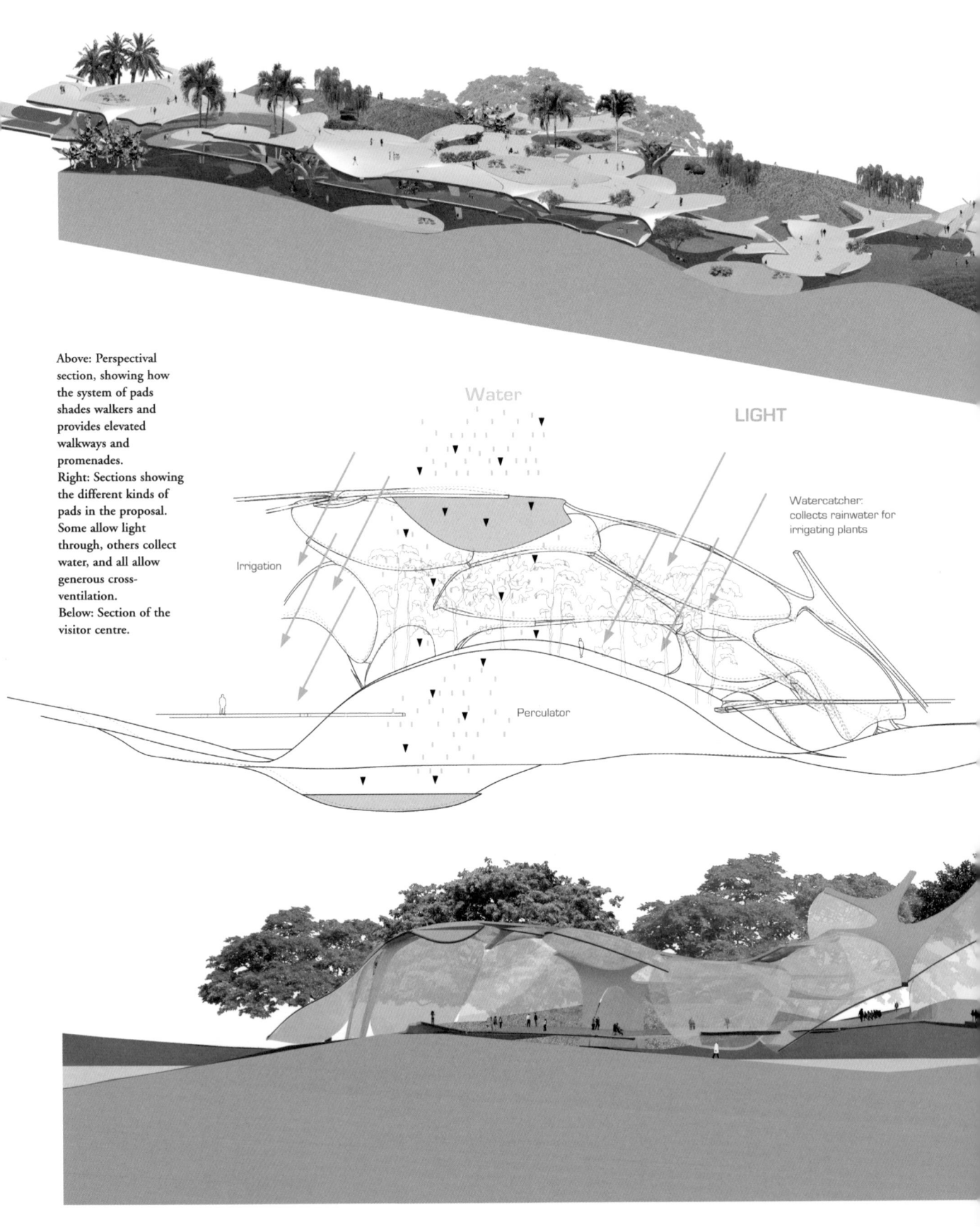

Above: Perspectival section, showing how the system of pads shades walkers and provides elevated walkways and promenades.
Right: Sections showing the different kinds of pads in the proposal. Some allow light through, others collect water, and all allow generous cross-ventilation.
Below: Section of the visitor centre.

Water

LIGHT

Irrigation

Watercatcher: collects rainwater for irrigating plants

Perculator

with underground parking, grassy landscape on the ground, and ramps and platforms up to second-floor level that would have allowed the promenading public views of the scenery from many different heights and angles. The conservatory rose up to become a massive winter garden, covered with an inflated ETFE skin of a roof. Paths also lead through the landscape to a waterside event space, composed of lilypad-like patches, and a spectacular pedestrian bridge over the water.

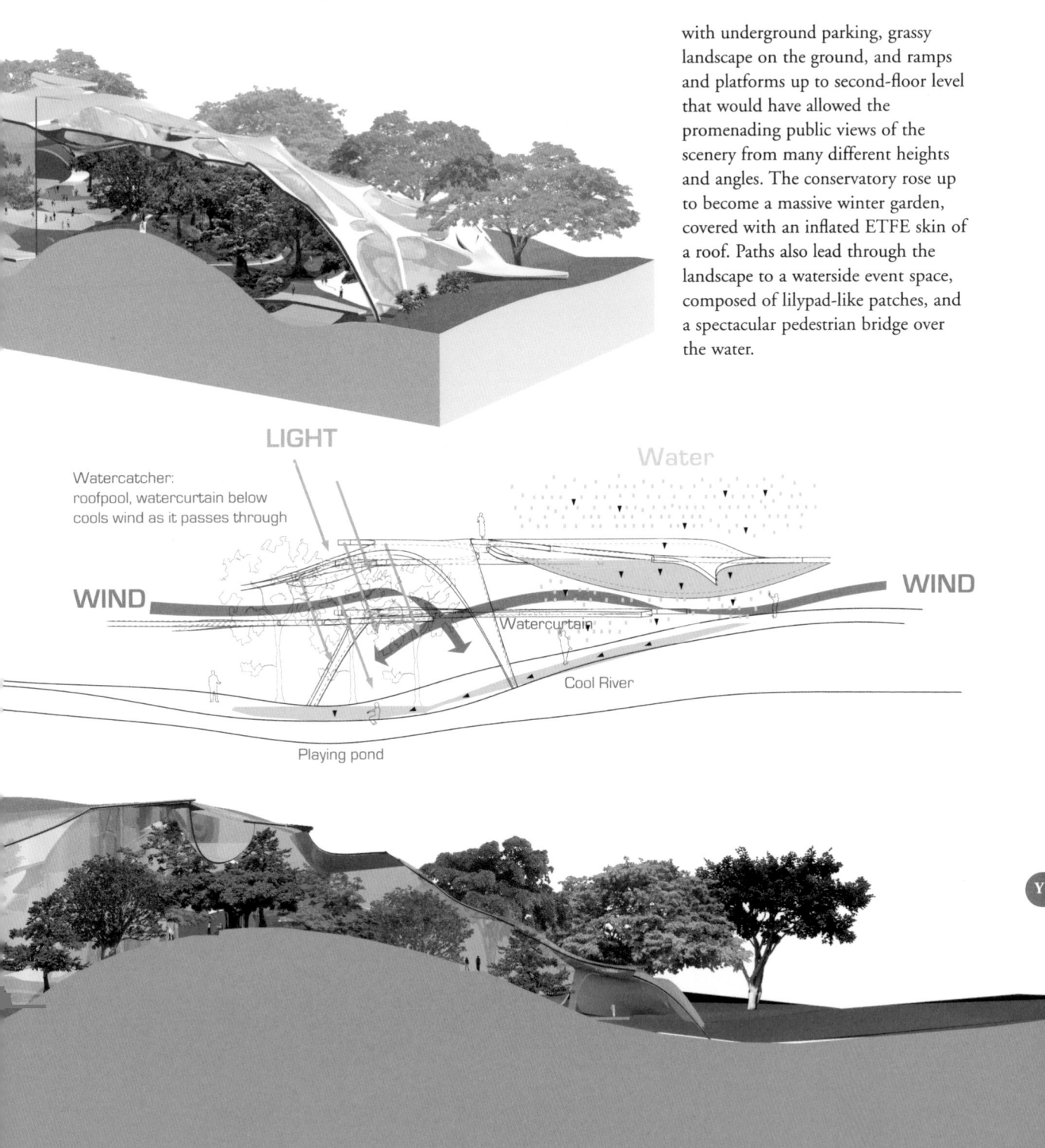

LIGHT

Water

Watercatcher:
roofpool, watercurtain below
cools wind as it passes through

WIND

WIND

Watercurtain

Cool River

Playing pond

Y

# Zellner Plus

The Sweeney Gallery at the University of California Riverside is a 604sq m (6,500sq ft) space that Peter Zellner fitted out in 2006 in a historic banking building in downtown Riverside in Los Angeles. The gallery, which sits within UCR's ARTSblock context, consists of a 372sq m (4,000sq ft) main gallery and two smaller project galleries, as well as office and art-handling and storage spaces. The project was built in collaboration, with California architect HMC as executive architect.

The intervention is subtle. The plan of the gallery is slightly off-set from the windows of the existing building, to allow the gallery to address the adjacent pedestrian mall. Inside, a new faceted reception desk addresses the visitor on entrance, before the gallery itself is revealed, skinned in white.

Zellner, who is active as a writer and curator, curated an exhibition at the Sweeney Gallery in 2007 called *Trans-Aestheticization of Daily Life*, which looked at the interaction of 'cultural production, urbanism and identity', with artists such as Ruben Ochoa, Walead Beshty and Alex Slade.

This spread: Images of the reception desk and gallery of the Sweeney Gallery in Los Angeles by Zellner Plus. The pictures on the right are of the exhibition *Trans-Aestheticization of Daily Life*, curated by Zellner.

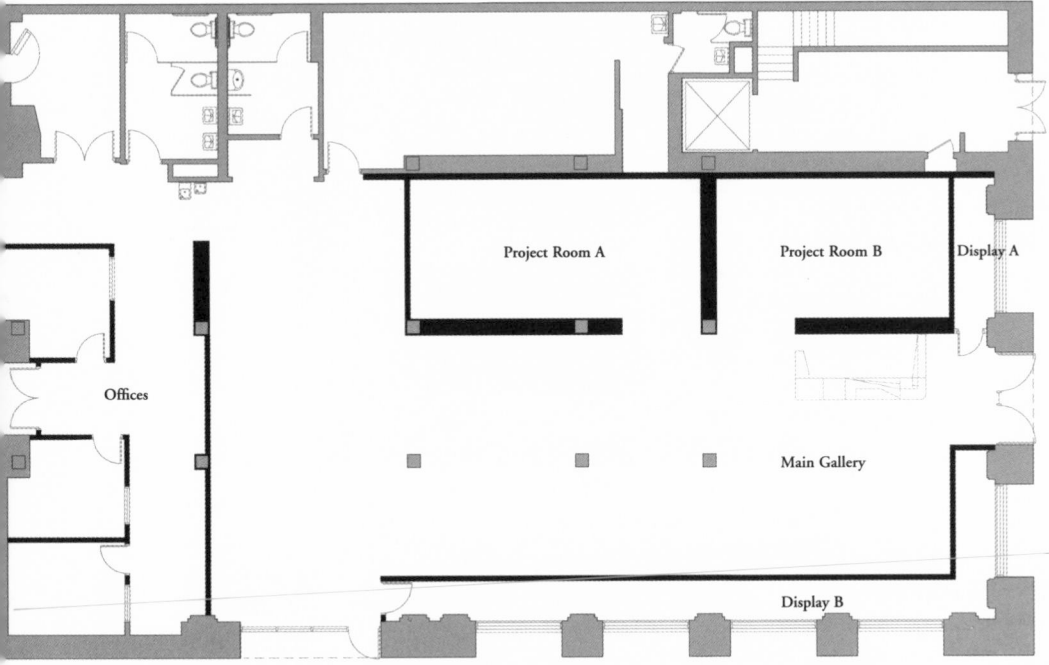

| Location | Los Angeles, USA |
|---|---|
| Nationality | Australian |

Zellner Plus is the practice of Peter Zellner, who studied for his first degree at RMIT University in Melbourne in his native Australia, before moving to the USA to study at Harvard. He runs his practice in Los Angeles, which he started in 1998. He now teaches at SCI-Arc in Los Angeles. Recent projects have concentrated on art spaces in Los Angeles, including Kinkead Contemporary (2006), Sweeney Gallery at UCR (2006) and the LAXART non-profit gallery, of which Zellner is a board member. Zellner is also a prolific author, with books behind him such as *Southern California: A Megalopolis in the Making* (with Andreas Ruby, G&B, 2000), *Sign as Surface* (Artists Space, 2004) and *Pacific Edge* (Rizzoli, 1998). He has also worked as a curator, and recently started a series of lectures and debates in Los Angeles called Outlet.

Project Room A   Project Room B   Display A

Offices

Main Gallery

Display B

University Avenue

Peter Zellner's *Project:Gallery* and other art space projects have been located in the unlikely but now vigorously up-and-coming art district of Culver City in Los Angeles, which hosts around 30 galleries along La Cienega and Washington Boulevards. The pioneer in this location was the Blum & Poe Gallery, whose space was designed by Escher GuneWardena (pp. 98–99).